Metal, Rock, and Jazz

MUSIC / CULTURE

A series from Wesleyan University Press

Edited by George Lipsitz, Susan McClary, and Robert Walser

Published titles

My Music by Susan D. Crafts, Daniel Cavicchi, Charles Keil, and the
Music in Daily Life Project

Running with the Devil: Power, Gender, and Madness in Heavy Metal Music
by Robert Walser

Subcultural Sounds: Micromusics of the West by Mark Slobin

Upside Your Head! Rhythm and Blues on Central Avenue by Johnny Otis

Dissonant Identities: The Rock'n'Roll Scene in Austin, Texas by Barry Shank

Black Noise: Rap Music and Black Culture in Contemporary America
by Tricia Rose

Club Cultures: Music, Media and Subcultural Capital by Sarah Thornton

Music, Society, Education by Christopher Small

Listening to Salsa: Gender, Latin Popular Music, and Puerto Rican Cultures
by Frances Aparicio

Any Sound You Can Imagine: Making Music/Consuming Technology
by Paul Théberge

Voices in Bali: Energies and Perceptions in Vocal Music and Dance Theater
by Edward Herbst

*A Thousand Honey Creeks Later: My Life in Music from Basie to Motown
—and Beyond* by Preston Love

Musicking: The Meanings of Performing and Listening by Christopher Small

*Music of the Common Tongue: Survival and Celebration
in African American Music* by Christopher Small

Singing Archaeology: Philip Glass's Akhnaten by John Richardson

*Metal, Rock, and Jazz: Perception and
the Phenomenology of Musical Experience*
by Harris M. Berger

HARRIS M. BERGER

Metal, Rock, and Jazz

PERCEPTION AND THE
PHENOMENOLOGY OF MUSICAL
EXPERIENCE

WESLEYAN UNIVERSITY PRESS

Published by University Press of New England

Hanover & London

WESLEYAN UNIVERSITY PRESS
Published by University Press of New England, Hanover, NH 03755
© 1999 by Harris M. Berger
Printed in the United States of America   5 4 3 2 1
CIP data appear at the end of the book

"Turn for the Worse," by Dia Pason, copyright © 1994 by Chris Ozimek, Brian Exton, Steve Christen, and Alfredo Ricci, is transcribed herein and used by permission of the artists.

"The Final Silencing," by Sin-Eater, copyright © 1991 by Dann Saladin, Rob Toothman, Brandy Smith, John Ziats, and Erik Rueschman, was transcribed from a local demo LP and is used here by permission of the artists. Dann Saladin is doing a new version, to be released in 1998, copyright © Dann Saladin.

For my parents and my wife

Contents

✧

List of Illustrations ix

Acknowledgments xi

1. An Introduction to Central Issues in Ethnomusicology and Folklore:
Phenomenology and Practice Theory 1

I. *The Ethnography of Musical Practice*

2. Commercial Hard Rock in Cleveland, Ohio: Dia Pason and Max Panic 31
3. Heavy Metal in Akron, Ohio: Winter's Bane and Sin-Eater 56
4. Two Jazz Scenes in Northeast Ohio 76

II. *The Organization of Musical Experience and the Practice of Perception*

5. The Organization of Attention in Two Jazz Scenes 119
6. The Organization of Attention in the Rock and Metal Scenes 149
7. Tonality, Temporality, and the Intending Subject (1):
Chris Ozimek and "Turn for the Worse" 174
8. Tonality, Temporality, and the Perceptual Subject (2):
Dann Saladin and "The Final Silencing" 200
9. Conclusions: Perceptual Practice and Social Context 242

III. *Music, Experience, and Society: Death Metal and Deindustrialization in an American City*

10. Death Metal Perspectives: Affect, Purpose, and the Social Life of Music 251
11. A Critical Dialogue on the Politics of the Metal Underground:
Race, Class, and Consequence 276

12. Conclusion: The Scope of Ethnomusicology 295

Notes 299

Glossary 311

Selected Bibliography 315

Index 325

Illustrations

FIGURES

Figure 1. Map of the Akron Agora 36

Figure 2. Map of Mr. E's Tavern 68

Figure 3. An accompaniment pattern for "Take the 'A' Train" 96

Figure 4. Another accompaniment pattern for "Take the 'A' Train" 97

Figure 5. A third accompaniment pattern for "Take the 'A' Train" 97

Figure 6. Basic jazz groove 98

Figure 7. An older jazz groove 99

Figure 8. Simplified jazz groove 99

Figure 9. Map of Rizzi's Jazz Lounge 101

Figure 10. "Turn for the Worse" 177

Figure 11. Approximation of the harmonic implications
of the second fill in "Turn" 190

Figure 12. "The Final Silencing" 201

Figure 13. An example of a rock groove 243

Figure 14. A fill played against the implied groove 243

Figure 15. A second fill played against the implied groove 243

Figure 16. Synthesis of identification in harmonic rhythm 244

PHOTOGRAPHS

Dia Pason (Chris Ozimek, Brian Exton, Steve Christen, and Alfredo Ricci) 40

Max Panic (John Carr, Ken Barber, George Chapman, and Jeff Johnston) 41

Dann Saladin 63

Winter's Bane (Terry Salem, Dennis Hayes, Timmy Owens, and Lou St. Paul) 65

Larry Whisler 79

Dick Schermesser 81

Bill Roth 82

Jack Hanan 84

Jerome Saunders 87

Eric Gould 88

The Whisler Quartet at Rizzi's Jazz Lounge
(Bill Roth, Larry Whisler, Jack Hanan, and Dick Schermesser) 100

Larry Glover 144

Dann Saladin at home 263

OUAM Hall 293

Acknowledgments

It is difficult for me to find the words to express my appreciation and gratitude to all of the people that have supported me in preparing this text. I must, of course, begin with my parents, Judith and Charles Berger, whose ceaseless warmth, kindness, and generosity have been the most certain foundation in my life. I also thank my aunt and uncle, Karl and Lynne Nisoff, and the Del Negro family for their ongoing concern and affection, and my sister, Alexa Murphy, who first introduced me to the pleasures of popular music.

This book is based on work begun during my graduate studies in the ethnomusicology program of Indiana University's Folklore Institute. Throughout my graduate career, Ruth Stone provided me with a constant source of guidance, insight, and wisdom, without which this book would not have been possible. I am especially grateful to Richard Bauman, whose perspectives and support have been crucial to my intellectual life both at Indiana University and in the years since. I also express warm appreciation to Bonnie Kendall and Greg Schrempp, who, as scholars and mentors, have showed me the meaning of critical thinking and humane scholarship. Charles Bird, Henry Glassie, Dorothy Lee, Roger Janelli, and Portia Maultsby all nurtured my growth and encouraged me in my work.

Robert Walser's ideas have had a key influence on my research; I deeply appreciate his perspectives on drafts of the text and his support during the publication process. I also extend warm thanks to Deena Weinstein and Anthony Giddens, both of whom read drafts of the work and provided valuable ideas for revision.

In the classroom or the kitchen, conversation is the place where ideas have their most vigorous life, and over the years I have been lucky enough to have colleagues that continually provoked and inspired me. From the foothills of the Berkshires to the bottom of the Brazos Valley, discussions with Stuart Svonkin have challenged my thinking about music and social experience. The awesome curiosity and rigorous reflections of Cornelia Fales and Patrick Leary broadened my understandings and continually reminded me why a person might want to engage in human research. I also express my appreciation to Cathy Brigham, Jean Freedman, Doreen Klassen, and Nathan Light, whose insights and perspectives have been crucial to my work. Over electronic mail or cups of coffee, Chip Fredericks, Sharon Hochhauser, Jimmie Killingsworth, Rebecca McSwain, Leon Marr, Sue Tuohy, Susan Schmidt Horning, Kati Szego, Jeremy Wallach, and Linda Williams have all shared their ideas with me, and I have benefited from their kindness and insights.

At Texas A&M University, conversations with Alan Houtchens have expanded my thinking, and I greatly appreciate his creative mind and generous spirit. The Ethnography/Theory Group—Kathryn Henderson, Mary Bucholtz, Tazim Jamal, and Jeff Cohen—has been an endless source of rewarding dialogue; the perspectives on practice theory and social life that developed in the group have been critical to my work. I also extend my thanks to Art Thompson of *Guitar Player* magazine, who generously shared his expertise on guitar technology during my research on related projects.

As an undergraduate music major at Wesleyan University, my thinking about music was profoundly shaped by the late William Barron and by Tony Lombardozzi. I am still benefiting from the kindness they have shown me and the musical life they helped me to find.

My first contacts in Cleveland came about through the help of Bruce Harrah Conforth, Jerome Saunders, and Anastasia Pantios; without them, the project would never have been undertaken. Most important, I express my abiding gratitude to the musicians who were so open and generous with their time, ideas, and sounds: Tanya Baldwin, Ken Barber, Trent Berry, Leonard Burris, Steve Christen, Duncan Crooks, Jesse Dandy, Alvin Edwards, Brian Exton, Eric Gould, Larry Glover, Dennis Hayes, Jack Hanan, Jeff Johnston, K.B., Dean Newton, Wilbur Clarence Niles, Timmy Owens, Chris Ozimek, Lou St. Paul, Keith Porter, Miles Reed, Alfredo Ricci, John Richmond, Bill Roth, Erik Rueschman, Dann Saladin, Terry Salem, Jerome Saunders, Dick Schermesser, Brandy "Chuck" Smith, Rob Toothman, Larry Whisler, and John Ziats. I thank Heights Guitars, Lentine's Music, and the Northeast Ohio Jazz Society for their cooperation in this project. I also extend my appreciation to Maria Magliolese.

During the writing of my dissertation, my great friend Valerie Jane Gulick passed away; there is no way to acknowledge the warmth and love she showed me. I am deeply honored to have had her friendship.

I extend my thanks to Patrick Leary who helped copyedit an earlier version of the manuscript and to Barbara Weis and Michel Leonard who prepared the transcriptions. I am also grateful to Suzanna Tamminen of Wesleyan University Press for her kindness throughout the publication process. Texas A&M University provided funding for a follow-up field trip for this project, and a grant from their College of Liberal Arts helped with one stage of the writing, for which I would like to express my appreciation.

Finally, I offer my deepest gratitude to folklorist Giovanna Del Negro. A wife, colleague, and friend, she has provided me with a constant source of insight, wit, love, warmth, and intelligence. I shall never know if I have learned more about expressive culture from our conversations or our everyday life together. I do know that I shall never be able to express my full appreciation to her.

November 1998   H.M.B.

Metal, Rock, and Jazz

ONE

An Introduction to Central Issues in Ethnomusicology and Folklore
Phenomenology and Practice Theory

We are forced, finally, by the nature of meaning itself as the construct of a reader always already situated within an interpretive context, to conduct empirical research into the identities of real readers, into the nature of the assumptions they bring to the texts, and into the character of the interpretations they produce.   Janice Radway, *Reading the Romance*

This is a study of four music scenes in northeastern Ohio: the commercial hard rock scene of Cleveland, the death metal scene of Akron, the African American jazz scene of Cleveland's east side, and the European American jazz scene of Akron. The research for the study was conducted in 1992 and 1993 and involved fourteen months of participant/observation fieldwork and more than four hundred hours of interviews and live musical recordings. Part I presents a general ethnography of the musical life in the four scenes. Like most ethnographies, these chapters describe what I call the "medial level" of social life: everyday practices and typical contexts of music making, the overall sound of the music, and the main meanings of the music to the people who make it and listen to it.[1] Throughout the study, the descriptive, ethnographic aim is yoked with a theoretic one. In Part I, I compare the four ethnographic portraits to reveal how seemingly natural musical activities (composition, rehearsal, performance) are at once deeply informed by social context and are actively achieved by the participants. The central concept here is the doubly constitutive nature of musical practice—that musical activity constitutes both the meaning of the music in the participant's experience and the music scene as a social group.

Part II tightens the focus to examine the participants' experiences of musical sound and speaks to questions of meaning, affect, and aesthetics. Chapters 5 and 6 show how musicians from the four scenes achieve the tasks of performance by foregrounding and backgrounding the various elements of their experience: reflective thought, affect, and perceptions of the musical sound, the other players, the audience, and their own bodies. By comparing across metal, rock, and jazz, we see how the musician's organization of attention is tied to musical goals and broader social projects specific to each scene. Chapters 7 and 8 further narrow the focus and explore how participants from the rock and metal scenes experience particular songs. Comparing traditional harmonic analyses of the songs with the participant's own descriptions, these chapters show that the tonality of a piece of music is not inherent in the sound but is an artifact of the listener's perceptual arrangement of that sound in the living present. Taken as a whole, Part II depicts perception as a kind of social practice, conduct both actively achieved by the practitioner and profoundly informed by his or her social context.

Part III shifts the focus again and explores the relationship between situated musical activity and large-scale political and economic conditions. Chapter 10 examines the musical uses, encompassing aesthetic projects, and broad social beliefs of death metal guitarist Dann Saladin. Chapter 11 presents a dialogue between Saladin and myself on the politics of death metal. Tacking between academic criticisms of metal and insider perspectives, the dialogue sheds new light on complex issues of race and class in American society.

Finally, building on the traditional insights of ethnomusicology, the Conclusion suggests how the notions of practice and experience can be used to understand the full range of social and musical life: from the micro-level constitution of musical meanings in perception, to the typical acts and routine situations of the everyday world, to the large-scale social and historical forces that inform music making.

The emphasis on practice and experience is part of a broad trend in the twentieth-century intellectual arena. Pursued from a range of scholarly traditions and with differing amounts of programmatic self-consciousness, this trend has been particularly important in my home disciplines of folklore and ethnomusicology. The first half of this Introduction examines how this trend has played itself out at selected moments in these fields. My goal here is not to produce an exhaustive disciplinary history but to examine key achievements and point out ripe opportunities which currently exist for research organized around these concepts. The second half of this Introduction explores and synthesizes ideas from phenomenology and practice theory and suggests how such a synthesis can forward this larger trend. Although this study examines the lives of musicians playing specific styles of vernacular music in a specific locality, its findings provide new insights into the interpretation of musical experience and the role of expressive culture in society.

Folklore and the Problem of Study Object

An intellectual tradition whose history spans over two hundred and fifty years, folklore studies is a logical point of departure for those interested in popular music. Folklorists have long been concerned with the relationship between expressive culture and its social contexts, and in everyday life, jazz and rock are often casually referred to as types of "folk music." By examining how past folklorists have conceptualized the study object of their research, we can shed light on the broader theoretical issues that animate this study.

Folklore's historic geographic tradition presents an interesting starting place. The historic geographic method is an approach to literary history that uses documentary evidence to trace the diffusion of folklore across large tracts of space and time. For example, in his canonical "Folklore Methodology" ([1926] 1971), Kaarle Krohn presents exquisitely detailed ground rules for teasing out the historical relationships between archival texts. The thoroughness and reason of Krohn's method is astounding and far exceeds much of the diffusionist anthropology of the time. His intense focus on the literary artifact, however, draws attention away from the fact that "the text" is only useful here as a record of tales told and tales transmitted. While the historic geographic folklorist Carl Wilhelm Von Sydow (1948) depicted "tale migration" as an epiphenomenon of practices of tale telling and the contingencies of social history (migration, culture contact, social organization within a community), most of his contemporaries took the text as a thing-in-itself rather than as a problematic record of past practices and experiences. Here I shall use "textual empiricism" to refer to any scholarly approach that treats the text alone as its object of study. Such a treatment is more complex than it may first seem and entails the severing of a variety of critical links between the text, its constitution in experience, and its social production.

The dominant paradigm of pre-1960s folklore was collection, classification, and analysis, and this approach can be used to illustrate some of the difficulties of textual empiricism. Publishing decontextualized and unanalyzed collections of ballads or proverbs, writers like George Lyman Kittredge (1905, 1907, 1908, 1909) and Archer Taylor reflected the prevailing idea that the "text itself" was folklore's object of study. While this work has served as an invaluable primary source for countless research projects, the assumption underlying such collectivism was that meaning resides in the text and is uninfluenced by the event in which it emerges, the fieldwork process, and any larger social contexts. Research on generic classification employed similar perspectives. In Andre Jolles's classic *Einfache Formen* (1965), or Max Lüthi's phenomenology of German fairy tales (1948), characteristics inherent in the text are believed to locate it in a particular literary category. The same orientation underlies Stith Thompson's great motif index (1955). Dissecting texts into individual motif units and organizing those units into a massive system, Thompson assumes that the motif units are implied by the literary work itself and that the text is comprehensible in its autonomy. This approach is most pronounced in grand analytic projects like Sir James Frazer's *Golden Bough* (1911) and Kittredge's *Witchcraft in Old and New England* (1929). These scholars mined ethnographies and folklore archives for descriptions of the beliefs and practices of cultural others and treated decontextualized items of folklore as the basic unit of analysis. While Frazer and Kittredge saw their texts as records of social activities, their treatment of custom as an isolatable unit of data severs the practice from the situated event and broader cultural milieu. Setting aside the biases inherent in the larger evolutionist project of these works, this kind of radical decontextualization distorts the meaning of the folklore and jeopardizes any theoretical conclusions to be drawn from it.

If textual empiricism separates the text from practices of production and experiences of meaning, a variety of folklorists in the pre-1960s period moved in more humanistic directions. While many of Franz Boas's publications focused on artifacts or texts (1955; 1966; 1970, 58–392), there was almost always a sense in his work that the textual evidence implicated human practices, and similar approaches can be seen in his students' studies of expressive culture (for example, Bunzel 1929; Benedict 1969; Reichard 1928). In a related vein, many scholars of folklore's literary tradition (Lomax and Lomax 1938; Korson 1938, 1943; Botkin 1944) surrounded their collected texts with descriptions of social context. Such text-context "sandwiches"[2] vivified their studies and suggested the situated nature of meaning. For all the diversity of folklore scholarship before the 1960s, however, the problem of study object did not become the focus of theoretical debate until the development of performance studies. In foundational works such as Albert Lord's *Singer of Tales* (1960) or Dell Hymes's "Ethnography of Speaking" (1962) and later statements such as *Towards New Perspectives* (Paredes and Bauman 1972), we see both literary and anthropological attempts to interpret folklore texts as evidence of situated expressive practices. It was in this period that textualism versus contextualism became the central debate in folklore studies.

If the text is a record of a performance, and if the performance is the object of study, then, performance theory suggested, the text must expand to represent all the dimensions of the performative act. From this insight emerged research into the ethnopoetic study of verbal art (for example, Tedlock 1972; Bright 1979; Sherzer 1987; Woodbury 1987) and the folkloristic study of kinesics (Fine 1984). While these scholars substantially increased the scope and richness of folklore studies, their work treated the text as a representation of events in the objective world, as behaviors rather than actions or experiences. Such an approach detaches the text from the act of performance and the experience of meaning, and reestablishing those linkages in analysis produces problems of significance, intention, and method. Elizabeth C. Fine's *The Folklore Text* (1984), for example, augmented verbal transcriptions with schematic representations of the gestures that accompanied the performance. While Fine's transcripts are highly suggestive, it is not clear which of the transcribed gestures are significant or what they might mean. Similarly it is not clear which if any of the gestures were intended, when such intention emerged, or with what detail. Such problems bring us full circle to the process of transcription. Without addressing the problem of intention and significance, how does the transcribing scholar know what level of detail to notate? Are only gross movements of the limbs worth transcribing, or should facial expression and hand gesture be depicted as well? Similar inquiries can be made of the enriched texts produced by those from the ethnopoetics school. Scholars like Sherzer and Woodbury transcribe the pitch contours, pauses, and grammatical structure of oral poetry and use the transcriptions to search for structural relationships among those features. While such scholarship sheds light on previously ignored dimensions of expressive culture, similar questions emerge: What level of detail of pitch contour or prosody is worth transcribing? Do the structural relationships between the features have meaning? Are they intentional? Do they emerge in the participant's experiences? If so, how? How can we determine if the structural relationships are spurious correlations? If they are not, what is the significance of those correlations?

A different perspective on the problem of study object comes from looking at some specific programmatic statements in performance theory. Richard Bauman's 1989 essay "Performance" in the *International Encyclopedia of Communications* lays out three definitions of the word *performance* and offers crucial insights into the achievements and challenges of the performance school. Bauman's first definition equates performance with enactment (for example, the performance of a play as opposed to the script). Though this sense of the term is infrequently used as a formal definition of performance studies, the general orientation toward situated activity animates much of contemporary folklore scholarship. A second definition narrows the first to construe performance as a special mode of conduct—heightened, aesthetic action oriented toward an other in communication. Such a perspective is reminiscent of Alfred Schutz's phenomenological sociology (1967), seeking as it does to use structural features of interaction to reveal universal categories of expressive behavior. As a formal statement of theoretical orientation, however, the most widely employed is the third definition—performance as opposed to competence. Such a perspective finds its roots in Dell Hymes's "Ethnography of Speaking" (1962) and its fullest flower in Charles Briggs's *Competence in Performance* (1988). In designing his seminal program, Hymes modified Chomsky's vision of competence as an unconscious, synchronic system of grammatical rules to include knowledge of interactional norms and generic categories. Competence's diametric opposite, performance, is modified to include the application of past cultural knowledge to present contexts. Such modifications serve to humanize the purely formal systems of grammar that Chomsky envisioned as descriptions of the neurological basis of language.

But modifying competence and switching the emphasis to performance does not overcome the difficulties of these structuralist assumptions. Even in highly sophisticated studies like Briggs's,[3] competence is seen as a synchronic system; as a result, change is difficult, if not impossible, to account for. Further, the system of competence is understood as subconscious and completely outside of the subject's experience. As a result, competence is divorced from the subject's meaningful action and the study object recedes into a realm that is, by definition, inaccessible to both the participant and the researcher. I have argued elsewhere that change and agency mutually implicate each other (Berger 1991), and here that connection is vital. If a person can neither experience nor change the underlying system of competence, then it is difficult to see linguistic behavior as the product of *agency*—the subject's active intervention in the world. Hymes's modifications of Chomsky's performance fail to convert it into practice or fully remove its antihumanism in the same way that Talcott Parsons's "action" fails to have any relationship to agency or responsibility (on Parsons, see Giddens 1993, 21–22). Like the posited objective reality in subjective idealism or the unconscious in Freud, the vision of competence as *a priori* inaccessible turns Chomskian linguistics—and any orientation that defines performance, however modified, in opposition to competence—into a kind of metaphysics. Throughout, I shall use "metaphysics" to refer to any theoretical orientation or philosophical approach that defines its study object as essentially inaccessible to the subject's experience. Understood in this way, most forms of phenomenology can be understood as attempts to overcome metaphysics.

In scholarly practice, the interplay between these three differing definitions of performance (enactment, heightened expressive activity, subconscious expressive system), has influenced much folklore research in the last thirty years. Theoretical works like Bauman's *Verbal Art as Performance* (1977) and Roger Abrahams's "Rhetorical Theory" (1968) have sensitized scholars to the way folklore is created and used in performance events. Rich ethnographies like those of Linda Dégh (1969) or Henry Glassie (1982) illuminate the connections between expressive culture and the everyday life from which it emerges. Recent research in verbal art has focused on the ways that performers connect text and context by weaving references to the ongoing event into their performances (see, for example, Briggs 1993; Butler 1992; Parmentier 1993). Even in the specialized field of pareimiology, Peter Seitel (1972) brought the study of the proverb, the most easily reified of all genres, far closer to living experience.

In a well-known statement on the state of discipline, Alan Dundes (1980) once argued that the folklore scholars had shifted their focus from text to texture (performative features like prosody and kinesics) and context (the immediate situation and broader social environment in which the text emerges); the description still applies today. While contemporary folklorists understand expressive culture as the outcome of human activity, we can gain new insights and forward the performance perspective by continuing to reexamine our vision of study object. One way to do so is to treat folklore as experience and explore the ways in which expressive culture is actively constituted in situated acts of perception. Such a vision retains the wealth of kinesic, prosodic, and contoural data garnered in ethnopoetics's enriched texts; it also, however, explores how such features are arranged in experience. Such a vision is able to represent the participant as an agent because it sees the constitution of perception and the construction of expressive forms as social processes that are both present for experience and actively achieved. Such a vision is well suited to handling the tight relationship between context and meaning, because the subject's meaningful engagement with an item of expressive culture is always an activity performed in and influenced by the immediate situation; likewise, the active engagement that forms experience is constrained and enabled by the subject's social history. The focus on experience in phenomenological approaches is often confused with a kind of brain-in-a-vat, anything-goes idealism. Nothing could be further from the case, because phenomenology emphasizes that the world thus engaged is a genuine other. As a result, the complex dialectic, within experience, of the social subject and the genuinely other object is the phenomenologist's central concern.

I shall develop these ideas in more detail. One of the difficulties of inter-disciplinary work, however, is accounting for related but distinct strands of intellectual history. With basic concepts like textual empiricism, the contex-tuality of meaning, and enriched text in place, we shall be able to move quickly through the related developments in ethnomusicology and popular music studies.

Ethnomusicology, Popular Music Studies, and the Issue of Context

Transcription issues and the concern with form

From Béla Bartók's formal analysis of Hungarian folk song ([1924] 1981), to Helen Roberts's ([1936] 1970) areal classifications of Native Amer-ican musics, to the collectivist and salvage work of Francis La Flesche ([1914] 1970, 1928, 1930, 1939), Fletcher and La Flesche ([1911] 1972), and Francis Densmore (1939, 1972), a wide range of scholars in the first half of the twentieth century were concerned with questions of musical structure and problems of transcription. The main methodological challenge for this generation was that standard Western music notation is often unable to capture the sonic details of non-Western musics. In response, special mark-ings and symbols were created to adjust for the limitations of the five lines and the staff. Opening up new possibilities for descriptive accuracy, the works of Bartók and Roberts set the standard for ethnomusicological transcription. From the founding of the Society for Ethnomusicology in 1957 until the mid-1970s, however, scholars began to problematize this ap-proach.[4] First, writers such as Charles Seeger (1958), Mantle Hood (1963), and Bruno Nettl (1964) argued that transcription was necessarily a selective process and that the transcriber's cultural background invariably influenced that selection. Soon after, others observed that the basic visual features of even modified Western notation projected Western European assumptions about music onto any sonic form it was used to transcribe. Bar lines and time signatures, for example, imply an underlying pulse grouped into units with a hierarchy of strong and weak beats; note shape, staff position, and multistave scores construct pitch, rhythm, and timbre as independent sonic elements. Scholars such as James Koetting (1970) and James Reid (1977) worked on new notation systems that could reflect non-Western ideas about musical sound. Against the evolutionists' textual empiricism, this work suggested that ethnomusicology's study object should be the "native perspective" on the music.

Approaching the problem from a different angle, other writers enlisted mechanical transcribers to overcome the selectivity of the scholar's ear (Seeger 1957; List 1974; Reid 1977). Perhaps the most suggestive idea of the period came in an undercited article by Nazir Jairazbhoy in *Ethnomusicology* (1977). Criticizing the idea that a mechanical transcriber can produce purely objective transcriptions, Jairazbhoy pointed out that human neurology and the body's bulk itself attenuate musical sound in a way that is not represented by the mechanical transcriber's output. While mechanical transcribers can be designed to account for such filtering, Jairazbhoy's comments are significant because they suggest concrete and unavoidable links between musical sound and the experiencing subject. Jairazbhoy notwithstanding, the growth of structuralism in ethnomusicology siphoned away interest from transcription issues. A form of textual empiricism, structuralism treated transcriptions as unproblematic raw data. Searching for the deep structures believed to be implicit in the surface text, the work of John Blacking's structuralist period (for example, 1970, 1972) and Robin Cooper (1977) neither questioned the status of the transcription nor related their analyses to the research participant's experiences.

Though transcription issues received diminishing attention, intriguing questions of study object still remain. Is the music a physical object, existing independent of any person (composer, musician, listener) and capable of being fully described by an objective transcriber? Is the music the research participant's intention? Is the music the performance? If the music is an independent object, how can we account for features of the sound that are constructed by the listening subject, such as the underlying sense of pulse? If the music is a research participant's intention, how can a transcription reflect the fact that intentions are influenced by the act of performance itself, that intentions vary over time, and that intentions range from the minutest sensual detail to the broadest of structural features? If the music is the performance, what is the relationship of the music to the transcriber's or performer's experience? One way beyond these apparently irreconcilable perspectives (music as fact, music as idea, music as act) is to see that even the most fundamental, seemingly objective aspects of the music imply the existence of a listening subject. Without a spatiotemporally specific subject engaged with sound waves, there is no now, no before and no after, no loud or soft, no accent (just changes in amplitude), and no underlying pulse. It takes a subject—always an agent and always social—to hear a period of sound as linked together in a phrase, to hear a phrase as present or past, to stand close to or far from a sound source, to constitute a pulse. And if these basic, "objective" aspects of the sound imply a listening subject, the affective and more complex formal dimensions do this all the more. Before the designation of any musical feature as an objective sonic fact or a subjective mental construct is our prereflective engagement with the world, our immediate experience of music. If we think of our study object as experiences actively and social constituted by perceptual subjects, than spectrograms, interview data on musical intentions, and ethnographic descriptions of performance can be understood as different moments in the project of transcription.

The ethnomusicology of form and meaning:
From evolutionism to functionalism

Alongside the concern with form, the discipline has always been interested in the problem of music and emotion and the relationship between musical activity and larger social contexts. Until the 1950s, these issues were largely taken up by the evolutionists. Scholars like John Comfort Fillmore (1888, 1895, 1899), Helen Roberts ([1926] 1967), Jaap Kunst ([1950] 1974), and Miczyslaw Kolinski (1961, 1965) all proffered variations on the idea that non-Western musics are both simple in structure and unchanged since prehistoric times. Interpreting the music of "primitive" peoples as a direct reflection of emotion, ethnomusicological evolutionism rests on the belief in a universal system that links musical form and emotional content. Setting aside evolutionism's obvious and objectionable racism, such a position is problematic because it assumes the existence of an underlying system and locates any new data within it, rather than treating this system as a hypothesis and collecting data to test its validity.

The seeds of a new approach to these issues can be found in the descriptive passages of Helen Roberts's work and in the ethnographies of Edwin Burrows (1936a, 1936b, 1945). Juxtaposing musical transcriptions with evocative accounts of performance events, these writers suggested that music's affective content is tied to its situated context and cultural milieu. Occupying a similar place in ethnomusicology's history as the "Ethnography of Speaking" does in folklore, Alan Merriam's *Anthropology of Music* (1964) made the implications of these text-context sandwiches explicit. The *Anthropology* is based on the notion that music is the product of social activity and argues that the affective power of musical form is culturally specific. Problematizing the assumption that music only exists to evoke affective and aesthetic responses, Merriam charged ethnomusicologists with the task of discovering the variety of uses to which music is put in world cultures. In so doing, Merriam and his functionalists contemporaries (McAllester 1954; Nettl 1964; Ames 1973; Johnston 1973; Irvine and Sapir 1976) repudiated the notion of a universal system of musical meaning and exorcised the spirit of evolutionism from academic ethnomusicology.

While functionalist research represented a major advance for the discipline, its level of focus presented two difficulties. The functionalists all agreed that cultural context gave musical structure its affective power, but most of these scholars took that affective power for granted and concentrated their attention on how that power plays itself out in society. Of course no single work can examine all aspects of musical phenomena, but the consistent functionalist focus on "macrolevel" problems drew interest away from the question of how musical form evokes affective experiences. As a result, functionalist ethnomusicology never developed a detailed theory of music and emotion to replace the one from evolutionism that it dismantled. A second difficulty was one to which all forms of functionalism are prone: the problem of agency. While Merriam's *Anthropology* took social activity as the basis of musical phenomena, the focus on typical behaviors and large-scale patterns tended to reduce situated practices to a mere expression of larger social forces. Thomas Johnston's analysis of Tsonga beer drink music (1973) is a case in point. Here, the diversity of situated practices in musical performances is reduced to routinized behaviors and society's need for solidarity is seen as the music's source. Within and beyond ethnomusicology, functionalist work tends either toward a synchronic antihumanism that ignores agency and social change or toward after-the-fact attempts to reconcile individuals' uses with society's functions.[5] Here, structuralism and functionalism are parallel. Structuralism strays into metaphysics by treating experience and action as epiphenomena of a neurological system that is, by definition, inaccessible to the subject; functionalism strays into metaphysics by treating experience and action as epiphenomena of social forces that are also, by definition, beyond the actor's control.

The difficulty here is broadly social theoretic and not narrowly ethnomusicological. As Anthony Giddens has argued (1979, 1984, 1993), the problem emerges from the false idea that society is a thing in and of itself, an entity independent of the people that constitute it. Giddens's solution is the notion that society is the ongoing intentional and unintentional outcome of individuals' intentional action in the flow of history. Within ethnomusicology, we can use the notion of practice to gain insights into both the problem of music and affect and the relationship between musical activity and large-scale social context. On the "microlevel," musical structure and affective content are constituted in the practice of perception. As a kind of practice, this musical perception is both deeply informed by the practitioner's situated and broader social contexts and actively achieved by the subject. On the "macrolevel," the historical emergence of relatively stable forms of the social life of music (performance events, musical cultures, and subcultures) are indeed informed by functionalism's "larger social contexts." Social "context," however, is not an anonymous force separate from individual human conduct; rather, it is made up of the intentional and unintentional consequences of past practices. Similarly, the typical performance events and musical cultures that functionalism describes are themselves constituted by the diverse practices of social actors. This doubly constitutive nature of practice in musical cultures is a theme I shall return to throughout this book.

Form and meaning since the 1970s:
Ethnomusicology

The 1980s and 1990s have seen a wide variety of intellectual approaches to the issues of affect and context. Probably the best-known musical ethnography of this period is *Sound and Sentiment* (1982), Steven Feld's study of music among the Kaluli of Papua New Guinea. Brilliant in his synthesis of Lévi-Strauss's structuralism and Geertz's interpretive anthropology, Feld expends copious and fruitful field time in understanding the Kaluli perspective on music. Arguing that the various domains of cultural knowledge are structurally homologous, Feld suggests that Kaluli ornithology and mythology serve as a metaphor that connects musical form and its affective content. Feld's study object can be interpreted as "the native perspective" and his text an attempt to unearth the mechanisms that produce that perspective. The notion of "native perspective" is fundamental for most recent humanistic research in ethnomusicology; by examining this concept we can illuminate the achievements and challenges of the contemporary discipline.

The idea of "perspective" implies a specific spatiotemporal point, a subject located there and a world grasped from that vantage; the word "native" locates the subject in a society and suggests that culture informs perspective. In the best tradition of Merriam and the 1960s transcription theorists, the idea of native perspective highlights the profoundly social nature of experience. But social context is only one-half of a complex dialectic that informs culture; the other half is agency, and the notion of native perspective often obscures historical change, differences within social groups, and the active component of human conduct. *Sound and Sentiment* powerfully evokes the everyday life of Kaluli villages, but in the text's most reifying moments, "the native" ceases to be a social individual, actively constituting his or her perspective. Here, the "native" is a reified norm, an ageless and genderless Kaluli, structuralism's ideal speaker/hearer whose perspective is produced by an underlying and inaccessible system, itself formed by functionalism's larger social forces. Here, native perspective is not the partially shared elements of diverse Kaluli experiences, but an autonomous set of metaphors that relate abstract systems of myth, ornithology, and music.

In analyzing the interplay between different domains of knowledge, Feld achieves powerful insights, but it is unclear how his model operates in concrete situations. Do all Kaluli know the master myth and the system of ornithology? If not, how does the music's affective power operate for them? Do all Kaluli experience the music in question as embodying the same affective contents? Can Kaluli grasp the music in different ways and experience different emotional contents? The very notion of structure would seem to prevent this. What of differences across age, gender, or other affiliation? Though Feld amasses his transcriptions through participant observation, he analyzes those transcriptions as a purely formal system, without regard for their emergence and use in situated practice or their various meanings in the participants' experiences. Such an analytic treatment disconnects the transcription from its grounding in daily social life and operates as a kind of textual empiricism. Lived meanings can hang together in tightly coordinated sets of relationships, and these relationships may be partially shared among diverse social actors. But when we take underlying structures as our study object, we disengage meaning from the social practices that constitute it.

In the period since *Sound and Sentiment*, ethnographers from a variety of intellectual traditions have helped to orient music scholarship around the concepts of social activity and lived experiences. Judith Vander's *Songprints: The Musical Experiences of Five Shoshone Women* (1988) is one of the most sensitive ethnographies, musical or otherwise, written in recent years. Ruth Stone's *Let The Inside Be Sweet* (1982) and *Dried Millet Breaking* (1988) are landmarks of phenomenological ethnography. By taking entire events, rather than decontextualized texts, as her study object, Stone made a major step toward returning musical sound to its foundation in situated practice. Her approach to interaction and time perception is foundational to this study.

In the 1990s, scholars such as Christopher Waterman (1990), Peter Manuel (1993), Jocelyne Guilbault (1993), Veit Erlmann (1996), and Barry Shank (1994) synthesized social history and participant-observation fieldwork to gain new insights into musical meanings. Exploring what folklorists would call the "genre problem" (the question of how individual works of expressive culture are organized into genres and the epistemological status of generic categories), Zouk, Guilbault's study of popular music in the West Indies, serves as a case in point. Content with neither a formal analysis devoid of people nor a social history devoid of musical detail, *Zouk* explores how musicians and music producers developed particular musical genres in creative response to particular social contexts. Highlighting the diversity of Caribbean perspectives and allowing ample space for local voices, Guilbault depicts the subjects of her study as agents, social individuals actively making meaning in their world.

The work of Paul F. Berliner (1994), Ingrid Monson (1996), and Stephen M. Friedson (1996) contribute related insights. Berliner's epic *Thinking In Jazz: The Infinite Art of Improvisation*, painstakingly traces out the process by which jazz musicians acquire and develop their improvisatory skills. Here, the focus on learning illuminates aspects of agency overlooked by other approaches and powerfully evokes the participants' diverse experiences. Treating the musical structures of jazz performance as the outcome of social interaction, Monson's *Saying Something* provides a detailed ethnography of performance that fails to disengage music sound from musical activity. Where Guilbault employs polyvocal writing techniques to highlight the multifaceted nature of musical meaning, Monson draws on W. E. B. Du Bois's concept of double-consciousness (the idea that African Americans always partake in both African American and European American culture) to shed light on similar social processes. Berliner's and Monson's perspectives on jazz has been foundational for this study. Friedson's ethnography of music in Tumbuka healing rituals, *Dancing Prophets* (1996), uses Martin Heidegger's vision of the mutually constitutive relationship between the subject and the world to suggest the transformative potential of musical activity. While Freidson's use of Heidegger is quite different from my approach to phenomenology and Monson's notion of interaction is distinct from my idea of practice, their research provides a path related to the one I wish to chart here. From social history to the development of musical skills, to the unfolding of performance event—in all of these studies the theme of emergence highlights different dimensions of agency and illuminates the relationship between musical form and meaning. I hope to forward this approach by focusing attention on the constitutive act where most meanings are established: perception. By treating perception as social practice, I show how such seemingly individual and microlevel acts are informed by and go to build up historical currents and the relatively stable forms of social life.

Form and meaning since the 1970s: Popular culture studies

Based on foundational works like Dick Hebdige's *Subculture* (1979) and Simon Frith's *Sound Effects* (1981), the British popular music studies of the last twenty years have provided another set of approaches to the problems of music research. Frith's work debunks romantic ideas about rock's resistance to the music industry and sheds light on issues of race, class, and gender in Britain and the United States. Hebdige uses the semiotics of Roland Barthes and Julia Kristeva to reveal the complex ways that signs can convey meanings in popular music subcultures. Both authors interpret the musics and fashions of youth subcultures and use those interpretations to develop theories about the relationship between music and society. Once again, problems of research method shed light on fundamental issues of study object. One difficulty here is that these authors provide little information about the process by which they collected their data and made their interpretations. In Hebdige's work, it is never clear if the meaning ascribed to a given item of expressive culture (the mod's tie, the punk's Mohawk) is based on mass-media reports, informal interviews, or the scholar's own interpretive work. Hebdige has clearly spent time in popular music scenes, but his failure to describe his research methods makes the status of his readings unclear. While he provides ample citations for his sources in semiotics, he never grounds his readings of style in feedback interviews or specific examples of participant observation. While Frith supports some of his interpretations with quotes from critics, media interviews with performers, or biographies, many of his readings—of "black music" as "immediate and democratic" (16–17) or of "country music" as dominated by feelings of "shame" (25)—are given with no support at all and seem to be only the scholar's view of the music. If past ethnomusicology had reduced the variety of local music meanings to a typified norm, the method of much of the 1980s British popular music studies seem to suggest that a sufficiently sophisticated scholarly reading of subcultural style is all that is needed to unearth local meanings—or even that participant perspectives are unimportant.

This last point is crucial. If our work is to explain the role of music in society, then our interpretations of music must be an attempt to understand the meaning of the music for the people who participate in it. If an interpretation of a genre of music or subculture is present for the scholar and no other social actor, I cannot see how it can be consequential for the larger society. As a result, the interpretation of music, fashion, and style must be understood as an attempt to share the experiences of the music's participants. As I shall argue in Chapter 11, this is not to suggest that musical participants cannot misinterpret their own musical experiences, that every scholarly reading must be verified by the research participant in feedback interviews, or that cultural outsiders cannot provide unique insights into the musical lives of others. This is to say, as Sara Cohen emphasizes (1993), that if we wish to understand how music operates in society, our interpretations must illuminate the ways in which musical meanings play out in the lives of a society's actors, and that ethnographic research is one of the most powerful tools we have for exploring this domain. While it is not always practical, or even possible, to do participant observation and feedback on some topics, I believe that we must conceptualize our study object as lived experience and interpretation as a partial sharing of meaning. To do otherwise is to jeopardize the data upon which any broader conclusions are built.

A related difficulty in the British popular music studies of the 1980s was the lack of work on musical sound. Here, the few writers that did look at music exemplified many of the problems of study object and method I have suggested above. For example, Richard Middleton (1985), Sean Cubbit (1984), and Barbara Bradby and Brian Torode (1984) interpreted particular songs and genres and sought to reveal the social meanings implied by their musical form. Treating musical meanings as both inherent in the sonic structure and unproblematically accessible to the interpreting scholar, this work ignored the fact that different audiences may interpret musical sound in different ways, that a single listener may garner a variety of meanings from a piece, and that situated context can have a profound impact on the ways in which listeners "read" songs. When Bradby and Torode, for example, interpret the lyrics of Buddy Holly's "Peggy Sue" and discover patriarchal ideas in the text, one can imagine their interpretation as a description of the sexist meanings the song subtly reinforces in the experiences of its listeners. Understood in this way, such interpretations are relevant to the beliefs and practices that constitute patriarchy in the world. But when these writers notate the rhythms of the guitar solo, capriciously ascribe lyrics to those rhythms, and then analyze the text they created, one is forced to question, not only the specious musical score but their entire interpretive project as well. A critical analysis only makes sense if interpretations describe the experiences of the people who make and listen to the music. How can meanings that are not present in participants' experience influence their conduct or inform the larger society? Middleton's analysis of the juxtaposition of styles in John Lennon's "Imagine" is highly sophisticated and rich in insight. Reading the text, however, one still wonders how different audiences interpret the song and how these stylistic references play out in situated practices of meaning making.

In the 1990s, musical sound began to receive greater attention in the research of rock scholars (Whiteley 1990, 1992; Josephson 1992; Moore 1993; Ford 1995; Hawkins 1996). One of the richest of these works, Allan F. Moore's *Rock: The Primary Text* (1993), presents a history of rock styles and shows how the traditional concerns of British cultural studies (authenticity, the historical development of music subcultures) can be forwarded by attending to the music. In the theoretical section of his work, Moore argues that the listener's perception of the song should form the basis of musical analysis and suggests that fans might apply different strategies to the act of listening. In the musical analysis, however, Moore focuses solely on the score, provides little discussion of listening strategies, and uses neither observation data nor feedback interviews to ensure that his sonic interpretations connect with the listener's perceptions. Like Middleton, Moore provides many insightful readings, but the lack of field data and the failure to account for situated context suggest the problems I have explored above.[6] Based on rich interview data, Rob Bowman's fine style analysis of the songs of the Stax record label (Bowman 1995) helps to connect the musicology of rock with ethnomusicological approaches.

With the broadening of the field of data has come a related expansion of interpretive approaches, and a number of recent scholars have sought to overcome the assumption that popular music is a solely regressive force in modern societies (Lipsitz 1990, 1994a, 1994b; Walser 1993; Garofalo 1987, 1992, 1997; Manuel 1993; Shank 1994). Peter Manuel's painstakingly researched study of the impact of cassettes on popular music in India, *Cassette Culture* (1993), refutes both Luddite condemnations and facile celebrations of mass-media technology. Manuel illustrates the complex range of consequences that cassettes have had and shows that it is not technology per se, but the way that technology is used that determines its effect on society. In all of this work, careful historical or ethnographic research replaces older speculations about mass media and enriches our understanding about the relationship between expressive culture and society.

Though the present study compares four music scenes, heavy metal is at its center, and recent work in this area has provided key directions for my research. Robert Walser's pathbreaking *Running with the Devil* (1993) combines ethnography and social history with a rigorous musical analysis. Placing the development of the genre within the context of Western deindustrialization, Walser connects subcultural styles with larger economic forces. Most important, his powerful interpretations of particular songs make the artistry of metal comprehensible to outsiders and show how the analysis of music can bring insights into issues of class and gender. Relating musical meanings, metalhead beliefs about virtuosity, and broader American ideologies of race and gender, Walser's work yields powerful insights into the role of metal in the lives of its participants. Related ideas emerge in Deena Weinstein's *Heavy Metal: A Cultural Sociology* (1991). Though Weinstein spends little time on the musical sound, her sensitive ethnographic work and comprehensive attention to audiences, performers, and music industry mediators produces rich understandings into this music. Further, Weinstein's wide knowledge of the genre allows her to reveal participant perspectives on the music and debunk many of the myths that surround metal. Like H. Stith Bennett's research on the everyday lives of rock musicians, Weinstein's rigorous fieldwork evokes the diverse experiences of metalheads. The focus on musical practices in Bennett's *On Becoming a Rock Musician* (1980) make his classic research another source of inspiration and insight.

Another study that has important connections with my work is Ruth Finnegan's excellent book *The Hidden Musicians* (1989), an ethnography of amateur music making in the English town of Milton Keynes. Applying approaches from folklore's performance school, Finnegan takes music making practices as her focus, and she uses her rich and detailed fieldwork to challenge many of the strictly theoretical criticisms of popular music leveled by mass culture scholars. Comparing a wide variety of musical scenes in the town, Finnegan shows how the organization of performance events, the acquisition of music skills, and the act of composition vary across musical cultures. Finnegan does not explore musical sound, and she repeatedly juxtaposes her own emphasis on musical practice with the music scholar's analysis of scores and recordings; one goal of this book is to reconcile these apparently opposed perspectives by showing how issues of musical structure can be understood in terms of the practices of musical perception and musical action.

Perhaps Finnegan's most important contribution is her attempt to replace older conceptions of the social base of music (such as "musical community") with her notion of the "pathway"—an organized pattern of music making conduct actively brought about by performers and listeners. Though Finnegan does not rely on practice theory, her concept of the pathway is compatible with my own vision of situated practice constituting music scenes; interpreting Finnegan in the language of Giddens, one could say that her powerful idea of the "pathway" accounts for both the structure of local scenes and the agency of their participants. While Finnegan sees her pathways as forms of social organization, she tends to focus on the personal and local dimensions of music making. For example, problematizing simplistic equations of popular music styles and the social background of their participants (i.e., rock as youth rebellion), her work places less emphasis on the role of power relations in local music making. Responding to materialist perspectives on culture, she argues that what is most important about music is its ability to provide a vehicle for creative activity, profound ritual experiences, and transcendent feelings of social connectedness in the performance event. Using concepts from Anthony Giddens, I hope to put more emphasis on the relationship between local music making and so-called larger social forces, without slipping into the determinism and reductionism that Finnegan so rightly critiques. Exploring the complex dialectics of situated practice and social context, I show how issues of race and class in American society inform, but do not determine, the music making practices in my field site.

Phenomenology and Practice Theory

The discussion so far has explored a variety of new ideas about the study of expressive culture. The rest of the chapter uses notions from Edmund Husserl, Maurice Merleau-Ponty, and Anthony Giddens to weave these ideas together and suggest a program of music research based on the concepts of practice and experience.

Foundational ideas from phenomenology: Experience and world, self and other

The concept of experience is central to phenomenology, but in everyday conversation and academic usage the term has a wide range of meanings. To clear the ground for our discussion of phenomenology we must first see what the word does *not* mean to phenomenologists.[7] First, experience is not some mysterious substance that stands in opposition to the real, objective world of things; experience encompasses both the objective and the subjective. Neither, as the empiricists would have it, is experience only sense-impression; to reduce experience to sensation is to weigh down our understanding of perception with unfounded assumptions. In my usage, experience is not some abstract entity possessed by a group (some ideal object like "The American Experience"); although experience is always socially constituted and potentially can be shared across individuals and groups, experience is always someone's experience and sharing is always partial. Finally, experience is not the opposite of book knowledge; while there is a genuine distinction to be made between perception and reflection, both are part of experience. As a first approximation, experience can be understood as the contents of consciousness: the ideas thought, the emotions felt, the sounds heard, the fragrances smelled, the flavors tasted, textures touched, and colors seen. By definition, therefore, experience is all we can ever know because it encompasses both the knowledge and the thing known. Here we have reached a truism and need to make our way more carefully. Husserl's idea of the *epochē* ([1913] 1931, [1931] 1960) will provide the path.

Husserl developed his work in reaction to an idealist philosophy that set up a sharp (and to some, commonsensical) contrast between experience and objective reality. According to that idealism, we are never in contact with the objective world of things; we have only experience, and this is completely distinct from objective reality. Wanting to give philosophy an absolutely stable grounding, Husserl argued that we must not begin with abstract arguments but must instead base our thinking on a rigorous description of that which is concretely given to consciousness. To make this radical return to the givens, we must place judgments about the objectivity or subjectivity of experience in an "*epochē*" (or set of brackets) and examine the things themselves. When we do this, we immediately stumble onto a thunderous discovery: *nothing has changed*; the objectivity of the world is retained in the pure experience that the *epochē* establishes. When I attend to the desk before me, for example, I not only see its brown color and its smooth texture; built into my experience of the desk is the sense that this object is independent of me, that it has sides that are hidden from me, that it is there for (sighted) others to see, for (sensate) others to touch. What Husserl concludes from phenomenological descriptions such as these is that the world—as persistent and independent as we know it to be—is there in and for experience. As a result, we are never to remove the *epochē* and find out what lurks behind experience, because the objective characteristics of the world are there given directly in experience.

Applying the *epochē* does not reduce the world to a mere idea. Objects in the world are not to be confused with ideas, because the two are grasped in different ways. Objects in the world are there to be experienced by any capable person who is physically present; thoughts are mine alone until I share them through some form of expression. Likewise, arguing that the world is there for experience is not to reduce perception to imagination. While we have a measure of control over the act of perception (think of the vases and the hourglass in the famed Rubin's Goblet drawing), the world in perception is not infinitely malleable. I cannot see the map of Connecticut in Rubin's Goblet and call my experience a percept. However, the objectivity and autonomy inherent in our experiences of the world should not blind us to the fact that those experiences are always had by a subject. Understood phenomenologically, the objective aspects of the world are better described as all of those aspects that are there for anyone to grasp. Husserl's phenomenology is a transcendental phenomenology in that it emphasizes that the world exists as something there to be constituted in experience; in that sense the world is constituted within experience. The existential phenomenology of Maurice Merleau-Ponty ([1945] 1989) differs from Husserl's in many ways, but on this fundamental level the difference is merely one of emphasis: Merleau-Ponty agrees that the world is there for experience, but he emphasizes that the subject is there in that world, as much constituted by it as he or she constitutes it (see Hammond, Howarth, and Keat 1991, 127–48).

This dialectic of the subject and the world is basic to all forms of phenomenology. Perceptual phenomena emerge as the outcome of the subject's active and meaningful engagement with the world, and both the object of experience (or *noema*) and the engagement (or *noesis*) that constitutes it are present in experience. Experience is not constituted in one unified process but in an array of *noetic modes:* perception, memory, imagination, and so on. In fact, it is because our modes of engagement are so varied that it is so easy to miss the foundational reciprocity between ourselves and the world. In Merleau-Ponty's words, "[Phenomenological] reflection does not withdraw from the world towards the unity of consciousness as the world's basis; it steps back to watch the forms of transcendence fly up like sparks from a fire; it slacks the intentional threads which attach us to the world and thus brings them to our notice" (1989, xiii).

Both parts of this dialectic are profoundly social. First, the world is a public world there for others. We saw before that when I experience this desk, I am not only aware of the surface that faces me, I am also aware that it has a back and sides that I cannot view. That is, built into my experience of physical objects is an awareness that objects possess features that are beyond my immediate grasp but may become the focus of future experiences. Pointing toward a world beyond the immediate givens, present experience entails the existence of other subjects: my self in the past or future, and others. The world is, in Merleau-Ponty's terminology, an *interworld*—a world partially drawn into the subject's experience and partially shared between subjects. Second, the subject itself is social in origin. As Husserl observed (1960, 103–28), assimilating the concept of subject simultaneously establishes the concept of the self and other. In one's first reflexive experience, one discovers that the counterpart to oneself as an experiencing subject is oneself as a body in the world. Encountering another body, one does not merely constitute him or her as physical object; one experiences him or her as an *other subject*, because one knows that the counterpart of oneself-as-object is oneselves-as- subject. Finally, the diverse acts by which the subject constitutes experience are radically social: informed by situated event and broader social contexts, actively deployed to achieve social ends, and potentially consequential for others and society as a whole.[8]

The dialectical, betwixt and between character of the social subject and the public world allow for a sharing of experience that is as real as it as incomplete. In everyday life, the fact of cross-cultural misunderstanding, as well as simple lying, attest to the difficulties of knowing another's experience. But while I can never possess the identical experiences of the other, experiences can be partially shared. As we have seen, perception is not capricious imagination; while it is true that the world never determines the experiences we constitute from it, the fact that we live in a common world allows a measure of partial sharing. Further, because the constitution of experience is a social act, we can learn to constitute experiences in ways similar to that of others. The fact of partial sharing makes social life possible and serves as the basis for any program of inquiry that can be marshaled to understand it.

Goals and methods of phenomenological folklore and ethnomusicology (1): Situational phenomenology

Differing ideas about subjectivity have led to sharp conflicts within phenomenology. Husserl believed that the meditating philosopher could distinguish the necessary, universal structures of subjectivity from culturally specific styles of constituting experience, and that such insights could provide an absolutely stable grounding for research. Most existential phenomenologists, however, have doubted the viability of this transcendental project. Whatever the status of the philosophical debate, approaches to music and folklore based in transcendental phenomenology have tended to underestimate the variety of ways in which a subject can engage with a "text" and the importance of context for experiences of expressive culture.[9] The notion of experience in its fullness can address these questions of study object and suggest new ways of using phenomenology to understand expressive culture.

Max Lüthi's 1948 *European Folktale*, a phenomenology of the Grimm fairy tales, is a case in point. Taking the tales as *noema* and the act of reading as *noesis*, Lüthi seeks to reveal the essence of the tales and the world they evoke, to shed light on the structures and meanings evident for anyone genuinely engaged with these narratives. The difficulty here is the conception of the study object. Lüthi focuses solely on "the text" and excludes from his analysis the situated context of tale telling, his own process of constituting the tales in experience, and the broader social history that informs that reading. As a result, Lüthi does not acknowledge that others with different cultural experiences and different purposes might constitute the tales in different ways. Though Lüthi produces valuable insights, he confuses his own, culturally specific style of engaging with the text with its necessary structures. Similar issues occur in traditionally conceived phenomenologies of music, such as Alfred Schutz's "Fragments on the Phenomenology of Music" ([1944] 1976) or Roman Ingarden's *The Ontology of the Work of Art* ([1957] 1989). Schutz rightly asserts that the phenomenology of music should focus on the subject's constitution of musical experiences. But by treating music as an "ideal object," his analysis disengages musical phenomena from particular performances and cultural contexts. Confusing culturally specific ideologies of music with the necessary structures of musical phenomena, Schutz suggests that musical instruments are "neutral" mediators that have nothing essential to do with music (26–28). While such an account may be a valid description of Schutz's musical experience, listeners in many musical cultures find situated context, other elements of the performance (dance, costume), and the idiosyncrasies of their instruments to be indivisible from, or even a type of, musical phenomena. There are many valuable ideas in the writings of phenomenological musicologists like Joseph Smith (1979) or Thomas Clifton (1976); however, like Schutz, these writers ignore situated context and overestimate their own ability to account for the impact of culture on their own constitution of experience. As a result, the study object for these writers is not experience in its fullness, but the *noema* of their own culturally specific engagements with the music.

What is needed is a Husserlian return to experience, a vision of study object that includes both the rich phenomena of expressive culture and their situated constitution by subjects living lives in society and history. Such an approach builds upon ethnomusicology's interest in the multi-channeled nature of communication and the holistic concern for production and reception found in the sociology of culture. Here, musical experience does not just refer to sound, but to any phenomena deemed "musical" by the people who make it and listen to it. Such experiences do not exist solely in performance, but in the full range of settings (composing sessions, rehearsals, listening events) where musical life is carried out. The constitution of musical phenomena is actively achieved social practice, powerfully informed by the situation, the participants' goals in the event, and a potentially endless range of larger cultural contexts; as a result, all of this falls within the purview of phenomenological music studies.

The musical experiences of the participants in the death metal subculture in Akron can illustrate this approach. Such a study object is vast: all of the musical experiences of a group of people, their practices of constituting experience, and any elements of their social life that impinge upon that constitution. For the sake of argument, let us limit that range to one person's listening to one song on one night. Here, the study object is a particular listener's experience of the formal and affective aspects of the song, the stage moves of the musicians, the moshing of the crowd, the taste of the beer, and any other elements of the event that the participant concretely grasps. The participant's constitution of these experiences is influenced by his or her purposes in attending the event (the desire to get out of the house, to hear intricate and furious music, to support the local music scene) and his or her perceptual skills (listening skills, knowledge of interactional styles in metal shows). These, in turn, are informed by past musical experience (years of listening to metal, an interest in hardcore punk, music classes in high school) and nonmusical experiences (a good day at work, local ideas about gender, a series of nonunion, service-sector jobs). Ethnomusicology includes this entire complex, all understood as experience.

Of course a deep exploration of this one research participant is only one selection from the possible range of phenomenologically grounded study objects. Alternatively, the focus of research could be the similarities between many participants' concrete experiences—in the bar on that night or in Akron over twenty years. As I shall suggest in Chapters 2, 3, and 4, by taking achieved practices and partially shared experiences as its object, such an approach is well suited to account for the blurring of boundaries between groups and the relational nature of identity. To highlight the subject's agency, one could explore alternative ways that the participants could have constituted their experience of the event. One can also compare the constitution of musical experience by listeners from different groups to display the role of social context in influencing the constitution of perception. In either broad or narrow studies, however, the scholar must take the full experiences of the musical participant as the horizon of the study object, even if some more circumscribed theme becomes the focus of the research.

The method of exploring such a study object is partial sharing, and the traditional techniques of the ethnographer and the historian can be understood phenomenologically. Although the research participant can misunderstand or misrepresent his or her experiences, survey, interview, and feedback interview techniques are basic ways in which the researcher can achieve partial sharing. Engaging in the routinized activities of the community, the fieldworker can also gain insights through participant observation. And just as performance theory applies to both archival and ethnographic projects (see, for example, Bauman 1986, Foley 1992), phenomenological approaches bear on historical research as well. Understood in this way, the reader of archival texts uses the mediating marks on the page to partially share the experiences of subjects from earlier times. Likewise, material culture and archeological remains give another kind of access to the experiences of past others.

Another aspect of method is dialogue and critique. Multifaceted and contextual, individual phenomena are complex, situated gestalts whose focal features imply dimensions and connections unseen at present but potentially available for future experiences. As a result of this richness, our reflective descriptions never fully capture the experiences they are meant to describe, and the research participant cannot be taken as the sole arbiter of ethnographic description. The interpretation of experience is a social process; in ethnographic dialogue the fieldworker and the research participant can work together to bring experience into focus. Further, phenomenology is not unable to recognize that the interpretation of experience is filled with "occlusions." Just as an occlusion in the eye prevents us from seeing the world clearly, power relations act as ideological occlusions, actively impairing our ability to interpret social life. Here dialogue and critique may be necessary to unearth richer understandings. This line of argument terminates in the problem of reconciling participant perspectives with critical scholarship and is the subject of Chapters 10 and 11.

With all this in place, the goals of situated phenomenological work in folklore and ethnomusicology can be easily stated. First, folklore and ethnomusicology can pursue an ethnographic and descriptive aim. As subjects necessarily situated in particular times and places, limited in our engagement with the world, and brief in our life spans, we all suffer from an inevitable provincialism. Even the best traveled and most sensitive can only hope to sample a tiny fraction of the food, music, thought, and feeling—the forms of social life—that the world presents. As a result, we constantly mistake the contingent for the natural, the particular for the universal. The ethnographic aim of situated phenomenology can partially overcome this provinciality by sharing experiences with others distanced by space, time, and identity. This project of cosmopolitanism can never be completed, but ethnography infinitely widens the scope of our lives. In its ethnographic goal, situated phenomenology is not unlike the novel or the poem (though these two may differ greatly from social research in their methods).

Yoked with the ethnographic goal is the analytic one. Here, phenomenology goes beyond the description of experience and tries to shed light on its dynamics; the range of possible projects here is immense. Chapters 5 and 6, for example, are a case study in the social basis of perception; by comparing the constitution of musical form by musicians with different social pasts and musical goals, I show that even the most minute aspects of perception are at once deeply influenced by our social context and completely open to our agency. The individual purposes of these analytic projects are as diverse as the problems they seek to solve. At its root, however, such research helps us understand how our minds and bodies operate, how experience is tied to the world, and how social life works. In this way, situated phenomenological research is practical, providing a sort of owner's manual for the experiencing subject.

Goals and methods of phenomenological
folklore and ethnomusicology (2):
Cross-situational reality and phenomenology

Although the foregoing discussion focused on so-called microlevel issues, phenomenology can also be used to understand cross-situational phenomena—events that extend beyond the boundaries of the immediate context. By relating existential phenomenology to Giddens's practice theory we can suggest how scholarship grounded in the notions of practice and experience can explore the full range of social life.

Addressing the problem of structure and agency, Giddens argues that social structure is not an autonomous entity that stands in opposition to intentional action. On the contrary, society is brought into being by the intentional and unintentional consequences of intentional action (1979, 1984, 1993). This action, however, is not some radically individual caprice, but is itself informed by past and present social context, understood here as the consequences of past and present acts. The process by which past intentional acts become objectified as the context for present acts is referred to as *structuration* and forms the central concern of practice theory. Mediated by the physical world or by memory, events from even the dimmest past may be consequential for the present situation; thus, Giddens holds that all action takes place in unacknowledged contexts and in turn entails unintended consequences.

All this would seem to be at odds with phenomenology, arguing as it does for a world beyond the subject's experience that constrains and enables his or her action. Giddens's critique of Schutz's sociology illustrates the problem. In *The Phenomenology of the Social World* ([1932] 1967) Schutz tries to depict the world of society through all the modes in which others appear to the subject, ranging from the most intimate and specific (face-to-face social interaction) through greater levels of mediation (the phone call or the letter) to ideal types (abstract knowledge of distant social groups). Giddens argues that "having adopted the starting-point of a phenomenological reduction [or *epochē*], Schutz is unable to reconstitute social reality as an object-world" (1993, 31). In other words, Schutz's phenomenology is unsociological because it strays into subjective idealism, reducing the objectivity of society to the subject's perception. But as we have seen, phenomenology does not represent the world as mere idea. The links between phenomenology and practice theory become apparent if we understand the world outside of the present situation—the world of the past and the large-scale spatial world—as experience; returning to the *epochē* will make this idea clear.

When we apply the *epochē* and explore the immediate givens of experience, our attention is first drawn to the situated context and the subject's engagement with the world. As Husserl showed, however, we experience the here and now of the situation as located within a horizon of other places and times. Typing away at my computer with focused attention, for example, I may momentarily forget that there is a world beyond this keyboard and these flowing ideas. When the frame is broken, however, I become aware that the foreground of my situation implies a background of a world larger than this room and a time before this scene. Engaged in perception, the world reveals itself to me as a field of potential experience that was there for subjects in the past and will be there for potential subjects in the future. As a result, the cross-situational chains of context and consequences that precede and enable my present action are there to be constituted in experience by anyone thinking historically or sociologically. Just as the South Pole was always there to be experienced before anyone explored it, the trains of context and consequence that extend across individual situations and tumble beyond the awareness of any given actor are there to be experienced through an examination of their traces.

Understood in this way, the concepts of practice and experience can be used to explore so-called macrosocial study objects. Take, for example, the topic of Chapters 10 and 11: the relationship between deindustrialization and death metal. Deindustrialization can be understood concretely as the intended and unintended outcome of a vast number of intentional practices; such practices include the cutting back of wages, the reorganization of distribution networks, the responses of labor, the building of plants in Third World countries, the activities of Third World laborers, the forging of global trade treaties, the purchase of Third World goods in First World countries, the closing of First World plants, and so on. As actions in the past world, this massive train of events is there to be grasped by any inquiring subject through its mediating traces: documents, material evidence, oral reports, and so on. In this study, the topic is not just deindustrialization, but its acknowledged and unacknowledged consequences for the musical experiences of metalheads in Akron. Among these consequences is that when young people in Akron read the newspaper want ads, there are few jobs and what few jobs there are pay little. The young people are free, of course, to respond to this situation as they choose, but the consequences of past practices form the context in which their actions operate. Here, phenomenological ethnomusicology seeks to understand how deindustrialization (understood as past and present acts in a world of experience) forms a context for the musical practices of metalheads and to explore the possible consequences that those musical practices might have for the participants' lives and the larger society. In sum, phenomenologically based research can explore historical or macrosocial topics because the vast trains of context and consequence that compose history and society can be understood as parts of the world, there to be grasped in experience.

From the smallest act of perception to the broadest historical movement, the scope of phenomenological research is the scope of the world. By taking the notions of practice and experience as guiding concepts, we can get beyond approaches that see activity and society, or experience and the world, as two unrelated orders of reality. Lived experience is the primary ground from which these dichotomies are abstracted, and the issues and problems of music research can provide us with unparalleled insights into its dynamics. In musical experience, the subject engages with the world in creative acts of perception; here, the participant plays a role in the social life of music and, to varying degrees, helps to constitute society as a whole. By returning to musical experience, we can gain powerful new perspectives on social life.

PART ONE

THE ETHNOGRAPHY OF
MUSICAL PRACTICE

TWO

Commercial Hard Rock in Cleveland, Ohio
Dia Pason and Max Panic

In this part of the book I shall introduce the reader to the practices and experiences of the participants of four music scenes in northeastern Ohio. This chapter focuses on the commercial hard rock scene of Cleveland; Chapter 3 focuses on underground metal in Akron, and Chapter 4, on the jazz scenes. If we are to gain insight into musical perception and the political dimensions of rock and jazz, we must first have some basic vision of the fashion and comportment of the audiences, the stage behavior and musical forms used by the musicians, the physical spaces and overall forms of the performance events, and the ensemble of meanings that these various expressive cultures possess. My first goal is to provide such an ethnographic background.

But there is another goal here as well: to focus on practice at its medial level and examine how the participants' practices constitute music cultures. When I say that social practice constitutes cultures, I use "constitute" in a dual sense. On the one hand, the participants' practices—acts of music making and music perception—constitute the meanings of the music in their experiences; on the other hand, the patterning and the reciprocities of the participants' practices, along with larger contexts and the unintended consequences of the participants' actions, constitute larger social groups (scenes, subcultures and so on). This double constitution, the constitution of immediately lived meanings and the constitution of social groups, gives practice its density; if we wish to understand practice, we must observe it at multiple levels of focus and seek connections among the data we have thus constructed.

While Part II focuses on the constitution of meanings in perceptual practices and Part III focuses on the trains of context and consequence that bind situated practices to history, this part focuses on practice at the medial level and fits in with our most quotidian understandings of life. By "focusing on practice at its medial level," I mean examining typical activities described in general terms, habitually settings of face-to-face social interactions, everyday purposes and perceptual experiences and their meanings depicted in broad strokes. Everyday attention rarely lets in the rich, sensuous details of our perceptual experiences, nor does everyday reflection commonly examine the broad historical and social contexts of our practices. Only artists or serious meditators examine the colors, textures, and meanings, for example, of their morning toast; only political activists and social scientists habitually reflect on the long-term consequences and complex social histories implicated, for example, in the act of buying fruit at the grocery store. As most of us live our lives, our everyday thoughts are focused on gross sensual description and the abstract, typical situations and practices of social life's medial level: "Time to make the toast; don't forget to pick up some bananas at the store." Information at the perceptual and cross-situational level tends to be esoteric, and not merely by virtue of the fact that it is frequently insider knowledge. To study the constitution of perception one must make an effort to focus attention on the smallest details of living experience; to garner knowledge about the large scale of history and society, one must tie together vast tracts of experience possessed by different individuals and mediated in different forms (documents, material culture, and so on). The medial focus, however, provides the most accessible image of practice and the easiest entrance into unfamiliar cultures.

Humanistic ethnography traditionally focuses on this level of social life. Unfortunately, much contemporary work in cultural studies takes the meanings of expressive culture as artifacts to be collected, the social actors they observe as mere examples of a type, and social formations such as musical scenes or subcultures as entities in their own right. Like cultural studies scholars, I explore meanings, patterns, and power relations; however, more in line with interpretive ethnography, I show how those meanings and social groups arise as the outcome of constitutive practices. Rather than merely describing styles of clothing and their meanings, I show how fashion and bodily stylistics[1] are actively achieved by participants in performance events. Rather than analyzing the abstract musical structures of rock, metal, and jazz, I show how musicians engage with the universe of sound in culturally specific practices of composition, arrangement, and rehearsal. And rather than taking subcultures as preexisting entities somehow divorced from the people who partake in them, I show how they are constituted by the various practices of their participants. Building on the insights of diverse music scholars such as Ruth Finnegan (1989), Jocelyne Guilbault (1993), and Barry Shank (1994),[2] I demonstrate how both the stability and the fragmentation of meanings within a scene are established through constitutive practices. Treating practice as both the achievement of concrete actors and deeply informed by social context, I show how even the most robust scene is built up from the practices of its adherents, and how even the most fragile and ephemeral musical coalition is informed by large-scale social context.

One final note of introduction: it has been my constant concern throughout the fieldwork to garner the participants' views of all of the meanings that I interpret. Feedback interviews with the musicians have confirmed or disconfirmed almost every point in the descriptions of the music, the musical scenes, and the broader political contexts. But because I have focused on the musicians and not the listeners, the descriptions of the practices in the clubs themselves and the audience members are based more on observation than on interview. Also, while I am interested in all settings of interaction in commercial hard rock, my focus will be on the practices of nightclub performance.

America's north coast and a building in Akron

Cuyahoga County is the practical and municipal body that surrounds and defines Cleveland, Ohio. A home to roughly two million people, the county sits on Lake Erie and is divided in half by the Cuyahoga River. In many ways the city reflects a number of central themes in American history: European immigrations to the area have given the city a variety of ethnic groups; migrations of African Americans from the South have provided racial diversity; a declining industrial base has left the city with its "rust belt" reputation as well as a working class whose real income has been stagnant since the early 1970s; racism has shunted the greater part of the economic damage onto the African American communities, and racial tensions are high throughout the city. To the south and slightly west, Summit County is Akron's municipal region. With a population of more than 250,000, Summit County is less ethnically diverse but more troubled economically. Akron was once America's tire capital; now, according to the Akron Development Office, the only tires made in the county come from a few specialty shops for race cars. Limited-access roads connect Cleveland and Akron, and though their suburbs form a roughly unbroken whole, the two regions have maintained separate identities in the minds of most people with whom I spoke.

In the early 1990s, commercial hard rock was one of the most established musical scenes in northeast Ohio. As Ruth Finnegan so rightly emphasizes (1989, 325–26), even the most stable scene is brought into being by the actions of its members (also see Cohen 1993). In Cleveland and Akron, the rock scene was constituted in a wide variety of typified settings and practices, including promotional work, recording, band rehearsals, nightclub performances, music store bull sessions, and parties; the style of music associated with the scene was known somewhat pejoratively as glam (short for glamour) or pop metal (not to be confused with underground metal). The musicians are almost exclusively white and male, and a large cadre of white women and men also participate in the scene as fans. Most of the band members know each other from playing gigs together, and, on nights when they are not playing, most musicians go out and see other bands; the scene regulars know each other from spending time at clubs. Through performance, recording, promotion, and socializing, the bands grow in local success, and—contextualized within the international music industry and American society as a whole—it is the relatively stable pattern of these activities that make up the scene.

Musical scenes are often constituted in opposition to other scenes, and alternative rock and the punk and metal undergrounds were the main musical others against which Cleveland's commercial hard rockers defined themselves. Composed of a variety of scenes and genres, "alternative" includes the Seattle or grunge style, the Grateful Dead subculture and their numerous imitators, and the jangly, post-Byrds "college rock" style spearheaded by REM. Industrial and various kinds of dance musics have also been labeled as alternative, although the commercial hard rockers were generally less aware of them. While the rockers I spoke with had no consistent terminology for discussing alternative, these generic designations describe the rockers' fairly uniform musical and sociological intuitions.

Grunge (or, as it was known at the time, Seattle style) was the most important other for Cleveland's rockers. Associated with both a scene and a musical style, grunge is commonly understood as a reaction against the excesses of commercial hard rock. Where rock bands employed extensive effect processing to produce a smooth guitar distortion, grunge bands like Nirvana used improvised, older, or low-tech equipment to produce a rawer guitar sound. Reacting against the rockers' concern with visual appeal, the fashions of grunge bands are self-consciously unmannered. Intended as more serious than the party-hearty glam bands, their lyrics are often political or obscure; grunge revived the punk critique of rock's instrumental virtuosity as silly macho posturing. A similar reaction against glam, REM-styled college rock combined the chimey guitars of 1960s folk rock with richly layered vocal harmonies, serious lyrics, and an intense pop melodicism. Perceived by the rockers as more generically distant than alternative, Cleveland's country scene followed the national trend and exploded in the 1990s, while the varieties of hip-hop claimed a loyal following among rock's traditional audience.

From its roots in the independent record labels and college radio stations of the 1980s, alternative grew from an obscure motley of genres to the mainstream rock music of the 1990s. When I arrived in Cleveland in the fall of 1992, most commercial hard rockers had heard of alternative; when I left in December 1993, the biggest of the commercial hard rock clubs had closed, and the scene was in a rapid decline. Because of the large size of the rock scene and the relatively limited number of venues in Cleveland and Akron, alternative fans could often be found at commercial hard rock shows in 1993 (though rockers were rarely seen at alternative shows). As an entrance into the social life of commercial hard rock, let us explore a typical night in the spring of 1993 at one of the area's main commercial hard rock clubs—the Akron Agora.

You get to the Agora by car, a trip that for most Agora regulars would take forty-five minutes to an hour, often in wet or snowy weather. Cuyahoga County folklore has it that Cleveland and Liverpool, both declining industrial cities, share exactly the same paltry number of sunny days per year. While numerous Cleveland rock musicians have hoped that their town would copy Liverpool in its nurturing of great rock bands, no Cleveland Beatles have ever emerged. Like most suburban rock clubs, the Agora is a plain rectangular building sitting in an immense, un-snowplowed, poorly paved parking lot. The keynotes for performances at the Agora are energy, excitement, and the promise of soon-to-be-won fame. Most local bands do not even half-fill the lot, giving their performance a somewhat amateurish look even before one enters the club. Opening bands usually begin around ten-thirty, and, when I arrived on the evening of April 30 at quarter past ten, the half-filled parking lot indicated a fairly busy crowd. A tube-shaped water tower sat to the south of the club, well lit, and with a spiral stairway running around it. I parked next to a Camaro and went inside the club.

The Akron Agora is one of the largest rock clubs in the area (see Figure 1). After paying the bouncer, you walk west through a dark, narrow hallway into a large room divided roughly into three parts, the southern third immediately in front of you. The sections of the room are at different levels, and each section in turn is articulated into smaller spaces by the lighting; low walls and Plexiglas barriers divide the sections, while short stairways afford passage at odd intervals. The walls and floors are covered in a red

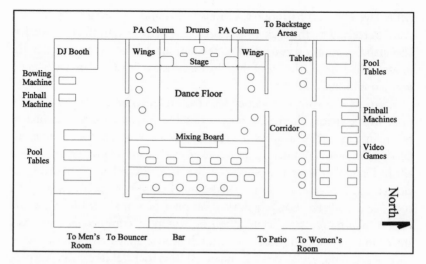

Figure 1. Map of the Akron Agora

and black carpeting, while the tables are covered with flyers advertising future shows. The walls are largely devoid of decoration and the room as a whole is dark but not dismal. Even on a quiet night, the air is thick with cigarette smoke. After any night at a rock show, my hair would have a burned, ashen smell.

The southern section of the room is mostly empty except for a few pool tables and video games; it only becomes crowded on the busiest nights. The central section, with its stage, dance floor, and bar, is the focus of the club. High off the floor, the stage is flanked by two large PA columns (speakers) and covered by an array of colored lights. An elaborate drum kit is set on risers in the center of the stage, while amplifiers, strobes, pyro effects, and other equipment are arranged around the space. The bands own all of the equipment on the stage except for the PA and ceiling-mounted lights; thought to be essential for giving the musicians a professional look, this equipment eats up a good deal of the bands' money and time. The dance floor is on the lowest level of the club, and with its intense, multicolored lighting it is the visual center of the space. A series of tiers with large round tables ascend to the bar level, each a step above the last. The bar area itself is spacious and well lit; centrally located and with a commanding view of the dance floor, this area becomes a hot spot between sets. The high-traffic corridor connecting the back stage to the bar and patio is another focal point, as strutting participants and purposeful roadies constantly traverse its length. Behind the stage is the band's "dressing room," a large empty room covered floor-to-ceiling in graffiti, the layers of spray paint and Magic Marker an archeology of the local rock scene. The northern third of the room is the highest in the club and the most insulated from the music; people come here to take time out from the social displays below, talk, or shoot pool.

Typical of larger rock clubs, the overall effect of the architecture is to create an image of both spectacle and intimacy. The special lighting, loud PA, and spaciousness give the Agora the ambiance of a big-time rock venue, of celebrity, spectacle, and fun; the articulation of the room into nooks and crannies allows small groups to personalize the space—parading in the thick of things or observing from the sidelines, seeing and being seen. Taking a broader view, we can understand the physical environment as a kind of highly mediated communication among the architects, decorators, management, musicians, and nightclub goers. From this perspective, musical performances, bodily stylistics, fashion, interior decors, and architecture can all be understood as genres of expressive interaction, differentiated only by the durability of their mediators (sound, body motion, clothing, and building materials). In this sense, designing, decorating, and using the space are practices that constitute the event, rich in meaning and ripe for interpretation.

Some people at the Agora

On a busy night of commercial hard rock, the participants at the club employ a wide range of fashions and bodily stylistics. Greg, a participant in an earlier study of mine, suggested that if I were interested in people watching at rock shows, I should start with a type he called the Silent Men. Musicians or critical listeners, these men are there to judge the bands, said Greg. Dressed in worn but not ripped jeans, work boots and T-shirts, they avoid both the self-consciously showy look of the commercial hard rocker and the self-conscious carelessness of the Seattle-style grungester. As the bands play, they stand off to the side of the dance floor and view the musicians with a critical glare; between the sets they position themselves at the margins of the action, leaning against the walls and avoiding the dance floor and bar area. Such men always go to shows with a friend. Arms folded across their chests or one hand holding a plastic cup of beer, they talk little and drink just slightly more. They gaze critically at both the musicianship of the bands and the boisterous displays of the participants. This observation, however, is not lecherous. While sexuality and spectacular display are major themes in all of these events, the disdain of the Silent Men's glances seems aimed equally at the loud and expressive men as well as the provocatively dressed women.

Positioned at the margins and stony in demeanor, the Silent Men clearly mark themselves as observers, but most of the other participants at the Agora are performers. While all public behavior is enacted with an awareness that others are present, performance, in folklorist Richard Bauman's sense of the term, occurs when we self-consciously try to present our behavior to others, drawing special attention to our aesthetic competence (1989). A commercial hard rock show is a place where people go to see and be seen, and when the Agora becomes busy, dress and comportment range from the slightly giddy to the sharply stylized. Far from a monolithic display of style, the practices of dress and comportment at the Agora range wildly. *Agora* is the ancient Greek word for marketplace, and any busy night at the Akron Agora in 1993 would present the observer with what Ted Polhemus has called a "supermarket of style" (Polhemus 1994, 130–34).

Sexuality, extravagance, and display are keynotes for the glam metal look. Men's fashions in this scene might include tight-fitting, faded but not ripped jeans, spandex pants, silk button-downs, or T-shirts; hair could range in length from the shoulder to the mid-back, and hair weaves were not unheard of. As is true in the broader society, women's fashions were both more varied and more complex: in the summer, skin-tight jean shorts or black miniskirts; in the winter, skin-tight jeans or spandex pants. T-shirts were acceptable in this scene, but tight, summer halters, short-sleeved shirts, and elaborately laced blouses were also common for tops. Black leather jackets and handcuffs through belt loops provided a tougher image for some of these women, while tight and lacy black dresses in the style of singer Stevie Nicks were still popular, even though that performer hadn't been in the limelight recently. High heels, long permed hair with mousse-coated bangs, and thick layers of makeup were common. Such a style is actively put on for shows and marks the wearer as part of the local hard rock scene.

With commercial hard rock acts still common at local venues, alternative fans not totally alienated from glam could be found on busy nights at the Agora. More rips than fabric, baggy jeans or loose-fitting plaid shorts were common in this style, as were plaid shirts, long, unstyled hair, vests, and Dr. Martens boots; men often wore goatees. A 1960s retro-alternative look with ties to the Grateful Dead subculture was also familiar. Imported Guatemalan wear, tie dyes, and other Dead paraphernalia were part of this style, as was the peasant dress. Side-by-side with these spectacular subculturists could always be found more mundane collegians. Men in polo shirts or sweatshirts with college or beer insignias and neat, medium-fit jeans could always be found with women in quiet dresses. Office wear was also common for women—white linen pants, understated floral blouses, and blazers. Uniformly white and boisterously heterosexual, the crowds ranged from mid-teens to late twenties with a few casually dressed people in their thirties and forties also in attendance. The bustling atmosphere of a busy commercial hard rock show in the declining days of glam was nothing if not eclectic, but I never saw any tension or antagonism between participants with different styles.

The notion of performance is not merely meant to awaken us to the social nature of aesthetics, but to emphasize that performances are enacted, actively achieved by their participants. While the participants make an effort to dress themselves up for an evening at the Agora, it is their comportment and bodily stylistics that pushes their behavior from mere socializing into performance. As the bands set up or tore down their equipment, their friends would charge seriously around the club hauling equipment and running miscellaneous errands; above the crowd's insignificant pursuits, their crucial missions tinged them with some of the limelight the soon-to-be famous band members basked in. Women wearing the glam style would storm along the main corridor from the dressing room to the bar, each aggressive step a performance of popularity and sexuality. A strange parallel to the Silent Men were the Black-Clad Glam Women. The disdaining, icy glance of these women drew attention like a magnet; always congregating in groups of two or three, they sent the unmistakable message: "Don't mess with me." Wispy Deadhead men in Guatemalan shirts cavorted with women in peasant dress and drew glares from the Silent Men. By and large the grungesters portrayed a tougher and more standoffish demeanor, and the collegians and other conservatively dressed participants held to the background. With the main corridor serving as a fashion runway and the bar area a stage, the tiers of central tables and the section with pinball machines functioned as festival seating for the less performative audience members. In the dressing room, one of the few places in the bar where the music didn't quash conversation, friends of the band talked in quiet groups.

Imagine yourself at one of the tables along the main corridor in the Agora on April 30; all around you, rockers, grungesters, deadheads, and mundanes are performing their scene. A flier on the table advises you that the Metal Bratz, a local glam band, will be playing here next week. Their heads close together to hear each other over the noise, two women in tight black jeans and loose blouses fervently share some of the latest gossip at a table fifteen or twenty feet away; they are scanned by three men with beautifully permed hair leaning against the side of the bar. A short woman in a low-cut red top and tight blue jeans steams past your table on an urgent

Dia Pason (left to right: Chris Ozimek, Brian Exton, Steve Christen, Alfredo Ricci)

errand to the backstage area. In her wake, a woman in a long peasant dress flows past and, unnoticed, is given a disdainful look by two Silent Men with folded arms and concert tees; they themselves had been dismissed with a glance by the short woman in red. Sipping your soda (you avoid alcohol to stay sharp) you observe the collegians shooting pool in the odd glow of the big-screen TV. The quick and decisive movements of roadies and musicians on the stage have stopped, the recorded music ends abruptly, and an announcer's voice tells us that Out Of The Blue is about to take the stage.

In many ways, the April 30 show was one of the more successful nights of commercial hard rock in the waning days of northeast Ohio glam. Two years earlier, larger and far more homogeneous crowds of hard rockers were common, but in the spring of 1993, an Akron Agora only three-quarters full and attended by Deadheads, grungesters, and mundanes was seen as a pretty good show.

If the image of celebrity, energized sociability, and irresistible fun are the desiderata of a hard rock show, the March 24 show at the Agora was far less successful than the April 30 gig. When I arrived at quarter past ten, the parking lot was mostly empty. The first of three acts was a power metal group called Gothic. At several generic removes from Gothic were two commercial hard rock bands, Dia Pason (pronounced DEE-uh pas-OWN) and the headliner, Kid Wicked. A weeknight show with generically dissimilar bands held during the declining days of the scene, the Agora felt more like a quiet get-together than a party. Four or five guys shot pool in the southern section of the room. In the central section, a woman in black leather in the bar area casually spoke with a friend. Two women in glam attire danced halfheartedly on the illuminated floor, while their friends sat at a table to the north. A few others were scattered around the club, and I wandered back to the dressing room and chatted with the people I knew from Dia Pason, the group whose music is the focus of Chapter 6. Gothic played as a crowd of no more than twenty listeners gently rocked their heads in time with quarter notes or stood stock still. After their sets, about thirty more people arrived. Alternative guys in Guatemalan shirts cavorted with expansive gestures on the dance floor; with no one to impress, they quit their free-spirited antics and wandered quietly to the bar. Unlike the night of April 30 with its performing crowd, this night's audience was more interested in getting out of the house or supporting their friends in the bands than seeing and being seen. Dia Pason came on after a half-hour break.

Max Panic (left to right: John Carr, Ken Barber,
George Chapman, and Jeff Johnston)

The band and the crowds

Dia Pason's instrumentation and personnel have changed radically since its inception in the late 1980s. A fan of Cheap Trick and Poison, lead singer and bass player Chris Ozimek[3] was the band's main songwriter and founder. Alfredo Ricci was the rhythm guitarist and backup vocalist; musically inexperienced, he spent much offstage time doing promotion and building special effects. KB (Kirk Spork) filled in on lead guitar while his own band, The Atomic Punks, was between regional tours. This show was one of drummer and founding member Steve Christen's last musical performances. Chris hoped to book regional shows in the coming months, and Steve, recently engaged and with prospects for a good local job, was leaving both Dia Pason and the scene.

Even with a small crowd, the band's props and instruments spoke of spectacle, energy, sexuality, and fun. Set in the back of the stage, the big double bass drums and endless percussion instruments of Steve's kit evoked feelings of musical capacity while its circus colors tempered power with fun. Two sets of plywood steps built around disused speaker cabinets led up to the drum risers, a small-scale approximation of the walls of speakers with which national acts display sonic power to their crowds; the band's logo was painted in orange and white on two large bedsheets. As this was a midweek show, the band's smoke bombs, strobe-lights, and fireworks were all left at home. A more complex bricolage, the band's fashions projected an image that was equal parts vaudevillian comedy, Chippendale sexuality, and zoot suit extravagance. Chris wore tight black jeans, while a loud black-and-white vest (no shirt) showed off his muscular arms and chest. Chris would eventually grapple with pop metal's decline by cutting his hair, but at this show it extended to the middle of his back in sensual, carefully styled waves. Al, who was later shocked by Chris's post-glam coif, wore a flashy silk shirt, black jeans, and straight, brown, shoulder-length hair. Roughly strat shaped,[4] his flashy Jackson guitar sported the image of a women in a bikini lounging on a beach. Always clowning, KB wore oversized black high-tops, elaborately ripped jeans, and a denim vest covered with countless buttons.

Like the strutting audience members, the musicians of Dia Pason achieve their performance through bodily stylistics as well as costume. Though Dia Pason had less space available to them than the headliners, Chris, Al, and KB used every inch of the stage. Tied to the mike while singing, Chris gestured as much as he could, kept time with his heel, and marked phrases and hits with his body. Freed from the mike during instrumental breaks, Chris spun away from the literal and figurative center of the performance, walking in exaggerated, loping steps (that I would mentally label "the Godzilla walk"), gesturing with his guitar in tandem with Al, or directing his stylized movements at Steve. Nervous on stage, Al maintained a much more low-key stage persona, responding to Chris's gestures and making the choppy motions with his guitar neck so well known in rock performance. Running from one end of the stage to the other, cavorting on the risers, gesturing to members of the audience, and leaping upward while kicking out his calves (Eddie Van Halen's signature move), KB was clearly the stage clown. Largely hidden by his drum kit, Steve would occasionally twirl his sticks and articulate drum parts with his head. All of the musicians except for Steve would jerk their heads in a stylized gesture used to clear their hair from their faces. Both observation and interviews revealed that fun, effortless musical engagement, and virtuosic skill was the message their bodily practices were intended to convey.

As ethnomusicologists have long known, every musical culture has its typical and desired style of audience response, and the audience's activities are just as important as the musicians' for a successful performance. At a commercial hard rock show, listeners will foot tap or move their heads gently in time with the quarter notes; if they know the original songs or, more likely, the cover tunes, they will mouth the words. Women occasionally dance, but men almost never do, and it is not uncommon for friends of the band to parody the musicians with imitations of their stage gestures; at all but the most successful shows the Silent Men stand stock-still. Most bands try to involve the audience with devices such as between-song patter, sing-along sections, eye contact, and a vocabulary of flashy stage antics. There is virtually no audience conversation during the songs (talk in front of the PA columns is virtually inaudible); those who are bored walk away. The images of fun and raucous good times that the rockers seek to evoke is ideally greeted by an audience that moves to the music, neither engaged with elaborate dancing nor set in the immobile attentiveness of a Western art-music concert.

Each musical culture, however, doesn't merely possess norms of audience response; it also possesses a unique social organization of attention in the event—a culturally specific style of partially sharing experiences between audience and performer. One of my most robust discoveries in Cleveland was the rock musicians' desire to compel the audience's attention. All of the rock musicians I spoke with said that their aim was to pry the listeners from the bar or pool table and rivet their attention to the music; reciprocally, the audience expects that a good show will be compelling, and they wander away from the dance floor when a band does not draw them in. In contrast, jazz musicians are mostly unconcerned with inviting attention; over and over, jazz musicians told me that the fickle nature of their crowds and the demanding nature of their music made it impossible for them to try to compel the crowd's regard. The best they can do, they said, is focus on their own playing, create good music, and hope the audience might make the effort to share their aural experiences. Rock musicians are afforded no such luxury; for both the audiences and the musicians, a successful performance has only occurred when the show becomes an irresistible attraction in the audience's consciousness. In such a situation, the rockers said, the meanings the music projects (energy, fun, sexuality, the sparkle of soon-to-be-won fame) are amplified and fed back to them by the audience's responses—body motion, cheering, and so on. In this sense, the music is just one element, albeit a crucial one, in the participant's constitution of meanings in the event. Fun, abandon, and capacity (the musicians' capacity to compel attention, the audience's capacity for release) are not merely the central themes of the music; they inform the styles of interaction and the modes of sharing experience in the event. We shall explore the social organization of attention in the event (or, for brevity's sake, what I shall call the "sociology of attention") in greater detail in Part II, but for now it is important to observe the intimate connections between the meanings of the performance, the styles of audience-performer interaction, and the culturally specific patterns of partially sharing experience in a performance event. At this level—the social constitution of experience by the situated subject—meanings and practices are inextricable, and it is from the constitutive practices of performance and partial sharing that all the more artifactualized descriptions of meaning emerge.

Music and words (1): The practice of composition

More than gesturing bodies, the rock show is a musical performance, and the preceding sections lead us right to the verge of the musical sound. A difficulty in the treatment of musical sound by past ethnomusicological ethnography has been the trope of the "musicological sandwich"—the juxtaposition of descriptions of situated context and musical structure at the level of chapters or paragraph subheadings (see Chapter 1). While historically, this kind of rhetoric served as an important first step in contextualizing musical transcriptions, it ultimately reaffirms the boundary between text and context and disengages musical structures from the practices of perception and action that constitute them. Seeking to emphasize their links, I must pause in my description of the performance event and explore the practices of composition and rehearsal that precede and enable the live performance; comparing rock and jazz compositional practices in Chapter 4, I shall emphasize the ways such practices are culturally specific.

The processes often begin in the practice room. Because of the sheer volume of sound a rock band produces, rehearsal space is often hard to find. Dia Pason practices after hours in the basement of a music store, while other bands rent commercial warehouse space, attics, or barns. Bands typically rehearse one to four times a week, but the length and content of rehearsals vary. Most rehearsals start by warming up with familiar tunes. When a band is performing frequently, practice may entail little more than running through the set list, but when bands have gone through a long period of steady work, they often get tired of performing the same songs and start composing. Broadly speaking, we can understand composition in rock or metal as falling within a continuum from group composition to leader composition.[5]

Among group-composition bands, seed ideas for sections of songs often occur to individual members while noodling on their instrument, driving, or working. When the rehearsal session turns to composition, anyone who has composed a seed idea during the week will present it, and the other musicians will either learn it or try to compose a part to go with it. When no one has a seed idea to start the process, one player may just start to play and a seed will emerge in spontaneous, improvised composition. Jeff Johnston, guitarist for the hard rock band Max Panic, explains that ideas will often develop during breaks in the rehearsal, and while half the band is drinking a beer, the other members may be composing a section of a song. How a section is composed depends upon where the seed idea comes from. For example, a common seed is a short, memorable series of guitar chords that acts as a melodic fragment. Given this, the guitar player may sing or tap out his or her ideas for a drum groove,[6] and vocal melody may be fitted with the guitar part; in other situations, an entire song may be composed before vocals are added. Short bass ostinati, vocal melodies, and distinctive drum grooves may also be the seeds for new songs. When the group is composing as a whole, they will play, modify, and elaborate the seed until an entire section is composed and everyone has at least some tentative part to play.

As to the content of the seed ideas, most commercial hard rock seeds are in 4/4 time, with the snare drum hitting strong accents on the second and fourth beats. The bass or "kick" drums articulate and decorate the first and third beats, while the high hat cymbals typically count the quarter notes. The repeating pattern of snare, kick, and hats is the rhythmic backbone of the song and is referred to as the groove or beat. While all rock drummers have a vocabulary of standard grooves, in the practice of composition, drummers creatively develop new grooves to compliment the other players' seed ideas. Weaving together single-note lines and chords, the guitarist's seeds often serve double duty as melodic fragment and harmonic accompaniment; other seeds arpeggiate major, minor, or suspended triads and fulfill the traditional role in Western song of outlining the harmony. Blues harmonies and stock progressions employing the I, IV, V, and iv chords[7] are most common. (Chapter 7 explores the harmonic and melodic content of commercial hard rock in detail.) As Walser (1991, 1993) repeatedly emphasizes, timbre is crucial to the aesthetics of rock and metal. At their very inception, most guitar seeds are imagined with specific configuration of distortion, time-domain effects (echo, reverb, chorus, and so on), and amp settings; for guitarists, the practice of developing ideas may just as frequently involve the creative adjustment of equipment as it does the manipulation of note choice. Similarly, rock singers employ a wide range of vocal articulations and timbres, all of which are foundational aspects of their musical ideas. From even the first stage of composition, Chris defines the glissandi, embellishments, and timbral features of his vocal lines as well as their pitches and their durations.

With one section complete, the band may introduce an old seed or search for a new one with which to begin the next section. As they develop the seeds, the players are usually aware of the type of section (verse, chorus) the part will become, and, during the first composition sessions, the players will develop a tentative outline for the order of the parts. Commercial hard rock songs tend to employ six types of sections (verses, choruses, bridges, solos, intros, and "outros") and arrange them into typical forms. The chorus is the heart of the song; a 16- or 32-bar section, choruses usually contain the hook—a short memorable vocal or guitar melody intended to stick in the listener's mind. Each iteration of the chorus usually has the same lyrics and is intensified with backup vocals. In contrast to the chorus, verses tend to be less energetic. Each iteration of the verse usually has different lyrics, and background vocals here are often less prominent. If a story is told in the song, each verse develops some phase in the narrative; if the song is trying to make a point, each verse elaborates a different example to display it. Bridge sections, either vocal or instrumental, link verses and choruses, and it is often difficult to tell the difference between the second half of a two-part verse and a bridge. Often featuring flashy guitar work, instrumental solos usually occur after the second chorus. Bridges and solos give the listener relief from the alternation of verses and choruses, while intros perform the same role as the hook. Grabbing the listener's attention and drawing him or her into the music, intros often employ a foreshortened version of the hook. Outros, any new material played at the end of the song, frame the composition and give the band a chance for a spectacular finish.

The most common song form is *intro, verse, bridge, chorus, verse, bridge, chorus, solo, verse, bridge, chorus, chorus, outro*. Given this backbone, however, the composing band has great flexibility. For example, *verse, bridge, verse, bridge, chorus, verse, bridge, chorus, outro* is a common form that teases the listener by holding back the hook until halfway through the song. When verses have hooky, repeated final lines, composing bands sometimes eliminate the chorus altogether, producing forms like *verse, instrumental bridge, verse, instrumental bridge, verse, instrumental bridge, solo, verse*. The overall form of the song tends to be climactic, with the solo increasing the energy and the outchoruses and outros bringing the song to its highest point. These typical song forms and the section names are common knowledge in the commercial hard rock scene.

Treating music as artifact, the analyzing scholar may view the typical forms of commercial hard rock as empty placeholders, the synchronic structures of a genre into which ideas are mechanically slotted. In the practice of composition, however, we see that the musicians creatively interact with their knowledge of form, orienting their overall design of the song to their expectation of the listener's interest. The final form emerges in a dialectical interaction between the unique parts of this particular song and the relatively stable, though dynamic, stocks of formal knowledge.[8] At the early rehearsals, players start to solidify the order of the sections, repeating or deleting a sections, and adding bridges, solos, intros, and outros. The lyrics of the second verse often repeat in the third verse, and the second bridge is less common in contemporary hard rock than it was in the 1970s. As the form becomes more stable, the band elaborates the song with background vocals, fills, and hits. Drum fills are brief rhythmic phrases, usually played at the end of four- or eight-bar sections; they often show off the drummer's technique and almost always mark the phrase structure. Guitar and bass fills are melodic phrases that similarly show off the player's technique, frequently playing response to the singer's call. Hits—tightly coordinated rhythmic accents in the bass, drums, and guitar—may occur during a vocal phrase or follow the vocal phrases like a fill. Harmony vocals can be quite elaborate. Bands typically keep the songs interesting by varying drum grooves, accompanying patterns, and dynamic levels across the sections; the density of fills, hits, and harmony vocals is often increased in the later verses and choruses to build the song to a climax.

In the last stage of rehearsal, the form, fills, solos, and backing vocals will be set, and the band will practice playing through the song as a whole. Internalizing the form, smoothing out the transitions, coordinating the hits, keeping track of the form, and getting the vocal intonation correct are the central concerns here. A song may take weeks or months of practice to make it from rehearsal space to the stage, and very difficult songs may be scrapped if the band can't perform them adequately. Chris Ozimek refers to this period of the song's first performances as the time when "the song is young"; young songs may go through a number of changes. After watching the audience response carefully during performance, musicians may (in later rehearsals) change the form, the solos, and the backing vocals to make the song work better; difficult high notes, fills, or hits may be modified. It is in this period that the solo is given a more or less fixed form, and many fills or vocal parts that were once left to improvisation slowly become sedimented. In all but the most rigid bands, songs can change even after they have been performed for a long time. Musical styles shift, and songs are altered accordingly; shifts in the band's personnel almost always involve modifications in the songs. If a song is recorded it may undergo even more transformations, which may or may not make it to the stage. And, after a period of a year, most songs are played out. It is a point of pride with local bands to keep writing new material, and those bands that stick with the same set list for too long are seen as lazy. Occasionally a band may shun one member's song, and it may make its first appearance only when the player has found a new group, sometimes years after it was composed.

This outline describes the most group-oriented form of composition. However, many bands are led and dominated by a leader-composer, and in these groups different dynamics apply. At various periods in Dia Pason's history, Chris Ozimek served in such a capacity. Ideas for vocal melodies and bass parts would occur to him while practicing by himself, driving, or falling asleep. Recording these on cassette, Chris would come to the rehearsal with bass parts, lyrics, and a sense of the song's overall form.[9] Chris would then explain to the drummer and guitar players what kind of musical ideas he had in mind, and the exact parts would be negotiated between them. Later, Chris would compose the backing vocals, and across the span of several rehearsals the form of the tune would sediment. Chris was one of the more flexible leader-composers. He welcomed input from different band members, and, in the periods when Dia Pason had a stable lineup, group composition was the norm. Many local rock musicians have spoken of bands with dictatorial leader-composers who specified all of the drum, keyboard, and guitar parts as well as the vocal melodies. While leader-composer bands are common, most players feel that it is intrusive for a leader-composer to specifically determine every part a musician must play, and this kind of directiveness is only tolerated from the best-known figures on the scene (see Weinstein 1993, 214–15).

It is important to note that there is no correlation in the data between a band's use of leader or group composition techniques and their social or political orientations. Numerous strands of 1970s-era ethnomusicology (for example, Hood 1971; Blacking 1973, 122; 1979, 8; Herndon and McLeod 1979) held that the microsocial, face-to-face interactions of musical production are necessarily a reflection of or template for broader forms of social life. In his structuralist period, Blacking suggested that both macrolevel social structures and microlevel musical forms are coded in the basic patterns of the human brain, and that their homology is a kind of structural necessity. In the romantic variant of these ideas, other theorists argued that deep, culturally based notions about the nature of human relationships determine both the form of social interaction in musical activity and broader social structures. My data suggest both types of this reflectionist argument are problematic.[10]

For example, KB's own band, The Atomic Punks, operates almost solely through group composition, but this communitarian spirit is far from present in their broader social views. KB was the first research participant to tell me that a band is a small business and that the goal of that business is nothing less than top international stardom. It is not too much of an exaggeration to assert that the ideology of celebrity is a kind of individualism, and yet, KB—proponent of communal composition—is one of its greatest adherents. In Max Panic the communal spirit is so great that it is considered bad form to bring anything but the smallest seed idea to rehearsal. Adamant followers of conservative radio personality Rush Limbaugh, the communitarian Panic members are free-market capitalists, the individualistic ideology par excellence. Aside from Max Panic, the commercial hard rockers I spoke with were rarely politicized, and I found no correlation between individual styles of band interaction and larger social beliefs.

Though these data are far from a statistically valid sample, a focus on practice suggests a theoretical difficulty with these macrosocial/microsocial arguments. By contradicting the reflectionist argument I do not suggest that there is no relationship between musical experience and larger social forces; music is deeply informed by broad social contexts, but not because of abstract homologies. Large-scale social structure does not generate a "cultural style" of interaction that somehow descends upon each individual to determine his or her musical interactions. How could something as divided by power relations and historical change as a society produce a single "cultural style," and how would such a concept explain the vagaries of contingency or agency? Neither does any "deep structure" code the entire abstract form of a society within each individual's brain, and then express itself as some structural transformation in musical performance. How could something as systemic and emergent as a society's social structure be coded in each individual brain? Social structure is not some abstract Platonic form; it is constituted in history by the intended and unintended consequences of diverse, on-the-ground actions. Social structure informs present practice, not as an abstract formal system, but as a context for action, as a material and social history mediated into the present. American capitalism impinges upon musical performance, not as a cultural style of individualism or a formal structure, but as a concrete context of wealth and poverty, of hard-to-come-by jobs and low wages, of messages of consumerism endlessly repeated in the mainstream media and voices of agreement or resistance spoken in bars and bedrooms. While a pattern of individualistic worker-boss interaction is well known to most Americans and may be replicated in a dictatorial composer-musician relationship, musicians may seek to avoid such a relationship in their musical life, and the intellectual framing of musical and social ideologies does not guarantee an inevitable pairing of democratic musical relationships and broader democratic beliefs.[11]

Purpose and meaning: The threshold of the event

At this point in the discussion, we have an outline of the various practices by which the participants constitute commercial hard rock performance events. Differentially interpreted by participants from opposed scenes, and only partially shared by participants of the same scene, the meanings of these various practices are informed by the participant's broader purposes for taking part in the event. Why do people go to the Agora? In a quotidian sense, they go to drink, search out sexual partners, people watch, socialize, listen to music, see a spectacle, buddy-up to local celebrities, sneer at people from other scenes, get out of the house, support friends in a band, or work. Musicians go to perform, make an incremental step to fame, watch the competition, promote their band, prospect for new band members, or feel out the changes in scene. And at one time or another, everyone attends out of habit. Purposes and practices have a complex and often contradictory relationship as they emerge in the flow of history; nevertheless, we can achieve a richer understanding of the scene by exploring the participants' larger purposes in attending the event and examining the complex links between those purposes and other aspects of their social lives. Comparing the celebratory perspective of Al Ricci and Chris Ozimek and the more critical view of Max Panic guitarist Jeff Johnston will reveal some of the range of interpretations present in the shows.

When I asked Al and Chris why someone would go to a Dia Pason show, their responses were clear; you see this band to have fun. Al repeatedly described commercial hard rock as an energetic release from the pressures of work and bills, and, while Chris applauded bands with political messages, he said that Dia Pason is not one of those. Fondly recalling his first sports arena rock show, Chris said that the members of Poison looked like they were having the time of their life on stage. Eager to pursue that fun, he dropped out of college, got a job in a music store, and devoted himself to a career in rock. Al remembers endless afternoons in high school pumping iron and pumping himself up to the commercial hard rock of the day—Ratt, Poison, Def Leppard, and Arrowsmith. After high school, Al roadied for local headliner Neil Zsa Zsa; for Al, Zsa Zsa's onstage facial expressions typified the ambiance of a good rock show, "He (Zsa Zsa) looked like he just pulled something off . . . like the cat that ate the canary." Al said that whereas metal bands want to overturn society, a commercial rock band merely wants to pull a little harmless mischief. Stage antics and self-deprecating humor are important to Al's stage persona, and he has many tales of mischief and silliness on stage. Messing up guitar parts and laughing at himself, running into other musicians on stage or falling off the drum risers—it's okay to look silly, Al said, as long as the audience laughs. For Al, the fun of commercial hard rock is situated within a systemic interpretation of popular music styles: while the heavy drum parts and distorted guitars of metal, punk, and alternative are energetic, the aggression of these musics takes the fun out of the sound; where pop dance music is lighthearted, it lacks the irresistible energy of guitar-based rock.

Beyond the situational goals of fun, most rockers join bands in pursuit of fame and wealth, and many listeners go to shows to be around potential celebrities. Several rockers suggested to me that the quest for celebrity was an attempt to sidestep the stultifying life plan of high school, college, family, and work. When I offered the parallel between sports stardom as an exit route from the inner city and rock stardom as an exit route from the responsibilities of traditionally conceived working- and middle-class manhood, the rockers heartily agreed. With his love of amusement parks and rock music, Chris described himself as "*obsessed* with fun." The day-to-day life of local rockers is, unsurprisingly, one of poorly paid day jobs, stingy club owners, and squabbling bandmates; as we shall see in Chapter 7, the pursuit of fun often presented Chris with stresses as great as any of those experienced by a wage-earning family man.

For Al and Chris, the musical sound is a direct reflection of these purposes. In their experience, chunky bass lines, powerful snare accents on two and four, and the guitar's distorted power chords are the aural embodiments of energy. The glissandi and timbral devices of Chris's melodies give them a floating quality that contrasts with the driving instrumental parts, putting a human face on the music. Backing vocals sweeten the hooky melodies, filtering the anger from the snarly guitar timbres and resulting in a

distillate of pure action and fun. And while the guitar solos are often a virtuosic display, KB's cool smile suggests that the soloing is effortless, a mere
flourish. Obscured by in-jokes and poor sound systems, the lyrics of his
song are often lost on his listeners, Chris said, but they should always
"sound cool," and individual phrases should stick in the listener's ear.
Typed out in the liner notes of Dia Pason's demos, the lyrics focus on
themes of glamour and power, rock stardom, romance, and veiled stories
of scene gossip.

A rather different view of commercial hard rock emerges from Max
Panic's guitarist, Jeff Johnston. The 1993 version of Max Panic was a reaction against the commercial hard rock scene of the late 1980s and early
1990s in which his own bands had headlined; while Jeff was no friend of the
alternative scene, his attacks on glam are reminiscent of the grungester's critiques. Though Jeff maintains his admiration for the very best of 1970s and
1980s era commercial hard rock—Led Zeppelin, Van Halen, Pink Floyd—
he feels that most local rock musicians cared too little for the music and too
much for the spectacle. Jeff depicted the typical male band member as a
musical incompetent seeking to achieve sexual conquest with flashy technique, while the female fans were starstruck innocents or emotionally dam-
aged abuse victims. From his years in the scene, Jeff told many narratives of
exploitive promiscuity, misogyny, drug abuse, and musical ineptitude.
While delusions of imminent stardom and subadolescent maturity
rounded out the list of glam's social vices, Jeff elaborated a long list of musical vices as well. The classic hard rock bands, he explained, produced rich
distortions with top-quality equipment (Fender Stratocasters, Gibson Les
Pauls, and Marshall amps); they used tight band coordination and good
songwriting to make their music energetic and expressive. By contrast, Jeff
said, the glam guitarists play inferior Hamer or Jackson guitars; cut in out-
rageous shapes, painted with gaudy images, and sporting low action, these
instruments facilitate fast playing but have a thin tone that is exacerbated by
the glam rocker's extensive use of effect processing. The overall musical in-
competence of these bands makes the time unstable, robbing the pounding
rhythm of its power. The infectious melodies and sweet harmonies of early
nineties glam ring false to Jeff's ears; he hears overgrown adolescent men
impressing foolish women, not the engaging contrast of floating melodies
with crunchy guitars. In line with this vision, Max Panic's post-glam sound
melded industrial keyboards, Les Paul through Marshall distortion timbres, and politically conservative lyrics; Jeff sought venues for this music in
the cracks between the alternative and commercial hard rock scenes.

It is important to note here that my juxtaposition of Jeff's and Chris's
views does not mean that Jeff was commenting on Dia Pason specifically.

His critique of pop metal was directed at the Cleveland scene in general, not at any band in particular. In that scene, Chris and Al had a reputation for kindness and for avoiding the exploitive sexuality so common in pop metal. Jeff was not the only one to find fault with the musical style of early nineties pop metal; others had similar perspectives and said that Dia Pason's music displayed many of the problems of this style. During one interview, I related Jeff's critique of the music to Chris and asked Chris what he thought about it. He said that Jeff had a point and that some of Jeff's criticisms applied to Dia Pason. Toward the end of my fieldwork, Chris began to update his band's sound.

Music and words (2): The event

While individual genres of expressive culture (fashion, bodily stylistics, musical structures, patterns of audience and performer interaction) are separable in scholarly reflection, they form a rich, often contradictory constellation of meanings in the participant's experience of the performance event.[12] To put the Humpty Dumpty of expressive genres back together again, we must return them to the whole from which they were abstracted, the flow of constitutive practices in the event. To conclude this introduction to commercial hard rock and synthesize the previous descriptions, we must return once again to the Agora, this time on March 12, 1993.

Sitting in the club, I am aware that this room was designed to hold a bustling social scene: bouncers, roadies, and tough female rockers strutting purposefully and displaying status through sexuality or connection; the latest gossip screamed into a girlfriend's ear in a performance of busy sociability; masculinity and quiet judgment emanating from the intense stares of the Silent Men in the corner; seeing and being seen. Such a scene is literally history. Framed by both the memory of past spectacles and the active absence of spectacle in the empty space itself, tonight's Agora feels dead. The recorded music is louder than usual because there are no extra bodies to absorb the sound; the dance floor is brighter, with only a few dancers outlined by the flashing lights. "A quiet gathering of friends," is how a singer for a hardcore band once sarcastically described a night in which only the band's friends showed up for the gig. That phrase describes tonight's turnout, but the members of Dia Pason seem to take it pretty well. Checking out the crowd in a mild and friendly manner and chatting with those they know, Dia Pason waits to go on. It's hard to get upset about a quiet Wednesday.

Watching their performance on stage, their attempt at spectacle jars slightly with my recent memory of their quiet, friendly conversation. Nevertheless, the ten friends of the band listening on the dance floor are joined by a crowd of twenty or so reasonably enthusiastic strangers, probably from Kent State or the University of Akron. They stand in distinct but not unfriendly bunches; the bright lights and smoke effects give Dia Pason some of the energy that the small crowd and absence of drum risers take away. So does their professionalism. Steve uses massive kick drums and many long double bass passages; you can't help feeling them in your chest, and they almost propel the band into a heavier generic bracket. Chris's vocals are clear and powerful, the influence of Cheap Trick evident in his swooping, nasal glissandi and uncoarsened tone. The first few songs run one into the next, with Steve starting the groove of each new song as soon as the previous one is finished. Commenting upon Max Panic's new, tougher style, Al Ricci once said to me that Panic's singer's new short haircut "looked like they sound." The same could be said about Chris. Carefully styled, long, dirty-blond locks waving past his shoulders, his hair evokes the sensuality and celebrity of the nationally famous rockers to which the hooky melodies, elaborate special effects lighting, and even the Agora's own architecture also point. By the same token, the hair is framed by what it is not—the long, straight, greasy mass that hangs in the faces of the grunge kids, that literally accompanies their tense, gruff vocal sounds. As I listen closer, beats 2 and 4 on the snare frame the hooky guitar parts, above which are layered the intricate backup vocals. The guitar's crunchy tone gives the music energy and power, says Chris, but the Beatle-esque harmonies are his real love. Artfully arranged, they come through tolerably clearly on the Agora's PA system and garner disgusted looks from the leftover Gothic crowd that listens from behind the Plexiglas wall at the north section of the club. Chris stops between songs to ask the audience how they are doing in an affected southern accent. The verses blur by, and even though Chris enunciates clearly, only hooks and fragments remain in my experience: "It's all in your head, . . . wheels go spinning round." "Sidewalk walkin' round the blockin' [ensemble guitar melody with coordinated hits]; Turn your back and look who's talking." Chris's friend Marcia and two of her buddies on the dance floor mouth every word along with Chris. A few of Steve's more original fills pop out of the mix and draw the listeners' attention; projecting the song from one section to the next, their exact form is forgotten though their effect remains. Chris, Al, and KB perform the stylized gestures of commercial hard rock and are parodied affectionately by Marcia and her friends. Al's guitar blends in seamlessly with KB's during the rhythm, and only with great effort are his particular parts made audible. KB's solos, all speed and flash, come across as a blur, the register and distorted tone being the only facets present in experience with a

PA of this quality. Hits and coordinated fills pop out of the general flow of the tune and, fitting in with rock conventions, are articulated by the gentle head rocking of the crowd. A power ballad written to appeal to the sentimentality of adolescent women, "It Happens" seems to be about the loss of a love affair, and only months later do I learn that it is about the death of Chris's friend. Dia Pason has been playing for thirty-five minutes; the presence of that quantity of material, metaphorically lurking off the stage of the present moment of consciousness, is the ostensible cause of the feeling that there isn't much more of the set left. Jeff Johnston has told me time and time again that a band's first job is to sell beer. About 75 percent of the audience has stayed on the floor through the set and remained moderately interested in the music. While Dia Pason has not actually sold them beer, they were professional enough to capitalize on the energy the crowd gave out and feed it back to them though gestures and sound. The end of this song starts to pick up and I know we are heading toward the end. KB's slow, composed, melodic lines—a part of the song and not a part of the solo—are audible now, unlike the speedier phrases of his solos. The pyro goes off on the headstocks of Chris's and Al's guitars, the dance floor lights come up, and the announcer says that the headliner Kid Wicked will be on in a little while. So have another beer.

THREE

Heavy Metal in Akron, Ohio
Winter's Bane and Sin-Eater

In this chapter, I move from northeast Ohio's commercial hard rock scene to its metal scene. As before, my dual goals are to present a general introduction to the music and to understand how both the meanings of metal and the social organization of its subcultures are the outcome of the participant's constitutive practices. While the meanings of contemporary commercial hard rock and underground metal differ greatly, their common origin in the rock musics of the late 1960s has left both scenes with similar categories of practice: group or leader/composer composition, nightclub performance, promotion, and casual social interaction. But the metal scene is constituted through a variety of practices not found in commercial hard rock, and the stylistic differences and subcultural divisions within metal are far more complex than those in rock. While I am interested in all of the varieties of underground metal and all practices that constitute the scenes, my focus is on death metal and the practices of nightclub performance. We gain our first entrance into the social life of metal by exploring the history of this music.

History and social organization of
Ohio's metal underground

The metalheads of northeast Ohio are nothing if not enthusiastic exegetes, and they delighted in providing me with a detailed description of metal history. A living element of the metalheads' present experiences, this history can provide us with a first entrance into the contemporary scene.

Almost without exception, the metalheads depict the history of their music in a progressive fashion, moving from metal's initial break with the perceived chirpy banalities of commercial rock to its steady achievement of ever-greater heights of emotional intensity. Releasing their first album in 1970, Black Sabbath was credited by all of my research participants as the originators of metal. The band brought elaborate compositions, aggressive drumming, heavily distorted guitars, themes of fantasy and the occult, and aggressive or morose affects into a constellation of features that has been the touchstone of metal to this day. Perceived as both more musically sophisticated and more emotionally intense than the mainstream rock of its day, Black Sabbath is spoken of with awe by all the metalheads I interviewed. Sometimes called power metal, progressive metal, or the second wave of British metal, Judas Priest and Iron Maiden broke new ground in the late 1970s. Rob Halford, singer for Judas Priest, explored new territory by deploying a huge vocal range and an array of vocal timbres that ran the gamut from the pure to the growly, from the whispery to the piercing. (After the period of my research, one of the participants in this study, Timmy Owens, later went on to replace Halford as the lead singer in Judas Priest; see Chapter 5.) Iron Maiden pushed the boundaries of 1970s metal with ever more elaborate two-guitar arrangements and longer instrumental sections.

Born of its initial rejection of pop, metal's virtuosity has always been crucial to its evocation of power and aggression, but the 1980s saw metal reach ever new heights of emotional intensity by borrowing the raw energy of punk. While the punk and metal scenes were quite distinct in the 1970s, some 1980s bands moved back and forth across the border and many listeners kept in touch with both scenes. As Donna Gaines observes in *Teenage Wasteland* (1990, 194–204), the early 1980s thrash bands were the first products of such interactions, combing metal guitar sounds with low, gruff vocals to bring a raw new aggression to metal. Speed metal followed quickly on its heels; playing at accelerated tempos, these bands fused the frenetic energy of punk with some of the lyrical themes and chord progressions of metal. By today's standards, speed metal was slow, and it quickly gave way to grindcore with its even more accelerated tempi. Death metal, the focus of much of this book, began in the mid-1980s and refers to a variety of styles characterized by noisy, unpitched vocals. The subdivisions of death metal refer less to discrete scenes than to styles and themes. For example, black metal refers to bands that explicitly discuss Satanism; contrary to popular misconception, black metal is a relatively small part of the metal scene and most metalheads are in no way connected with Satanism.[1] Gore metal refers to death metal bands whose lyrics are primarily concerned with images of mutilation. Somewhat distinct from death metal, doom metal refers to a style that emphasizes extremely slow tempi, morose affects, and low-pitched, spoken vocals. 1992 and 1993 saw a period of growth and expansion for death metal, and bands experimented with nontraditional instruments like violins and synthesizers and an ever-expanding range of musical techniques.[2]

Metal history is most often summed up by metalheads as a progressive quest for ever-heavier music.[3] A rich and complex concept differentially interpreted across scenes, "heavy" refers to a variety of textural, structural, and affective aspects of musical sound and is crucial for any understanding of metal.

First and foremost, "heavy" describes distorted guitar timbres. Walser (1991, 123–24) observes that distorting an electric guitar's signal adds a substantial noise component to the timbre, increases sustain, and boosts the upper and lower harmonics. While the increase in noise aurally emphasizes the guitarist's use of technology, the expanded sustain and harmonics serve to amplify the guitar's natural timbre; as a result, observes Walser, distortion and heaviness are heard as the sonic equivalent of power. Metal guitarists talk about the history of guitar technology as a progression toward ever-heavier tones (see Berger and Fales 1997), and throughout the music industry, the gargantuan distortion sound common in contemporary metal is referred to as the "scooped-mids death tone."[4] Other timbres may be heavy as well. Bass guitar timbres are heavy when they give the aural impression of great size. Like guitar sounds, bass drum sounds and the overall equalization of a recording are heavy when the extreme low and high-end frequencies are emphasized; more than mere harmonic expansion, the emphasis on lower frequencies provides the instruments with their power and tactile punch, while the boosted upper harmonics give the individual parts definition and prevent the mix from becoming muddy. Heavy vocal timbres are produced when the vocal folds are left partially open and air rushing through the glottal space produces a noisy, nonharmonic component in the sound waves. The vocal analog of distorted guitar timbres, such sounds are often described as "guttural" or "growly." Pitched vocals with a rough, noisy component can be referred to as heavy, while the heaviest death metal growls have no identifiable harmonics whatsoever. Both the contemporary bass drum sounds and contemporary death metal growls are recent developments in the metalhead's quest for heaviness.

Beyond timbre, the composition or performance itself can be heavy if it effectively evokes morose or aggressive emotions. While the heavy songs of the 1970s and early 1980s employed a vocabulary of minor chord progressions, the late 1980s and 1990s saw metal bands push the envelope of heaviness with variations of the harmonic vocabulary that break up the minor tonality and obscure the tonal center. (Such developments are the subject of Chapter 11.) Likewise, the 1980s experimentations with extremes of tempo was part of the quest for heaviness, and both slow dirges and frantic grindcore numbers can be heavy if performed well. In terms of time and band coordination, local musicians told me that a stiff rhythmic feel is heavy and aggressive, whereas a looser feel is lighter and more "happy." Effectively performed music that is cheerful or merely snide is not heavy to any of my research participants, nor is poorly performed music heavy, no matter the composition or the intended affect. In sum, any element of the musical sound can be heavy if it evokes power or any of the grimmer emotions, and the history of metal is commonly understood as the pursuit of greater and greater heaviness.

Such a history of pioneering bands and style periods serves as a useful entrance into the metal universe, but, like all Great Man histories and linear narratives, it disengages history from the practices and experiences of the fans and local musicians who are key to its constitution. Both earlier fieldwork in Bloomington, Indiana, and my Ohio research uncovered a surprisingly robust genre of personal experience narratives that describe the local musician's participation in the history of metal. The metalheads begin these narratives of their musical lives in their early teens. Only marginally interested in music at this point, they describe listening to commercial hard rock on the radio and owning a few albums. The pivotal moment comes when an older sibling, friend, or a lucky accident introduces the would-be metalhead to his or her first metal album. More powerful than any music he or she has ever heard, the music is interpreted as an epiphany, a complete break from the pablum of commercial radio. Budding metalheads play the recording until the grooves are worn off and proceed to search out every metal recording they can find. Like a drug addiction, numerous participants joked, they start out with the lighter stuff, and keep searching for heavier and heavier music. Unlike drug use, however, the highs do not diminish; they increase. The vast majority of people I talked with explained that just when they thought that metal was as heavy as it possibly could be, a new variety emerged that was even heavier than the last. From casual music purchasing, budding metalheads proceed to acquiring their first instruments, to hanging out in practice rooms, to spending time at clubs, and, sometimes, to forming their own bands. It is through these involvements that the local metalheads, along with the music industry and the innovators, help to constitute the scene and its history.

While a focus on personal narrative helps to reconnect the participant's practices and the larger history, the linearity of the participant's narrative obscures the complex ways in which patterns of practice emerge, persist, and dissipate over time. Histories of artistic styles typically construct linear narratives by ticking off the emergence of new styles from old ones. While, as the linear narratives suggest, the development of new styles may sometimes bring about the wholesale abandonment of a older style by its adherents, eclipsed styles may also be preserved or incrementally altered by a core of listeners who reject the changes. By the same token, even styles that are maintained through the most studious preservationism constantly change—if only through recontextualization and entrenchment. Treating style periods as relatively stable patterns of musical practices (such as composition and performance), we can understand how a history of musical styles is deposited into the present as a social organization of scenes. In the northeast Ohio of 1993, a variety of styles from the history of metal were supported by a scene referred to as the underground. An assortment of subgenres of death metal were present in the underground, all related through their use of nonpitched vocals; 1980s-style thrash bands with rough, pitched vocals were present as well. While I know of no local band that played exactly in the style of early 1970s Black Sabbath, a number of power metal acts—updated with heavier, 1990s-style guitar and drum timbres—were also popular. The scene also supported cover bands (groups who only play songs by other musicians) and tribute bands (cover bands that play the songs of just one famous act and imitate the stage performances of that act as well as their repertoire). A variety of punk styles can be found in the underground as well, including straight edge and hardcore, though no punk tribute bands or punk cover bands exist.[5]

More than a motley collection of styles, the local underground is constituted and internally organized through practices of composition, performance, nightclub attendance, and socializing, and their attendant aesthetic and political ideologies—vegetarianism, left- or right-wing views, musical eclecticism, and heavy progressivism. Almost everyone in the local underground—metalheads and punks—dismisses commercial hard rock and other mainstream musics (pop, country, pop alternative, and so on) as banal; they avoid both rock music and the rock scenes. Primarily identifying themselves in opposition to commercial hard rock,[6] the metalheads see rock's "heaviness" as long superseded by the musical developments of metal. The main division within the underground is between punk (now called hardcore) and metal. While there are listeners and musicians who only attend metal or hardcore shows, many listeners go out to see bands in both styles.

Within the metal underground there is a sharp division between death metal and the other styles—thrash and power metal. Self-consciously eclectic, many death metal fans attend thrash and power metal shows, follow the bands and listen to their records; while respecting the other underground metals, they interpret death metal as the cutting edge of heaviness. On the contrary, many power metal devotees find death metal to be unpleasant nonsense rather than incarnate heaviness; vaguely aware of the bands, most power metal fans avoid death metal shows and never listen to death metal recordings. Death metal fans are also more likely to attend hardcore shows. The divisions within death metal refer to styles of composition and performance, not larger patterns of social interaction. An individual listener might prefer doomy bands, but there is no doom metal scene of which I am aware; there are a large number of gore bands, but no gore metal scene per se. While the death metal fan's eclecticism is an actively pursued value, it is informed by the larger demographics of northeast Ohio. The population of the Cleveland-Akron area is large enough to support the underground, but not large enough to sustain smaller groups within the underground as autonomous scenes. As a result, the fans of less popular styles (death metal and its subgenres) must either embrace related musics (hardcore, power metal) or spend most nights at home. A similar dynamic occurred within the alternative scene of early 1993. A result of the unintended consequences of intentional action, the structural dynamics of large and small scenes in a medium-sized music market like northeast Ohio engenders a variety of responses in the local music fans, among which is death metal eclecticism.

Political affiliations divide the underground. Hardcore has both extreme left- and right-wing factions that, unsurprisingly, are opposed to one another. Death metal, on the other hand, is most often actively apolitical or antipolitical. Within death metal there are a small number of Satanic bands. While most non-Satanists in the underground have a neutral attitude toward the Satanists, there are some who actively oppose them; by the same token, many Satanists criticize bands that merely employ Satanic imagery, and the Satanic bands commonly accuse each another of being mere poseurs. Except for the most exclusive left, right, and Satanic fans, most listeners are actively and self-consciously eclectic, engaging with the music that attracts them and leaving the ideologies behind. As recent research has shown (Hakanen and Wells 1990, 62–63; 1993, 60, 66) the metal scene is largely white, and working-class. Most, though not all, metal musicians are male.

While metal is similar to commercial hard rock in its reliance on band composition and nightclub performance, a number of its constitutive practices are unique to the underground. Commercial hard rock groups develop a local network of fans through face-to-face interaction, and when their local success grows, they play across a large region; while regional bands may know one another, the rock scene has little coherence beyond the local level. But because the underground is so much smaller, a much more integrated national culture is possible in the underground, and one of its main vehicles is the fest. Listeners travel literally thousands of miles to attend these all-day shows, which often feature dozens of bands on multiple stages. At these events, relationships begun through the mail are made concrete in face-to-face meetings, and bands that tour nationally are able to meet with audiences from across the country. On both the national and international level, death metal is bound together through amateur publications called "fanzines" (a contraction of fan magazine) or "zines." Often written, edited, xeroxed, and circulated by a single individual, zines editorialize on the scene and review metal demos and independent recordings. A rich and extensive "cassette culture" (Manuel 1993) has arisen through the zines, with bands exchanging personal correspondence and demo tapes throughout the world. Death metal guitarist Dann Saladin, for example, corresponded with literally hundreds of musicians and listeners from United States, Scandinavia, Western Europe, East Asia, and South America—most of whom were contacted through zines.

The practice of composition in two metal bands

Many of the practices of leader composition and group composition that make up commercial hard rock are also found in metal. Leaders or band members form seed ideas on the road, at work, or while noodling on their instruments. During rehearsal, fragments are shared with other band members and fleshed out into full-fledged songs. Chords, melodies, grooves, and hits are solidified; fills and solos are outlined. Songs are rehearsed until they are tight, and eventually the band performs them. Demos are recorded. Bands change lineup or styles change, and the songs are modified and eventually rotated out of the set list.

These similar practices aside, nowhere is the metalhead's oppositional identity more evident than in the *content* of the music thus composed. Commercial hard rockers tend to employ either simple diatonic chord changes or blues-based variations of that harmony. Sometimes a series of power chords is more melodic than harmonic, serving as a countermelody to the vocal line; at others times the changes operate more traditionally, setting out the harmonic context for the melody layered above. While short single note lines or power chord melodies are the most common seed ideas for both rock and metal composers, the similarity between the styles ends there. In an effort to avoid the diatonic or blues-based harmony that metalheads see as commercial and "light," death metal seed ideas frequently disturb the listener's sense of tonality with unexpected half steps and tritones (see Friesen and Epstein 1994, 9; Harrell 1994, 93–94). Another technique

Dann Saladin

that defies the listener's tonal expectations is the pitch axis. Like a diatonic melody, a pitch axis melody establishes one note as a tonal center; unlike diatonic melodies, all eleven other pitches are treated as equal. Clear patterns of half steps and whole steps and driving rhythms balance out the tonal ambiguities and make these melodies accessible to the listener. Woodchucking is another common technique. In woodchucked seeds, the guitarist plays a constant flow of muted eighth notes on the lowest or second lowest string of the instrument, occasionally broken with power chord stabs in the octave above. The overtones of a highly distorted guitar woodchucking blend smoothly with those of the snare drum, producing a driving and irresistible rhythm. Rarely are death metal's guitar parts meant to define periods of harmonic function. In Chapter 8, I shall return in detail to the issue of tonality in death metal and problems of method in the interpretation of musical structure.

Formal concerns and styles of performer-audience interaction unique to metal engender a variety of compositional practices not shared with commercial hard rock. Rock songs tend to be brief, and their forms are readily understood in terms of verses, bridges, and choruses; death metal songs are usually longer and poorly characterized by the traditional section designations of pop music. For example, death metal leader-composer and guitarist Dann Saladin would typically go to a rehearsal with five to ten different seed ideas, each a potential section. One completed song ran to twenty-six distinct sections. Intros, outros, and solos are present in most metal tunes, but the alteration of verse and chorus that forms the backbone of rock songs is largely absent in death metal. Death metal composers develop their forms to orchestrate the ebb and flow of the audience's interactions. Moshing, once known as slam dancing, is a kind of audience activity at metal and hardcore shows in which participants swing their elbows or forcefully knock one another about with their shoulders. Hooky, aggressive, medium-up tempo sections are the ones that typically induce moshing, and in designing forms, bands seek to deploy the moshy parts at just the right point in the song to stir the audience into a frenzy of moshing. Changes in tempo and groove are also important, and one of the most powerful effects in metal occurs when there is a sudden shift from fast to slow tempo or vice versa.

In the death metal band Sin-Eater, for example, Dann and drummer John Ziats were the main composers. In the early stages of the process, Dann would teach a seed idea to the other guitar player, Erik Rueschman, and the two bass players, Rob Toothman and Brandy "Chuck" Smith. John would then compose grooves for the section, sometimes radically reinterpreting the more obvious rhythmic implications of the guitar parts that Dann had written. When the section finished, the process would be completed until all the parts were learned. A form would then be developed, and the song would go through several different versions before a final form would take shape. Connective material was composed as the form was worked out, with short, coordinated band fills smoothly linking even the most radically different grooves and tempi. When development of the parts was called for, Dann and the other string players would experiment with harmony lines for the various instruments. With rhythms identical to the lead melody, most Sin-Eater harmonies employed parallel thirds, fourths, and fifths; sweet and less tonally ambiguous, diatonic harmonies were rarely used. Where commercial hard rock's briefer structures only employed cues for intros and outros, the complex and unique form of the Sin-Eater tunes required more substantial cuing. Ideally, members of Sin-Eater would have the exact number of repetitions of each phrase memorized and the order of the form fully internalized by first performance. The players, however, were not always able to feel these long periods, and during the middle and latter stages of rehearsal the musicians would compose subtle drum, vocal, or guitar cues that would help them keep track of the form. In the final stages of rehearsal Dann composed the lyrics and set the phrasing for the chanted, growly vocal parts that characterize the genre.

But not all underground metal is death metal, and the musical forms of local power metal band Winter's Bane illustrate some of the differences within metal. The music of Winter's Bane was intended as a corrective to what its founders (guitarist Lou St. Paul and drummer Terry Salem) saw as

Winter's Bane (left to right: Terry Salem, Dennis Hayes, Timmy Owens, and Lou St. Paul).
Photo by Ron Burkett.

the inaccessibility and excessive formal complexity of the metal of the early
1990s. Several orders of magnitude heavier than the heaviest commercial
hard rock group, Winter's Bane sought to stake their place at the commercial end of the underground metal spectrum. Despite long solos, forms of
up to seven major sections, exclusively aggressive or morose moods, and
displays of extreme virtuosity, a backbone of verse/chorus forms are per-
ceptible in all of their songs. Though their 1993 independent release involved an elaborate, six-track song cycle, most Winter's Bane tunes have
hooks and few last more than five minutes. The band's harmonic and melodic structures also help them to stake out their ground, falling neatly
between the anarchic atonality of death metal and the commercial diaton-
ism of glam. Like Dann Saladin's, Lou's guitar parts involve power chord
melodies and extended woodchucking, but he also has sections where the
chords outline periods of harmonic function. While some songs rely on the
established metal vocabulary of minor chord progressions, those progressions are frequently skewed with half steps and tritones that give the music
a heavier, contemporary quality. All of singer Timmy Owens's vocal lines
form pitched melodies, but he keeps the band solidly within the metal
camp by deploying an arsenal of vocal qualities that can range from clear
tones to growly rasps.

Purpose: Metal and meanings

Practices of composition and rehearsal enable acts of recording, listening, and nightclub performance. But before I can discuss the heavy metal performance event, I must touch on the broader social contexts and purposes in metal. As I have suggested earlier, the underground is rent by sharp ideological divisions. While all underground music is in some way tied to the grimmer emotions, the shadings of those emotions and the larger ideologies they serve vary wildly across the segments of the underground. One ideology that serves to heal these divisions is eclecticism, and many death metal fans are actively eclectic. Committed in their aesthetics to the underground's emotional core and skeptical of any all-embracing dogmas, eclectic metalheads frequently cross generic boundaries. While Dann Saladin is committed to death metal, he keeps up with the full spectrum of the punk scenes, and dips into noise, gothic, and experimental musics. His main criteria are aesthetic: Is the music heavy? Do the musicians command their instruments with virtuosity and authority? Are the musical or political ideas interesting? None of this is to deny that ideological clashes and even physical confrontations are found within the underground, nor is it to suggest that all metalheads are eclectic; however, rejecting what they see as the banality and narrow-mindedness of mainstream music, many death metal fans champion a broad social and aesthetic eclecticism.

Closely related to death metal's eclecticism are themes of critical thinking and tolerance. Over and over in interviews, metalheads said that punks tend to be preachy and dogmatic in their politics. Endless hardcore songs about corrupt politicians, televangelists, and environmental destruction—or, alternatively, songs celebrating racial hatred and "patriotism"—have left many underground fans bored and disaffected. In contrast, death metal lyrics often criticize dogma and emphasize critical thinking. The explosive power of a death metal performance, Dann Saladin said, is intended to break the listener free from the comforting clichés of any party line and to inspire critical thinking and self-determination. Tolerance is also a major theme. As long as they don't cause fights, people from any scene are welcome at a death metal show, said many metalheads. Tolerance, however, is a complex concept, and in interviews, metalheads agreed that death metal tolerance included a tolerance for racist bands. Perhaps the most important theme in death metal is personal motivation and personal responsibility. While the mostly working-class death metal fans are largely apolitical and could be in no way understood as standard-bearers for class consciousness, they are also sharply aware of the frustrations that everyday life brings to working people in the America of the 1990s. In this context, the thunderous power of a death metal performance is intended as a motivating force, a way of rousing the listener from the tedium of school, a spur to achievement, and a goad to accepting responsibility for one's own destiny. Counterbalancing these individualist ideas is the theme of solidarity within the underground. Subscribing to zines, buying demos, attending shows, and socializing in the scene, many metalheads are active community builders. Death metal rage, the tension between individualism and communitarian spirit, and the broader relationships of death metal practice to issues of class and race are explored in detail in Part III.

If we turn from the broad purposes of death metal to those of the self-avowedly more commercial power metal bands like Winter's Bane, a different constellation of meanings comes into view. Dann and the death metal fans spoke as much about the broader personal and social consequences of the music as the aesthetic effects they seek to achieve. While Winter's Bane's music presents a range of aggressive and morose affects, no one in the group ever spoke to me about politics. These musicians describe their music as cinematic—gripping narratives that entertain and engage the listener in the manner of a thriller or horror movie. In fact, most of their 1993 shows were devoted to a song cycle whose plot was distantly reminiscent of the movie *Body Parts*. Although Lou spoke of stirring a club audience to frenzied moshing, Timmy spoke of portraying the emotions of the characters about which he sang, and Terry spoke of conjuring images and entertaining a crowd, none were interested in politics or larger social consequences. Unlike the members of Sin-Eater, there is little sense of an underground identity among the members of Winter's Bane. Mainstream commercial success is anathema to many in the underground, and the growth of death metal in the early 1990s has been seen as a mixed blessing by many fans with a strong underground identity. Positioned at the commercial edge of underground metal, the members of Winter's Bane feel no ambivalence. They have little interest in building the underground, and focus solely on creating good heavy music and developing their careers.

Moshing at Mr. E's

Talk of purposes can be misleading when separated from practice, and we can gain another perspective on the scene if we take a look at a death metal performance event. Much smaller than the Agora, Mr. E's Tavern is a neighborhood bar in a white, working-class section of Cleveland's west side. A rectangular room whose long dimension runs perpendicular to the street, the space is divided roughly in half, making it seem narrower than it actually is (see Figure 2). I arrived around quarter past ten on a cool, rainy

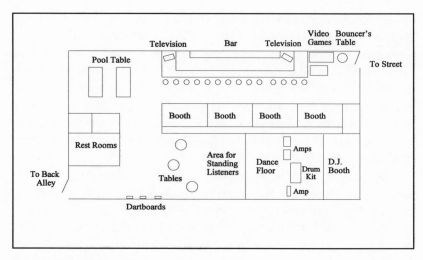

Figure 2. Map of Mr. E's Tavern.

night in August to hear two local death metal bands. Near the front door, the bouncer stood at a small round table next to an ancient "Birdie King" video game; behind it, the long wooden bar extended two-thirds the length of the building. All night long, the Indians-Expos game played on two large TVs that hung above the hundreds of bowling and baseball trophies on the back bar. High, red lunch-counter stools stood before the bar, and the floor was covered with a checkerboard of black and white linoleum tiles. The booths across from the bar were covered in red vinyl and the ivory Formica tables were stippled with brown dots. A low wall framed the booths, which overlooked the slightly raised DJ's platform and the small, checkerboard dance floor. A few disco lights hung from the low ceiling, and the wall was covered in smoky mirrors. Behind the dance floor a few tables stood in an empty area covered in dingy, red carpeting. Neon beer signs and dart boards hung on the flat black walls, and the ceiling was scarred with white primer.

The crowd was small, ranging from forty early in the evening to seventy during the headlining act. Three large men in jeans and T-shirts ("America, Love it Or Leave It," "Allman Brothers," and "ZZ Top") sat at one end of the bar all night long, watching the ball game and ignoring both the crowd and its music. A group of three women in their late thirties or early forties sat at the other end of the bar; mothers, aunts, or friends of the band, they spent the night in relaxed conversation. The majority of the crowd were metalheads. Ranging in age from their early teens to their late twenties, their dress was uniform. Unlike both the carefully manicured look of glam and the actively disheveled style of grunge, the metal costume is relatively unaffected for a "spectacular" youth subculture. Most had worn but un-ripped jeans or cutoff shorts, although a few younger kids had the faded blue-and-green plaid baggy shorts of the grunge scene. Almost all wore black T-shirts with the names of death metal bands picked out in a variety of gothic, blood-dripping fonts—Cemetery, Hideously Mangled, Death (with a scythe for the D and the T an inverted cross). With the summer heat, few wore the characteristic black leather jacket. The men's hair was shoulder-length or longer and clean, but a few had buzz cuts; the women were dressed like the men, though some had purses and a few wore a small amount of makeup. While large underground shows often bring out both punks and metal fans—and occasionally engender violent confrontations—the T-shirts and haircuts of the Mr. E's crowd made it clear that mostly metalheads were present.

About two-thirds male, the grouping of the crowd was similar to that of a commercial hard rock show: pairs or trios of men or women, small, mixed-gender groups, and no single women or male-female couples. The bands mingled with the crowd, and despite the bloody imagery of the T-shirts and the lyrics, the crowd was low-key and convivial. Friends or ac-quaintances stood in small groups, sipping beer and chatting; none of the elaborate flirting or urgent errand-running of the rock scene was found at Mr. E's. While bigger metal shows draw large, excited crowds, neither the rock star posing nor the endless displays of sexuality of glam can be found at even the biggest death metal events. Out to see friends, support the bands, and listen to good, heavy music, the death metal crowd neither seeks nor expects the I-knew-them-when thrills of the rock scene. Without the Agora's elaborate sound systems and lights, Mr. E's was a relaxed scene, and the bands mixed with the audience between shows in relative quiet. One of the groups sold demos and T-shirts between sets; a member of an-other local band sold his own recordings at a small round table in the back of the room, and Dann passed out flyers advertising his group's upcoming tape.

The bands set up on the dance floor near the DJ's booth. A black, double-bass drum kit sat unmiked in the center of the floor flanked by amps and speaker cabinets. While the guitarists used their own amps, the same drum kit and bass amp were used by both bands, and the two PA col-umns sat behind the bands on the DJ's platform. Gutted, the opening act, was a four-piece unit. Their bass player–singer stood in the center of the space wearing green and blue plaid shorts not baggy enough to mark him as part of the grunge scene. The rest of the band wore cutoff jeans, sneak-ers, and goatees; shirtless and with hair to the middle of their backs, they all played instruments finished in a flat black paint. While commercial hard rock musicians employ a well-established cannon of stage moves, the repertory of gestures in death metal is more limited and stylized. The two muscular guitar players stood with their instruments slung low, legs planted in a wide stance, and knees bent; exuding an air of menacing intensity, they did not move more than six inches from the one spot throughout the show. Throughout the night they head-banged (bobbing their heads in time with the quarter notes) or did whirlwinds (swung their neck in a circular motion creating a distinctive pom-pom effect with their hair). They kept their chins lowered; that and their long hair obscured their faces for most of the night. While singing, the bass player looked out at the audience, but otherwise his gestures were identical to those of the guitar players. While bigger crowds and larger stages sometimes evoke more spacious gestures, the head-banging–and–whirlwind approach is common in death metal. Viewing video tapes of his own band, Dann Saladin explained to me that the stripped-down stage moves of metal were part of the reaction against the (perceived) phony theatricality of commercial hard rock. The stage moves of death metal, he said, are meant to reflect the players' engagement with the sound; with fewer lights and effects, the death metal stage show is far more aural than visual. In any case, most of the spectacular kinetic performances come from the audience.

The crowd at the Gutted show was divided into several clearly marked sections. At the edge of the dance floor stood a row of four or five male metalheads listening to the music and head-banging lightly; later on, these were the listeners that moshed. As the show progressed, a group of listeners assembled in a semicircle behind them; the people that formed these back rows were listening with a powerful, motionless intensity. This group bled off continuously into couples or individuals standing further back and listening to the show with less interest; others shot pool, watched the baseball game, or chatted at the bar. At the beginning of the set, there was little movement among the listeners. After a few songs, however, they became more engaged in the music, and the front-row crowd started to head-bang more vigorously, bowing their heads deeply and bobbing them from the lower neck. When the band finally shifted into a very fast tempo, the men in the front row responded by head-banging with new intensity, bobbing with strong motions from the neck and shoulders; others began to lope around the empty space with a characteristic gait: hips back, legs canted forward, eyes on the floor. As the fast section developed, sheepish grins formed on the faces of two high school–aged friends in the front row. With an air of faked apology, they began to shove each other casually with their shoulders; after a short while others joined in, running in five- or six-foot circles, body-checking each other, head-banging fiercely, and taking up large amounts of space on the dance floor. The term "mosh pit" refers to the space in front of the musicians where the participants mosh; once the mosh pit was established, a tall, heavy-set man with buzzed hair began rolling his shoulders in huge circles, holding out his elbows, twisting his upper body in fast sharp arcs, and throwing punches into the air; all the while, the guitar player's hair spun in fierce whirlwinds, and the bass player sang with greater and greater power. The intense moshing continued until the end of the section and then quickly died out. No one outside the pit was involved in the moshing in any way, though everyone else moved backward once the pit got going.

Throughout the performance, the pit was in a constant state of flux between these fairly well-defined stages of moshing. The band played through medium, medium-up, and fast tempi; conducted by the song's form, the moshers stood stock-still, head-banged gently, moshed tentatively, or really threw themselves into the event. The endings of the tunes were extremely tight and no one moshed between the songs. At these points, the band's and the audience's demeanor became friendly and casual, songs were introduced in an everyday voice, and the guys in the pit wiped sweat from their faces or wandered back to the men's room to cool down. Plucked from the context, these men could easily have been amateur basketball players taking a breather between quarters. The crowd outside of the pit echoed those inside it, either standing stock-still or head-banging, while the rest of the people in the bar took little notice of the performance at all.

Dann Saladin describes moshing (in a quote for which he has forgotten the citation) as "good clean violent fun," and what must be understood about moshing is the tension between violence and order. Although I have heard of people getting out of control in the pit—bloody noses and broken fingers are common—I have never seen the pit turn into a full-fledged riot. On the contrary, moshing at most death metal shows is a remarkably controlled and ordered phenomenon, and the moshing practices at Mr. E's can serve as a case study in the gestalt structure of bodily display. When they started moshing, the two young men in the front row had the cat-that-swallowed-the-canary look of a guilty child feigning innocence. At this moment, the gentle body-checking portrayed, rather than enacted, violence; the theme of violence was pushed to the background and the foregrounded meaning was of two friends teasing one another. As the moshing became more intense, a deep anger overcame their faces and their pushing and shoving built to a fever pitch; however, as they body-checked one another, there was always the distant sense that no one wanted to do another serious damage. At these moments, the explicit message of violence was foregrounded, but the participants' carefulness acted as a frame and a defining background, coloring the focal violence with the subtle awareness that this was a mosh pit and not a riot.

Unlike these two friends, the tall buzz-cut man's expression was dour throughout the evening. When the participants started moshing, he swung his elbows strongly, but stood far away from all others; like a gun brandished but not fired, his swinging elbows were a sign representing violence, not violence itself. When the pit was really going, however, he took up huge amounts of space on the dance floor and his elbows and fists were truly menacing. Even though a broken nose was merely inches from reality during the pit's wildest moments, no one got hurt. What we see here is both a genuine expression of aggression and the control of that aggression. Like a figure and a ground, neither eliminates the other; to do so would destroy the meaning and the image. Had the buzz-cut man actually smashed someone, or had the two friends given up their awareness that moshing was for sport, the event would have collapsed into a melee; had the images of violence been removed altogether, no moshing would have taken place at all. Coordinated by the musicians' tempo changes and the audience's active musical perception, the themes of violence and camaraderie constantly shifted from foreground to background in the ebb and flow of activity in the mosh pit. In death metal performance, the bodily practice of moshing is the representation and enactment of violence, constantly tempered with the representation and enactment of ordered social interaction and fun.

The action in the pit of a major show is similar in many ways to the moshing described above. While a large pit may run continuously throughout the set and involve a hundred or more people, the music still conducts the intensity of the moshing. Large shows have a broader range of audience activities, including stage diving (in which the listeners or musicians jump from the stage or speaker columns and are supported and tossed about by the upraised arms of the crowd), launching (in which one participant garners a toehold in another's interlocked hands and leaps onto the stage) and skanking (in which the participants mosh in a circular pattern). The tension between violence and order that characterized the pit at Mr. E's can be found at big shows as well. While the margin of the pit at a large show is not well defined, most of the participants are careful not to have contact with someone who doesn't want to mosh, and there is an unspoken balance between the listener's prudence and the mosher's consideration. While people do get hurt moshing, most people emerging from the pit to cool off in the rest rooms are markedly courteous and careful to avoid contact with those merely listening in the surrounding crowd. In general, men outnumber women in the pit.

Even in this relatively unified scene, the meanings of the event are complex and multivalent. At a death metal show, the pounding rhythms, artfully twisted harmonies, and heavy textures evoke anger, aggression, sadness, doom, depression, and grandeur in a thousand subtle shades. Oriented toward the moshing in the pit, built on a past of (perceived) aesthetic progress and opposed to the (perceived) vapidity of commercial hard rock, the music is inextricable from situated and larger social contexts. Moshing presents both the reality and the representation of violence, their shifting figure/ground differentiating the practices in the pit from a riot. Here the forms, varieties, and meanings of that aggression range broadly: aggression as a symbol represented; aggression as a reality enacted. Aggression released through catharsis; aggression created in events for its own end; aggression as an aesthetic form to be explored. Performances are more than pure affect, and, in the participants' experiences, the emotions are implicitly and explicitly bound to the rest of their social lives: aggression as a response to various forms of authority; aggression emerging from the frustrations of economic disenfranchisement. Aggression as a spur to personal motivation; aggression disengaged from its social contexts; aggression as a stance against the banality of mainstream popular culture; aggression as the focus of community. All of this is set in the convivial sociability of the bar—chatting and drinking, selling demo tapes and promoting up-coming shows, a ball game playing on the TV, and friends of the band talking at the bar.

Segue from rock to jazz

In these last chapters, I have begun to explore the nature of double constitution—how meanings are constituted by social practices and how social groups are constituted from on-the-ground actions. Describing the practices of dress and comportment by the participants of the Akron Agora, I have shown how commercial hard rock fans engage with the architecture and the other participants in the event to make the club a buzzing marketplace—a literal agora—of social interaction. Exploring the sociology of attention in rock shows, I have suggested how performance events are achieved through the lived experience of partially shared attention. Examining the practices of moshing, I have demonstrated how death metal shows are the collaborative achievement of the musicians and listeners. Discussing the metalhead's personal experience narratives and grounding the notion of musical style in the practices of composition and nightclub attendance, I have illustrated how fans of metal actively create the history and social order of their scene. Exploring the practices of composition in both rock and metal, I have highlighted the links between musical structures and musical experience.

But, as Anthony Giddens has suggested (1984), the social theoretic emphasis on constitution and agency should not be confused with a program of radical individualism; individual practices are informed by past social history and present social context, geared toward the experiences of others, and consequential for the actors of the future. In a variety of situations, we have seen how meanings are constituted differentially and in complex relationship with perceived others: metalheads select and craft ideologies relative to the diverse politics of the underground. Glam rockers, deadheads, and grungesters deploy their fashions at the Agora relative to one another and to a complex history of subcultural styles. Musical forms are composed and interpreted as heavy by both rockers and metalheads with respect to a history of popular music and a sociology of styles. The limited and stylized stage moves of death metal musicians are performed in opposition to the perceived shallowness of the glam spectacle, and the shorter songs and simple forms of Winter's Bane are crafted in rejection of the burgeoning inaccessibility of metal. Further, we have seen how the participants' practices aggregate in complex ways and constitute scenes whose structure—while always a product of the participant's actions—is not always of their own choosing. Thus, the size of the Cleveland-Akron area results in a limited number of death metal and alternative shows, to which many participants respond with a structurally based eclecticism; by the same token, the members of the larger and besieged commercial hard rock scene find themselves entertaining alternative crowds, though the rockers rarely feel the need to see alternative shows. Finally, larger social contexts—from the entertainment industry to the globalization of the American economy—impinge directly on the structure of the scenes and the practices of the participants. The responsibilities of traditionally conceived manhood make commercial hard rock's lure of sexuality and celebrity a substantial attraction; similarly, the frustrations of working-class life in a deindustrializing economy inform—but do not determine—the titanic energy of death metal. The rocker's search for stardom is oriented toward the international music industry, while the metalhead's grassroots community building is at least partially intended as a reaction against the industry.

While the minor cross-cultural comparisons between commercial hard rock and metal have suggested the cultural specificity of musical practices, a quantum leap into jazz will reveal more thoroughly how cultural context informs musical action. The patterns of practice that constitute the jazz scenes are so different from those that constitute the rock scene, however, that they call forth a different rhetoric. In the past two chapters I have explored the rock and metal scenes through a rhetoric of typification; ubiquitous in ethnography, the rhetoric of typification describes common practices and shared values. Rhetorics of typification make sense when they describe patterns of practice that are highly stable over time and highly shared among their practitioners. The difficulty with such rhetorics is that they tend to represent individuals as mere instances of larger patterns, rather than agents carrying forth actions that could have gone otherwise. While I have tried to emphasize the creativity, historical specificity, and internal differentiation of the practices of the rockers and metalheads, the rhetoric of typification foregrounds the sharing of practices and meanings within a community and backgrounds the differences.

If the rock scene is a giant castle whose walls have been breached by invading soldiers, and the death metal scene is a tightly unified outpost whose residents visit neighboring lands, then the European American jazz scene in Akron is a fragile coalition of diverse parties without a homeland. The African American jazz scene of Cleveland's east side is a relatively stable musical scene, but little jazz "scene" exists in Akron. The Akron jazzers I worked with the most have very different backgrounds and interests. Complementary skills, partially shared histories, and overlapping musical goals allow the players to constitute their performances, but it would be difficult to describe the barely extant Akron scene by using the trope of "typical" participants. The rhetoric appropriate to this situation is one of family resemblances, a Venn diagram of biographies and abilities that allows the fragile coalition of jazz musicians and listeners in Akron to come together. Like Finnegan's metaphors of musical world and musical pathway (1989, 304–5), the rhetorics of typified musical cultures and family resemblance differentially emphasize structure and agency, stability and fluidity in the constitution of music scenes. The key point here is that *both* the coherence and the fragmentation of meaning, both the stability and fragility of constituted social groups are effects of social practice. Even the most highly shared meanings and robust patterns of social practice are produced by agents who may do otherwise and whose unique interpretations are never fully identical; even the most polyvocalic riot of meanings and fragile coalitions are informed by large-scale social history, constituted through social interaction, and made meaningful by the actions of others. By comparing across scenes of such wildly different patterning, I throw into relief a small range of the interdependent relationships of creativity and sociality that can emerge from the practices of musical life.

FOUR

Two Jazz Scenes in Northeast Ohio

My research into Ohio jazz focused on two very different scenes: the mostly European American jazz scene of Akron and the mostly African American jazz scene of Cleveland's east side. My main contacts in the Akron scene were the members of the Whisler Quartet, a group that played 1950s style post-bop; throughout 1992 and 1993, their regular venue was a club called Rizzi's Jazz Lounge. Mostly in their mid- to late thirties, the four African American musicians that I worked with the most were never part of a single band; during my stay in Ohio they were regulars in Cleveland's east side jazz scene and played a style of post-bop characteristic of the period from the mid-1960s to the present.

While I am concerned with both scenes in this research, the study focuses more attention on the white jazz musicians. Let me explain: though I was able to do extensive interviews with African American jazz musicians, it became clear to me early in the research that the African Americans were less interested in participating in the research. While more than 50 percent of my appointments with musicians, white or black, ended up as cancellations or no-shows, even getting the African American players on the phone was a serious challenge. One reason was that, unlike most of the European American musicians, all of the African American players with whom I worked treated music as their primary occupation and were busy trying to break out of the local scene; their rehearsal, recording, and performance schedules were much more hectic, and, as a result, they had less time for interviews. But there was more to the story, and it was very clear that some of the African American musicians were wary of me. This was verified toward the end of my research by one of the African American players with whom I had developed a rapport. In the past, white academics and journalists have often misrepresented African American music, and some of the African American musicians did not completely trust me.

As a result, I have focused more on the European American jazz scenes than the African American jazz scenes, but in no way should this focus suggest a false reading of jazz history. Although there have been important European American jazz musicians, historically jazz has been an African American music; its greatest innovators and the bulk of its performers and nurturing audiences have been African American. Further, jazz history reflects the racism of American history: white record companies have excluded or exploited black jazz musicians; white performers have stolen songs and innovations from black musicians. In my research, the understandable reticence of the African American musicians has had the unintentional consequence of directing more attention toward European American jazz.

But that focus is not entirely negative. The music industry has lavished undue attention on white jazz celebrities, and African American studies, rightly redressing racist readings of music history, has focused mainly on African American jazz. Local, noncelebrity European American jazz scenes, however, have received little attention in ethnomusicology, and the present study seeks to address this gap. Describing my research to various audiences, I have often been confronted with disdain for studying anything as "mundane" as "white" jazz played in Akron, Ohio. Setting aside the fact that the music is of the first quality, and in no way denying the seminal role of African Americans in jazz history, the Rizzi's scene is worthy of study because it is important to the lives of its participants. If music means something to someone, it is a valid object of attention, and exploring the Akron scene can help us turn away from the snobbery that I have encountered and set our sights on the life of music in human experience.

My first goal in this chapter is to explore the constitution of these two music scenes. Jazz scenes and rock scenes are constituted by their participants through very different practices, and we can gain our first entrance into the complex social life of Ohio jazz by exploring how jazz musicians form bands and get gigs. Although rock and metal groups form and disband with great rapidity, band membership and band identity are the norm, and no rocker thinks of himself or herself as an individual player working single gigs. Jazz musicians of all scenes do occasionally form stable, ongoing bands, but the most common practice is a kind of freelancing. An individual musician scouts out a date at a local venue, usually with one or two colleagues in mind for key seats in the band; when the date is set, the leader (the musician who set up the gig) lines up colleagues to play the job.[1] Some jobs last for months or even years, but many are for just a few nights. Being "part of a jazz scene" largely means being known by the leaders that dominate the venues and getting one's name in their phone books. One result of this pattern of practices is that a jazz "scene" can be anything from the tightest of cliques to the vaguest of networks.

A number of factors make the constitution of the scenes more complex. The Akron jazz scene is small and undifferentiated. In 1992 and 1993 there were just two main venues, Rizzi's Jazz Lounge and Jazz Etc, and they employ mostly European American musicians and attract mostly European American audiences. Many of the players in this scene are in their forties or older and perform jazz in the post-bop style of musicians like George Shearing, Bill Evans, and the Modern Jazz Quartet. Cleveland, by contrast, has several jazz scenes, some serving mostly African American musicians and listeners, others catering mostly to European Americans. Little avant-garde jazz is performed in Cleveland, but jazz-rock fusion, "modern" (post-1960s) small ensemble jazz, and big band all have venues. There is also a smaller New Orleans–style jazz circle and a variety of blues scenes. As in rock, larger scenes have unequal relationships with small scenes: most Akron players know the Cleveland scene, but only the older Cleveland players to know the Akron scene well. While some players move between scenes and do so habitually, the most in-demand Cleveland players rarely cross the county line.

Several dimensions of identity interact with stylistic concerns in the constitution of the scenes. For example, many African American musicians I worked with emphasized that the scenes are sharply differentiated by race, but most of the European American players were either unaware of the differences or disputed their existence. Stylistic animosities between the different scenes are related to generation. Most of the older European American players I spoke with strongly dislike avant-garde jazz, and many of the post-1960s stylistic developments—the work of musicians as diverse as Keith Jarret, McCoy Tyner, and Herbie Hancock—are not well liked by these players. The African American musicians tend to have an undisguised hostility toward the commercial fusion scene and a general disinterest in the 1950s and early 1960s post-bop that the Akron players employ. A textbook case of oppositional identity, these racial and generational issues affect the venues the players choose, their readings of music history, and their visions of the local music scene. Gauging the situation was complicated by my never-invisible identity—a young, white, Jewish academic, a guitar player with an interest in rock musics and the mid-1960s style of post-bop. As I suggested at the end of Chapter 3, the best way to understand these fluid social forms is to employ a rhetoric of family resemblance rather than a rhetoric of typification; by exploring the biographies of each of my main research participants, we shall see how each particular belief or practice constitutes, or diverges from, broader patterns.

A tall man in his early sixties, Larry Whisler is the son of an electrical contractor in Akron. He played marimba in a school band and enjoyed the music he played there, but as his teens passed, he became more and more interested in the popular jazz of performers like Woody Herman, Art Van Damme, and George Shearing. Soon Larry switched from marimba to vibraphone; vibes are much less physically demanding than marimba, and Larry soon found himself more accomplished in technique than most of the young percussionists in the area. But technique was one thing and the ability to improvise was another, and Larry's school band experiences did not prepare him to improvise in a jazz context. Stimulated by his love of this music, Larry and his friends began attending jazz clubs in the African American community of Akron, broadening his musical perception in ways that soon showed in his playing.

Larry fondly recalls road trips with his friends to New York City. A young man from a small city, Larry was excited by the vibrance of New York's nightlife and thrilled by the live performances of his musical heros. Thinking back to those trips from the vantage point of age sixty, Larry's face brightened as he recalled for me the famous clubs and sheer energy of New York in the late 1940s and early 1950s. For a short period of time, Larry wanted to be a professional musician himself, but he quickly discovered that the irregular schedule and unstable, itinerant life style was not for him. I interviewed Larry in the living room of his modest suburban

Larry Whisler

condominium; two of his adult sons live at home, and, between their polite intrusions and glasses of iced tea, Larry described the poverty of the local Akron scene as compared with the cutthroat vitality of the New York scene. Without rancor, Larry returned again and again to the rich ferment of the New York scene, and after several hours it became evident to me that, more than forty years later, the interview process was stirring old career regrets.

However, the security of a regular income and family life was a boon to Larry. He married, and after a few years at the University of Akron and Kent State, he got a management position at Goodyear Tire where he remained till the mid-1980s. Throughout the years, Larry continued playing jazz in local clubs, but the scene has gone progressively downhill since the mid-1960s when rock music siphoned audiences away from jazz. Universally loved for his gentle and good-natured manner, Larry allows a bit of frustration to creep into his voice as he describes how rock—in his eyes simplistic, talentless, and amusical—has almost totally destroyed the local jazz scene. Akron's many jazz clubs dwindled to two, young people stopped listening to jazz, and older people listened to less music of any kind; these days the jazz is harder and harder to find on the radio. The more aggressive avant-garde jazz that blossomed in the mid-1960s appeals to neither Larry nor his friends, and when jazz-rock fusion emerged in the 1970s, Larry's tastes became more deeply entrenched in the styles of his youth. Throughout the 1960s, 1970s, and early 1980s, Larry played Akron clubs and "society gigs" (weddings, parties, dances) and watched as venues closed, his audience aged, and the many, nearly full-time Akron jazz musicians dropped out of the scene.

In the late 1980s, Goodyear offered Larry early retirement, and he and his family moved to Florida, where he played a variety of society gigs. Though he found many talented musicians there, he disliked having to play (to him) simplistic pop tunes like "Moon River" and yearned for more challenging instrumental jazz. Missing friends and family, as well as the local jazz scene, Larry and his family moved back to Akron in the early 1990s. He approached local club owner Joe Rizzi for a gig soon after returning and assembled a band from what was left of his musician's phone book. The Whisler Quartet played the first weekend of every month at Rizzi's for all of 1993, during which time Larry also picked up parties and weddings. Because of a bad back, he didn't like moving his vibes for single-night performances, and, not needing the money, he soon avoided these jobs.

Though ten years younger than Larry, pianist Dick Schermesser tells a similar story. The son of a mortician in suburban Akron, Dick's love of jazz

Dick Schermesser

began in his teens. While jazz artists like Stan Getz and Oscar Peterson have always been heroes to Dick, he was, from a young age, also attracted to Western art music and feels that this tradition, up through atonalism, has produced some of the world's finest music. Nonetheless, despite his love for Western art traditions, Dick aspired in his early twenties to be a professional jazz musician. He went to college for a few years, but regarded music scholars as shallow thinkers and inept performers. Attracted by its more vibrant jazz scene, he moved to Cleveland, dropped out of college, and played in a variety of European American and African American clubs. He also studied with local pianist and music teacher Phil Rizzo; Dick credits Rizzo with educating him in the universal musical principles that underlie jazz, classical, and all "serious" musics. Eventually, Dick moved to New York to pursue his career. Before long, however, he began to feel that the New York scene was built more on personal connections and visual appeal than talent, and he soon returned to Akron. Eligible for the draft, Dick enlisted in the Army Musician Corps.

Upon returning home, Dick swore off the reckless ways of his youth. Though unrepentant in his dislike of music scholarship, Dick returned to school, married, and took a position in his father's funeral parlor. Dick shares Larry's musical preferences, but his feelings are much more pronounced the vibist's. He has an undisguised dislike for all of the developments in jazz after the mid-1960s (avant-garde, modal, fusion, and so on), Western art music after impressionism, and all forms of rock. In all of these styles, he feels, the participants are little more than technicians, artistic poseurs, or charlatans, and his disgust with changes in jazz led him to quit music for much of the 1980s; during this period he neither played, practiced, nor listened to music. For reasons that are still not clear to me, Dick eventually returned to music. In 1992 and 1993, he played a small number of society gigs in Summit County as well as jobs at Rizzi's and Jazz Etc.

Bill Roth, the Whisler Quartet's drummer, is one of Akron's few full-time jazz musicians. A native Akroner in his early fifties, Bill started playing drums as a teenager. Big band drummers like Buddy Rich and Louis Belson were early inspirations to Bill. Always open-minded, Bill also played the then new rock and roll of the late 1950s, as well as blues and Latin musics. He attended the University of Akron for a few years but soon felt that academics weren't for him; after dropping out, he followed a less formal but equally rigorous musical and personal education by participating in the musical life of the city. In the 1960s, one of Akron's jazz scenes was mostly composed of Italian Americans, and throughout that decade Bill involved himself with these players, performing popular jazz standards in the numerous Akron clubs and theaters. Later, he shifted to a primarily African American scene and accompanied local pianist Count Head. Throughout the 1960s and early 1970s, Bill played in local rock bands. During this period he constantly listened to the various waves of Latin music that hit America's shores. Always interested in spirituality, Bill experimented with different forms of meditation and even some psychedelic drugs. To keep body and soul together, Bill taught drums in local music stores and played a wide variety of society gigs.

Bill Roth

The end of the 1960s saw the breakup of Bill's first marriage. Unlike Dick Schermesser, however, Bill has never known a period in which music was not his main occupation. He led various Latin ensembles throughout the 1970s and 1980s and was often frustrated by local musicians' ignorance of musics originating outside the United States. By the end of the 1960s, Bill had lost interest in commercial rock. Throughout the 1970s, however, he played in jazz-rock fusion groups, and to this day bands like Oregon and the Mahavishnu Orchestra continue to inspire him. From the 1980s to the present Bill has continued to play jazz and society gigs, as well as running a marimba band with his second wife. So-called world music is his greatest interest these days, and Bill's spiritual and musical lives cannot be separated. Once a year Bill attends drumming workshops at the Omega Institute, a New Age education center in Rhinebeck, New York; he also leads workshops on drumming, improvisation, and creativity, and teaches more conventional drum lessons at a local music store.

Bill feels little or none of the animosity toward rock and avant-garde jazz that Larry and Dick do; his feelings are shared by bass player Jack Hanan, the only member of the band who is not an Akron native. Born and raised in Cleveland, Jack is the youngest member of the group. As a teenager, Jack listened casually to the commercial rock of the day, but his real interest in music exploded when he heard the jazz-rock fusion of the Mahavishnu Orchestra on a local radio station. Jack was soon a bass player, and jazz was really the only music ever to engage his attention. After high school, Jack moved to Boston to study jazz at the Berkeley School of Music. Though Boston had a lively music scene, Jack felt constrained by the education he received at Berkeley and returned to Cleveland after a few years. There, he married a local jazz vocalist and the two played a variety of area gigs.

The critical force in Jack's music education was not Berkeley, but the circle of older African American jazz musicians that adopted him after his return to Cleveland, and he credits pianist Ace Carter as his most important mentor. Throughout the 1970s, Jack's primary occupation was music, but the birth of his two children in the 1980s and his subsequent divorce left Jack needing a steady income. While managing a downtown discount store owned by his father, Jack played bass in a local circle of younger, mostly European American musicians that centered on a popular Cleveland club. These musicians play the demanding, mid-1960s style jazz disliked by Larry and Dick. He eventually removed himself from this scene, and by late 1992 was looking for a new musical outlet. It was then that he got the call to play at Rizzi's. His sixty-hour-a-week schedule and desire to spend time with his children kept Jack's musical career at a slow simmer, but nevertheless he found time to play the Rizzi's job and a few jazz gigs in both the Cleveland and Akron areas.

Jack Hanan

A common social scientific approach to such widely divergent data would be to separate the idiosyncratic from the shared and construct some "typical" Akron jazz musician. While the biographical sketches given above are too brief to give anything more than an introduction to these player's lives, we can indeed extract from these stories a set of shared themes. But in the fragmented social life of Akon jazz, divergence is just as much a part of the story as commonality; embracing a rhetoric of family resemblance, I shall instead focus on the highly specific relationships of the various life stories to one another and the broader social conditions that nurtured them. My goal is not to describe a consistent "musical culture," but to highlight the commonalities and the differences in the actors' responses to social and musical context and to examine the impact of their practices on the current jazz scene.

The alternating currents of fluidity and stability in the Akron scene are best illustrated by the contrast between Jack and Bill on the one hand and Larry and Dick on the other. Jack has a very wide musical network and has shifted between different scenes as the years have passed. Although Dick and Larry know of the younger European American clique and the older African American players that Jack has performed with, neither has played much in those Cleveland scenes. Bill's experience reflects a slightly different set of movements in the social space. He is a stalwart of the Summit County jazz scene, but he also played rock in the 1960s and fusion in the 1970s; his interests run far beyond jazz to New Age and world music and he has cultivated opportunities outside of the usual venues—improvisation workshops, world drumming jam sessions, and marimba band gigs. It is easy to see how the Akron scene—served by musicians with various stylistic commitments and constrained by a shrinking audience and limited venues—is constituted by the practices of its actors; indeed, should ten or fifteen of the Akron players drop out, the scene would either disappear altogether or be taken over by musicians from Cleveland. But within this fragmentation there exist enough recurrent patterns of practice and partially shared expectation to speak of a small "scene" and an attendant set of styles and aesthetics. Though idiosyncratic and shifting, the practices are never radically individual but are always dependent on a partially shared social past (1950s style post-bop jazz) and oriented toward a common social present (the expectations of the audience and the management).

I shall return to racial dynamics below, but it is important to observe here that generation and style interact in complex ways in these players' life stories. For example, Larry's and Dick's musical preferences were formed in the period from the late 1940s through the early 1960s. As 1950s post-bop passed into the more experimental approaches of the 1960s, these players found themselves increasingly alienated from the assertive musical styles of players as diverse as John Coltrane, Cecil Taylor, and Miles Davis. As a result, the innovations of their heros from the 1940s and 1950s slowly sedimented into a period style in a process structurally similar to those we have observed in power metal. Dick's and Larry's emotional responses to the changing musical climate—respectively, undisguised aversion and bemused dislike—neatly reflect the range of negative feelings toward contemporary jazz and rock found among the Akron players. These attitudes also connect to broader social changes; for example, Dick interprets the perceived artistic pretensions of post-bop and the perceived amusicality of rock as an outgrowth of "the kid revolution"—the moral decline of American parenting since the 1960s. Not surprisingly, the younger Jack has none of the aversion to rock or avant-garde jazz expressed by his older colleagues. While attracted to the older styles of his bandmates, Jack has a breadth of taste that reaches back to Larry's youth, but also embraces the Miles Davis of the 1960s, the Chick Corea of the 1980s, and a thin slice of the rock pie. Bill presents an even more interesting picture. Though older than Dick, he didn't spurn the jazz innovations of the 1960s or rock developments of the 1950s through the early 1970s; further, his interest in spirituality drew him from jazz toward musics outside the United States. Bill and Jack have both engaged in some of the style period dynamics discussed above, but, at a number of points in their musical biographies, they have explored other avenues and accepted different influences.

These data bear upon the question of the systematicity of culture. Familiar with similar recordings, commonly nurtured in the African

American jazz scene, and driven by the ubiquitous need for cash, Jack, Bill, Larry, and Dick have enough shared knowledge of songs and improvisational techniques to allow them to perform together comfortably and satisfy the audience and the management. But none of this guarantees the sharing of wider values or experiences, and, in many ways, the players are extremely dissimilar. The immediate point is that for actors to constitute a scene, they need not have identical—or even highly similar—social histories or beliefs; all that is necessary is enough shared or complementary knowledge to enable interaction. Built around an emergent and fragmentary sharing of interests and enabled by a variety of contextual factors, many scenes are more like political alliances than traditionally conceived folk groups. The larger point is that practice is the foundation of both cultural cohesiveness and cultural fragmentation. Although—as in the metal example—histories, beliefs, and social experiences can be intensely shared and patterns of practice can have great stability, the only requirement for a scene's existence is enough sharing and complementarity to enable interaction. Practice is the primary reality from which all reifications, the scholar's and the participant's, are formed. [2]

Many of the these players' attitudes and experience reflect wider patterns in contemporary jazz. Jack's eclecticism, Dick's animosity toward avant-garde jazz, Larry's more gentle spurning of that music, and Dick's and Larry's shared feeling that rock's popularity destroyed their scene are all common beliefs. Bill Roth's embrace of the great breadth of jazz history, 1960s rock, New Age music, world music in general and various Latin and African musics in particular is more unusual. What is ultimately unique here is the constellation of features, formed by contingency and agency, that make up each individual biography and the Whisler Quartet as a whole. How these musicians play out their biographies on the bandstand will be explored below, but, because patterns are always grasped more clearly in contrast, we shall gain a richer understanding if we turn to the musical biographies of my African American research participants.

Jerome Saunders, a native of Cleveland and a pianist in the African American, east side jazz scene, was my first contact in Cleveland. The main theme of my conversations with Jerome was eclecticism. In the early 1970s Jerome attended the famous Verde Valley High School, an experimental institution where students were encouraged to work outside the school and guide their own education. A pianist since his early teens, Jerome's interest in music exploded during his college years at Antioch. At this liberal bastion, Jerome immersed himself in a wide variety of musics. Post-bop from a variety of traditions, older jazz from King Pleasure to Ella Fitzgerald, rhythm and blues, a variety of musics from the Western art tradition, and

Jerome Saunders

the avant-garde jazz of Antioch professor Cecil Taylor all graced Jerome's turntable at the time. Practicing eight hours a day but still not considering himself a musician, Jerome eventually went to the New England School of Music in Boston to polish his craft.

Holding down two jobs, playing in several bands, and attending music school full time, Jerome's Boston period was one of growth. There he sampled the musics and social cliques of the full range of Boston's club scene and formed a "general business" band that played anything from pop to rock to a wide variety of jazz musics. After two hectic years in Boston, he left the New England School and moved to New York; though the range of musics and sheer vitality of the city fed Jerome's yearning for variety, he found it very difficult to get a foot in the door of New York's competitive jazz cliques, and he played many more private gigs than nightclub jobs. After five years in New York, Jerome went back to school to earn his master's degree in psychology from Howard University. He moved back to Cleveland, got a job doing psychiatric evaluations, and slowly returned to music.

Though largely involved in the east side jazz scene, Jerome is one of the more varied musicians I spoke with and performs in a wide range of contexts. Two nights a week he and a local bassist play traditional post-bop jazz in the lobby of an expensive Cleveland hotel, and Jerome is also the pianist in a long-standing Cleveland jazz quintet. Beyond his forty-hour-a-week job and those two time-consuming musical commitments, Jerome is frequently called to play pickup gigs. Although he keeps busy, Jerome is often frustrated by the conservative nature of the Cleveland scene. Members of

Eric Gould. Photo © Herbert Ascherman, Jr.

the tight musical circles, says Jerome, neither call outsiders to play nor listen to musicians from other scenes; clubs are reluctant to try any new kind of music, and little avant-garde jazz is performed in the area. For all these reasons, in the early 1990s Jerome was planning to leave Cleveland as soon as his finances would permit.

Pianist Eric Gould's experiences are similar in many ways to Jerome's. Eric cites banging on pots and pans as a toddler as his earliest musical experiences, and, as he grew up, Eric was surrounded by a variety of musics. He listened to his older brother's band explore free improvisation and jam over rock chord structures, and when he grew older he sat in with them. Elementary school music lessons on recorder led to ten years of clarinet and the flute; in high school, he used these skills to play in a variety of rhythm and blues bands. His father's tastes ran to jazz, and when Eric heard Miles Davis's *Bitches Brew*, neither the rock nor the jazz elements came as a great surprise. In the late 1970s, Eric attended the University of Cincinnati and majored in communications, but, like Jerome, he found himself practicing piano eight or nine hours a day. He soon returned to Cleveland and dedicated himself to a career in jazz.

The 1980s were a period of great musical expansion for Eric. He studied classical piano at Cleveland State University and developed a disciplined practice routine. In the first years of the decade he played electric keyboards and led a variety of jazz/funk groups. During this period, Eric says, the scene was fairly active, but the other players' increasing drug use made stable musicians hard to find; as a result, Eric turned to more mainstream post-bop jazz. During this time, he went to Cleveland State to finish his undergraduate degree, collaborated with a local artist on a music and slide-show presentation, played concerts with a local trio and orchestra, taught at the Cleveland Music Settlement House, and did administrative work there. Eric feels that as the 1980s came to an end, the jazz scene shrank. Clubs closed down, and the ones that stayed open hired only a small group of musicians. When I spoke with him, Eric was avoiding the local club scene. During the three nights a week Jerome has off, Eric took his place playing piano in the hotel lobby gig, and one weekend a month he played a similar style of jazz at a bar in a wealthy suburb. He was also making a demo tape and playing on several recordings of Cleveland players. Family illness has kept Eric in town, but his main goal at this point is for his wife and him to leave the area and expand their musical careers.

Alvin Edwards (not his real name) is another local musician looking to get out. He began playing trumpet in high school and performed in a wide variety of rhythm and blues bands. His sister was an avid jazz listener, and after Alvin heard an old Miles Davis record, jazz became his focus. Although he didn't perform with a group strictly devoted to jazz until after college, Alvin played with a jazz influence and picked jazz tunes for his high school bands to play. His high school groups achieved some success, opening for national rhythm and blues acts when they came to town.

Feeling that music was a pleasant avocation that would merely impede his serious studies, Alvin left his instrument at home when he left for college in the early 1970s. A semester later he realized the importance of music in his life and every spare moment was filled with playing. After transferring to a local university, Alvin majored in engineering but minored in music, taking piano lessons and theory classes. After college he landed a series of high-paying jobs in business, but music took up every moment of his spare time. By the early 1980s he began playing the aggressive, post-bop mainstream jazz that so enthralled him, and, with the support of his family, he finally quit his job to pursue a career in music. Among his diverse projects in jazz were several duo groups with local pianists from the east side jazz scene. In 1984 Alvin left for Philadelphia where he played funk and jazz pickup jobs.

Personal reasons brought Alvin back to Cleveland in the late 1980s. Honing his skills on the flute and trombone, he did part-time consulting work for a local design firm. Always broadening his abilities, he garnered a variety of gigs including a seat in a respected Western art quartet and several jobs in the pit band of touring musicals. While Alvin enjoys these performances, it is jazz that he likes the best, and when we spoke he was playing frequently on the east side. In Cleveland, his best musical hopes were pinned on an octet that included pianist Eric Gould and several other players in the east side scene. Alvin feels that Cleveland has many fine jazz musicians, but they have not demanded the respect due them from local club owners. While Alvin is offended that jazz is merely background music in most clubs, he reserves his main scorn for contemporary fusion. Fueled by changes in technology and a variety of musical innovations, a light, jazz-rock fusion scene began garnering greater public attention in the early 1990s, and a number of Cleveland clubs began booking local fusion acts heavily. Alvin occasionally takes calls in this scene, but during my stay in Cleveland he became disgusted with what he saw as the banal and stultifying commercialisms of the genre. More and more, Alvin grew to dislike this so-called fuzak (fusion Muzak), and when we spoke he was hoping to leave the area.

The story of Leonard Burris (not his real name) follows Alvin's closely. This Cleveland native began playing trombone at age twelve. The popular music of the day like Earth, Wind, and Fire, Cameo, and Chicago stand out in Leonard's mind as the music of his teens. In the seventh and eighth grades, Leonard took private lessons at a local supplementary center where volunteers gave music lessons, but the center closed and Leonard's family was unable to afford private instruction. Throughout high school, Leonard joined various rhythm and blues bands and played the occasional talent show or party. At the time, he also listened to fusion, and in our interviews he chuckled when he recalled how he had confused fusion with jazz. Except for his mother's gospel there wasn't a lot of music in his household, and Leonard had no exposure to jazz.

Student loans enabled Leonard to pursue higher education, and the transition from his inner-city high school to a rural college in the West was quite a shock. Though considered a top-flight player in high school, Leonard's lack of training left him with bad technique, and a beloved college music teacher (whom I will call Ken Jones) taught him proper breathing and forced him to relearn the instrument from the beginning. It took two long years to retrain his technique, but Jones was always supportive and this training gave Leonard the potential for much greater musical growth. Leonard defines himself as a loner, and during his college years he practiced four or five hours a day, spending the rest of his time working on theory or composition. Though the school offered no classes in jazz, the jazz lab band exposed Leonard to Duke Ellington's music, and soon his interest in popular music began to diminish. He eventually began organizing small jazz groups of his own. It was hard, however, to find good musicians in a western college town, and Leonard has many stories of inept or irresponsible side players. The 1980s cutbacks in student loan programs made it impossible for Leonard to afford college, and he dropped out and returned to Ohio in 1986. During that year, Leonard got a job backing a touring reggae band, but he disliked the raucous scene and eventually quit.

The late 1980s were a hard period for Leonard; gigs were difficult to come by, money was scarce, and Leonard spent as much time as possible practicing. Eventually, he quit his day jobs and enrolled in a local college to focus solely on music. Making contact with some of the best-known local African American jazz musicians, Leonard began to break into the scene and gain what he called real-world jazz skills. His return to religion and intense focus on jazz are all part of what he describes as his overall recovery from the ravages of the 1980s. When we spoke, Leonard was fully devoted to his music and only worked day jobs when his finances demanded. Picky about the gigs he plays, Leonard resents clubs where music is a mere background and avoids them whenever possible. Believing that the soloist should lead the small ensemble, he dislikes playing with musicians who are insensitive to the musical directions of his solos and is careful in picking side players for his jobs. During the period of our interviews, Leonard was still playing occasional gigs at east side clubs, but his main focus was on developing his quintet for concert venues and building his career. He left Cleveland for New York in 1996.

With these biographies presented, we can again explore the fluidity and stability of the scene's constitutive practices. Unlike the Rizzi's group, the generational and regional affiliation of these players is much more uniform; all share an ascriptive identity, long-term career goals, a grounding in popular music, and a relative lack of interest in Akron. But there are differences as well. Although Alvin and Leonard occasionally mention eclecticism, Eric and Jerome have a deep commitment to this concept. Although primarily playing in the African American, east side scene, Jerome likes to think of himself a player that can bridge scenes and stylistic differences. With his voluminous collection of recordings, he also keeps up with a broad range of musics within and outside jazz. As we shall see, Jerome's main concern is to bring the broadest range of musical approaches and harmonic materials to bear on his improvisation. Similarly, Eric Gould's music draws on a broad range of styles from jazz history, as well as rhythm and blues and the "art rock" of the 1970s. Like Jerome, Eric's musical goal is a constant broadening of the stylistic palette. Finally, where Alvin and Leonard are less self-conscious about their eclecticism, these two possess backgrounds in African American popular musics and cite them as important touchstones.

Region, generation, and race all characterize the differences between the African American and the European American scenes. The clearest oppositions are along regional lines: the Akron players are all much more aware of the larger scene to the north than vice versa; though our spoiler Jack plays in the Akron scene, he is by and large more aware of the Cleveland players than those in Akron—if only because the former outnumber the latter. Similarly, the acceptance of popular musics and the style period dynamic in both groups are related to age and generation: all of the younger players (the African Americans and Jack) began with some interest in popular musics and none have an animosity toward pop; Dick and Larry have a very hard time accepting most of the rock-based musical innovations of the last thirty years, and, although Bill has some warm feelings about older rhythm and blues and rock, he has little interest in contemporary popular music.

The generic other for the African American players is fusion, not rock. Jerome rarely has a bad word for any music, and his all-embracing eclecticism seems boundless. Though accepting some forms of 1970s fusion, Alvin, Leonard, and Eric see the 1990s fusion of players like Kenny G and Nagee, and even the slightly older fusion of David Sanbourne, as part of the white music industry's crass commercialization of jazz. Through a sharply differential identity, their music is set off from the contemporary fusions. All of the players (African and European American, main and secondary research participants) view fusion from the 1970s to the present as outside of the mainstream of jazz history.

The comparison of style period dynamics shows some interesting similarities. For example, the jazzers said that, for all its emphasis on innovation and experimentation, the mid-1960s post-bop style has undergone few dramatic developments in the last thirty years. When I played recordings of local African American jazz performances back to my research participants, the players usually agreed that the music could have been recorded anytime since the mid-1960s. Jerome Saunders holds that even avant-garde jazz has become conservative and changed little since the first innovations of players like Cecil Taylor and Ornette Coleman. Thus, while long-lasting jazz masters like Chick Corea and McCoy Tyner and more recent heavy hitters such as Joshua Redman or Henry Threadgill have developed unique forms, my research participants agree that no stunning innovations like those of Charlie Parker or John Coltrane have developed recently. With the popular historiography placing fusion off to the side, the post-bop mainstream can be seen as a kind of period style largely unvanquished by a stylistic successor. Given this situation, my African American jazz research participants—players who depict themselves as artists and experimenters—participate in a period style dynamic similar to that of Larry and Dick.

While age and region are important to these scenes, the critical factor to explore here is race. I set aside special interviews with all of my research participants to discuss the relationships between race relations, jazz history, and the contemporary music scenes, and here, clear differences emerged between the two groups. While the African American players emphasized that there have been important European American musicians, they all took pains to represent jazz as an African American music; while the European American players were aware of jazz's African American roots, they presented a much more desegregated view of jazz history.

But readings of history are much less significant to our current understanding than the racial dimension of the biographies and practices. Power relations tend to solidify patterns of interaction, and four hundred years of inequity in America has, of course, affected these musical scenes in complicated ways. Early in their careers, all of the European American players spent time learning jazz in largely African American scenes. While the younger African American players' first musical experiences were with both white and black pop, black jazz scenes nurtured their jazz skills. While Jack and Bill still play in African American scenes, Larry and Dick have moved away into primarily European American jazz circles. By contrast, the African American musicians have continued in both European American and less segregated venues, even as they focused on the black, east side scene—if only because of the greater number of venues. Though deeply formed by racial politics, the Rizzi's and Jazz Etc scene has no self-conscious racial identity. By contrast, the African American players see themselves as rooted in an African American music history and as members of an African American community. When playing in mostly white venues, the black players' sense of differential identity emerges from being African American, rather than merely from being a musician.

In sum, we can see that these two groups interact infrequently and have little awareness of one another. Dick and Larry live in a suburban, middle-class world where music provides meaning and enjoyment and is far distanced from the economic realities of everyday life; there are few African American players or audience members in their scene and neither racial tensions nor racial awareness are foregrounded in their experience. The other that frames their musical life is a generational one: the youth of the 1960s, 1970s, and 1980s that abandoned their music and stole their scene. Eric, Jerome, Alvin, and Leonard are still engaged in the all-consuming struggle for survival as musicians. Their musical experiences stretch beyond a racial minority but are firmly rooted in a racial awareness; differential identity for Alvin and Leonard means a stand against commercial fusion, not the pop music that nurtured them and still garners their affection. For these career-minded musicians, the local musical scene is not a home to be made comfortable, but a stepping-stone to national success and greater stylistic innovations.

What every jazz musician knows:
Musical structures and musical knowledge

The best way to explore musical sound is by observing how those sounds are created and grasped by participants. Those musical practices depend on past experiences, however, and describing practices of acquiring jazz fundamentals would entail a large ethnographic project of its own.[3] To avoid this, I shall first present some abstract musical knowledge and then describe how that more-or-less stable knowledge is applied. This division of the presentation should not be taken to imply the existence of two distinct domains of study; as I have suggested in the discussion of rock fundamentals, abstract knowledge is best understood as sedimented practice.

The most basic piece of shared knowledge is the head-solos-head form. In the small ensemble, pickup band jazz scenes with which I am concerned, a tune is defined by its head—a short, abstract outline of the composition that defines a melody and chord changes. The 32-bar AABA form is the most common shape a head may take; it begins with the A section, eight bars of melody and accompanying changes, usually divided into two 4-bar units. The phrase is then repeated exactly or in variation. Next comes eight bars of new material called the bridge or B section; the form ends with the A section's return. One full performance of the head is called a chorus. When a tune is called (selected for performance), the band plays the melody and chord changes of the head. After one or two choruses, the rhythm section (piano, bass, and drums) continues playing the head's changes, and each musician in turn improvises a solo over that repeating accompaniment. A player may solo for one or more choruses, and musical and visual cues are used to indicate when a player is about to end his or her solo and another player should begin.

Except in trio settings, the rhythm section players almost always solo last, and often in the order piano, bass, and drums. Bass players occasionally miss a solo; drum solos are even less common, and the band may instead play "fours." There, the player that soloed first will solo again for four bars, and then the drummer will solo for four bars; after that, either the first soloist or a succession of additional players will trade 4-bar solos with the drummer until one or more full cycles of the head have been played. When the drummer is finished soloing or the fours are over, the band will play the head once or twice and the piece will be over. This general form is found both in the Akron and Cleveland jazz scenes and has been the foundation of small ensemble jazz since before bebop. Its ubiquity allows players who have never met to coordinate their activity and put on an entire evening's performance without reference to written music; a tune is called and the form simply unfolds from there.

The shared knowledge about any particular tune varies widely between musical scenes, genres, and periods, but much of the knowledge about any single tune is knowledge about the head. In defining a song, the head specifies the melody and chords. Though some parts of some melodies must be played very strictly, melodies are typically varied, and the extent and the style of their variation depends on the genre of the tune, the musical scene of the players, and the type of job at which the tune is played. The soloists must know the head melody, and the rest of the band should know it as well.

Everyone but the drummer must know the chord changes, but "knowing the chord changes" is a more complicated matter than knowing the head melody. Unlike chords in rock (which, as I have suggested above, can serve melodic, harmonic, or nontonal functions) the chords in the head of a jazz standard lay out the harmony against which the head melody or solos are played. In most cases, knowing a tune's chord changes does not mean memorizing particular notes and rhythms. On the contrary, the chords to a tune (often referred to as the harmonic rhythm or the changes) define periods of harmonic functions (tonics, dominants, and so on) within tonal centers or changes to new tonal centers, each of which lasts for a set number of bars or a fraction of a bar. Many different chord qualities based on one root serve the same harmonic function; for example, if the tune requires a C chord as a tonic, the player can play a C major seventh, ninth, eleventh, or thirteen—all of which indicate to the listener that that chord is a tonic. Further, the player is free to voice the chord (stack the notes of the chord in different octaves) as he or she chooses. While each style has typical chord qualities and voicings, the chordal players (usually keyboardists and guitarists) improvise their specific accompanying parts on the bandstand. They are also free to employ passing chords, substitute new chords, or even superimpose new chord progressions, as long as the parts they play give the right tonal sound and don't interfere with the head melody or the improvised solos. Occasionally, chord qualities, specific voicings, or hits are more specifically defined.

For example, here is a typical lead sheet defining the changes for the first eight bars of Duke Ellington's classic "Take The 'A' Train."

/C Maj7/ % /D 7 flat 5/ % /D-7/G 7/C Maj 7/ % /

(In standard jazz chord notation, the slashes refer to bars and the percent sign means to repeat the last bar.) The first two bars tell the player to play any chord that gives a C major sound. Figures 3, 4, and 5 are three possible comping (accompaniment) patterns a pianist could play for the first eight bars of the tune and still be performing a valid version of "Take the 'A' Train." Figures 3 and 4 are two common ways of playing the changes; Figure 5 breaks the stylistic rules of jazz but is still a valid (if avant-garde) interpretation of the harmonic rhythm.

The chords fulfill a similar role for the other members of the rhythm section as they do for the soloist. In some styles of jazz, the bass player largely plays walking bass—a constant flow of quarter notes that serve to define the harmonic and rhythmic framework of the tune. In more contemporary styles, the bass player may break free from the rhythmic restraints of a walking bass line. In either case, the notes the bass player chooses always emerge in relationship to the changes. In older styles of jazz, the bassist tended to play the roots or fifths of the chords on the first beat of the measure to make the changes as clear to the listener as possible; in more recent styles the player has become freer in his or her note choices.

Knowing a tune, however, means knowing more than just the head melody and changes, and it is at this point that specific aspects of style within each musical scene can be elucidated. The phrase "head arrangement" refers to knowledge of hits, accents, elements of form, and typical voicings that are specific to each particular tune. Larry and Bill are particularly frustrated playing tunes with younger players who don't know the classic head arrangements of the jazz standards. Some head arrangements are specific to the players of a local scene, while others arise from famous recordings, and the line between required head arrangement and optional musical device is both blurry and contextual. Bill Roth tells how one night at a club he was

Figure 3. An accompaniment pattern for "Take the 'A' Train"

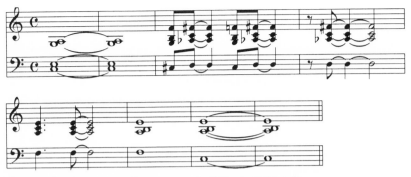

Figure 4. Another accompaniment pattern for "Take the 'A' Train"

asked to sit in on drums for a few songs with a group of musicians that he had never played with before. The other players called the song "Get Me to the Church on Time," a favorite of Bill's. In a well-known recording by André Previn, the drummer on the recording filled the space between the end of the head and the beginning of the first solo with a press roll on the snare. Familiar with the recording, Bill played that press roll and gave it special emphasis; in doing so, he alluded to the recording and let the other musicians know he was really a jazz musician. In his words, the others' heads spun around, and "they played their asses off." Here, the press roll is not so much a required aspect of the head arrangement as it is an in-group reference, but the distinction between the two depends on the players and the setting in which they perform.

The drummer's knowledge of a tune is somewhat different from that of the other musicians. As a nondrummer, I asked Bill Roth to introduce me to the drummer's basic musical knowledge; he explained that the two

Figure 5. A third accompaniment pattern for "Take the 'A' Train"

things a drummer must know if he or she is to play a song are its tempo and groove. Referred to by a number of terms, the concept of groove is not commonly taught in the basic Western musical education but is essential to all forms of drumming in jazz and Western popular music. In Western music classes, the most basic rhythmic unit is defined as the pulse, a procession of events such as clicks or foot taps with equal amounts of time between them; the amount of time between the pulses (referred to as tempo) can be long or short, and tempo is measured in pulses per minute. A time signature defines the number of pulses in a unit, called a bar, and also specifies if the pulses are to be treated as quarter notes, eighth notes, or sixteenth notes; the smaller fraction notes are meant to have short durations, so time signature has implications for tempo. Time signatures also imply a hierarchy of strong and weak beats. In a typical music skills class, the first and third beats are said to be "strong" or naturally accented; the second and fourth beats are weaker and the off-beats (subdivision of the beats) are seen to be weaker still.[4]

A groove is a pattern of accents and timbres that is layered on top of the time signature. (Confusingly, jazz musicians and ethnomusicologists also use "groove" to refer to the sense of rhythmic energy and vitality that takes place in a successful jazz performance.) The essential feature of most jazz grooves, understood in the former sense of the word, are the accents on beats 2 and 4 and the feel of swung eighths; Figure 6 shows a basic jazz groove. In contrast with the usual pacing of the chord changes and the traditional hierarchy of strong and weak beats, the primary accents in jazz grooves fall on the second and fourth beats, here played on the snare drum. The relatively rapid flow of eighth notes is played on the high-hat or ride cymbal, and these eighth notes are of unequal duration. Bill explains that the swung eighth notes of jazz are really just the first and the third of a flow of eighth-note triplets. Some jazz authorities disagree and say that while the pulses must be metronomic, swung eighth notes can vary in duration from a triplet feel to an almost equal division of the quarter note. Each style has a vocabulary of grooves, and the drums and cymbals upon which these patterns of notes and accents are played have varied throughout jazz history. Figure 7, for example, is an older variation of medium jazz, with the four pulses articulated on the bass drum, and Figure 8 is a stripped-down

Figure 6. Basic jazz groove

swung eighths

ride cymbal
snare
bass drum

Figure 7. An older jazz groove

swung eighths

high hat

Figure 8. Simplified jazz groove

groove used to accompany the solos of quieter instruments like the double bass. Bill explained to me that most local jazz gigs require no more than seven grooves: ballad, several Latin feels, medium jazz, up-tempo jazz, jazz waltz, jazz-rock, and Latin rock.

In all styles of jazz except avant-garde, playing the groove, or "playing the time," is the drummer's first responsibility. Beyond knowing the tempo and the groove, Bill explains that ideally drummers should have other knowledge about the tune as well. While they can get by without it, drummers should be able to sing the melody in their minds; knowing the melody's specific rhythms, larger phrasings, and affective contours helps them coordinate punches and fills and keep track of the form. While drummers need not know the exact chord changes, knowing when the changes come and having a general feel for the patterns of tension and release serves similar functions. It is often crucial that drummers know the head arrangement, because they often lead the band in its coordinated hits, fills, intros, bridges, and codas (ending sections) as well as changes in groove, tempo, or time signature.

Musical structure in the event: Some soloists

The basic knowledge of jazz described above applies equally well to the African American and European American scenes. We can begin to understand the differences between the scenes if we explore how the abstract knowledge sedimented from past practices is employed on the job. In the chapters on rock and metal we were able to follow the evolution of a song from composition through rehearsal to performances and recordings; in jazz scenes, the situation is quite different. While several of the members of the Whisler Quartet write songs, the Rizzi's audience come to hear standards, and original tunes are extremely rare in Akron performances. Further, the Whisler Quartet doesn't rehearse. Playing pickup gigs, receiving low wages, and leading busy lives, few Akron players get together before the gig. Bill and Jack bemoan this fact and claim that it has negative consequences for performance: loose intros and endings, dead periods between songs as the players pick the tunes, and occasional confusion about the changes. Most of the standards that the Whisler Quartet plays are from the 1940s, 1950s, and 1960s; because Dick, Bill, and Larry learned many of these tunes when they first were released, it was very difficult to explore how they learned the songs. Many songs were picked up by ear from recordings, while others were learned through lead sheets or on the fly during gigs. Detailed knowledge of the head arrangement and form arose both from the popular records and from spending time in the Akron scenes. The African American players do compose songs; these play an important part in their concerts but are less frequently used in their nightclub jobs. The Clevelanders rehearse more frequently than the Akroners, but they also complain that rehearsal is much less common than it should be.

All of this leads us to the threshold of the event. To get a clearer picture of a Whisler Quartet performance it will be helpful to know something about Rizzi's Jazz Lounge, the place where the performances occur (see Figure 9). Located in the heart of a suburban commercial strip, Summit Mall is a fully enclosed shopping complex in the style of the late 1970s or early 1980s. Rizzi's is found in the back of the mall, and by 9:00 P.M. it is the

The Whisler Quartet at Rizzi's Jazz Lounge (left to right: Bill Roth, Larry Whisler, Jack Hanan, and Dick Schermesser). Photo courtesy Bill Roth.

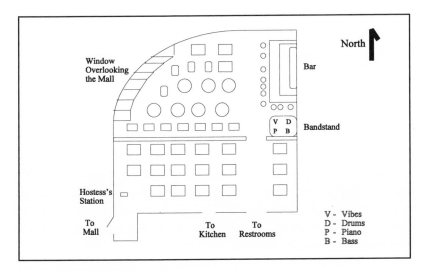

Figure 9. Map of Rizzi's Jazz Lounge.

only establishment left open. Entering the mall's wide corridor, you see an array of darkened shops and hear music from speakers inset in the ceiling. Stepping inside Rizzi's, you are greeted by a hostess wearing black pants, a white shirt and a bow tie. On most nights the wait for a table is short. Immediately before you is a large rectangular space divided in half; tables for two and four fill the dining section, and a low wall and two small steps up mark the edge of the lounge. The far wall of the lounge section sweeps across the room in a long, dramatic sweep; against the wall are set big, comfortable booths that overlook the shop-lined mall corridor. The wall's tinted glass makes the empty stores look like an abandoned movie set. The bar and the bandstand take up the opposite side of the lounge. Tall bar chairs with white metal legs and turquoise padded seats stand next to the bar, and tables fill the center of the room. Only one step above the house floor, the tiny bandstand is too small for the quartet, and Bill's drums and Jack's equipment are jammed together at the back of the stand. Larry's vibes are set up in front of the drums, and the house piano, a dilapidated white baby grand, is set up in front of Jack. A sticker bearing the name "Steinway" has been pasted above the keyboard, but all the band members agree that this infrequently tuned instrument did not come from that august manufacturer.

Offering a bar, live music, and Italian dinners priced between seven and twelve dollars a plate, Rizzi's seeks an image more upscale than national chains like Chili's or Applebee's, but more casual than the expensive restaurants of downtown Cleveland. The room is softly lit but not dark, with its recessed lighting, vaguely Art Deco decor, and turquoise and mauve color scheme. Though the band may play hard, the sound level is never deafening. Jack's acoustic bass runs through a small amp, while the vibes, piano, and Dick's vocal mike go through a house PA that feeds speakers set in the ceiling of the dining room and mall corridor. The PA is very soft and the sound always seems to come from the instruments themselves. Joe Rizzi, the owner, has several restaurants in town; once a professional jazz pianist in New York, he occasionally sits in with the band.

The club's clientele is mostly European American and range in age from their late twenties to their early sixties. Men are casually dressed in slacks, knit shirts, and sweaters, and women wear skirts, pants, and blouses as they arrive at the club to eat and chat. Three or four older patrons, well known to the band, sit at the bar and listen intently, and usually a few of the younger listeners at the tables are there for the music as well. Most patrons, however, don't hesitate to talk, eat, and ignore the group completely. Typically, the bar and tables are full until about 10:00 P.M. Food is served until much later, but the crowd begins to wane around 10:30, and by 11:30 only the jazz fans remain.

For their part, the musicians are aware of the audience but do not play out to them. Starting at 9:00, the group plays four sets before it finishes around 1:00 A.M.; Dick usually sings the head melody of the last song in the second and third sets. Though Dick quietly introduces the musicians at the end of every set, he rarely announces tunes or engages in stage patter. Between sets, however, the musicians are very alive to the audience, talking with listeners and musicians from the ever-shrinking scene. Though it is never difficult to hear the band, crowd noise and a shrill blender at the bar can become quite loud. The staff makes a small effort to keep things quiet during the music, but this is definitely not the Bop Stop—a Cleveland club where music is the venue's focus and there is no talking or ordering during the performances. Rizzi's does not exist to serve the jazz listener.

Occasionally, tunes are called in the Whisler Quartet that one of the players doesn't know, and a jazz fake book (an omnibus collection of tunes) is the answer for those situations. Each tune in a fake book is represented in the most minimal form, providing just the name of the tune's groove and/or tempo, head melody, and chord notation. Dick occasionally used fake books to remind him of the lyrics of the one or two tunes a night that he sang. For the first year of the gig, Larry relied on his memory and brought no music; feeling that the group's repertoire was too small, he eventually brought a fake book to the job. When relying on the music, Larry simply read the head melody and occasionally glanced at the changes to find his way; once the changes were internalized, he soloed without the book. Neither Jack nor Bill ever use music; Jack knew almost all the tunes and quickly picked up the changes for those about which he was unsure. On rare occasions Bill had to play a tune he didn't know, but as long as the other players told him the tempo and groove he had no problems.

When a tune is called, Larry almost always takes the head melody. Dick may double the melody in unison, but because doubling requires the kind of coordination that only arises out of rehearsals, this practice is uncommon. More often, Dick just comps with chords and fills. Jack usually walks (plays walking bass), and Bill plays time. During the head, Larry rarely plays the melody the same way twice, and extensive variation is critical to his style. The desire for melodic complexity, however, is tempered by his constant concern for accessibility. Larry knows that his audience has listened to these standards for years and developed strong attachments to them. Playing the melody exactly as it would be written on a lead sheet would be too boring, but varying the melody too much might lose the listeners. Holding the basic melody in his mind as a defining background, Larry may add fills and runs, alter the rhythmic values of notes, or introduce chromatic passing notes or diatonic arpeggios; however, the general melodic contours are always maintained and the song is always recognizable to the regulars at the bar.

The head played, Larry almost always solos first, and the developments of jazz improvisation since the mid-1960s are largely absent from his playing. Recounting the experiences of his youth, Larry explained that his first impulse in soloing was to simply arpeggiate the chords of the tune (play the notes of the chord in succession). This guaranteed that none of the notes of his lines clashed with the chords, but to his ear the effect was choppy and unpleasant. It was only by learning how to tie several chords together with scaler ideas and more extended arpeggios that Larry was able to get the sounds he was after. Listening to Dick's comping (accompanying) and his own internal imagination of the changes, Larry doesn't stop to reflect about the harmonic material of his solos. Rarely venturing outside the key area of the section, altering the chords, or substituting new harmonic structures over the harmonic rhythm, Larry's solos clearly reflect the harmonic terrain. With his constant concern for accessibility, Larry often phrases in the 4- and 8-bar patterns older jazz fans expect and frequently quotes the head melody in the B section of his solos so that the listeners can follow the form.

A more contemporary player might become bored with Larry's traditional application of harmonic materials; however, the art in Larry's solos is in his melodic approach, and to find fault with his harmonic palette would be to miss the point completely. Larry's ongoing concern is to keep the music interesting, and he achieves this by constantly varying the runs he uses to tie the changes together. Larry says that the clearest way to illustrate the changes is to play straight scalar runs that lead from the third or seventh degree of one chord to the third or seventh degree of the next important chord, but this approach quickly becomes tedious. He keeps his solos lively by using a variety of melodic devices. For example, rather than merely running a line straight up the scale (1, 2, 3, 4, 5, 6, 7, ^1, ^2, ^3, and so on), Larry might apply one of his extensive repertoire of scalar or arpeggio patterns, such as: 1, 3, 2, 4, 3, 5, and so on; 1, 2, 3, 2, 3, 4, 3, 4, 5 and so on; 1, 3, 5, 7, 2, 4, 6, ^1, ^3, ^5, ^7, ^^2, and so on.[5] Within any pattern, he can vary the direction and the phrasing, string together two different patterns, or select from a wide range of rhythmic values. Often, Larry will begin or end a run with a bit of contour from the head melody or some other well-known fragment. Keenly aware of the grouping of phrases into larger sections, Larry actively organizes the overall structure of his solos.

These abstract descriptions of Larry's playing would effectively capture the details of a written transcription of a Whisler solo, but how are they heard and experienced? This question is the topic of Part II but a few impressionistic comments here can make things clearer. Hearing Larry improvise, one is mainly aware of contour, pattern, and texture. To me and to the players in the band, Larry's lines are fast and agile; as a result, they are heard less as a series of individual notes and more as long, flowing contours running from one range of the instrument to another. The patterns he runs through the scales are immediately evident to the ear and emerge as the clearest aspect of the lines. As Larry rarely plays over each chord change, one is less likely to hear individual changes as one is to hear tonics, generalized dominants, and changes of key area.[6]

Anyone who listens to Larry will realize that many of his solos use stock formulas; such a collection of techniques and licks (set phrases) is referred to in jazz as a *vocabulary*. All players have vocabularies, and part of the interest of Larry's playing arises from the manner in which he employs his patterns, the nuances with which his licks are performed, and the process of combination and contextualization that occurs in each solo. Larry's forty-plus years of experience and his early training in the physically demanding marimba have left him with nimble physical technique and an ability to cover standard jazz changes with lines that all of the other members of the group find extraordinarily flowing and delicate. And though his harmonic palette is less varied than that of players of contemporary styles, this fluidity remains interesting, even to players like Jack who were weaned on contemporary soloists like Keith Jarrett and Chick Corea. Larry's solos usually end after two or three choruses; they are often recognized by polite applause, and after he is done he will either remain next to his instrument or descend from the stand to freshen his drink and listen to the other players.

To really understand the kind of harmonic approaches that Larry employs, we need to compare them to the methods of somewhat more contemporary players like Dick Schermesser and significantly more contemporary players like Jerome Saunders. Dick's playing is more harmonically adventuresome than Larry's. Though he will engage in long flowing runs, Dick employs a variety of other melodic and harmonic devices; frequently, Dick will take motives (fragments of contour) and actively apply to them the devices of melodic variation (inversion, extension, and so on). Where Larry's lines simply follow the gross outlines of the tonality, Dick's solos will follow the changes at several levels of detail. For example, in one chorus Dick may play a part that outlines each individual change; in a second chorus he may play over just the tonics or dominants, while a third chorus may be still more harmonically abstract, reflecting just the gross changes in key area. Dick will use notes from outside the key area in small ways by applying chromatic embellishments to arpeggios of the chord changes, inserting passing chords, and trying out a few altered dominant sounds. While Dick occasionally uses Whisler-style patterns, the nature of his instrument allows him to explore larger chords and contrapuntal parts as well. To the ear, the immediate difference between Dick and Larry is in the phrasing. Larry's long, flowing patterns span a large percentage of his instrument's range, while Dick's phrases are of a wider variety of lengths, use more varied rhythmic values, and tend to cover a smaller range of pitches. In Larry's playing, the harmonic aspect of the lines is fairly straightforward and the changes are clearly laid out to the listener's ear; Dick's soloing is harmonically richer, providing a greater variety of textures and sounds.

The "modern," more assertive sounds of Jerome Saunders and the other Cleveland players clearly point up the difference in musical approach and intent between the older style of the Akron players and the more contemporary style. Jerome's constant goal is to expand the range of sounds and effects he can coax out of his piano. Dick's solos may enfold a brief key change or a secondary dominant into a larger key area; Jerome, on the other hand, may connect much larger groups of chords. This approach enables a broader range of sounds but requires greater effort on the part of the listeners to keep the contour and form of the composed melody and changes in mind. Playing lines that relate to each individual chord ("cutting each change"), Dick will play brief chromatic parts or apply a fairly small number of altered scales; Jerome will apply a much larger range of scales and even substitute a series of new and harmonically distant scales. Again, the increase in the number of harmonic textures available moves the improvisation further away from the composed tune and places a bigger burden on the listener to connect the improvisation with the composition.

A bit of phenomenological exploration will reveal some interesting complexity. As I shall suggest in Chapters 7 and 8, harmony is an effect of the subject's constitution of musical sound in perception. In listening to Dick, the changes implied by the improvised solos, comping, and composed head are the same. To grasp the music, all the listener must do is constitute one consistent, overarching harmonic rhythm. In Jerome's playing, the changes implicit in the improvised solo may be distant from or opposed to the tune's harmonic rhythm; as a result, the listener has to make a greater effort to constitute the harmony in perception. If the solo is harmonically distant from the comping, the listener may have to make an effort to hear the underlying changes that the solo line suggests. If the composed changes and the harmonic implications of the solo are actually opposed, the listener has to constitute the separate harmonic implications of the solo line and the changes and then actively relate them to each other to appreciate the full effect. If the listener fails to do all this, the music will sound like a rushing blur that is unrelated to the composed song, rather than a colorful improvisation over the standard.

Musical structure in the event: Some comping

Jack's and Bill's solos will be discussed in the next section, but not even this brief outline of the musical practices of the Whisler Quartet can be understood without discussing comping. In comping, the pianist's mandate is to make the changes clear. As I have suggested above, this can be achieved in a wide variety of ways, and a basic issue in comping for Dick, as well as Eric and Jerome, is voice leading. Voice leading refers to the relationship between the notes of the chords across time. The term is a metaphor from choral music, in which the sopranos sing the highest note of every chord, the altos the next highest note, and so on; similarly, the musical phrase formed by the highest notes in each chord is referred to as the top voice, the series of the lowest pitches in each chord is the bass line, and the other series are the inner voices. The norm for all three pianists is smooth voice leading; here, the players choose and stack the notes of the chords in such a way that the voices form linear parts with few large leaps and little parallel motion between the voices, all the while producing the appropriate harmonic function and quality. Standard changes call up standard voicings and voice leading, but both the Cleveland and Akron pianists constantly listen to the bass player so that their piano parts do not interfere with the bassist's lines. At the other end of the spectrum, the pianist must attend to the soloist to make sure that the voice leading complements the improviser's part. For Dick, this largely means avoiding voicings in Larry's range and playing mostly in the spaces between his phrases. Players from the Cleveland scene share similar concerns. More contemporary soloists, however, juxtapose a wide range of harmonic materials over the tune's changes; as a result, Eric and Jerome must also be aware of the harmonic materials that the soloist is employing and take care not to contradict or confine the soloist with their voicings.

Though voice leading is important, it is not the whole story. Pianists play fills, passing chords, and contrapuntal lines, experiment with large textural comping parts, and play chordal sections that have a melodic character of their own. Further, Bill and Dick both explained that many common piano comps have arisen from big band horn section parts. Standard tunes, many of which come from the big band repertoire itself, usually employ 4- or 8-bar melodic phrases; big band arrangers, and later drummers and pianists in small ensembles, often place their fills in the spaces at the end of these phrases. Bill explained that he typically kicks accents or small fills at these points to mark the form of the tune for the audience and other players; the comping parts that Dick plays often employ the rhythms, phrasings, and voicings of horn arrangements. When Bill hears Dick use one of these standard patterns, he is immediately able to play fills and kick punches that mesh tightly with them.

The jazz musicians I spoke with commonly describe the history of their music as a constant procession toward greater and greater musical choices for the musicians and less and less articulation of the composition. Observing similar processes, Monson (1996) has argued that the interplay between "solid" and "fluid" parts (parts that articulate the song's musical framework and parts that improvise around it) is central to all jazz improvisation. We have seen how this idea applies to the soloists and the piano accompaniment, and it describes the drummer's comping as well.[7] When a tune is called at Rizzi's, Bill can either play the standard groove or reinterpret the part with a different groove. With a groove selected, his first responsibility is to just to keep time, and this can be achieved in a variety of ways. When the band switches between soloists or from solos to head, the drummer can change the texture of the ensemble by playing the same pattern of accents on a different set of instruments; for example, when Dick starts to solo, Bill can shift the eighths from the rivet cymbal, with its constant ringing, to the high-hat, with its sharp attack and complete lack of sustain. Various repeating patterns can be added to the basic groove to make it richer or change the texture.

Beyond the groove, Bill can add all manner of kicks and accents on the bass, snare, toms, or cymbals to respond to the soloists' lines. Isolated hits and accents can be formed into fills; falling in the spaces between phrases, these usually come at 2-, 4-, or 8-bar intervals. As the playing gets more intense, the fills can take the form of ongoing rhythmic phrases; overflowing the spaces between the soloist's phrases, fills can evolve into lines of their own and serve as a continuous rhythmic dialogue with the soloist's lines. In more contemporary styles, the groove and pulse are no longer played, and the drummer overlays the implied time with continuous rhythmic phrases and parts from other time signatures. In sum, the jazz drummer has a scope of rhythmic approaches that range from articulating the basic pulse and groove, through the addition of accents and fills, to playing a constant flow of complex rhythmic phrases and leaving the pulse and groove implied. The choice of groove, texture, punches and accents, fills, and ongoing rhythmic phrases depends on the song, the other players, the setting of the gig, the location in the set, and the player's chops.

Bill's choices are informed by the venue and his desire to support the other musicians and please the audience. Early in the evening when the Rizzi's crowd is still dining, Bill plays more time and keeps the dynamics soft; as the evening wears on he is more likely to apply a busier Latin groove or introduce chatter on the ride or snare. Ever aware that the audience likes to follow the song, Bill rarely employs any of the polyrhythmic innovations of more "modern" players like Elvin Jones, and the pulse is usually present somewhere on Bill's kit. The changes and head melody are always present in Bill's awareness as the tune proceeds, guiding his accents and fills and keeping his parts close to the tune. The interest in Bill's drumming lies more in tasteful parts and solid grooves than in dense, post-bop experimentation.

Most of the night Jack comps with a straight walking bass line. While his note choice is not constrained by the need to provide the listener with the roots and fifths of the chords, he is otherwise a fairly traditional bassist, playing parts that are "inside" the chord changes. Part of the rhythmic drive of jazz emerges from the subtle effects in coordination between bass player and drummer. Taking care not to rush or slow down, the bass player may intentionally play his notes a bit after the drummer's quarter-note pulses (so-called playing behind the beat) to give the tune a looser feel or anticipate the pulses (playing ahead of the beat) to give the impression of driving the tune forward.

And so the tunes are played. Larry lays down the head melody with numerous embellishments, syncopations, and fills, but the knowledgeable listener is never confused about the name of the song. "Underneath" these melodies, for such is the metaphor of the genre, Dick lays down chords and fills with rich, extended harmony; Jack keeps the tune swinging with walking lines, and Bill plays time and kicks punches. The harmony falls into the background of the listener's experience as Larry's long solo lines arc across the instrument, smooth and flowing with their evident patterns; a chatter of kicks and accents keeps the head melody just on the edge of attention, and Dick's parts act as melodic counterpoint to the improvised line. Larry's solo ends; Bill switches the time to the high-hat to make sonic room for Dick; Jack pulls back, too, and the band becomes a trio. Dick's comping parts thin out, but he uses a wider range of scales, arpeggios, and patterns, and the overall harmonic effect is richer. Perhaps Dick tries to build the form of the solo as whole; he increases the voices in his righthand chords and his melody lines become denser. Bill keeps playing time on the hats, but the chatter on the snare and bass is busier and Jack begins picking up the bass accents, playing anticipations of the walking quarters and accenting the off-beats. As Dick's solo ends, Jack may solo for a chorus while Bill keeps time on the hats; later Bill may solo, playing phrases across the kit that tie into the rhythms of the head melody. Eventually visual cues are exchanged, Larry comes back in for the head melody of the out chorus, and the tune ends with a stock phrase or fade-out.

Musical practice, purpose, and the constitution of events

We can weave together the various threads of the discussion by exploring the relationship between the players' partially shared purposes for performance and the musical practices that are guided by them.

Larry Whisler's main concerns while soloing are smoothness and accessibility. He is well aware that players in the more contemporary styles of jazz articulate less of the song's structure, and he blames the decline in jazz's popularity on this development. In opposition to this trend, he wants his audience to identify the song quickly and follow easily the form of the composition as he solos. To that end, Larry uses harmonic materials that straightforwardly imply the changes and occasionally quotes the fragments from the head melody. Offering a clear invitation to the audience's attention, Larry's goal is to create rolling lines that both dazzle with their technical fluidity and charm with flowing contours. Ballads, medium swing tunes, and the occasional up-tempo "barn burner" offer a range of tempi and energy levels, but no matter the particular effect of the tune, Larry always wants the older members of the audience to recognize the tune and enjoy the smooth sounds.

Jack shares some musical goals with Larry. While comping, Jack feels no need to play tricky harmonic substitutions or stray from the chord changes; on the contrary, his main concern is that the band grooves (that is, that the time is metronomic and swinging and that the bass lines and drum parts are tightly coordinated). While soloing, Jack's aim is to avoid any hint of the contrived harmonic cleverness that he hears in the less able contemporary-style players; he seeks to create phrases that follow each other effortlessly. Like Larry, Jack wants the music to flow, but there is a distinction between Jack's and Larry's usage of those terms. The "flow" to which Jack aspires is the effortless passage of musical ideas from aural inception to physical articulation on the instrument; the "flow" to which Larry aspires is an endless rolling wave of melodic contour that smoothly connects the changes. In both cases, the ultimate intended aesthetic effect is the same, a smooth continuity and a dynamic beauty, but this similarity should not obscure the differences that exist. Jack does not dislike the broadened contemporary harmonic palette that Larry derides, and he would play a limited range of substitutions if he felt he could produce them without sounding forced or too clever. But though Jack enjoys contemporary styles, his goal in this venue is the same as Larry's: smooth and accessible sounds.

Like Jack, Bill feels that groove is paramount. Though he has an arsenal of Latin grooves and West African derived polyrhythmic parts, Bill feels his first responsibility is to get the band to groove and "make the music dance." He is also concerned with accessibility; aware that people are dining, Bill keeps the dynamics low early in the evening and rarely lets chatter, fills, and phrases overwhelm the time. Playing parts appropriate to the scene is a key goal, and Bill's spirituality is a factor here. Viewing music as an expression of love, Bill told me repeatedly that he was always playing from the heart, always playing for the other musicians and the audience. But where some find the older style of jazz at Rizzi's to be a soothing relief from the overintellectualized style of the contemporary post-bop scene, and where Larry feels he has virtually all of the musical freedom he needs, Bill occasionally feels constrained by the strictures of the Rizzi's gig. Though on many nights Bill felt that the band was cooking beautifully, and though he genuinely enjoyed bringing pleasure to the older set at the bar, there were times when he wanted to "stretch out" a bit. Dense Latin grooves threaten European American audiences, said Bill, and the busy "modern" styles are less acceptable to older listeners. Bill is no frustrated avant-gardist and enjoys the laid-back Rizzi's atmosphere, but he would like more musical options.

Where the ideas of making a connection with the audience and manifesting love constantly enter into Bill's conversation, Dick is mostly concerned with musical structure. In our interviews and conversations with others, Dick represented himself as sandwiched between the overintellectual posing and technique-ridden posturing of contemporary jazz and the mindless amusicality of rock and pop. To Dick, all music must follow climactic form, proceeding from a point of low energy through greater and greater intensity to a climax and a denouement; Dick likens this form to the movement of the seasons, the cycle of sexual arousal, and the life cycle. Similarly, says Dick, universal laws of melodic development and harmony control the manipulation of musical structure; while valid styles of musics are yet to be discovered, none exist outside of these laws. Avant-garde jazz musicians such as Ornette Coleman and modern Western art composers such as Schoenberg failed, Dick contends, because they tried to manipulate musical structures without attending to the universal aesthetic laws that guide them; pop and rock musicians fail because of a willful ignorance of musical structure itself. Avoiding anti-intellectualism, Dick embellishes the changes with chromatic devices and a range of harmonic colors; avoiding overintellectualism, Dick keeps close to the composition, avoids strictly rhythmic or textural experimentation, and keeps his solos melodic. And while Dick is not averse to an appreciative audience, he is unconcerned with accessibility; he would rather quit the job than modify his playing.

The connection of all these disparate goals and practices in the performance is a study in partial sharing and the fluidity of culture. No end of contradictions are present in the players' tastes and perceptions: Dick and Larry dislike all of the post-bop that Jack and, to a certain extent Bill, enjoy. Bill likes a variety of new age and fusion musics that few of the other players even know, and Larry's musical background in older jazz ranges far beyond that of the other players. Larry and Jack want the music to be accessible to the crowd; Bill wants the audience to enjoy the music but occasionally finds them to be constraining, and Dick simply doesn't care about accessibility.

Given all of these contradictions, how were the players able to constitute performances for over a year? One piece of the puzzle is power relations: Joe Rizzi wants the music to draw a crowd, and Bill knew that if he played intense Latin grooves during dinner, he would be out of a job. Partially shared musical goals and a partially shared social history play a role: Dick, Bill, and Jack all want the crowd to like the music, and they rely on a shared social past to select and display the styles and skills the crowd will enjoy. Contingency plays a part as well: Dick simply plays what he likes, and he has the good fortune to live near a venue that will pay him to do it. A little verbal negotiation between the sets and a lot of musical negotiation on the stand enable them to choose tunes and play in ways that satisfy (or at least do not strenuously displease) one another, the management, and the varied audience members. But even this sharing is only partial, and the players occasionally voiced frustrations with their bandmates' styles. Through a combination of compromise, negotiation, and interaction, the differences were temporarily overcome, a coalition of players, management, and audience was built, and performances were constituted.

That this constellation of goals and practices is culturally specific is most evident when compared with the purposes and approaches of the Cleveland players. While Larry was determined that his runs never become repetitious, none of the players are as self-consciously devoted to the notion of eclecticism as Jerome and Eric. Both players repeatedly explained that their overarching project was to find as many harmonic approaches to the changes as possible. But eclecticism for them didn't merely refer to harmony; Jerome and Eric constantly spoke of broadening their range of textural, improvisatory, and stylistic perspectives. Shifting from long flowing melodies to sharp, staccato polyrhythms; plotting and planning out some passages and letting other lines and parts flow forward without reflection; juxtaposing post-bop, avant-garde, rock, and older stride styles—Eric and Jerome spoke of all parameters of improvisation as "textures," and their only overriding goal was constantly to broaden their range.

Alvin and Leonard spoke less frequently about eclecticism; intensity and complexity were more important to them. Alvin's overriding concern was to play intense and profound music, and he often expressed disgust with the popularity of "easy-listening" fusion. Alvin and Leonard did value the connection between audience and performer; however, they felt that the listeners should make an effort to understand the music, and musicians should never compromise their vision to appeal to an audience. While Eric would never want to be restricted to just one affective feel or style of band interaction, both he and Leonard agree with Alvin on one point—their dislike of the club scene. All three prefer playing jazz in a concert setting where the listener is attentive and the music is the focus. Though Jerome does not want to play background music all his life, he served his usual gadfly function when he expounded on the pleasures of playing music for an audience whose attention was otherwise engaged; the background role, he said, allows the player greater latitude in performance and the opportunity to affect the crowd in subtle, almost subliminal ways.

Juxtaposing the player's goals in music-making across scenes—accessibility and smoothness versus eclecticism and complexity—helps us appreciate the diversity within jazz. While the musician's goals are never fully realized in performance and are only partially shared among the participants, goals are an entrance to the rich meanings of the performance event. More important, the focus on goals helps us to reconnect musical structures with the musical practices that constitute them. But to discuss the player's goals in music-making puts us on the never-ending path of discussing the purposes of purposes, the uses of uses, and the values of values. Such goals neither originate nor terminate with the individual musician; they are informed by the players' social history, are oriented toward the possibilities of the present social context, and entail future consequences that are never fully intended. Exploring the ways in which race, region, and generation inform the player's ideas and practices, I have tried to suggest the large-scale dimensions of past and present social context. To complete the temporal triad, Part III of this study will discuss some of the possible future consequences of musical practice in the death metal scene.

Conclusions

The concept that unifies the diverse materials of Part I is constitutive practice. In the case of death metal, intensely shared meanings and stable patterns of practice were the themes. Framed and informed by the immediate others of commercial hard rock and alternative, the clothing, musical structures, lyrics, styles of interaction in the performance event, and larger social and aesthetic ideologies form a tightly systematic network of meanings. The practices of attending shows, performing, rehearsing, partying with friends, and doing mail constitute a closely knit scene. In Akron jazz, fragmented meanings and fragile patterns of practice were the touchstones. The player's involvements in other musics, the disappearing venues, and the dwindling audiences all made Akron's jazz scene a tenuous coalition rather than a robust musical community.

As I have emphasized throughout, the larger point is that both the stability and the fragility of the scenes are grounded in constitutive practices. As practices, the conduct of the participants is at once fully informed by social context and actively achieved by the participants. Even the most unstable scene and fragmented set of meanings cannot be called radically individual. However differently the participants interpret it, the Rizzi's scene is enabled by a common social and musical past: 1950s post-bop jazz. However differently the players orient themselves toward it, the performance is enabled by a common social present: Rizzi's Jazz Lounge and its various patrons. However different their purposes, the musicians all pursue social ends: pay, applause, or a night of good music. By the same token, even the most stable scene and the most systemic set of meanings are actively achieved by the musical participants. The history of metal is only a social context relative to a historical subject; performance events do not occur by themselves, but are creatively enacted by participants who may choose to do otherwise. While particular forms of social organization may become more or less interesting to scholars at different moments in intellectual history, it is the job of ethnomusicology to recognize all the forms that the social life of music may take, cohesive or fragmentary. And the wide variety of forms that musical life can take should never blind us to the fact that musical life is always constituted through practice, which is no less social for being actively achieved and no less actively achieved for being grounded in a social history and lived social context.

Another theme in Part I has been the cultural and historical specificity of musical practices. In a classic 1974 article, Bruno Nettl suggested that the stages in the production of music may vary widely across cultures, and he called on ethnographers to explore the various ways in which improvisation and composition are defined in different musical traditions. In a related vein, Ruth Finnegan (1989, 165–79) identified three general modes of musical composition in the diverse local musics of her fieldsite—written composition for Western art music, "composition-in-performance" for jazz, and "prior-composition-in-practice" for rock (also see Sawyer 1996). By briefly comparing the data on composition, arrangement, performance, and improvisation presented in Part I, we can better understand how the medial level musical practices of the four scenes are culturally and historically specific. In Chapters 5 and 6, I shall substantially develop this analysis by comparing the differing ways that musicians from the four scenes organize attention in the performance event.

In the small ensemble jazz of Akron and Cleveland, composition means specifying harmonic function, melody, and groove. Arrangement largely refers to hits, melodic fragments, changes in groove, and aspects of the form; arrangements may originate from a seminal recording or sediment from the improvised performances of the local players over the span of years—much like the traditionally conceived "folk process." Here, performance usually entails improvisation within a framework or variation on an abstract musical model, and only rarely is performance the exact enactment of practiced parts.

In rock and metal, things are quite different. Composition is mainly a group activity achieved in rehearsal. The range of materials specified in a composition are much broader: particular pitches and rhythms for the chords, melodies, and vocal harmonies, contours for the guitar solos, hits, locations of fills, and the overall form of the tune. As we shall see in the next section, the melodies themselves are defined in very different ways. Nonpitched sounds, changes in timbre, discrete notes, and what I call "monadic glissandi" (structurally basic scoops and slides) may all be foundational elements of the melody. Further, the compositional stage is shorter in jazz than it is in rock and metal; in the latter scenes, compositions emerge slowly and constantly change throughout rehearsal, performance, and recording. In rock, the line between composing and arranging is blurred; for most bands, it is difficult to say when the basic compositional ideas are set in stone and when the issues of form and ensemble parts are taken up. In jazz, these two stages are sharply differentiated. Finally, performance in rock is somewhere between the nineteenth-century Western art-music ideal and jazz. In most of their performances, rock players seek to breathe life into a set of planned musical forms. Some guitar solos, however, have spontaneously created elements within the strictures of contour and lick; drum fills, coordinations between bass and drums, and a number of the dimensions of the vocal line are also substantially varied on stage.

In an undergraduate music seminar, musicologist Jon Barlow once suggested to his students that all musical performances entail aspects that are preplanned and aspects that are created on the spot.[8] With only the musicians' instruments determined before the performance, free jazz may form the extreme case of improvisation (Sawyer 1996); with even the most minute elements worked out in advance, some styles of Western art music may be the extreme case of the enactment of composition. Barlow's remark directs our attention to the nonidentity of all performances and the inevitable connection of each performance to history. But beyond the general necessity of the planned and the spontaneous, the data of rock and metal show that the actual forms of musical practice are endlessly varied, historically particular, and culturally specific. Ideas like "composition" and "performance" describe culturally specific patterns of past practice that have been sedimented into concepts; such concepts guide, but do not determine, present musical actions.

But concepts guide perception as well. When an educated listener—a listener who is deeply connected to the musical scene—hears music, the terms *composition* and *arrangement* are more than reflective descriptions of the music's structure: they describe the immediate shape of the sound experience itself. Culturally specific notions like composition and arrangement deeply influence the listening subject's constitution of sound experiences, and it is in this way that the social history of the music intimately informs the participant's lived experiences. The rock listener, for example, *hears* the guitar's power chords as composed parts and *hears* the guitar and drum fills as elements of the arrangement or improvisations; the jazz listener *hears* the tonal implications of the harmonic rhythm as the composed song, and *hears* the voicings as this particular player's comping. Of course, the listener may constitute the sound inappropriately, hearing a fortuitous group hit as part of a traditional head arrangement. But in any case, the social history of the music is sedimented in the listener's acts of music perception. As Stith Bennett has observed (1980, 214–15), shaping perception and organizing attention are crucial, culturally specific skills that all musicians must acquire. As I shall show in Part II, we can gain new insight into such processes if we treat perception is a kind of practice.

Our medial focus has taken us as far as it can. To go further, we must focus our inquiry tightly and explore how the listening subject uses his or her lived social past to constitute present musical experiences. In terms specific to this study, this means taking all of the forms of musical sound—notes, changes, melody, vocal timbre, affect, glissandi, and so on—that we have merely referenced, and seeing how they are actively and socially constituted in the subject's experience. The experiences that are juxtaposed with the device of comparison must now be interrogated in phenomenological description. It is only there, in the constitution of experience, that the terms *culture* and *agency* are revealed for what they are: partial descriptions of our dialectical engagement with the world.

PART TWO

THE ORGANIZATION OF
MUSICAL EXPERIENCE AND THE
PRACTICE OF PERCEPTION

FIVE

The Organization of Attention in Two Jazz Scenes

Introduction

From medial to micro

In Part I, I made a first step toward understanding the diverse experiences of local jazz and rock musicians. There I focused on the medial level of social life: typical practices described in general terms, habitual settings of face-to-face social interactions, everyday situational purposes, and perceptual experiences and their meanings depicted in broad strokes. This focus fits with our most quotidian understanding of life. Everyday attention rarely lets in the rich, sensuous details of our perceptual experiences, nor does everyday reflection commonly examine the broad historical and social contexts of our practices. As most of us live our lives, our thoughts are focused on gross sensual features of the world and the abstract, typical situations and practices of social life's medial level.

Much ethnographic work focuses on the medial level, too. Because it is so closely aligned with our everyday modes of reflection and attention, such a level of focus has the marked advantage of making unfamiliar musical lives easily accessible. But to understand unfamiliar musical experiences more fully, we must tighten our focus and explore the ways in which those experiences are constituted by actors. This is the first sense of the term *double constitution* that I introduced in Chapter 2: constitution as the subject's active, social engagement with the world that establishes perceptions and meanings. Elaborating this vision with a tight focus, my broadest aim in this section is to show that the constitution of perceptual experiences and meanings is a kind of practice. As practice, perception is the practitioner's active achievement; at the same time it is deeply informed by the practitioner's social history, oriented toward his or her present social context, and is potentially consequential for a larger social future (see Berger 1997, In press).

Phenomenology, humanistic and formal: The process of cross-cultural communication

As an exercise in phenomenological ethnography, this part has two interdependent goals: to share the research participants' experiences with the reader and to garner insights into the nature of experience in general. Attention to the first goal, the goal of "humanistic" phenomenology, implies an awareness that the individual's experience, and the partially shared experiences of an intimate group, are essentially significant and worthy of study; where transcendental phenomenology in academic philosophy passes over the merely factual in its quest to lay bare the structure of all potential experiences, the humanistic goal of empirical social inquiry is to acquaint us with people in the concrete world of particulars. Attention to the second goal, the goal of "formal" phenomenology, implies an awareness that experience *can* be shared, that concrete experience itself has some public dimension, and that some of the dynamics of those experiences can be mapped out.

Central to my vision of phenomenology is the awareness that these two goals are interdependent, that experience is always both the concrete experience of a historically and culturally particular subject, and that this subject is also a member of the human race with the potential for learning about others and partially sharing experience. Because the general structures of experience always emerge in a dialectic with "contingent factors," and because those structures are always the possession of living human beings, "formal" phenomenology is always a kind of humanism; because a phenomenology concerned with partially sharing the experiences of others is always dependent upon the necessary structures of experience, "humanistic" phenomenology is always formal. The two aspects are inseparable.

We can synthesize the humanistic and formal approaches of phenomenological ethnomusicology in the project of facilitating cross-cultural communication. The goal here is to present such an accurate picture of the musical experiences of others, and to so vividly portray the modes through which they actively and socially engage with the world, that the reader is able to organize musical perceptions as the participants do. Such a project serves the humanistic aim of allowing the reader, however partially, to concretely experience the world as others do and to gain insight into their lives;

the project serves the formal goal inasmuch as the reader thereby gains insight into the general processes by which experience is constituted.[1]

The first step in partially sharing the experiences of another is understanding his or her organization of experience. As we move through life we are constantly assailed by feelings, thoughts, bodily awareness, perceptions of the outside world, awareness of others, and, perhaps, experiences of the divine or spiritual. To make sense of the sheer quantity of information impinging upon us, we must hold one or more types of experience in the foreground of attention, hold other realms in the near background, and push others outside of awareness. This chapter and Chapter 6 will explore how musicians from the four scenes of interest achieve the various tasks of music making by highlighting and backgrounding their experiences of the body, perceptions, emotions, thought, and imagination. To provide a visual metaphor, this chapter paints a two-dimensional picture of the musicians' experience, laying out the figure and ground of those experiences.

Experience, however, is not a fixed image but a dynamic reality, and Chapters 7 and 8 flesh out our understanding by shifting the focus from the lifeworld as a whole to musical phenomena in particular. Because experience is not a static object but a lived procession, I shall focus on the temporal dimension of musical experience and examine how players from the different scenes structure their awareness in the thickness of the living present, variously "protending" (anticipating upcoming sections) and "retaining" (holding in living awareness past chunks of musical material) to form experiences of phrases and sections. Chapter 7 will introduce these ideas by exploring the temporal dimensions of Chris Ozimek's experiences of a commercial hard rock song, while Chapter 8 extends these insights with an examination of Dann Saladin's experiences of a death metal tune. In both chapters, my formal aim is to show that harmony, usually thought to be somehow inherent in the musical sound, is in fact an effect of the subject's grasping of the world in its procession and change.

Continuing with my visual metaphor, I have shifted our representation of musical experience from a two-dimensional picture to a kinetic sculpture. As we live our lives, they are heated by our emotions and colored by our purposes and goals. Both Chapters 7 and 8 deal with the emotional dimension of musical experience, and, throughout this part, we shall see how the musicians' perceptual practices are informed by their situational goals and broader projects. The concern with affect and purpose connects the constitution of perceptual experiences to its social context, and in Part III we shall bring this concept to its fulfillment by exploring the ways in which musical experiences may themselves be consequential for larger social and historical forces.

The Organization of Attention to the Event as a Whole

As we move through our lives each day, we are bombarded by a varied and complex motley of experiences. Sounds, plans for future activities, the awareness of the position of our limbs, emotions, smells, the words and ideas of others, flavors, memories—experience is nothing if not heterogenous. But just as we are bombarded with an endless stream of experiences, we are also aware that the stream of experience is organized. For example, as I type these words, the ideas I want to express are clearly presented in the center of my experience. The clicking of the computer keys is also present, but since each click is insignificant as anything but a confirmation that I have typed a letter, the sound of the keys is held in the background of my experience. Further, our experience constantly changes and the change itself is organized. At one moment, for example, the sight of my drinking glass is literally on the edge of my attention while my ideas for this paragraph hold me in thrall; in the next moment those ideas have receded and exist as a living past, while a parched feeling in my throat rises into the center of attention. The parched feeling shares the center of experience with a split-second plan to drink: the glass is grasped and relief shares the stage with the emerging ideas about the next few lines. Nothing could be more prosaic or intuitive.

What causes experience to be organized? In some situations, it is clear that we actively arrange our attention. Distracted by the sound of a fly, for example, I may make an effort to ignore its buzz or, just as effectively, I may shoo the fly away (Ihde 1976). In other situations, our experience of the world is something we cannot control; the loud backfire of a car engine arrests me for a moment, and only expert meditators could keep such a loud blast from captivating their attention. Most important, *the organization of our experience is something that has its base in our social lives.* Knowing what to listen for—or knowing that we should listen rather than watch—at a performance of Western art music is just as much based in our social context and social history as the notes played or the clothes worn. If we wish to share and understand a person's experience, we must first learn about its gross organization—what parts are experienced richly and fully, what parts lurk with vague detail, what parts are actively focused upon, and what parts actively ignored. In the pages that follow, we will make a first step toward ethnographic partial sharing by exploring the phenomena that populate the musician's experience during performance and examining how their overall experience is organized.

Foreground, background, and gestalt

In a fieldwork seminar I once attended, a student voiced the concern that the ethnographer may distort the experiences of the people he or she is trying to study by overreading the symbols and messages found in their culture. A noted folklorist present in the seminar responded that while the student's concern was legitimate, the problem of overreading was unavoidable. Likening cultural meanings to objects in the physical world and likening the ethnographer's exploration to a flashlight's beam, the folklorist said that the goal of ethnography was to shine the beam as widely and intensely as possible. Casting light from every angle would remove all of the shadows and distort the experienced reality, of course, but this distortion was an inevitable result of rigorous and thorough inquiry. My general admiration for this folklorist not withstanding, I find myself in disagreement with these ideas. What is primary for human research is the lived reality of meanings, not some ideally rich universe of cultural objects, and this visual/physical metaphor is particularly apt for explaining the point. The everyday world of lived social experience is always *perspectival*. Some meanings stand out sharply illuminated, others wallow in the shadows, vague and colorless. More important, the relationship between sharply articulated and intense meanings and dimly perceived, marginal meanings provides experience with a texture—a depth and quality—that is just as important as any individual meaning present.

Such "textures" come about as a peculiar effect of the foreground/background structure of experience. Again the metaphor is visual, and the famous glass/silhouette diagram (known in psychology as Rubin's Goblet) will make the point clear. In the diagram, the viewer can either see the profile of the two faces or a symmetrically shaped goblet. Which image you see depends on how you treat the parts of the diagram; if you see dark spaces as a background, the light space emerges as a goblet; if you see the light space as a background, the two faces become foregrounded silhouettes. The first point to be garnered is that objects in experience are partially formed by the background against which they appear. Upon closer examination, the illustration helps us to defeat the reism of our commonsense thinking about experience. We usually think of objects in experience as autonomous from both their context and the experiencing subject; one point of this well-worn chestnut is that the perceptual object is really part of an inseparable object/context whole.[2] The entire image is referred to as a *gestalt*, a constellation of a foreground and background that mutually define each other and form the basic unit of experience.

More important, the illustration displays the subject's role in perception. Given even a moment's experimentation, the viewer can learn to see either the faces or the goblet and switch back and forth at will. Without venturing too deeply into questions about the relationship of experience to reality (see Chapter 1), the picture illustrates that the subject has a measure of control over the organization of experience, and that such control extends not only to imagination but also to perception. Lest the reader suspect that such an idea leads to an anything-goes idealism, we would do well to observe that it is hard to see anything in Rubin's Goblet but the faces and the hourglass. The illustration suggests that perception always has two components. On the one hand there is always the subject, actively and socially grasping the object and present in experience as the order of that experience; on the other hand there is the object, always there for experience but also a genuine other and not a creation of fantasy. The subject's active engagement with the world is referred to as the *constitution of perception*; this is the first sense of the term *double constitution*.

The notion of foreground and background and the insights into the constitution of individual phenomena that we have already explored also apply to the organization of experience as a whole. For example, the typing and drinking illustration given above is a gestalt of experiences with a dynamic foreground and background structure. In the first stage of the illustration, the ideas I am composing are in the foreground of my experience as a whole, and the clinking of the keys and the emerging dry sensation in my throat are part of the background. That the various elements color one another and form a gestalt should be readily apparent: the full living experience of writing with no physical discomfort is very different from the experience of writing with a physical distraction—as anyone who has suffered an annoying headache at work can attest. To make our analysis more precise, we can differentiate between two kinds of backgrounds. I shall use the term *defining background* to refer to phenomena that are located just outside the center of attention,[3] can easily shift into that center, and strongly color the other phenomena in experience; our experience of the parched throat is just such a defining background. The term *receding background* will be used to refer to situations in which a phenomenon is dimly present for the subject but has only a minimal impact on the texture of the experience as a whole. As I type, the quiet buzzing of the cicadas is just such a receding background; it is occasionally and vaguely present in my experience, but it has little impact on my focal thoughts and perceptions. Finally, it is crucial to keep in mind that both foreground and background are simultaneously present in experience; while less intensely grasped, phenomena in the background are not absent, but dimly and marginally present—as the defining backgrounds of the Rubin's Goblet example and the nagging thirst of the typing example so clearly show. With these ideas in place, we can begin to explore the musician's organization of attention.

The Whisler Quartet

Jack's comping: Experiences of the other players

One of Jack's main roles on the stand is comping (accompanying the other players), and his number-one priority in comping is time. "Laying down the time" or "grooving"[4] not only means playing a metronomically consistent string of quarter notes; it also means making sure that his part has a loose and flowing feel that is well coordinated with the drummer and other players. If the tempo seems to be slowing down and speeding up, or if Jack isn't coordinated with the drummer, Jack "locks on" with Bill.[5] In concrete terms, this means placing the sound of his bass and the sound of the drums in the center of attention with the goal of coordinating and negotiating a constant tempo. Such an intentional act forms a unique constellation of phenomena in experience. When locking in, Jack isn't attending just to the bass or just to the drums; on the contrary, Jack draws the sound of the bass and the drums together in a gestalt and places that gestalt in the center of his experience. Further, Jack doesn't lock on with any random selection of drums, but rather focuses on the snare and high hat or cymbals—the instruments on which Bill consistently articulates the tempo. Because the notes flow past too quickly for Jack to reflect on each note and control its duration, the mere act of forming this constellation of experiences is often enough to tighten the coordination of the two players. The groove is a top priority for Bill Roth as well, and if things are "edgy" (if the time is not metronomic and swinging) he will lock on in a precisely complementary way.

As George Herbert Mead observed long ago, reflection tends to occur when everyday activity becomes problematic.[6] Ideally, said Jack and Bill, careful attention to the other player should solve the problem of an "edgy" groove; however, when focusing attention doesn't solve the problem, the players must actively reflect on the situation. When another player speeds up, for example, Bill has a choice: he can stay at his tempo and let the other player correct him or herself (with the possible consequence of sacrificing band coordination), or he (Bill) can change to the other player's tempo (with the possible consequence that the other player will speed up again and the whole band will continue to go faster and faster). Bill posed the problem in almost moral terms; by standing firm, Bill said, you are prizing your correctness over the band's solidarity. By moving to the other player's tempo, you fail to point up his or her poor craftsmanship, and you may even appear to be admitting that your own tempo is wrong. Nevertheless, Bill said, he usually opted to keep the band coordinated by changing to the other player's tempo—even if it meant a kind of losing face. Jack said that most of the time, he changes tempo as well.[7]

In sum, we can say that when the band isn't grooving, Jack and Bill place the bass and the timekeeping percussion together in a tight gestalt in the center of their experience. When the other players speed up or slow down, Jack or Bill will actively reflect on the situation (hold a flow of reflective thought in or near the center of attention), decide whether or not to change tempo, and then carry out that decision. Such "reflections," of course, are not slow and ponderous. More like a fleeting cognition than an internal speaking voice, the player's thoughts vie for the center of experience with the sound of the band and occur in that quick, on-the-fly manner in which the vast majority of decisions in performance situations are made.

To Jack, groove is a constant priority in music making. When the band is having a good night, the groove is experienced as a kind of defining background. Just as a dull headache chronically lurks on the fringe of experience during a bad day and colors all of the day's phenomena with a grim affect, a good groove—concretely experienced as tight coordination of the instruments and the flowing-yet-metronomic consistency of the tempo—is present as an ongoing background for all the other experiences during the evening and infuses them with a light, rolling quality. Because groove is important in a variety of musics, the act of "locking in" is not unique to Jack and Bill; drummers, bass players, and other instrumentalists in both rock and jazz go through similar procedures. As we shall see, the quality of the desired groove—"flowing" in jazz, "heavy" in heavy metal—and the style of temporal negotiation vary sharply between the musical scenes.

But the bassist's lines must not only swing, they must also articulate the song's harmonic rhythm; to do this, the bassist must "hear the changes." "Hearing the changes" does not merely mean hearing the chords that the pianist plays. When a player cannot hear the changes, it means that he or she cannot experience the harmonic qualities and functions of the chords in the song as part of an ongoing series. A metaphor from speech will clarify the point. During conversation, we are not aware of the words we say *only* at the moment we say them; as we speak the present word, we have a dim potential awareness of the words we are about to say as well. In almost all experiences, the future lurks as a kind of anticipated background to the dynamic present. Husserl's term *protention* refers to this living awareness of the anticipated near future during the present, and the next three chapters will examine this concept in detail. A jazz musician who knows the changes to a tune can sit in a quiet room, count out the time with his or her foot, and imagine the chord qualities and functions of the changes; more important, at each moment, the player will also protend the upcoming chords, and those protentions will color the quality of the chord in the now-point. "Hearing the changes" means hearing and feeling those sounds as qualities and not merely imagining musical descriptions or names of notes. When a player knows the changes well, that process is effortless. As we shall see, a player can hear the changes in a great variety of ways: protending far in the future, hearing each chord as a distinct unit, hearing the chords as subsumed within larger key areas, and so on. Like keeping time, articulating the harmonic rhythm is basic to almost all jazz performances.

Since the Whisler Quartet sticks to jazz standards, Jack is quite familiar with the harmonic rhythm of almost every tune that is called. Ideally and on most tunes, Jack effortlessly hears the changes as a flow of quasi-sensual qualities and functions. The changes in imagination require neither reflective thought nor effort and form a defining background to all of the particular parts the members of the band play: Jack's own lines, Dick's comping chords, and Larry's improvised solos. On occasion, however, Jack may be unfamiliar with a tune, or he and Dick may have differing concepts of the tune's changes. In such a case, a complex ballet of attention ensues. Here, Jack will carefully attend to the imagined flow of the changes, trying to "hear" the chords that fail to emerge effortlessly; he will also listen carefully to Dick's voicings and Larry's lines to figure out the harmonic implications of the particular notes they are playing. Simultaneously, Jack may apply his knowledge of music theory and, in that quick and on-the-fly manner described above, actively reflect upon what the chords should be. In such a case, other aspects of experience (such as the drummer's parts and the groove) drop into the background while the various flows of perception and reflection described above hold the center of his experience. Though such a process may seem rushed and frantic, Jack rarely has a serious problem on the stand, and the chord changes are always fixed by the end of the first or second chorus. Just as Jack and Bill may organize experience in reciprocal ways when they lock in, Jack and Dick manage their experience in reciprocal ways when they try to negotiate a set of changes. This process is common across the various traditions of jazz.

As the band's bassist, Jack must not merely hear the changes; he must produce a walking line. While some players wish to manage their comping parts reflectively, Jack's goal is an effortless flow of quarter notes that unambiguously lay out the harmonic rhythm and groove with the band. Of course the sound of his line and its harmonic implications will be central in his experience, but ideally and most often there will be no accompanying flow of reflections about note choice or harmonic implication.

To get deeper into Jack's organization of experience, we must examine how the arrangement of the sensorium as a whole is coordinated with the foregrounding and backgrounding of aspects of the individual phenomena; an example from everyday life will make this concept clearer. Talking with a friend at a party, I keep the sound of his voice in the center of attention, his body language in the near background, and the taste of my drink in the far background. Focusing on the sound of his voice, however, I still must organize my experience of the numerous aspects of that sound: his word choice, his meaning, his prosody and contour, his accent, his syntax, and so on. At one moment I can attend to the accent and almost completely ignore the meaning, while at another I can hold his word choice and tone of voice in the center of attention and forget his accent. In the same way, musicians focus on different elements of the other player's lines. For example, Jack chronically monitors Dick's parts, constantly shifting them between the foreground and the near background of attention. But Jack doesn't merely locate the sound of Dick's piano in the overall field of his experience; he also organizes his attention to the various aspects of the piano sounds—the phrasing, the timbre, the note choice, and so on. Because Jack's priority is to play lines that do not conflict with Dick's chords, Jack focuses on Dick's range. If Dick is playing voicings that are in the bass's range, Jack must take care to play above or below the chords. Similarly, if Dick—or the rest of the band—is building to a climax in dynamics or playing softer, Jack must play along as well. As with the time and the changes, Jack's goal is immediate, unreflective response to changing musical conditions. In sum, Jack usually places the sound of Dick's piano in the near background of his experience as a whole, and, within the piano phenomena, he focuses on dynamics and range.

Larry's and Dick's solos are also important for Jack as he comps. Though Dick's piano parts are always audible, the vibes are a quiet instrument, and Jack must often make an effort to hear Larry's lines. While the harmonic substitutions of more contemporary soloists require the bass player to pay special attention to note choice, Larry and Dick do not engage in such practices, and Jack rarely focuses on the harmonic implications of their solos. Jack mainly listens to them for dynamics, texture, and density, adjusting his parts to the mood they set. On occasion, Jack may pick out particular melodic contours from Larry's or Dick's parts and incorporate them into his lines; in general, however, the textural and affective components are foregrounded in Jack's experience of Larry's and Dick's solos.

With the introduction of the issue of dynamic, texture, and affect, we can see a central element of Jack's experience: the social interaction of the players. As Ingrid Monson has observed (1996, 83), the jazz musician's goal is to "be so thoroughly familiar with the basic framework of the tune that he or she can attend to what everyone else in the band is doing," and Monson takes such interactions as the very heart of the jazz performance. Being aware of the other players' dynamics, texture, and affect doesn't merely mean recognizing that the band is building to a crescendo or that a drummer is playing a few fills; on the contrary, I suggest, those features are themselves experienced as evidence of social interactions on the stand. When a pianist plays large, spread chords loudly on every beat, Jack is aware of him or her not merely as loud but as busy and intrusive. There is a limit to the amount of sound a listener can assimilate at one time, so a busy player is one that hogs the "aural space." As a result, volume and density are interactive and social factors as well as purely acoustic ones. Jack is, therefore, constantly aware of how the other players' parts force themselves on his experience. A pianist's comping, for example, may rest pleasantly in the defining background, articulating the harmony and informing the solo held in the center of attention; alternatively, comping may obnoxiously disturb the focal solo, obscuring it with loud chords or too-frequent fills.

With this much of the discussion presented I can draw together some of these ideas and make them more precise. When the groove, the changes, or the interactions with the comping pianist are in any way problematic, Jack will actively move them to the center of his experience. Here, flows of reflection and imagination may supplement actively organized attention to help Jack fulfill the basic musical requirements of jazz—the changes and the time. When these foundational aspects are not problematic, however, there is no need to attend to them actively, and they recede into the defining background without any effort on Jack's part. Here, Jack may attend more freely to a wide variety of aspects of the musician's parts. Listening more for density, texture, affect, and style—the primary aesthetic features- —Bill's fills and accents and Dick's fills and voicings steal in and out of the center of Jack's attention. Just as a melody is typically focal in a composed song while the accompaniment forms the defining background, the solo line will typically hold the center of Jack's attention for a large percentage of the performance. Keep in mind that when a phenomenon is foregrounded, the backgrounded experiences are not absent. As I have suggested above, experience is always a dynamic gestalt of foregrounded and backgrounded elements. When Jack locks onto the drums, therefore, Dick's chords still play in the near background; because experience is not only polyphonous but also dynamic, Dick's comping may emerge at any moment from background to foreground.

This brings us to the topic of Jack's experiences of those phenomena usually labeled as "self": reflections and the body. Jack told me that, ideally, performance should be minimally reflective. While sharply focusing perception, planning action, and monitoring the enactment of those plans may be necessary to correct problems, Jack's preferred performance is an effortless and nonreflective flow filled with nothing more than the sound of the instruments. For Jack, and the rest of the Whisler Quartet, reflection is a means, not an end. This point is crucial; throughout our conversations, Jack explained that he never wants his parts to sound contrived and that he wants the bass to "play itself."

For virtually all the jazz musicians with whom I have spoken, the body is a means to an end and only enters into experience when it is problematic. This is true for Jack as well, and the ways in which he is aware of his body are unique to jazz bassists. The stand at Rizzi's is extremely small. Jack is crushed in the corner between Dick and Bill and forced to hold the bass in uncomfortable positions that, if not adjusted for, would adversely affect his intonation. When he notices that his intonation is off, or when playing in the thumb position (the high register of the instrument), Jack may actively attend to his back and hand postures. Most of the time, however, his body is experienced as a receding background. Unsurprisingly, Jack is always aware of the sound of his own bass. When another player's part becomes problematic or requires scrutiny, Jack's own playing may slip into the near background, but it must never be too far from the center of attention—if only to ensure good intonation and tone.

The affective dimension of the parts played by the musicians is a constant accompaniment to the performance. A unique aspect of Jack's organization of experience is his attention to the lyrics. Though many standards were originally vocal tunes, they are often performed as instrumentals, and many musicians don't know the lyrics to the tunes they play. Jack has often surprised other musicians with his voluminous knowledge of the lyrics to jazz standards. For Jack, this knowledge specifies the mood of the tune and acts as a defining *affective* background just as the changes act as a defining *harmonic* background. The lyrics not only conjure the song's mood, they help to make Jack's playing specific to the tune. This quality is crucial to a successful performance. Most tunes employ standard chord changes; while poor players treat every "/ii V/ I/" the same way, a good player is one whose solo lines are tailored to the overall mood and style of each individual song. Monson (1996) refers to this aesthetic need for playing specific and personal parts as "saying something." Jack's knowledge of the lyrics acts as a defining background to his performance, evoking the song's unique mood and allowing him to "say something" rather than mechanically reproduce the jazz vocabulary.

Jack's solos: Self and other

Jack doesn't just comp; he solos as well, and his organization of attention in soloing requires special consideration. During Jack's solos, Larry never comps and Dick only comps occasionally; Bill almost always plays on a smaller portion of the kit and with fewer fills and accents. Unsurprisingly, Jack is solidly focused on his own playing during his solos; though he may attend to Bill if he feels himself to be rushing, there is none of the emergent flitting to and fro within the sound of the band as a whole that we saw above. As in his comping, Jack avoids reflection in his soloing, and his goal is for melodies to emerge effortlessly from his instrument. Unlike some players of his generation, Jack feels that reflective plotting and planning of musical structures tends to lead to a contrived solo.

This is not to say that Jack's solos are empty-headed. On the contrary, because chordal parts rarely accompany his solos Jack must hear the changes by imagining the flow of harmonic rhythm, protending and retaining the functions and qualities of the chords of the head. Further, Jack not only imagines the flow of changes but also protends the lines he plays several bars ahead. It is not uncommon for jazz musicians to sing along with their solo, and Jack does this on occasion. This procedure acts as a kind of "policing," Jack said, and he does this on nights when his mind may be wandering to focus his attention on the solo. This point is critical. Jack repeatedly asserted that, for the experienced player, mistakes in performance almost never come from an error of fingering. If a player is playing a composed melody and hits a wrong note, he said, it is because he or she didn't learn the melody well enough, didn't incorporate it into his or her memory and imagination with sufficient detail, didn't protend it richly enough in performance. The point is perhaps easier to understand in improvisation. When musicians are intensely engaged with improvisation, they *hear* their parts in rich detail; that hearing includes both the present sounds grasped in perception as well as the protention of the rest of the phrase. When players are distracted or disengaged, the parts are not imagined with clear detail; mistakes arise in this situation, if only because the arms and hands are unable to articulate a part that is not specifically defined.

While Jack may reflect slightly about the overall form of the solo or the solo's ending, his goal is to hear parts effortlessly and play them. This kind of "hearing" involves intense aural protentions, a process quite distinct from reflective plotting and planning (Husserl [1929] 1964; Schutz 1976, 58–60), and we can use this situation to deepen our understanding of the notion of protention. Reflective plotting and planning is the active production of a discrete flow of phenomenon that serve as plans for future action. Such a reflective flow can take the form of words—the "voice inside the head" we experience in everyday life—or musicological concepts. Alternatively, plotting or planning may also take an imaginative and perceptual form; here, the musician imagines the sound of a line to be performed and then enacts it. Protention is quite unlike the first and has only distant ties to the second. The hearing Jack refers to is no such linguistic or imaginative plan, but the anticipation and vague awareness of the upcoming parts that runs continuously into the present perceptual moment and beyond that into the recent past. It is unlike conceptual plotting and planning in that it is an experience of sounds and not concepts or words. It is unlike the imaginative plotting and planning described above in that Jack doesn't close his eyes, imagine a line, and play it; instead, the protentions run smoothly into the part being played at present.

The notions of protention and retention come from Husserl's *Phenomenology of Internal Time Consciousness* ([1929] 1964) and Henri Bergson's *Time and Free Will* (1913); a foundational application of these notions to issues in music occurred in Alfred Schutz's "Fragments on the Phenomenology of Music" (1976).[8] The great achievement of these authors is to show that we do not experience life as an infinitely thin moment passing into the future. Instead, we exist within a "thick" living present in which anticipations of the near future and retentions of the recent past form an ever-changing gestalt. Building on Ihde (1976), I shall explore this point in greater detail in Chapters 6 through 9, but the point to be gained here is the sharp differences among *protention*, planning in imagined perceptions, and planning in concepts; Jack employs the first process, some of the second process, and actively avoids the third. Though none of the musicians use the term protention, this idea of "hearing the part" emerged in interviews with all of the jazzers.

Jack and the audience: The sociology of attention

How a player attends to the audience is one of the most culturally specific features of his or her structuring of the lifeworld. The topic is complex because the players not only organize their attendance to the audience, they also orient their actions to their interpretations of the audience's awareness of the performance. For example, as I have suggested in Chapter 2, the rock musician's flamboyant stage antics are calculated to draw in the audience's attention, while jazz musicians are less aware of the crowd and make no effort to compel their attention. Each musical culture has its own unique social dynamics of partial sharing, and the manner in which the players orient themselves toward the audience is central to their experience. For present purposes we can observe three parameters in what I have referred to above as the "sociology of attention": how intensely the player attends to the audience, when the player attends to the audience, and how the player orients his or her action to the audience's attention.

Early on in the interview process, Jack pointed out that he was aware of the audience in performance and gained energy from their attentive listening. As the discussion progressed, Jack made it clear that he made no effort to reach out to the audience and draw in their attention. In fact, because jazz is so complex, he said, all he can do in performance is focus on the music and play in a way that invites the audience to attend. Because audiences are capricious and largely outside the musician's control, Jack explained, compelling their attendance is pure folly. Jack is aware, however, of how the audience is listening to the music: if the audience is listening with rapt attention, they serve as a defining background, tinting his focal experiences with energy and excitement. If they are talking and drinking and fail to applaud for any of the solos, they are simply a distraction to be edited from his awareness, and his performance becomes oriented to the other players. Jack's approach is typical of both African American and European American jazz musicians.

In broad strokes, the foregoing discussion describes Jack's organization of attention on the stand at Rizzi's. Ideally, that experience is a flow of perceptions of the other musicians and his own bass; the textural and affective dimensions of the rhythm section's parts weave a counterpoint with the soloist's lines in the center of Jack's experience and appear against the defining background of the flowing groove, the changes, and the affective tenor of the lyrics. During his solo, Jack's attention focuses more narrowly on his own performance and his bass; parts are protended and played, emerging pretty and effortless. Again, in the best of all worlds, the audience is also a defining background and a source of energy. When this ideal situation does not emerge, groove, changes, negotiation of space within the band, or Jack's own body may take center stage in experience; tightly focused attention, often followed by plotting and planning, time-share with the sound of the band, changing the character of the overall experience. On a particularly bad night, a boisterously inattentive audience exists for Jack as a distraction to be edited out of awareness.

Bill Roth

At the level of abstraction at which this chapter operates, Bill Roth's and Jack Hanan's experiences are quite similar.[9] Bill's first priority is to keep time. On a bad night the central feature of his experience will be locking in with the bass player and keeping the time solid. Bill repeatedly brought up the question of responding to players whose tempi changed, and he said it was generally better to keep the band together than insist on the correctness of your tempo at the cost of ensemble cohesion. Further, on a bad night, Bill explained that he would limit his punches, accents, and fills and just play time.

On a better night, however, groove will recede into Bill's defining background, just as it will in Jack's. Also in the defining background are the changes. Bill has no formal training in harmony and cannot name chord changes or key areas. For most jazz standards, however, he is aware of the points at which the changes fall, their pattern of tension and release, and their place in the overall form of the tune. A more important defining background for him was the head melody and head arrangement. Bill explained that one could play the same groove over dozens of jazz standards; like Jack, Bill observed that musicians need ways to keep track of the form and play parts that are specific to the tune. The constant flow of the head melody playing in his imagination locks Bill in with the form and provides a constant background against which he kicks a counterpoint of accents and fills. Bill stressed that he rarely has to conjure the head melody actively in his imagination. Playing the tune, he "hears" the head melody the same way Jack hears the changes.

While Bill will actively listen to Jack if the groove is a problem, he backgrounds the bass and foregrounds the piano when the band is swinging. The chordal accompaniments that Dick plays often fit the pattern of big band horn arrangements, explained Bill; his familiarity with the rhythms of these standardized comping patterns enable him to anticipate the phrasing of Dick's parts, kicking accents and playing fills that mesh tightly with them. Thus, where Jack foregrounds the range and dynamics of Dick's comping figures, Bill is more focused on their precise rhythms. Bill also listens to Larry's lines and may play accents and fills that relate directly to them.

After numerous feedback interviews, I began to get the sense that Bill paid more attention to Dick than to Larry; this idea was confirmed by further questioning. Because Dick attends most intensely to Larry, a typical chain of influences developed in the band. Larry would improvise lines based on the changes, largely listening to the chordal qualities of Dick's comping. Dick comps, largely attending to Larry's phrasing and employing standard rhythmic patterns from the big band repertoire. Bill attends mainly to Dick, and responds with accents and fills that fit with his comping parts. Because Dick's parts emerge from interaction with Larry, and Bill's emerge from Dick, Bill's parts automatically coordinate with Larry's. In terms of the organization of attention, Jack's exact part is often backgrounded (but nevertheless present) in Bill's experience; Larry's may be foregrounded, but frequently it is the rhythms of Dick's comping patterns that hold Bill in thrall. Further, where Jack is more likely to be aware of the general textural and affective components of the other players' parts, Bill is just as likely to play to the others' exact rhythmic phrases as he is to their general density or style.

What Bill is unlikely to do, however, is reflect on any of those responses. The opposition between actively reflective and more directly responsive players is an issue for all of the players, but nowhere do you find a more ardent opponent of on-the-stand reflection than Bill. Throughout the interview process Bill repeatedly explained that there are head players and heart players, and that he was a heart player. "Don't let your head get in the way!" is Bill's credo; his broadest goal was to hear the other players and effortlessly respond with dynamic grooves and parts. Flows of reflective thought, to Bill, are nothing but a hindrance, and he eliminates them as a distraction whenever they are not absolutely necessary to overcome some momentary problem.

Attention to the audience, however, is not a distraction. Bill explained to me that the drummer's throne was an unusually advantageous spot from which to watch the crowd. For years, he said, he has watched northeast Ohio nightclub audiences from that vantage point. Ideally, he is aware of the audience and plays to please them, but like Jack, he has no desire to compel their attention. If the audience is drinking and talking, he plays for the other musicians; in the worst of all possible worlds, one in which even the other players are not paying attention, he plays for himself. Bill is not only aware of the audience's attention, he is also influenced by it. As I suggested in the previous chapter, Bill matches his playing to the listeners' moods, keeping things quieter early in the evening and using Latin grooves and polyrhythmic parts sparingly.

Dick Schermesser

The themes that emerged in the interviews with Jack and Bill continued in my conversations with Dick. Like Jack and Bill, Dick said that the time was a foundational aspect of the music. But because the time is set by the bass and drums, the procedure of locking in is less important to Dick, and in the interviews he never listed negotiating the groove as one of the central aspects of his experience. While comping, Dick's attendance to the bass complements Jack's attendance to the piano. Dick listens for Jack's range so as not to conflict with him and constantly adjusts his voicings to provide the correct harmonic implications to go with Jack's ever-changing line. Like Jack, he listens intently and reflects if he is unsure of the changes, but most of the time he simply responds. In a similar fashion, Dick may have to listen intently to the drums during an unfamiliar Latin groove, attending carefully to find a comping patterns that fits the flow of accents, but in general the drums require neither active attendance nor reflection. Ideally, fills and hits, as well as the density and dynamics of Bill's playing, are the aspects of the drumming that steal into the center of Dick's attention, and those do so only occasionally.

With Jack's note choice and range and Bill's accents and style forming a defining background, Dick places Larry's solos in the center of his experience. Often, said Dick, Larry is difficult to hear. On the level of basic proficiency, Dick focuses on Larry's phrasing to avoid rhythmic conflicts, on his range to avoid voicing conflicts, and, occasionally, on his harmonic content to echo the intervals of Larry's lines in his own note choices. When these basic coordinations are happening effortlessly, he foregrounds the affective and textural aspects of Larry's part in order to play sensitively and responsively. Like the other players, Dick is only aware of his body when it becomes a problem.

While soloing, Dick is more focused on his own playing than on the bass or drums. Here, he mainly attends to the other members of the rhythm section to make sure he is synchronized with the groove and the form; when those aspects are unproblematic, they recede into the defining background. Like the others, Dick is a staunch opponent of reflective plotting and planning in the act of soloing, though he may sing along with his soloing occasionally to "police" his attention. He explains that at the beginning of an improvised phrase, he may actively imagine the first part of the melodic contour and some aspects of the line (note choice, rhythmic approach), but soon his "hands take over" and lead the line to unexpected places. Strongly antireflective, Dick points out that without plotting and planning, his hands can direct his improvisation and lead the line to places he could not have predicted. Ideally, during the solo the other instruments recede into the defining background, and the sound of his parts dominates his experience, presaged by short-term protentions but unencumbered by reflection.

Of all of the members of the Whisler Quartet, Dick is least aware of the audience. At first, he said that he is never aware of them on the stand. On further reflection, Dick changed his mind, adding that he enjoyed a positive crowd response and that his main motivation for performance was emotional expression. Dick explained, however, that he is primarily aware of the audience only after his solo is over or between tunes, when the audience applauds or fails to do so. Dick strongly related to the opposition between inviting and compelling attention and explained that he had no desire to draw the crowd into the performance. On the contrary, his goal is to "enter into the music," holding the sound firmly and richly in the center of experience; the audience, he said, can follow him there if they so chose.

Larry Whisler

As we leave the rhythm section, we note other differences and similarities between the players' experiences. Larry plays the head melody and solos but only rarely comps. Because he has difficulty hearing the exact parts that Jack plays, Larry largely experiences the bass as an indistinct flow of quarter-note rhythms that fill out the lower registers. Beyond listening to his own parts, Larry is keenly aware of Dick's comping. Though he is well familiar with the changes and could solo without any accompaniment, Larry holds Dick's parts near the center of experience and listens for the rich, extended chords that Dick plays. While Larry has no problem hearing the changes, the rich chords Dick plays make the music fuller and allow Larry to enter into the music more intensely. During his solos, this rich flow of harmony shares the center of attention with Larry's own lines and stands out against the defining background of Jack's and Bill's flowing groove and his own protentions of the changes and form.

Like the other members of the Whisler Quartet, Larry believes it is a mistake to plot and plan on the stand. During our interviews he suggested that the current generation of schooled jazz musicians have been taught too much theory. Trying to cleverly apply that theory during solos, he said, they often become confused; the music zips by too fast to plan out lines, and good improvisation only occurs as an effortless flow of action unencumbered by reflection. Larry softened this antireflective stance slightly during the feedback interviews. There, he observed that he does not merely hold his solos in the center of his attention; to prevent boring repetition, Larry chronically monitors his solos to ensure that he does not overuse any one technique or contour. Occasionally this monitoring results in reflection upon and plans for melodic techniques, but most of the times he merely listens and responds. Ideally, Larry wants his performance to be unencumbered by plotting and planning; if he does reflect during his solo, he will do so as briefly as possible and solely as a means to an end.

The audience is an important part of Larry's experience, and he is as active as Bill Roth in orienting his playing to them. Like Bill, Larry explained that he is continuously aware of the head melody as he solos. Rather than spinning out the head melody to keep track of the form, Larry hears the head melody in order to quote from it or relate his lines to its melodic contours. Like Bill, Larry is intent upon making his music accessible to the listener, and quoting from the head melody gives the listeners an aural reference point and enables them to follow the solo. All of the quartet members allow the audience to lurk in the defining background if they (the audience) are attentive to the music, and all the players censor the crowd from experience when they show no interest in the music. However, Larry and Bill differ from Jack and Dick in that they allow their expectations of the crowd's tastes to lurk in the background of experience and influence their playing.

Four Jazz Musicians from Cleveland's African American Scene

Eric Gould

One of the most articulate and intelligent players I interviewed, Eric was clear and certain about his responses to my questions. When I asked the question, "What do you pay attention to on the stand?" he elaborated a detailed scheme that both fit in with my previous understandings of the musician's organization of experience and extended them. His first move was to define the term "parameter." To Eric the parameters are the defining, structural elements of the tune that set up a context for improvisation. The parameters of improvisation can differ widely across genres. In standard jazz, Eric explained, the parameters are the changes and the time. In Eric's experimental piece "The Joker," there is no harmonic rhythm against which the players are told to improvise; instead, they have brief, 2-bar periods in which they may improvise any part in a specified range. Here, the parameters are the range and the brief period for which the improvisations are set.

Eric explained that when one is unfamiliar with a tune or when there is some problem on the stand, one must actively attend to and deal with the parameters; ideally, however, one's negotiation of the parameters is effortless or even "subconscious." When the parameters can be moved into the "subconscious," the player is only aware of his or her direction and a brief anticipation of the sound of the first few moments of his or her part. Eric defined "the direction" as a split-second plan for the upcoming phrase. "Anything can be a direction," Eric explained: a plan to play with a certain physical technique, to aim the melodic contour at a particular note, to employ a type of harmonic materials or to play in a certain style. Though the planning of the direction only lasts a split second, he said, it is crucial; without it, the playing becomes vague and lifeless. Further, he said that while a player may plan a direction in concepts, the player may also "pre-hear" the first few moments of the phrase before playing it; "prehearing" only short passages leaves the player open to respond to the endless unexpected events that occur in improvisation.

After Eric had described his scheme, we spent some time coordinating his insights with my questions about the organization of attention. When he described the differences between the two levels of attention, I offered the terms foreground and background, and he readily accepted them.[10] Further feedback confirmed that his idea of direction was indeed a split-second reflection, a brief plotting and planning; his notion of prehearing is roughly equivalent to short-term protention. As a result, we can see some initial similarities and difference between Eric's organization of experience and those of the players in the Whisler Quartet. Both Eric and the Quartet members recognize the importance of protention in improvisation. Unlike the Quartet members, however, Eric values reflection in performance and actively employs it. And while Eric stressed that the planning of direction was a split-second process, he explained that the overall form of the solo emerged in slightly longer reflections during key moments in the solo. Such extended planning typically occurs, he said, at the very beginning of the solo, in the longer spaces between the phrases, and just before the solo's end.

Important similarities and differences also emerge between Eric and the Akron players on the topic of attention to the other musicians on the stand. Like Dick, Eric chronically monitors the bassist to avoid range and voicing conflicts with his lefthand piano accompaniments and chronically monitors the soloist for similar conflicts with his right hand. The drummer is especially important to a piano player, Eric explained, because of the drum's ability to overpower the piano. Soloing, Eric is likely to get rhythmic ideas from the drummer. Echoing the sentiments of the Akron players, Eric indicated that the management of harmonic conflicts, the coordination of tempo and aural space, and the negotiation of the changes all function like parameters do; only when they pose a problem should they enter into the player's experience. Ideally, all such concerns should languish in the distant background while perception, direction, and "prehearing" should stand in the foreground, richly imbued with affect and flowing effortlessly from past to future.

The similarities between Eric's and Dick's experiences come from the piano's serving a similar role in both their styles of jazz; beyond these similarities, however, important differences emerge. Where Dick and the other

Rizzi's players could quickly identify the types of interactions they had with the other players, Eric was eager to explain that, aside from the basic coordinations, his interactions with the other players were unpredictable. The difference between the two groups here is largely one of emphasis. All of the jazz musicians I spoke with agreed that when a band is cooking, the band member's attention flits among the interesting parts the other players perform. The Rizzi's players, however, felt comfortable isolating typical schemes of interaction within the band and their resulting dynamics of attention. In contrast, Eric stressed that the other players' parts were never the same twice, and he resisted any attempt to specify either the kinds of parts his bandmates might play or his constantly changing attention to them. This point also connects with his previous position on prehearing; one cannot protend too far in the future, Eric explained, because the unpredictable band interactions will constantly demolish your expectations and plans.

While Eric parts company with the Rizzi's players on the topic of reflection, his perspective on body awareness was echoed widely by all the players, regardless of genre. Like the members of the Rizzi's group, Eric is rarely aware of breathing or postural concerns on the stand, though he does attend to his body as he practices. Eric explained that he is mainly aware of his body inasmuch as it constrains or enables his performance. Because jazz improvisation is technically demanding, Eric must constantly assess his body's capacity to enact his musical intentions. Less a central focus than a backgrounded limit on capabilities, Eric is always distantly aware of the agility of his fingers, his digital accuracy, and the span of his reach, and instantly tailors his musical goals to his present physical capabilities. When I offered Eric's account to the other jazz musicians, most immediately agreed that it accurately describes their experience.

Eric plays a much wider variety of jobs than the members of the Whisler Quartet do. He performs in both a quartet and a duo setting, as well as in the studio, at nightclubs, and in concerts. Eric views the club setting as a "workshop" for experimentation. Drinking and socializing are the focus at all of the area clubs that have jazz, said Eric; as a result, the audience is largely a distraction to be actively placed outside of experience. With no one listening carefully, Eric feels freer to take risks and experiment with new techniques and approaches. This attitude must not be understood as indifference to listener enjoyment. Eric stressed to me that when an audience does listen intently, it can become part of the unpredictable mix of influences in performance, one of the myriad foci of attention. The air of expectancy and the subtle reactions of audience members to the emerging music is a welcome addition to any performance, though such a positive contribution mostly occurs in the concert setting. With an attentive concert crowd, Eric is less likely to take big risks and experiment. The point is carried further in the studio. While it may appear that the possibility for endless rerecording and editing may make a performer more likely to take chances in the studio, Eric said that, because of the cost of the studio time, he is even more cautious at a recording session. Echoing Dick's sentiments, he explained that his goal is to "enter into the music," and, though he greatly appreciates it when the audience chooses to follow him, Eric makes no effort to compel the crowd's attention.

Jerome Saunders

Both the similarities and the differences between the Akron and Cleveland players deepen when we explore Jerome's experiences. Like all the others I have interviewed, Jerome's first concern is with the parameters. In both the duo and the small ensemble, Jerome listens to the bass player for tempo and groove. He hears the changes himself, and agrees that when comping, the good pianist is attentive to conflicts of voicing and range with both the bass player and the soloist. When I introduced the concept of protention, Jerome was quick to identify. He said that while soloing or comping, he often protends several bars in the future, and the exact temporal form of his protention depends on the tune and the quality of his attention on a given night.

Like the other players, Jerome said that in the best circumstances, concerns about band coordination and basic song structure were backgrounded. But Jerome spent little time on these issues and pointed out that once the basic coordinations are achieved, he mainly attends to the stylistic, affective, and textural components of the other player's parts. For example, Jerome's management of range and voicing conflicts with the bass was nearly automatic. Hearing the changes in his head and quickly locking in with the time, Jerome listens to the bassist for the density of his or her lines, approach to the changes, and rhythmic feel. Conflict management with the soloist was similarly automatic, and, while comping, his attention is less focused on individual notes and more on style, texture, and dynamics. Jerome sees the bass's pulse as the band's temporal foundation and views the drums as rhythmic embellishment; as a result, he listens to them to pump up his energy and focuses on their texture and style. Just as those engaged in casual conversation listen less for their interlocutor's exact words and more for his or her meaning and tone (what psycholinguists call "gist knowledge"), Jerome listens to the other players for style.

But listening for style is the only area in which Jerome allowed himself to be pinned down, and eclecticism is Jerome's main loyalty. Reflection in performance is one example of Jerome's eclecticism: on some nights, his main goal is to shut out the voice of reflection and play effortless and spontaneous flows of sound; on other nights, he does the opposite, planning complex substitutions or other harmonic approaches, reflectively juxtaposing textures or devices, and plotting out the form of the solo as a whole. When questioned about any of the diverse musical techniques that jazz musicians employ, Jerome always explained that his goal was variety: sometimes he would actively sing along with his playing to give his phrasing a particularly vocal quality; sometimes he would avoid this technique to achieve more rhythmic effects. Sometimes, Jerome would tap out all of the quarter notes with his foot to play with groove and drive; other times, he would actively avoid this tapping in order to play textural parts that moved outside of the time. Sometimes he experiments with playing ahead of the beat or behind the beat, and sometimes this is the least of his concerns.

Eric's refusal to specify his attention to the other players in the unpredictable flow of performance represents a kind of open-endedness; however, his goal is always to be a conduit for affectively powerful musical expression, to enter into the music with full emotional engagement. Jerome, however, was not even willing to sign on to this broad program. Sometimes, he said, his goal in performance was to express emotions, hearing the music in its full valual richness and playing each note with feeling. At other times, his goal was the construction of interesting musical structures rather than the expression of emotion. Jerome's only overriding goal was to broaden his textural palette, to be able to approach a tune in as many ways as possible and control as many dimensions of the performance as he can. Here, Jerome uses the term "texture" in the broadest possible sense. In academic music discourse, *texture* refers to the arrangement of the instruments in an ensemble (i.e., a dense or sparse ensemble texture, a monophonic or homophonic ensemble texture), although the term is sometimes used loosely to refer to the timbre of an individual instrument or the timbre of the ensemble as a whole. In Jerome's usage, however, different chordal approaches (such as block chords versus spread chords), different melodic approaches (lines with large leaps versus chromatic lines), and different harmonic techniques (playing inside the changes versus playing outside of them) all have their "texture," as do abstract approaches such as reflective playing versus nonreflective playing. Jerome is nothing if not eclectic.

Jerome is more aware of the audience than most of the players with whom I spoke. While there are some nights in which he enters into the music completely and is oblivious to the crowd, and while he will play for the other band members if the audience pays no attention to the music, Jerome usually has some awareness of the listeners. Like all of the players,

Jerome felt that an attentive audience acts as a defining background and gives the players additional energy. Jerome said that the moment at which the crowd enters into the center of experience (between songs, between solos, or continuously throughout the tune) depends on the evening. Unlike most players who resent playing background music for a crowd otherwise engaged, Jerome said that there is a certain pleasure that comes from laying low—setting a tone that subconsciously affects a roomful of people. Like the other jazz musicians, Jerome wishes to invite, rather than compel, the listeners' attention to the music.

Alvin Edwards and Leonard Burris

Reflection is important to both Alvin and Leonard. Alvin explained that he was not averse to having flows of reflection "accompany" (Ihde 1976) his focal attention to the sound. In reflection he may plan out chord-scale relationships, chord substitutions, or the use of some new lick; however, there are also times when he desires a performance experience unaccompanied by flows of reflection. The theme of eclecticism was echoed in my interviews with Leonard. He explained that his goal was to have as wide as possible a range of approaches to a tune. While Leonard did not explicitly discuss reflection on the stand, our conversation suggests that he frequently employs a kind of reflective plotting and planning during performance to vary his approaches. Ideally, however, his goal is to protend phrases and reflect only in abstract aesthetic terms like *tension* and *release*. African American jazz drummer Larry Glover[11] also spoke positively about reflection on the stand. Larry said that playing with a new group, his reflections are aimed at finding parts that will facilitate the group's coherence; playing with musicians that have had lots of experience with one another, Larry will reflect to search out new and creative parts.

The idea of "backgrounding the parameters" was one that rang true to Alvin, Leonard, and Larry. Leonard spoke about practicing scales until they could be called up effortlessly; Alvin spoke of soloing to an imaginary rhythm section so he could "hear the changes" by himself; Larry spoke of the primacy of tempo and band cohesion as defining features of the music and provided an account of locking in with the bass. Like the other players, Larry and Leonard both spoke of backgrounding the body in performance and occasionally highlighting it in practice.

Alvin and Leonard differed markedly from Jerome, Eric, and the Whisler players in their attitudes toward and awareness of the other musicians. All of the jazz musicians I interviewed recognized that the soloist was in a privileged position to direct the feel and direction of the improvisation.

Larry Glover

But where Jerome and Eric emphasized band interaction and the critical input they received from the comping rhythm section, Alvin and Leonard complained bitterly about rhythm section players that intruded too many ideas and failed to follow the soloist's aesthetic lead. Pianists should play sparsely and even sit out one or more choruses, said Alvin; drummers should just play time and not interfere. And no one should play a part that contradicts the aesthetic or textural direction of his solo. In the continuum ranging from interaction to leadership, both Alvin and Leonard pushed the balance far toward leadership. These statements have important implications for the organization of attention. That both players want the other musicians to play sparsely and follow their lead suggests that they do not want the other players to figure too greatly in their experience. I was unable to elicit feedback on these ideas, but it is not too great a stretch to imagine that Alvin and Leonard's own reflections and performances are more frequently held in the center of experience than are their perceptions of the other players' parts. It is even more likely that the others are held as background, and almost certain that when the rhythm section stretches out, Alvin and Leonard hear them as distractions.

The audience was the greatest stumbling block for both Alvin and Leonard. Both players deeply resented playing background music in clubs and took an inattentive audience as an affront to their musicianship; as a result, they had begun to absent themselves from the local club scene. Disgusted by audiences reared on the (perceived) pablum of fusion, Alvin explained that his first impulse when confronted with a request for Kenny G was to deliver a stern lecture on jazz history. Similarly, Leonard was disgusted with audiences that treated his music as background. Like the other players, Alvin and Leonard derive energy from an attentive crowd, and make every effort to ignore an inattentive or rude audience.

Summary and Conclusions

With these accounts in place, we have made an important step toward partially sharing the players' experiences. Jazz performance is a complex juggling act in which different flows of experience are arranged in a delicate and dynamic structure. All of the players hold musical sound in the center of attention. Ideally, they experience the time, the changes and the head melody—Eric Gould's "parameters"—as a defining background to the overall sound. Basic coordinations with the other players on the stand, including the negotiation of the groove and the management of harmonic conflicts, should ideally be held in the background as well. As a means to an end, the players say the body should be transparent in their experience; less a defining background than a receding one, it most often retreats into more distant awareness as the flow of action proceeds. When the basic coordinations are not achieved, the players employ a range of techniques (including both the active structuring of attention and reflective planning) to get the job done. But, in the ideal situation, such techniques are not needed. With the defining background set, the players are free to let their attention flit among the sounds of the various parts. Here, the players tend to foreground affect and texture, and for most players, the music becomes a flow of sound and emotion.

Not only can similarities be found among players within musical scenes, they can be found among players of the same "musical role" across scenes: pianists speak of managing range and harmonic conflict; drummers speak of locking in with the bass player; soloists speak of leading the ensemble. As Schutz has observed (1976, 64) the organization of experience is first and foremost practical, and similar ends call for similar means. Interestingly, the differences between the players across roles within a scene do not suggest a radical fragmentation of experience but rather a complementarity and reciprocity of experience: Bill attends to Jack and Jack to Bill, and both do so with the aim of sharing each other's tempo to coordinate the band more tightly. This point is critical because it enables us to find a kind of coherence in the sharing of experience where a radically individualist and empiricist interpretation would find only fragmentation. The organization of differences beyond the level of the individual is precisely the kind of situation that has led structuralist scholars to envision culture and society as somehow distinct from the participants who constitute them. As we shall see at the end of Chapter 6, the problem of reconciling abstract systems of meaning with agency dissolves when we conceptualize culture and society as the outcome of constitutive practice. Understood in this way, systematic relationships are revealed to be negotiated coordinations, structural effects are understood as unintended consequences, and society emerges as a social achievement.

The differences between the scenes are instructive as well. The players from the Rizzi's quartet hold reflection to be nothing more than a means to solving momentary problems of coordination on the stand; ideally, their experience should be nothing but a flow of perception, action, and interaction. The Cleveland players are not opposed to reflective plotting and planning: Eric and Leonard espouse the reflection of momentary "directions," while Alvin and Jerome both see reflective plotting and planning as one technique among many to bring variety to improvisation. Similarly, the players from the different groups differ in the dynamics of their attention to the other musicians. The routes through which the players' attention moves in the Whisler Quartet are numerous, but not so numerous that the players cannot describe typical patterns; on the contrary, the routes through which the Cleveland players' attention circulates are less predictable and the players were uncomfortable in trying to specify them.

In their experiences of and orientation toward the audience, the players exhibit both similarities and differences. All of the players hope for the audience's rapt attention to act as a defining background and source of energy, and none of the players make any effort to compel that attention. However, Bill, Larry, and, to a certain extent, Jack want their music to invite attention and adjust their playing accordingly; Dick and the Cleveland players are more neutral. While they all appreciate an attentive crowd, they make no special effort to tailor their playing to the listener's ear. Feeling that an engaged player is a better player, they concern themselves with making music and let the audience take care of their own attention.

While descriptive ethnography is one goal of this work, exploring the similarities and differences in the players' organization of attention can be used to shed light on broader issues. The fullest conclusions about the organization of experience can only be drawn when we have compared the data from the rock and jazz scenes, but even at this stage of analysis some results are apparent. First of all, we can identify specific techniques by which experience is managed: solving problems through reflection; policing attention by singing along; using the performance of audible players to mediate coordination with inaudible players. Further, we can see some abstract features of the organization of experience: people tend to focus on the problematic; reflection is only a small part of our overall experiences, and nonreflective action can be both voluntary and meaningful; experience is a rich and polyvocal whole structured in dynamic layers of foregrounds and backgrounds; experience is not held in the infinitely thin now but exists in the thick moment of the protended and retained past. The most important point is that experience—seemingly the most radically individual and idiosyncratic of all concepts—is in fact primarily social. All players constantly orient themselves toward the other musicians on the stand and the listeners in the room. Not only aware of the notes played or the intentions of the other actors, even at the most basic level each player listens for the others' attention and seeks to understand how he or she is emerging in the others' experience. Experience is not some radically subjective realm of the personal, it is partially public and partially shared before it is either subjectively mine or objectively there in the world.

Further, we see that our organization of experience is simultaneously based on our social history and our agency. As our cross-cultural comparison has shown, the organization of experience is influenced by the players' goals in music making, which in turn are influenced by the musical scene to which they belong. For example, it is certainly not an effect of individual caprice that the Akron players avoid reflection on the stand, while the Cleveland players all prize reflection; the Clevelanders' commitment to reflection is part of their larger vision of jazz as sophisticated artistic expression, while the Akroners' avoidance of reflection is tied to their rejection of the perceived artistic pretensions of contemporary post-bop. As I shall suggest in Chapter 6, such links extend beyond the musical scene to larger social and political contexts. But at the same time, no superorganic "hand-of-culture" comes down and imposes schemes of organizing attention on the players; the players' own experiences of effort on the stand attests that the organization of experience is something achieved by the subject. Neither capriciously individual nor socially determined, the organization of attention is a kind of *practice*; influenced by our social past, we actively constitute our experience to form a social present—a present of and for others.[12]

Before making the leap to rock and metal, we should remember that our understanding of the music scenes can only be hampered by making value judgments about the music in question. To share another's musical experience, one must take it on its own terms, if only temporarily. This is easier in some situations than in others, and one must avoid the temptation to equate sophisticated techniques for organizing attention with "better" music. For example, Jerome's eclecticism embraces both antireflective and reflective approaches, while Larry is solely antireflective. Jerome can employ the pattern techniques that Larry uses predominantly, but he also uses a variety of other melodic techniques on the stand and intentionally juxtaposes those techniques to achieve abstract "textural" effects. Because Jerome's techniques encompass Larry's, the reader may be drawn to the false conclusion that he is a "better" player. Setting aside the fact that Jerome can never fully play as Larry does, the logic of this value judgment is still flawed. When listeners hear Jerome, they don't merely hear this or that technique, they hear the full eclecticism of Jerome's juxtaposition of techniques; when listeners hear Larry's flowing lines, they hear Larry's commitment to that sound and style. Players are not the bearers of technique, the possessors of some musical competence; they are contextual *actors* who employ techniques to fit broader aims, and any judgment that is made must be of the players' performances and the broader musical goals that they serve. More important, the equating of variety and eclecticism with quality is itself an aesthetic ideology that must be suspended if we are to understand the players' musical experiences. These ideas are particularly relevant to the comparison between rock and jazz.

One final note before continuing. Beguiled by philosophy and psychology's search for timeless universals, the reader may too quickly focus on the similarities and abstract generalizations about experience given above and assume that they are the ultimate goal of the research. While it is true that organization of experience is influenced by the players' goals and that perception is always the subject's active and meaningful grasp of the world, the reader would do well not to take lived experience merely as an end to broader generalizations. As abstract descriptions, such generalizations have power and validity, but we should never think of them as superseding lived experience. No generalized musician has ever had an abstract goal and organized attention to achieve it. It is always one particular player who has had a specific goal at a specific time and shuffles his or her specific experiences into a specific configuration to achieve it. The search for universals, even the phenomenologist's search for universals in the subject's constitution of perception, should not distract us from the existential reality that is the fount from which those generalizations—no matter how interesting or powerful—emerge. As limited, specific subjects living in the contingent world we can never forget that concrete reality is greater than the sum of universal truths plus mere contingent facts. As such, scholarship is the child of experience and universal generalizations (either psychological or philosophical) are the children of ethnography.[13] With this in mind, we make a quantum leap in our empirical evidence, and turn to the experiences of rock musicians on the stand.

SIX

The Organization of Attention in the Rock and Metal Scenes

The comparison between the two jazz scenes in the previous chapter proceeded in a fairly straight-ahead fashion. With the introduction of the rock data, however, things become significantly more complex. Not only do we now have the potential for many more direct comparisons, we have an additional *level* of comparison: jazz as a whole and rock as a whole. Further, because rock and jazz are more different than Cleveland jazz and Akron jazz, comparison across the scenes is more abstract. And because of the vagaries of fieldwork, I was less able to find players of similar roles within the two different rock scenes; for example, I cannot directly compare hard rock drummers and heavy metal drummers. But while these difficulties present limited problems, the results from the last chapter show how such problems may be overcome. Comparing the experiences of Larry, Dick, Bill, and Jack, we saw how their partially shared musical goals influence their instrument-specific tasks, and how these in turn influence the players' organization of their experiences; as a result, the initial fragmentation of experience across the roles within a band are partially reconnected. Because music performance requires coordination among the players in the ensemble, many of the particular methods by which they organize their experience are reciprocal (as in Jack's attendance to the drums and Bill's attendance to the bass) or interactive (as in Dick's attendance to Larry's phrasing and Larry's attendance to Dick's rich harmonies). As a result, we can explore selected musicians from the rock and metal scenes and still gain insights into larger patterns of the organization of attention.

Cleveland's Commercial Hard Rock Scene:
Al, Chris, and Jeff

Coordination between players and the
experience of others on the stand

As I observed in Chapter 5, a central facet of any musician's onstage experience is his or her attention to the other players. The issue is complicated in all rock contexts in that the quality of the PA and the sound engineer varies from night to night,[1] and it is not uncommon for a player to be unable to hear the other musicians or even his or her own instrument. My conversations with Dia Pason's guitarist Al Ricci form an excellent starting place for our exploration of the commercial hard rocker's attendance to the other players.

Even unamplified, the rock drum kit is very loud, said Al; as a result, he can always hear the drums when he is performing. The lead vocals are usually audible through the side fills (the monitor speakers located on the side of the stage and used to deliver sound to the musicians). Chris's bass is also audible, said Al, because Chris's speaker cabinets are usually located on Al's side of the stage. The other guitar player's rhythm parts and solos are often inaudible, as are Al's own guitar parts if he stands on the other side of the stage. Given this kind of aural environment, how does Al stay coordinated with the other players? The trick for Al, and for all of the rock musicians I interviewed, is to treat the drums as a conductor. Al can usually hear his own parts, and he listens to the drums to define the tempo and cue him to the song's form. Emerging from the practical limitations of a typical bar's stage sound, this procedure is made easier because there is little improvisation in Dia Pason; while Steve varies his fills slightly and the guitar solos have improvised elements, the location of the fills and solos and the coordinated band hits are all worked out in rehearsal. Thus, the sound of his own parts and the sound of the drums form a gestalt in the foreground of his experience. The bassist and the other guitar player do this as well, and it is by syncing up with the drums that all of the players are able to present a tightly coordinated sound without always being able to hear one another. The use of drums as conductor is similar in many ways to the jazz bassist's practice of "locking in," but, as we shall see, there are important differences as well.

When Al can hear the other instruments, he locks in with them in specific ways. For example, Al has many runs that he plays in octaves with the bass. When he can't hear the bass, he uses the drums to mediate the coordination of these runs. He prefers, however, to hear Chris directly, and when the bass is audible, the octave bass and guitar runs form a gestalt in the center of his experience. Similarly, Al does have some unison breaks with the other guitar player, and he makes an effort to sync up with those parts whenever they are audible. Al can very frequently hear Chris's lead vocals. While the lead vocal helps him to keep track of the form, the sound of Chris's voice can cause Al to sing off-key during his harmony vocals, and he makes an effort to exclude Chris's voice from his experience during these passages.

Chris presents a similar story. His bass is generally audible through his speaker cabinets, which stand next to the drums; he also makes sure he can hear his vocals in his wedge monitor (the monitor speaker located in the front of the stage), because without them he will sing off-key. Beyond the sound of his cabs and monitors, Chris is mostly aware of the drums. For Chris, like Al, the drums are a touchstone for both tempo and overall song structure, and they form a gestalt with his own playing in the center of his experience. Of the instruments in the kit, Chris is primarily aware of the snare and bass drums (also known as kick drums), because they set the time; the toms and cymbals are mainly used for fills. Seeking comparisons with jazz, I asked Chris what he would do if the drummer's tempo changed. He explained that the drummer is the band's timekeeper and must be followed at all costs. Because the drums are the only instrument that are reliably present in the experience of all the musicians, deviation from the drummer's tempo is unacceptable—even if it means following a wavering drummer to a different tempo. Beyond attention to his own parts and the drums, Chris explained that he could almost always hear the other instruments when he moved away from the microphone. As band leader, the rhythm guitar, lead guitar, and backing vocals mostly enter the center of his experience when a mistake is made. Attempting to maintain a high standard of quality in his band, Chris is sensitive to the other players' mistakes and carefully notes them for correction in rehearsal.

The experiences of Max Panic's guitarist Jeff Johnston are similar to those of Chris and Al. Like the other players, Jeff explained that the other instruments are occasionally inaudible on stage, that his top priority is to hear the drums and his own parts, and that the drums are the coordinator of the band. The drums are always audible without amplification, said Jeff, so he tells the sound engineer to send the vocals and his own guitar to his monitor; this monitor mix is the bare minimum for effective coordination. Echoing Al, Jeff also said that he is more likely to lock in with the drums and other instruments during coordinated hits and more likely to attend to the drums alone on groove parts. Jeff emphasized that the contrast between groove parts and hits was critical to Max Panic's music.

My frequent queries into the organization of attention led Jeff to become exasperated with me during one interview. He explained that he made no special effort to attend to the other players, and in fact, the monitor mix (the relative volumes of the various instruments in his monitor speaker) was not a big issue to him. I asked how the sound could not matter in a live musical performance, and he explained that he was a professional: his job was to play guitar in a tight rock-and-roll band, and that he should be able to do that job no matter what the stage sound was like. When the sound is good, he just plays; when the sound is bad, he automatically compensates by tapping his foot in solid, metronomic time, coordinating with the drums if they are audible, and imagining the other parts in his head. His aural imagination supplements his perception and guarantees that he follows the form and synchronizes with the other players. Anything else, said Jeff, would not be professional. Al and Chris said they used similar techniques, but they put a greater emphasis on listening to the drums.

Taken together, the above data suggest a unique constellation of experiences, a special mode of organizing attention that is both echoed by the heavy metal musicians and distinct from anything found in jazz. This constellation depends on the vagaries of the rock performance situation (poor club PAs), the practices of composition and arrangement unique to the genre (composed songs with coordinated hits, complex forms, and improvised fills and solos), and the player's own creative skills in managing attention. Most frequently, nondrummer rock musicians will hold in the center of their attention a gestalt formed by their own part and the drums; of the drums in the kit, they will focus on the bass and snare drums; of the aspects of the bass and snare drum sound (timbre, accent, dynamic) they will foreground tempo. Other parts, like the player's own vocal or the other instruments, ideally form a defining background and occasionally pop into the foreground; when they are unavailable in perception, they are seamlessly replaced by imagination to guarantee tight band coordination.

This constellation of experience must not be confused with the locking in that goes on between the bassist and drummer in jazz. There was no consensus among jazz musicians about who was the primary timekeeper in a jazz band; some said the drummers and others said the bassist. In either case, all the players recognized that coordinating tempo required a kind of negotiation through mutual interaction and attention to the other players. Almost all of the rock players, however, said that the drummer was the band's timekeeper; here, band coordination depends on the musician's use of the drummer as a conductor and the adjustment of the other players's tempi to that of the drummer's, not a mutual negotiation. Jazz and rock are similar in that players from both traditions make reference to flows of imagination to keep track of their place in the form.[2] For the jazz musician, however, that flow consists of a quasi-aural cognitive model of the head melody and chord changes to which the players respond in their improvisations.

Commercial hard rock is largely a composed music, and the rock musician's flows of imagined parts are imagined substitutes for inaudible others.

Affect, reflection, and experiences of the self

The Akron jazzer's dislike of reflection on the stand is strongly echoed by the commercial hard rock musicians. Chris repeatedly told me that, ideally, his bass and vocal parts and all of the band's coordinations should emerge spontaneously and without any reflection; even on a bad night, Chris explained, he rarely had to make an effort to attend to his bass. Similarly, Jeff said that his goal was not to plot and plan musical structures or even actively reflect to control problems, but merely "to enter into the music"—even if "entering into the music" meant generating large parts of it in imagination! By the same token, body awareness was largely insignificant for these players. While both Al and Max Panic's keyboardist Ken Barber spoke of trying to relax their bodies on stage to give a more professional look, and though Chris spoke of actively relaxing his throat during the guitar solos, the body, to use Drew Leder's phrase (1990), is largely absent from these players' experiences.

The avoidance of reflection on the stand applies to soloing as well as comping, although the dynamics differ slightly. Jeff, the only commercial hard rock soloist that I interviewed extensively, said that his solos were largely composed. In his opinion, few rock guitarists truly improvise; their solos are merely unplanned strings of practiced licks. Jeff explained that when a Max Panic song is "young" (see Chapter 2), he may have nothing more of the solo planned than the outline of its overall form and contour. In the first few performances, Jeff improvises much of the solo; only after several shows do the specific phrases become set. When improvising, however, Jeff is adamant about attending neither to the agility of his hands (lest he fall into the trap of the technician) nor to plotting and planning (lest he lose the feel of the music). For him, improvisation means a flow of richly affective action free from reflection.

The avoidance of reflection on the stage leads us to the issue of affect. The reader may wonder how the musicians could play with feeling or have fun on stage in the aurally deprived conditions described above. I shall turn to this point in detail below, but for now we can observe that all of the players cite the excitement of live performance, the energy of the crowd, and "entrance into the music" as ways of overcoming the problems of a bad sound system. Further, Jeff's practice of "entering into the music" has important implication for our understanding of the role of affect in the rocker's organization of attention. The music, for Jeff, entails flows of sound phenomena, irrespective of whether they are imaginations or perceptions; "entering into the music" means experiencing these flows with great intensity and shuffling their affective aspects to the center of his experience. It is through intense attention to the "music," understood in the broad sense Jeff described, and interaction with the audience that a satisfying experience is achieved. For all the commercial hard rock musicians with whom I spoke, feelings of fun and energy are near the center of any good experience of rock performance.

Stage moves, audience interactions,
and the sociology of attention

The narratives presented so far, however, only tell half the story. In commercial hard rock, the vocal and instrumental performances are carefully worked out and rehearsed; as a result, the players say, the musical sound should emerge in experience as an effortless enactment of composed parts. This flow, however, constantly shifts from the foreground to the near background. Changing places with it is an intense awareness of the audience.

Al's first goal on stage is to interact with the crowd and project an image of lighthearted, almost goofy fun. Constantly shifting between the near background and the foreground of attention are Al's mannered stage moves and tricks of audience interaction. When he was a less experienced player, he had to make an active effort to loosen up and move around on stage without sacrificing his playing. As he became more comfortable with the stage and his instrument, he was able to focus less on the guitar and merely relaxing, and more on interacting with the audience, moving about the stage, and goofing around with the other players. Ideally, these stage moves should emerge effortlessly, but Al explained that on a good night he might reflect a bit—for example, planning to run over to the other side of the stage to perform a certain stage move or intending to gesture along with Chris or KB in a certain way. While most of these activities emerge spontaneously or involve the same kind of brief planning characterized by the jazz player's "direction," there are some commonplaces in Dia Pason's performance. For example, Al knows that whenever Chris is not anchored to his mike by his singing, he (Chris) will run around the stage, and this affords them the opportunity to goof around together.

Chris's story is quite similar to Al's. On most nights, his parts flow effortlessly from his instrument and voice and require no active monitoring. With his musical performance shifted to the near background, Chris is free to foreground his interactions with the crowd and the other players, experiencing and displaying the brash good humor that initially attracted him to the music. Like Al, Chris also explained that stage antics and gestures should develop freely in performance, but certain stereotyped moves become sedimented over a series of nights, and some activities— like lighting off the pyro at the end of the set—are planned ahead of time. Even for those moves that involve some reflection, the flow of stage antics and interactions with the audience should ideally mirror and display the player's fun; unfortunately, this is not always the case. In September 1993, for example, Chris explained that the band's unstable lineup and a variety of personal concerns made it difficult for him to enjoy himself on stage. Constantly monitoring the new players for mistakes and frustrated by a loose band sound, he was distracted from the flow of stage antics. Trying to have fun, like trying to relax, is a contradiction in terms, and it was several months before Chris finally gained perspective on the situation. Though he still monitored the other players, Chris explained that his new approach was to let the "energy"—the stage antics, interactions with the crowd, and his own sense of fun—emerge naturally on stage. When you put less effort into these activities, Chris observed, they tumble forth more readily by themselves.

More important than the stage antics are the player's interactions with the crowd.[3] Because of the stage lights, Al explained, you can only see the first ten rows of audience members when you are on stage; the trick to audience interaction is to connect with the ringside crowd that you can see, and to give the impression of interacting with specific individuals in the more distant crowd you cannot see. Similarly, Chris frequently spoke of making eye contact with the ringsiders and playing out to the crowd in general. Such interactions are not faked; the players constantly monitor the audience's reactions and do so for good reasons. On a most basic level, Chris and Al watch the audience to see how each song is received. While the players are not dictated to by the reaction of any one audience member, the audience responses are critical for determining whether or not a song stays in the band's repertoire or if it requires editing or elaboration.

More than this, however, all the players' actions are oriented toward the crowd; they not only have fun, they project the image of having fun and draw the listeners into that fun. As such, the audience is always in the near background of the rockers' experience, and their awareness of the *audience's* awareness is vital to the performance.[4] When there is no crowd or when the crowd is apathetic, Chris and Al "bounce energy off one another," performing their usual stage antics for their own and their bandmates' amusement. This "performing for each other" parallels the jazz musician's practice of playing for the band on a night when the crowd was inattentive. If there are even a few people in the club paying attention, however, their stage antics have a double function: they are both a display of fun for the audience and the experience of fun for themselves.

When we interact with an other, we are not only aware of his or her attention toward us, we are also aware of the affective tenor of that attention. As I talk with you, for example, I am not merely aware that you are attentive to me or distracted from me, I am also aware of the mood with which you constitute me in your experience—your rapt delight in my compliments or your riveted disgust with my insults. In precisely the same way, Chris and Al are not merely aware of the audience's mood and not merely aware of whether or not they are paying attention; Chris and Al are aware of the affective tenor with which the audience is attending to the band.[5] A crowd that head-bangs, foot taps, dances, sings along, applauds, and yells between songs, responds to Chris's patter, and even good-naturedly mocks the band with parodies of their stage antics is an audience that is not merely paying attention, not merely having fun, and not merely having fun because of the band. No simple English word captures the idea here, so a hyphenated phrase in the style of German phenomenology is required: such an audience is grasping-the-band-with-fun.

The band, however, is aware of more than the affective tenor with which the audience grasps them. Chris and Al told me time and time again that they "get energy from the crowd." Attentive to the affect with which the audience attends to them, the performers partially share the audience's energy. Ideally, their attendance to one another sparks a feedback loop in which audience and performer inspire one another to greater and greater levels of energy—a more and more heightened performance, a more intense grasping-of-the-other-with-fun. Finally, Chris and Al explained that their goal is not merely to make the audience have a good time, but to compel their attention, to force them into this feedback loop, to pull them away from the bar and the distractions of their lives, and to draw them into the performance. While the jazz musician's goal is to enter into the music and create sounds that invite the listener's active engagement, the rockers seek to bombard the crowd with such a powerful image of fun and such intense face-to-face interactions that they have no choice but to enter into the event. Though it appears to be simple, the notion of "partial sharing" actually entails an immense range of interactional dynamics, of which these data from rock and jazz are but two examples. Audience-performer feedback, grasping-the-other-with-fun, and compulsion are the key elements of commercial hard rock's "sociology of attention," a culturally specific set of practices through which audience members and performers constitute experience in the event.

While Jeff Johnston's stage persona is cooler and less frenetic than Chris's or Al's, his organization of attention and styles of interaction with the crowd jive with our previous observations and extend them. On stage, he largely stands in one place and uses few of the stereotypical stage moves that the members of Dia Pason employ. But beyond this difference of style, Jeff told a story similar to those of Chris and Al. As a professional, said Jeff, it is his job to entertain the crowd and compel their attention to the music, and Jeff pursues that end vigorously.

He explained good rock stage technique to me through the negative example of a inept band that once opened for Max Panic. This band wore street clothes that failed to set them apart as a group of performers. Max Panic is loath to indulge in the exaggerated fashions of other pop metal bands, but Jeff explained that his bandmates are always certain to wear special clothing on stage; such costumes sharply frame the performance, telling the audience that they take the gig seriously and drawing in their attention. The inept opening band spent half their time fiddling with their equipment. Though it is important to correct any flaws in the sound, excessive attention to the equipment, explained Jeff, draws the performer's attention away from the audience. It also distracts the audience from the show and tells them that the musicians are lost in their own world. Finally, Jeff said that the opening band failed to interact with the audience. While Jeff admitted that he has a cooler stage persona than players like Chris or Al, he said that he is always very aware of the audience and is careful to interact with them.

Jeff augmented the notion of compelling attention by making a distinction between giving and taking on stage. He explained that the flamboyant gestures and flashy guitar licks of many egocentric commercial hard rockers were employed in order to "get something" from the audience—attention, adoration, and, after the show, sexual favors. His band, on the other hand, aimed at *giving* to the audience, providing them with an evening of thoughtful lyrics and rocking grooves. Both the givers and the takers of Jeff's theory seek to compel the audience's attention; the difference is the ultimate end that that increased awareness is made to serve. The takers' goal is to aggrandize themselves with their audience's adoring attention, while the givers seek to uplift the crowd with the heightened awareness that comes from successful performance. To whatever end it is put, the compulsion of attention is a critical dynamic in the commercial hard rock event.

This culturally specific sociology of attention holds the key to the problem we have laid out earlier: How can rock performance be fun for the musicians when all they hear is a small and distorted portion of the music?

The answer, said Al Ricci, is the energy that comes from the crowd. Al explained that the sound of an average bar's PA is usually worse than that of a home stereo. As a result, fans of both national and local acts use recordings, not live shows, when they wish to appreciate the nuances of the musical sound. But what a CD, or even a video, can't replicate is the experience of the full event with all its audience-performer feedback. It is not merely that the clubs give up sound quality in exchange for volume, although this is true. It is the energy generated by this interactive partial sharing of experience that enables the musician to overcome the poor stage sound and enjoy the performance.

Power Metal and Death Metal

Coordination between players and the experience of others on the stand

In many ways, the organization of attention in commercial hard rock and metal are similar, and the experiences of the metal string players provide the easiest entrance into heavy metal performance. Winter's Bane's guitarist Lou St. Paul explained that on the stand he can always hear drummer Terry Salem, and he foregrounds Terry's snare to keep the time solid. Not surprisingly, Lou said that he always had to focus on his own parts, listening for coordination with the drums and making sure he was playing "with feeling." Though Lou prefers to hear Dennis Hayes's bass throughout the songs, his part is only crucial for Lou during his guitar solos; without a second guitarist, the bass forms the harmonic context of Lou's often improvised solo lines. Timmy Owens's lead vocals were Lou's lowest aural priority on stage; only when Lou was too lazy to follow the form closely would he need to listen to Timmy, and then only to cue section changes. Finally, like the commercial hard rockers, Lou explained that when the sound was bad or an individual player inaudible, he would imagine the other players' parts to mark his place in the tune and guarantee coordination.

Dann Saladin's story differs from Lou's in one important way; because Sin-Eater had more members than Winter's Bane, and because Sin-Eater rarely headlined, Dann often had to grapple with extremely poor sound systems. Frequently unable to hear anything but the drums, Dann and the other members of Sin-Eater know to listen to drummer John Ziats to conduct the tempo and sectional changes. Within the kit, Dann largely focused on the snare drum as the touchstone of the band's time; in sections where he plays a string of eighth notes on the low E string, Dann spoke of intently locking in on the snare. Though Dann's comping parts are largely composed, and therefore should ideally emerge for him as second nature, he said he would often have to attend carefully to his own playing. Dann is quite active on stage, and, with the combined distractions of the band, the poor sound system, and the crowd, he was always careful to keep his own playing and the drums fixed in the center of his experience. As a band leader, Dann echoed Chris Ozimek in saying that he often monitored the other players for mistakes; because the members of Sin-Eater improvised more than those in Dia Pason, Dann listened for interesting changes as well as flaws and errors.

Sin-Eater bassist Rob Toothman used the drums as conductor as well, but Dann was also a part of his experiential mix. While John was usually closer to the center of his attention, Rob said that he will occasionally shift focus to Dann if John's improvisations become confusing. Further, like Al Ricci, Rob Toothman would lock on with the other Sin-Eater bassist, Chuck, during the frequent unison or harmony breaks.

To this point, the use of the drums as conductor has emerged as a major theme for the string players. But what is the drummer's experience like? Terry Salem, John Ziats, and Keith Porter—the respective drummers for Winter's Bane, Sin-Eater, and the power metal band Shadow Play—were all quick to point out the importance of hearing their own drums. Keith explained that while he likes having all of the players in his monitors, the drums, particularly snare and kicks, must be loudest. The kick and snare are the loudest in Terry's monitor mix, with the guitar, then bass and vocals clocking in at successively lower dynamic levels. Terry was quick to emphasize that he always tries to be aware of all the instruments; when I explained that "foreground" and "background" imply multiple and simultaneous experiences, he agreed that his monitor mix reflects the centrality or marginality of the instruments in his experience. Likewise, John Ziats makes sure that his own drums are the loudest in his monitor mix. While he would ideally like to hear all the players, he rarely can.

Terry and Keith both spoke of the importance of the volume level of their monitors. The superamplified sound of your own drums blasting back at you, they explained, gives a drummer a sense of power and authority that is crucial for a good performance. Just as the player's and the crowd's attention to one another increases the overall intensity of their experience, Keith's and Terry's amplified perception of their own playing serves to pump up their performances. The immediate return of their actions to their perception forms a feedback loop like that described by James and Lange in their famous theory of human affect. Here, however, the affect is primed and, quite literally, amplified by the use of sound technology. While this is true for all rock instrumentalists, only the drummers emphasized this point in their interviews. Their emphasis underscores the fact that the drummers must not only hear themselves, they understand themselves to be the central focus and rhythmic touchstone of the band.

But even given blasting monitors, the practice of listening to one's own kit is not so simple as it seems, and the player's descriptions of the vagaries of stage sound were particularly vivid. Sitting behind the kit, Terry explained, all of the drums project their sound away from the drummer, and the sound that the drummer hears is like the hitting of "wet paper sacks." The cymbals, however, project their sound back at you, explained Keith, buffeting the player with a constant and distracting ring—a phenomena that Terry also observed. As a result, said Keith, the harder you play, the more you are lost in the buzzing ring of the cymbals and the less you hear. The monitors themselves add extra problems, Terry said. Though their enormous volume is crucial for pumping up the drummer's emotions, their close proximity to the player's head provides a strangely compressed sound that Terry likened to "listening to music inside a box." The problems of stage monitors and PA sound are so bad that "the bad monitor mix" narrative is a staple of the metal drummer's folklore. In one extreme case, Terry's kick drums and snares were fed into the monitors and cranked up to be extremely loud; just laying down the groove with this mix was a joy. The club, however, didn't include the toms and cymbals in the monitor mix, and they became inaudible when the rest of the band played. As a result, Terry's ears were nearly ripped from his head when he just played time, but he couldn't hear himself at all when he went for a fill. This made for an extremely challenging evening. In other narratives, Terry, Keith, and John all spoke of "playing blind," nightmarish performances in which they could hear none of the other band members. In a worst-case scenario, Terry explained, the other players' parts would be very difficult to hear, and the distortions of kit and mix would be so great that the other players' movements would seem to be out of sync with the parts they were playing.

To overcome the distortions of monitor mix and kit, the players employed a variety of techniques. Like Jeff Johnston, all the players spoke of filling in the other musicians' parts in imagination when they were unable to grasp them in perception. Most important, the drummers expressed a keen awareness that they are the rhythmic touchstone of the band. In clubs with poor sound, therefore, they focus intently on keeping solid time and play simplified versions of their fills to guarantee that they discharge their duties as conductor. Where jazz drummers negotiate the time with the bass players and the others on the stand, the metal drummers are the unquestioned arbiters of the time. This, combined with the superamplified centrality of their parts in their experience, shows that the string player's practice of organizing attention that I have labeled "using the drums as a conductor" has its reciprocal in the drummer's experience. By keeping their parts solidly in the foreground of attention, listening to the others but remaining unswayed by their changes in tempi, and, as we shall see, taking primary responsibility for maintaining the integrity of the tune's overall form, the drummers organize their attention in a pattern I call "conducting the band."

Beyond their unwavering solidity and the problems of mix and kit, drummers do ideally want to hear the other players. When I raised the point, both Terry and John said they were familiar with the practice of tightly locking in the kick drums and bass lines. Both, however, explained that their music relies more on melodic parts in the bass and guitars and less on constant streams of eighth notes or quarters; when the bass does play a steady flow of grooving eighth notes, the bassists and drummers actively sync up with one another, but this only happens occasionally. When the bass does not provide a steady flow, bass drum and bass guitar form an intimate rhythmic counterpoint, Terry said. Those coordinations were less important to John, however, who explained that bass and vocals are rarely audible to him on stage. One of John's compositional concerns was for the pitch contour of his tom fills to correspond with the overall melodic contour of the guitar parts. Of the other instruments on stage, John was mainly aware of the guitars. When he could hear them, the coordination of these contours was important to his experience; when he could not, he would fill in the guitar parts in imagination and still highlight that coordination.

The cuing of section changes is another area in which the drummer's attention to the other band members is critical. All of the players said that, as the touchstone of the band, they must be sure of the form and cannot rely on any other player to indicate the number of repetitions of a part in a given section. At the same time the players also listen to the rest of the band to make sure that the ensemble as a whole is together. When the drummers do get lost, a variety of techniques help them to cue off the other players. Keith and Terry listen to their singers to orient them in the song; less frequently, the bass or guitar parts cue changes in the form or indicate the number of repetitions remaining in a section. Keith added that if the sound is particularly poor, he would watch the other players' fingers and habitual gestures to find his place. Frequently playing in situations in which no one else was audible, John tried not to rely on the others for cues. As the conductor of the band, John often worked cues into the basic composition of his drum parts. In rehearsal, as the band decided the number of repetitions for each part in a section, John would compose a slight variation to the groove or fill on the next to last repetition to cue the band to the sectional change. In one long section, for example, John's part called for a fill on the crash cymbal at the end of every four bars. To articulate the form more clearly for both himself and others, John would switch the fill from crash to china cymbal every other time.

The players' attention to themselves:
Protention, the body, and reflexivity

This last practice of cuing the form emphasizes the drummer's role as conductor. Of equal importance for the string players and the drummers are specific techniques of protention and counting. As the song is composed in the rehearsal room, some of the band's main compositional work revolves around deciding how many times to repeat a lick in each section and in what order the sections will be played. As the song takes shape in rehearsal, the drummers generally watch the other players and cue visually. But as the song becomes set, the players become more autonomous in their knowledge of the overall form. At first, the drummers often have to count the number of repetitions of the guitar lick in the verse, foregrounding that part in perception and mentally counting each repetition. As the players become more and more familiar with the tune, they are able to retain the entire section in the living present and "feel" their way through the section. The process of protending upcoming sections is as common to string players as it is to the drummers.

Whenever the term *feel* is used in academic description, the reader is often left with the impression that the experience "felt" is some pure quality, immediately accessible to the "native" but incomprehensible to the outsider. As a basic aspect of experience, however, nothing could be less exotic than protention. "Feeling the form" provides the perfect opportunity to demystify this concept and build on our earlier discussion of protention. To illustrate the practice of organizing experience in its processuality, take this basic blues progression in 4/4 time:

/C /C /C /C/ F/ F/ C/ C/ G/ F/ C/ G/

In this standard nomenclature, the area between the slashes represents a bar of four beats. This "score" instructs the musician to play the chord C for four bars; for this exercise, the reader may just sing the note C on each pulse. Next comes two bars of F, two of C, one of G, one of F, one of C, and one of G. The difficulty for a beginning musician comes in singing sixteen C notes without getting lost. The obvious solution is to count each note and change to F at note seventeen. This system works; however, the effort of mentally counting each sung note is a distraction from singing even as simple a part as the one specified here. After a number of repetitions, another solution is to accent the first of every four notes and perhaps count those as one, two, three, and four. The group of four notes can easily be experienced as a temporal whole, the procedure is simplified and the singer can concentrate more on the sound than the numbers. Finally, after singing through the form enough times most people are able to "feel" the four bars and change to the F at the right time without any difficulty.[6]

What is going on here? In the early stages of the exercises, the beginner has to make an effort of attention just to sing an even pulse and go to the correct note. As the part becomes more familiar, however, most people become able to broaden the temporal "focus" (Ihde 1976) of their experience to include a moment longer than a mere note. The ever-fleeting "now" is still the foreground of attention, but a greater number of notes in the receding past are able, *simultaneously*, to stay within experience as a temporal background; similarly, an ever-longer period of the future is able to lurk in experience as a future background.

The whole process of "feeling a bar" can be described explicitly: (A) The note on beat 1 is experienced in the present foreground while the potential notes on beats 2, 3, and 4 are experienced in the future background. (B) This process slides into that of experiencing the note on beat 2 in the foreground while the note on beat 1 is experienced in the past background and the notes on beats 3 and 4 are experienced in the future background. (C) This process slides into that of experiencing the note on beat 3 in the foreground while the notes on beats 1 and 2 are experienced in the past background and the note on beat 4 is experienced in the future background. (D) This process slides into that of experiencing the note on beat 4 in the foreground while the notes on beats 1, 2, and 3 are experienced in the past background. When the singer can grasp more than one bar (that is, when the singer can begin to feel the entire first four beats as a unit) the next step has occurred: (E) As note 5 emerges, the first four notes form a temporal gestalt, and, as a whole, serve as a past background to the upcoming notes of the melody.[7]

When 4-bar units are taken as a whole, the notes in experience, no matter how "physically" identical, are no longer the same. We have seen before how phenomena experienced in the background color and affect those simultaneously experienced in the foreground and form an experiential whole. The point is true temporally as well as spatially. When we no longer have to count, the notes of the fourth bar are experienced in the context of the past three bars, and that context affects and defines them in the same way that the context of the two oblong shapes define the center space in Rubin's Goblet. As the notes of the fourth bar are experienced as now, three bars' worth of notes lurk in the background as past, coloring the notes of the fourth bar and forming a short-lived whole. The past background colors the foregrounded notes and imparts an experienced quality of instability, a sense that notes are piling up and another section is due. This form in temporal experience and its associated quality is precisely what is meant above when the players say they "feel" the section changes.

All the players said that "just feeling" the section changes was their goal. Terry explained that in some complicated sections, feel (protentions) guided the way to a change in section, but another player's part, like a guitar fill or vocal line, would cue the exact entrance. John also preferred to protend section changes purely, but this is difficult to accomplish in long and repetitious parts; there, he would augment his protention by adding subtly different kicks or fills every four or eight bars to mark the time sonically. Abrupt changes in tempo and groove between sections are critical to metal, making cuing particularly important. Keith explained that if you reflectively or imaginatively try to construct the upcoming groove, you will get confused; instead, the best course is just to flow along with the part and feel the section change. Terry and John both explained that when sharp changes in tempo or groove were found in the music, a fill that employed rhythmic aspects from both time signatures could help to connect the sections, and both players pointed these out in their music. Similar techniques of protending, cuing, and counting were found among the singers and string players; while they do protend and cue off each other, the drummers are most important for their cuing, particularly in situations with tempo and groove change.

We now turn to the drummer's attention to other aspects of the self. The body plays a much greater role in the metal drummer's experience than that of any other musician with whom I spoke. Like Eric Gould, all three drummers spoke of the physical rigors of performance. They all hit their drums hard, and Terry and Keith both explained that long passages of alternating sixteenth notes on the double bass drums are an exhausting workout for the legs. Postural concerns are key to John, who said that a straight back and a good grip on the sticks is the key to flexibility and endurance; while this was a greater problem in the past, said John, he is now able to place body awareness almost completely outside his experience and monitor it only when it became problematic in performance. Keith often spoke of cramped hands and arms, and the importance of stretching before and after performances. Keith and Terry both explained that their energy runs down during a show and that they must monitor their endurance constantly on most nights. The body shifts from background to foreground as the players tire, Terry explained, and on some nights he may even play simplified versions of his parts if he is extremely worn.

Except for certain special cases, the metal players I spoke with largely find reflection on the stand to be an encumbrance. Though Terry and Keith improvise fills and kicks, neither reflect about them; they say that reflection only interferes with the flow of performance, and the complexity of their tunes makes plotting and planning impossible. Terry added that in past bands he would plan out complex fills to relieve the monotony of simple cover tunes. The one important place where reflection is embraced is in the guitar player's soloing. Like Eric Gould and Jerome Saunders, Lou and Dann spoke of reflective and nonreflective performance of both composed and improvised solos.

The players and the crowd: Affect and compelling attention

Affect plays a similar role in the experiences of commercial hard rock and heavy metal musicians. All the metal players felt that the affective component of the musical sound should be central for themselves and the audience. While Keith wanted the players and crowd to come away from the performance with thought-provoking ideas, all of the players said that a good performance was experienced as a flow of sound in which the emotional dimension is sharply foregrounded.

Lou, Dann, and Rob further said they were careful to attend to the audience throughout the show and that they gained energy from the crowd. While drummers also stressed the importance of getting energy from the crowd, a subtly different story emerges there. Keith cited the importance of attending to the crowd and getting energy from them. John agreed with these points; however, he warned that if players focused too much on the crowd, they might be tempted to perform the exaggerated stage behaviors typical of commercial hard rock, and their playing might suffer. Terry went further, explaining that though he gains energy from the crowd between songs and sets, during a song he tries to seal out their distracting influence.

Why are these drummers less focused on the crowd? Several reasons seem plausible. While none of the drummers I spoke with felt they had to attend actively to the tempo to keep the rhythm solid, the responsibility of keeping the band together could be one factor in limiting their attention to the crowd. A more important point is their location on the stage. While Bill Roth explained that the drummer's throne at a jazz gig afforded a particularly good vantage point from which to observe the crowd, Keith said that tucked in the back of the stage with lights bearing down on them, rock and metal drummers were frequently unable to see the audience members. Even if the players can see the crowd, their potential for interaction is severely limited by their position—seated behind an elaborate and obstructing kit in the back of a glarey stage filled with mobile, expansive singers and string players. Only the sound of the drummer's playing reaches the crowd, and little of the crowd reaches them. As a result, it is not surprising that the drummers are less interactive with their listeners.

The goal of compelling the crowd's attention was shared by almost all of the metal players I interviewed. Discussing one of his compositions, for example, Lou explained that the function of a certain part was to "grab the listener by the balls," while John spoke of grooves and fills so emotionally powerful that the audience is stirred to a frenzy. For the death metal players, as well as for Lou, moshing was seen as the ultimate expression of this compulsion. When I asked John if he felt that a crowd that moshed wasn't really listening, he said that just the opposite was true: a moshing crowd was one spurred to near riot by the music. Similarly, Lou explained that there was no rush like the one of playing to a crowd of people and inciting them to the controlled riot of the crazed mosh pit. More distant from the death metal scene, Keith presented a slightly different view. While he was eager to compel the audience's attention, he was more concerned with their intellectual, rather than physical engagement. Focused on elaborate band parts and thoughtful lyrics, Keith's ideal is to look out from the drummer's throne and see row upon row of rapt faces and tapping feet.

A musical portrait of Timmy Owens

To emphasize the commonalities between the players' experiences, I have arranged the data of this chapter by themes rather than individual players. To provide a more synthetic view, I shall close the discussion of metal with a detailed examination of the organization of attention by a single musician: Timmy Owens. During the period of my fieldwork, Timmy sang for Winter's Bane and British Steel, a Judas Priest tribute band. Around this time, the real Judas Priest lost their long-standing lead vocalist, and the remaining members of the group began to look for a new singer. In a real-life Cinderella story, an amateur video tape of Timmy made its way into the hands of the pioneering metal act; impressed with his performance, Priest offered Timmy an audition and he soon became their new singer. My discussion of Timmy's organization of attention focuses on his days in Ohio.

On stage, Timmy hears all the instruments. In the changing and pragmatic mix of his experience, the drums are most often focal, cuing Timmy to tempo and form. Within the kit, Timmy largely "cues off" of the kick drums and cymbals. Unlike other players, he does not rely on the snare for the time, because, he says, it is often used for fills. While Timmy does experience the guitar and bass with the drums, they are more backgrounded. He largely relies on the guitar to supplement the drums in cuing section changes and entrances, while the bass is located in the furthest background.

All of this fits with the data already presented, but Timmy's attention to himself provides some surprises. Singing on stage, his own voice is always held in or near the center of attention; the aspects of the line he is most aware of are the so-called embellishments as well as the vocal timbres and dynamics. On stage, Timmy employs a great variety of vibrati and is centrally aware of their rate and depth as well as changes in rate and depth. Timmy's dynamics and vocal timbres—ranging from pure tones, through a wide and precisely defined spectrum of raspier tones—are critical to the performance and vie for the center of attention. The more backgrounded aspects of his vocal line are intonation (which is precise and requires little attention), contour, and rhythm.

Listing the focal aspects of the line, however, elides much detail. In composition, Lou comes to Timmy with a series of composed guitar parts, a general idea of what the vocal line should sound like, and the topic of the lyrics. When Timmy composes his vocals, he defines not only the contour (the pitches and durations of the notes in the melody), but also the timbres and embellishments that each line must posses. While turns, glissandi, the location of vibrati, and other devices are precisely specified, the types of vibrato to be used in each situation are left open and emerge spontaneously in performance. In rehearsal he plans out the points when he will breathe. But composing for Timmy is much more than specifying a flow of pitches, durations, lyrics, timbres, and embellishments; as a phenomenon in Timmy's experience, each line has a specific affective quality. Timmy views the singer's job as closely related to that of the actor, giving voice to the words of the character in the song. "Singing with feeling," Timmy's main goal, requires him to perform a complex juggling act of attention, one that deserves consideration here.

It is the middle of a Winter's Bane song in the middle of a set at Ron's Crossroads in Akron, Ohio; Timmy has just sung a phrase and waits in the brief rest before the next one. The key to a good performance, Timmy explained to me, lies in the singer's preparation for each line, but this doesn't mean actively rehearsing the upcoming phrase; to do so would make a singer fumble. The key, he explained, is to orient oneself toward the feel and affective content of the upcoming phrase. To that end, Timmy listens intently to the other players' parts. They relax him and distract him from the pressure of singing the next line; more important, these parts connect him with the sound of the music and align his overall mood to that of the phrase he needs to sing. As his entrance approaches, he takes a good breath, allows the affective feel of the line to steal over him, and sings.

Initially, Timmy said that this process should ideally occur without any reflective monitoring: attention shifts from the sound of the band, to his breath, to his welling emotion, and, finally, to his effortless flow of action. But this ideal is not always realized. Throughout the performance, Timmy is chronically aware of his "energy level." Unlike other players who actively relax particular muscles or focus on postural concerns (hands, back, and so on), Timmy's main experience of embodiment is an overall feeling of vitality and strength. Pragmatically, he knows that that vitality determines when he needs to breathe and how high he will be able to sing. When he is feeling strong, his energy level acts as a defining background, coloring all of the focal experiences throughout the night. When he is feeling weak, Timmy actively monitors his energy level, shifting it from background to foreground between the phrases. He uses the information gained from this monitoring to determine if he can sing the upcoming line or if he needs to modify it by removing high notes or planning extra pauses for breaths. In the interview Timmy added that he also may reflect during particularly high-energy nights. To take advantage of his extra power he may plan out additional high notes, longer phrasings, and even entire new melodies. Not unlike the African American jazz musicians I interviewed, Timmy is always pushing the envelope of his performance.

Like all other rock musicians, Timmy is concerned with the audience; they give Timmy energy, and he "feeds off them." But Timmy's awareness of and interaction with the crowd in performance is more limited than that of the nondrummer rockers and metalheads I spoke with. First, in performance, Timmy dislikes interacting with the crowd on a one-to-one basis. As a listener, he feels uncomfortable when a musician makes eye contact or points him out; as a result, Timmy relates to the crowd as a whole, talking to the audience in general, gesturing broadly, and looking out across the entire room. Further, Timmy does not elicit direct give-and-take with the crowd during his stage patter. Afraid they won't respond, he rarely asks the crowd to sing along or shout. And while Timmy does have a variety of stylized stage moves, he quickly disappears into the back of the stage when he is not singing in order to give the other players the spotlight. Timmy describes his stage gestures as clarifications of the lyrics or illustrations of the character's intent. While Timmy does employ many of the stage moves and devices common in metal, he is more concerned with engaging with the music than interacting with the crowd. Nonetheless, Timmy is always aware of the audience between songs; during songs, they act as a defining background to his experience.

Conclusions

With this discussion of rock and metal in place, I can begin to tie together some broader themes. Even a quick review of the data reveals that there are culturally specific styles in the organization of attention. The jazz players lock in and negotiate tempo; the rock and metal players use the drums as a conductor. The African American jazz musicians employ reflection on the stand; the rock players avoid reflection. The jazz players invite attention; the rock and metal players try to compel it. Such data help us to achieve the ends of humanistic ethnography. When we understand how the players from particular scenes organize their attention, we get a clearer picture of their experiences. Listeners unfamiliar with these musical traditions can use this information to approach metal, rock, or jazz more intelligently; listeners familiar with the traditions can use this information to explore the unreflected upon aspects of their experience.

The data, however, also serve larger theoretical ends. By comparing across musical scenes, we can see the complex dynamics through which the players' organization of attention—seemingly the most idiosyncratic and personal of all things—is informed by their social context. In the simplest dynamic, the players' shaping of experience is influenced by their goals in music making, and these in turn are influenced by the scene to which the players belong and the larger society in which they are situated. It is certainly not an effect of individual caprice, for example, that all of the Akron jazz musicians want performance to be an effortless flow of experience unencumbered by reflection, while the Cleveland jazz musicians all prize reflection on the stand. The Akroners' avoidance of reflection is part of their broader rejection of the (perceived) artistic pretensions of 1960s-era post-bop, which in turn is informed by their age and generation. The African Americans' reflection on the stand is also a means to an end: the securing of ever-wider expressive vistas; this goal in turn is tied up with the art-music aesthetic of contemporary post-bop and the politics of culture in the African American community. The commercial hard rocker's attention to stage moves and the larger techniques of compelling attention are informed by their desire to create performances that depict celebrity, power, and fun; as the literature on Anglo-American popular music has shown, these goals are informed by the ideologies of consumption and youth in American culture and the entertainment industry that fosters them.

While this chain of influence from large-scale social context, to musical goals, to the organization of attention helps us see the links between the performance event and society, other, less straightforward dynamics exist that connect the players' organization of attention to elements of social life.

For example, no exegetic tradition or explicit ideology is necessary for the organization of attention to be informed by social context. None of the rock or metal musicians I spoke with ever had to be told to use the drummer as a conductor; the practice of using the drums as a conductor came about through a combination of the players' musical goals (the desire to produce a tightly coordinated band sound) and the practical exigencies of the performance situation (poor sound systems that make the drums the only consistently audible instrument). Similarly, "inviting attention" is not taught in jazz studies classes. Seeking an interested audience, but unable to perform their demanding jazz and monitor the audience's attention, the Akroners simply enter into the music and hope the crowd will join them. In this dynamic, the players' musical goals and the practical demands of the performance situation together inform the players' organization of attention. If, as I suggested in Chapter 2, we understand musical instruments, sound systems, club architecture, and decor as the media in the complex social interactions of engineers, club owners, musicians, and listeners, then we can begin to grasp the variety of levels of social context that can impinge on the organization of attention. While the players may only partially share larger social histories and musical goals, even the largest-scale social context may be consequential for the players' organization of attention, and all techniques of ordering experience are informed by the players' immediate and larger social lives.

By focusing on partial sharing and systematicity, I have emphasized the social dimension of the organization of experience. But to get a fuller picture, we must understand the organization of attention as a kind of *practice*, equally the result of the practitioners' agency and the social context. Viewing the organizing of attention as practice can shed light on a key concern of contemporary research: the problem of culture and agency. Culture is often understood as a system of rules, ideas, or guiding principles that somehow condition or generate perceptions, affective responses, thoughts, and actions; it is traditionally seen as autonomous from both specific individuals and their experiences. Against this conception of culture we have agency, usually understood as self-determined conduct brought into being by specific actors in time and space; behavior is an example of agency when, in Anthony Giddens's celebrated phrase, one "could have acted otherwise" (1979, 56). Given this, it would seem that culture and agency could not be more opposed. As subconscious structure, culture emerges from something beyond the individual—social history, macroscale social life, or its own superorganic realm—and defines or produces behavior in a determined fashion. In this view, agency, the epitome of microsocial phenomenon, is by definition the nondetermined or paradoxically self-determined. Because there is no question that the phrase "cultural differences" points to something real, the relationship between culture and agency seems genuinely problematic. The data on the organization of attention in the jazz and rock scenes are exactly the kind of information that would traditionally be taken as evidence of culture; as a result, we can use these data as a case study in the problem of culture and agency.

When we examine these phenomena, the first thing we see is that the organization of experience is something that is actively achieved. On the stand, Timmy Owens foregrounds the sound of the band between phrases, but he could have acted otherwise, focusing on the crowd or running the next phrase over in his imagination. The reality of agency is nowhere so clear as when we address our own organization of attention. At this very moment, the reader can focus on the words on this page, fade off into daydreaming, or put the page down and attend to something else altogether; while we do not have complete control over the organization of experience, our everyday life viscerally confirms the fact that we exercise some free play in this sphere. In fact, our voluntary organization of attention is an exemplar of self-directed conduct, and musicians are the unrivaled experts in bringing this skill to perfection.

The second point that arises from our discussion is that a person's social history and social context has an enormous impact on the way he or she organizes his or her experience. It is not the case that jazz and rock differ merely in the artifacts produced under the aegis of each genre. As we have seen, the techniques of the organization of attention are unique to each musical culture: invitation is unique to the jazz players, while compulsion is unique to the rock and metal players.

The main point is that culture is not some underlying scheme that determines action; culture must be understood as a description of the patterns of similarities and differences in the *practices* of concrete actors. The problem of culture and agency comes about when we mistake such patterns of practice for an autonomous entity. Focusing on the patterning of practices, it is easy to believe that that patterning exists independently of the practices that constitute it. But while practice is deeply informed by social context, it is also actively achieved, and to think that the pattern exists independent of the practices that make it up is to place the cart of description before the horse of the practices it is meant to describe. A physical metaphor will make the point clearer. Sound waves are patterns of vibration in the air. Each air molecule responds in the same way to the wave and merely transmits the wave along. As a result, the individual molecules are irrelevant to the larger pattern, and acousticians are able to talk about sound waves as independent of the particular molecules that bear them. As people, however, we are more than mere bearers of the patterns of culture. Even when unconscious habit or coercive power relations cause us to reproduce a pattern of practice, we have the potential to act otherwise. As a result, we cannot talk about patterns of practice independent of their practitioners. The concrete conduct of real-world actors constitutes all larger patterns, and culture is best understood as a partial description of the relative stability and systematicity of patterns of practice. Understood in this way, it is not some abstract, autonomous system of meaning called "culture" that causes us to reproduce past practices; on the contrary, it is the concrete past acts of others, mediated into the present situation by memory, expectation, and material conditions, that informs our acts and causes practices to be reproduced.

Such an argument may seem to push us toward radical individualism and to a view of agency as unconstrained whim, but this is not the case. All practices are *social* practices. Every thought we have and action we make emerges from a social history over which we have no control and into a social context of concrete others, present or mediated through the consequences of their actions. As I have shown above, the organization of experience—so clearly the agent's achievement—is deeply influenced by the agent's goals in music making. Such goals do not emerge from the tabula rasa of radical individuality, but are deeply informed by the agent's social world: the concrete history in whose consequences the agent is bathed, the other actors in the situation to whom the agent responds, and the larger society of distant others upon whose future experiences the present action may impinge. The social world thus forms a field, a chronic context that makes any radically individualistic social philosophy unsupportable. Even the most unique and idiosyncratic practice or belief is only unique and idiosyncratic given a context of others. If we found a thousand rock musicians who all tried to compel their audience's attention and only one rock musician who tried to invite attention, there would be nothing "less social" about the inviter and nothing "less agentive" about the compellers; all of the musicians are engaged in practice. The inviter is only idiosyncratic in the context of all the compellers, and his or her act of inviting attention is still an action oriented toward the social others of the audience. Conversely, the thousand rockers compelling attention show no less agency than the unique inviter; even if they take for granted the act of compelling the audience's attention, they still have the ability to do otherwise, and, therefore, are still agents.

In sum, the organization of experience, seemingly the most private and "internal" reality is deeply and essentially social. Though social, it is neither determined nor produced by an underlying cultural system, but is rather an action achieved. Though actively achieved, it is informed by the broadest historical and social context through the musicians' everyday life, their musical goals, and the exigencies of the performance event. These ideas are not intended to reconcile the notions of culture and agency; when we reconcile two opposites we affirm their existence. My point here is to suggest that both culture and agency are after-the-fact, scholarly abstractions from a more fundamental social reality: the constitutive practices of social actors.

The ethnography presented so far describes the overall organization of the participant's experiences in the event. But "the sound of the band" is not some empty placeholder to be foregrounded or backgrounded in the context of "the body" or "the audience." Any ethnography of music that seeks to evoke the player's experience must at some point turn to the musical sound. Chapter 7 examines Chris Ozimek's experience of his song "Turn For The Worse," focusing particularly on issues of tonality and temporality. Chapter 8 deepens these ideas and explores the issue of affect in music by focusing on Dann Saladin's experiences of his song "The Final Silencing."

SEVEN

Tonality, Temporality, and the
Intending Subject (1)
Chris Ozimek and "Turn for the Worse"

We now turn from the organization of the entire field of experience to the more narrow topic of the player's constitution of the musical phenomenon. An entire dissertation could be written on one type of musical phenomenon experienced by one player in one genre, and a trilogy would not be enough to scratch the surface of any single genre.

The field work for this chapter and the next one is almost entirely based on feedback interviews: I recorded music at shows, collected live and studio recordings that others had made, and discussed the tapes with the musicians. The participants and I collaborated on the choice of songs, the level of detail with which to explore them, and the topics to be discussed. Some players had no interest in choosing a song for discussion, while others were insistent that a certain song be examined carefully. The level of detail was especially critical to the interviews. With all of the participants except Eric Gould, Alvin Edwards, and Leonard Burris, I was able to discuss at least one song in detail. Here, the players and I would talk about almost every note that they played and constantly linger to explore the ever-changing relationship of their parts to those of the other players. Though it provided key ethnographic insights, this process was almost always exhausting and frequently tedious. As a result, for most participants I have only one or two songs discussed with this level of detail; in most cases, these data were supplemented with lighter discussions of several other songs. The exception to this is Timmy Owens; his monumental patience provided me with exhaustive descriptions of numerous songs, and this material will be the topic of an upcoming work.

The goal in each interview, which I emphasized to the musicians repeatedly throughout the course of our conversations, was to arrive at a description of the players' experiences of the songs. Because the musical styles and musical roles of each player differed so much, the interviews ranged broadly in the kinds of descriptions that emerged. The process of rigorously observing one's constitution of musical experience is often difficult; as a result, the interviews were partly guided by my specific questions and issues of concern. To encourage their active participation in the interpretive process, I balanced my own specific queries with open-ended questions. Further, the players themselves brought up many points that were not part of my agenda, and they were rarely shy about correcting my misinterpretations. Since experience is always richer than our reflective descriptions of it, the interviews often led to places that neither the players nor I could have predicted.

At its best, the process was a collaboration, but such collaborations are asymmetrical and complex. The constant goal in the process is to share the participant's experiences. On the one hand, this sharing can never be complete. Because both perceptual experiences and their interpretations are situational and historical, the participant's experience is never the same twice, and its richness always exceeds even the participant's best description. Further, the ethnographer constantly influences both the descriptions and the experiences themselves. On the other hand, partial sharing is possible; the same richness that makes experience exceed its descriptions enables the ethnographer to engage actively in the interpretation and even suggest lines of inquiry. Over time, the ethnographer can learn to engage with the world in ways similar to those of the participants. With enough background and insight, the ethnographer can point out aspects of the participant's experience that had always been present but were never thematized.

When we recognize both the partiality and the possibility of sharing, the asymmetrical relationship between research participant and fieldworker can be clearly understood. The research participant must always be made the focus in both the research and the writing; to do otherwise is either to pass from ethnography into autobiography or to indulge in the narcissism so frequently criticized in the academic literature of the 1980s and early 1990s. By the same token, the fieldworker's role must also be recognized. To obscure his or her role in the fieldwork itself is to deny the social nature of interpretation and the positive influence the scholar can provide in coming to understand experience. To obscure the researcher's role when the fieldwork is written up is to deny the inevitability of his or her part in the descriptions presented and to proffer a strange objective intersubjectivity that is both paradoxical and dishonest. In this chapter and the one that follows I shall try to negotiate this dialectic.[1]

As the research progressed I collected a wide array of information. Based both on my own interests and the prompting of my research participants, the feedback interviews and their ensuing descriptions could be divided into three very broad categories: those focused on tonality, those focused on groove, and those focused on melody. Because of the chronic problems of scope and richness described above, I am only able to explore the issue of tonality here.[2] As always, the first goal of this chapter is ethnographic; here, this means partially sharing Chris Ozimek's experiences of his song, with a special emphasis on his experiences of tonality. Beyond the ethnographic description, I shall show that experiences of tonality are an effect of the subject's management of protentions and retentions. Rather than treating the music as possessing some autonomous structure, I shall illustrate how experiences of tonality come about as the result of the subject's perceptual practices, at once actively achieved and deeply influenced by the subject's social history.

The descriptions of the musicians' experiences of musical sound outlined below are in no way intended to be complete. Musical sound is just one component, albeit the focal one, in a musical event, and no matter how critical the music is to the participant's experience, the rest of the situation must be described for a more full understanding. The broader contexts—contemporary and historical, musical and political—are critical for understanding experience because they influence both the goals the players and listeners pursue and the ways in which they constitute experience. Though critical to any study of music, descriptions of musical sound are only a starting point.

"Turn for the Worse": Transcription issues

After my interviews on biographical background, band history, the sociology of the local scene, and the organization of experience, as well as interviews with other Dia Pason members and participant observation at numerous rehearsals and performances, I began to talk with Chris about the details of the music and lyrics of his songs. We explored two songs in phrase-by-phrase detail, "Notch in the Bedpost" and "Turn for the Worse" and several other songs less thoroughly. Figure 10 is a traditional transcription of "Turn."[3]

To those with music-reading ability, this representation will no doubt provide some general idea of what is going on in "Turn for the Worse."

Figure 10. "Turn for the Worse"

Figure 10. "Turn for the Worse" (*continued*)

Figure 10. "Turn for the Worse" (*continued*)

Figure 10. "Turn for the Worse" (*continued*)

Figure 10. "Turn for the Worse" (*continued*)

Figure 10. "Turn for the Worse" (*continued*)

But there are problems with such a representation as well, the greatest of which is the objectivism inherent in all "textual" presentations. It is a basic conclusion of phenomenology that experience, as the grounds of all knowledge, is always a duality of subject and object; as a duality, both parts are necessary and each implicates the other. In perception, the subjective aspects of experience are the orderings of that experience, and these emerge as the subject engages with the world. The objective aspects of perceptual experience are in fact best understood as those aspects that are there for all capable and present subjects; the objective aspects are those that project their consequences into experience irrespective of the grasping subject. One major goal of phenomenological research into any domain of experience is to tease apart its subjective and its objective aspects and understand the dialectics that bind the two together; arriving at an understanding of the objective aspects is the goal, and not the beginning, of an investigation. Musical transcriptions such as Figure 10 are problematic inasmuch as they purport to be representations of the objective pole of experience, but instead smuggle in a variety of subjective (and culturally and historically specific) orderings, such as time signature or the construction of discrete pitches. Here, I shall explore the dialectics of subject and object in Chris's experience of this song.

A more substantial problem with such transcriptions lies not so much in their claim to objectivity, but rather the value of such a claim. The aim of ethnography is the sharing of the other's experience; by definition, the "objective" transcription is minimally useful, because by definition it removes all of the subject's ordering and grasping. I intend to go beyond both of these problems (the smuggling of the scholar's subjectivity into the supposedly objective transcription and the limited usefulness of the objective representation for ethnography) and explore how Chris engages with his composition and, in so doing, constitutes both his experience of music and his own subjectivity. After achieving this description of Chris's experience, I shall draw together the themes that emerge and apply them to broader theoretical issues in the organization of experience.

Background to "Turn"

"Turn" was written during the early 1990s, when Dia Pason's lineup included Chris, longtime drummer Steve Christen, guitarist Brian Exton, and an additional backup singer. Fresh from a series of personnel changes, this particular collection of musicians had never written a song together, and at one rehearsal the band sat down to compose a song from scratch. Chris told Brian just to play something, and he (Brian) improvised until he stumbled upon the intro lick (see guitars in bars 4 and 5). Chris liked this part, and as a whole the band searched around until they found parts to go with it. Verses and chorus were later put together in a number of interactions, and eventually the form was decided upon. At this point, the song only entailed the drum groove, the guitar part, and the guitar part's octave double in the bass.

After all the instrumental parts were written, Chris composed the lyrics and vocal melody simultaneously. With no idea what the song was going to be about, the vocal melody and lyrics "Slipping slowly" popped into Chris's mind; this became the third line of the verse. Singing this over, the lyrics and melody for the first line of the first verse came to him: "Sidewalk walking, round the blocking." At this point, Chris began to have a good idea what the lyrics might be about. Brian entered the band to replace the departing Ken Barber. Ken was dissatisfied with the progress of the band's career as well as their pop metal sound, and eventually quit to join Max Panic. Though all of the musicians are on good terms now, there was a short period of tension between Chris and Ken after the breakup, and as soon as he composed the first line Chris knew that he was writing about Ken. The rest of the lyrics and melody emerged quickly after that. Even with the instrumental and lead vocal parts composed, the song underwent refinement and modification. The chorus was originally one long vocal melody rather than the series of "layered phrases" that we shall discuss below. In composing the lead vocal part, Chris also knew the general sound and style he wanted in the harmony vocal parts; in rehearsal he taught the other players the harmonies, and these changed repeatedly to accommodate the various vocalists of the band's constantly changing lineup.

The performance of the tune transcribed above and discussed below took place during a transitional period in Dia Pason. No guitarist had been found to replace Brian, and Atomic Punk's guitarist KB temporarily took over that role to help keep his friends in Dia Pason playing out. By the time of this recording, Chris had passed through a number of standard phases in his appreciation of the tune. After his initial indifference to it, "Turn for the Worse" became one of Chris's favorite songs. Given a few months of performing the tune and teaching it to successive versions of Dia Pason, the honeymoon had passed, and Chris eventually became tired of "Turn." During the first months of 1993, Dia Pason went into the studio to record a CD; with the decline of pop metal and the rise of the heavier grunge sound, Chris put relatively little effort into the recording of "Turn," which by now had become an old tune. As a result, he was disappointed with the final version of the song and was not especially excited about the tune during its March 12, 1993, performance. Discussing the live recording I made of that performance, Chris remembered how much he used to like the song, and as we began our interviews he said that he hoped our discussion would refresh that interest.

Method and the experience of tonality

Though I shall explore a number of other topics in this chapter, the focus of my description of "Turn" is Chris's experiences of tonality. Understanding this part of the ethnography requires a familiarity with basic concepts from traditional Western music theory, and the reader unfamiliar with these concepts may wish to go back to my review in Chapter 4. The one foundational element of rock harmony not covered in that chapter is the power chord. A power chord is a chord composed of just the root, the perfect fifth, and the octave, although less frequently the tritone or perfect fourth can replace the fifth; the third, as well as the seventh and the upper extensions, are always absent from the power chord, making it neither major nor minor. The power chord is essential to most rock musics, and a distorted guitar playing power chords in the lower register of the instrument is a trademark sound of the genre.[4] The standard nomenclature for power chords is the Roman numeral or Latin letter of the chord's root followed by the Arabic number "5" (representing the fifth above the chord's root). Thus, A5 is an A power chord (A, E, ^A) while I5 is any power chord treated as a tonic. Without its third, the power chord may be heard as major, minor, or neutral, and this ambiguity is central to rock and metal harmony.

After years of listening to rock musics and finding chords and melodies that defied textbook harmonic analysis I resolved to explore the musicians' experiences of the songs and to achieve a descriptive, rather than perspective, approach to tonality. "Turn" offers the perfect opportunity for such a study. It is important to reiterate here that Chris has little formal music education, and there is little tradition of harmonic analysis present in the local commercial hard rock scene or Chris's personal experience. This, however, does not invalidate Chris's experiences of tonality. Though there are many musics in the world in which the topic of tonality is irrelevant, many Western European–based musics are in some way tonal, and some kinds of traditional tonality are present in Chris's songs. As a result, my goal was to operate empirically, exploring Chris's experiences of tension and release in the chords and melodies of "Turn for the Worse" and allowing his vision of the tonality to emerge in the interview process. If the idea was wholly inapplicable to Chris's experience, that in itself would be a significant discovery.

Unlike other research participants, Chris didn't feel comfortable with leading the conversation, and although he was very firm on many points and changed the direction of the discussion many times, he wanted me to start the examination of the tunes and initially guide the dialogue. Before we started and throughout the interviews, I explained to Chris that I was interested in the topic of tonality, and by that I meant how he experiences some chords or melody notes as sounding at rest, while others sound as if they are tending toward other chords or notes. At first Chris was not completely at home with the terminology; however, after I illustrated the concept with some /V7/ I/ cadences, the most basic tonal transition, Chris said that he was familiar with the experience of tonality and that we could proceed. I also reminded Chris that I was not interested in what the chords should sound like or whether or not he intended a certain tonal effect. I was only concerned with how he experienced the music.

This last point is vital. Action/intention models of conduct are so deeply ingrained that it is often difficult to conceptualize meaning independent from them. Time and again, critics scornful of the analysis of popular music will say, "Your little account may be all well and good, but did the musicians *know* what they were doing?" Such comments completely miss their mark. Valid descriptions of music are descriptions of the living musical form in the experiences of the performers, listeners, and composers. Such living forms need not be reflectively plotted and planned to be extant in experience; all that is necessary for an account to be true is that it describes the participant's perceptual experience, regardless of reflection or intention. A parallel from the visual arts will make the point. An artist painting a still life may stop and think, "I will juxtapose the purple of the eggplant with the bright yellow of the squash to create a stunning chromatic effect," and a scholar later describing the artist's experience could rightly observe that the juxtaposition of color was an important part of the painting. But to be a valid description, the painter need not have actively reflected in the manner described above. All that is necessary is that the painter juxtapose the colors—either in sensual imagination or in the perception emergent in painting. Phenomenological description explores experience as a whole, and reflective planning is only an optional accompaniment to immediate perception.

One final point must be explored before continuing. The phrase "Chris's experience of the song," may be misconstrued as referring to some underlying mental object that is merely performed in a variety of contexts. In fact, it refers to an ongoing series of experiences of composing, rehearsing, performing, and reflecting about "Turn." When Chris and I try to achieve descriptions of his experience of the harmony, we are actually creating new experiences in this series; by examining Chris's grasping of the song in the interview, the goal is to shed light on his grasping of the song at other events in the series. Aiming at such partial similarities of experiences across situations, it may seem that I am actually analyzing the song as an "underlying idea." In fact, the analysis itself is a spatially and temporally situated event that is consequential for other situated events but in no way escapes its own particular location in the history. Chris's constitution of some aspects of the song are stable enough across events to make such generalizations useful; tonality, the focus of this chapter, is one such aspect. Other dimensions of the experience of the song, such as affect, change much more radically across the different events in the song's history. Still other dimensions, such as vocal embellishments, are intentionally left open to improvisation and are thus created and grasped anew in each performance. The reader will bear in mind that though this chapter focuses on aspects of the music that are similar across situations, I am in no way implying that these are more important than ones that are less stable across situations and the tune's history.

Descriptions of "Turn"

Given these "hermeneutic rules" (Ihde 1977, 32) and my brief explanation of the idea of tonality, Chris and I got down to the work of describing musical experience. We began with the intro, and Chris said that A was the tonal center of those licks, that all the notes seemed to center on A; given the conventions of Western music theory this was no great surprise.

The verse, however, is more complex. Chris explained that there are four parts to the verse; bars 12 through 15 make up the first part. A chromatic run (bar 11) connects the introduction, which centers on A, and the first line of the verse, with its vocal melody set against a D chord in the guitars; this is followed by a guitar and bass unison melody and then another vocal part with a D chord beneath. At first, I asked Chris what the tonal center of the verse was; he quickly responded that because the bass was "riding" on D, it must be D. Feeling that Chris might be mechanically applying a definition of tonality more than he was attending to his experience of the song, I responded that he could ride on D for an entire song and still hear it as the IV chord of the A. Chris listened to the part again, and he said that throughout that first line, the D chord feels stable and does not sound like it wants to move back to the A.

Elaborating the point, I referred to the chromatic run that leads us into the D. I explained that in my experience, the run in this context sounds as if it shifts the entire song to a new place, revving up the energy and kicking us powerfully into the verse. Chris thought this over and then strongly agreed. Referring to one of his other songs, Chris explained that he used the timeworn device of a half-step key change in the out-choruses to crank up the song's energy and bring it to a climax; the chromatic run in "Turn" achieved the same effect, he said, pushing the song to a higher energy level, but on the scale of a single section (the verse) and not the entire composition. Chris went on to explain that he likes to vary the parts of songs and make the energy levels change between sections to keep the music interesting. Though he had never articulated this interpretation before, he agreed wholeheartedly with my idea that the chromatic run and the move to D push the song into a new, higher, stable energy level.

Pushing the point further and bringing it back to the question of tonality, I asked again if this D chord feels like the IV chord of a tonic A or if it feels like a I chord on its own. Chris said that on stage, when he has finished singing the first vocal phrase (bars 12–13), he jumps away from the mike to allow the audience's focus to shift to the guitar; then, when the second vocal phrase of the verse comes up, he moves back to the mike to sing. As a result, he said, the vocal phrase with the D chord (bars 12–13) and the guitar part (bars 14–15) feel very distinct. Given all of this, we concluded that moving into the verse, D was the tonal center while it lasted.

Of course, as we observed above, tonality is more than tonal center; tonality entails scale and chord quality, as well. Turning to the vocal melody, the pitches all surround D, and again Chris and I found more evidence to support the contention that we are in a form of D. The pitch inventory gives us 4 Fs, 3 Ds, and a C. The guitar plays the standard rock power chord: a D with no third. I asked Chris if this chord implies a D-major, a D-minor, or suggests no third at all. To explore the point, I played the part three times while Chris sang—once with a D-minor, once with a D-major, and once with a D power chord. Chris was adamantly opposed to the minor chord, and said that either the major third or the power chord was fine.

Noting that he sings an F in the melody, I observed a contrast between the pitches of the line and those of the chord (that is, the chord's lack of F or F-sharp). The flatted third is a cornerstone of the blues and has been thoroughly assimilated into commercial hard rock as well. I offered that the flatted third is a classic tension note borrowed from the blues, and Chris agreed. This blues embellishment will be critical for our understanding of the idea of the listening subject below, but the foregoing is sufficient for the present purposes of ethnographic description.

The lyrics of this line and the details of the vocal melody would be the next logical aspect of the song to explore; while this would enrich our ethnographic understanding of the song, it also distracts us from the theoretical aims of the chapter. Thus, I turned instead to the next phrase, the guitar and bass fill. As a melody played in octaves without accompanying chords, the part's tonal and harmonic implications are more broad and open than those of the first line of the verse. Each note could be harmonized as a chord, the entire fill could be one harmonic period, or any number of tonal and harmonic implications could be present in Chris's experience of the part. To tease out that experience, I asked, "If you were doing an acoustic version of this song and a guitar player was to play chords against this line, what would be played?" After a little guitar and bass experimenting, Chris quickly concluded that an A-major or A power chord would ring through this part. Given the presence of a flat seventh in the pitch inventory, I asked if the A dominant would work, and Chris said no.

The various descriptive elements found in the preceding paragraphs require synthesis. Observe that A is the tonal center of the melodic part in bars 14 and 15. As such, the A is heard as most at rest, while the C is heard as a blues alteration of the C-sharp third, and the G is heard as the flat-seventh scale degree. Little questioning was required to reveal that Chris hears the part as a melody; thus we must understand that the C is protended when the first As and Gs emerge, just as the As and Gs are retained when the C is played. Similarly, little questioning was required to reveal that Chris hears bars 14 and 15 as a melodic *phrase*; thus we must understand that the flux of those bars is heard as a processual unit, a series of emerging events that are all conjoined.[5] Further, the A's centrality and the implicit scalar quality of the line are present in each note; indeed, the tonal implications of each A, G, and C *make up* that tonality.

Connecting this with earlier material, bars 12 and 13 of the verse are played over a D power or major chord; recapitulating our earlier conclusions, we recall that the A chord here would normally be a V chord of the I D, or itself could be a I chord of which the D was a IV. Chris, however, hears bars 12 and 13 as somewhat autonomous from bars 14 and 15, and though the mere note choices do not specify a new tonal designation, bars 12 and 13 are heard as two bars in D major, while bars 14 and 15 are heard as two bars in A major.

After the first guitar fill, the chords move back to a D power chord, which moves us into the second part of the verse, bars 16 through 19. Given the foregoing, it is no surprise that the new D chord is heard as its own area once again, with neither the A area of bars 14 and 15 retained as a V nor the present Ds heard as a IV. The melody here rides on an F note for the two bars, shifting only to an E at the end of bar 17. Again, I played while Chris sang, and he concluded that the chord is a D major or D power. As a result, Chris agreed that the F is to be heard as a blues alteration, a flat three tension against an implicit F-sharp, in the D major or a independent flatted third, free from any implications of the neutral D power chord.

Chris and I were not able to completely describe bars 18 and 19. Another melodic guitar and bass fill, the assertions about melody and melodic phrase applied to bars 14 and 15 also work here, but the tonality of these bars was more difficult to describe. With little listening, Chris quickly lighted on the idea that the first four and a half beats all emerge under the aegis of an E power chord; however, the second half of the melody, which descends from C to G, was more complex. I played a number of chords against bar 19, all of which grated against the harmonic implications of the line, said Chris. Pushing, I played a chord on each beat and other combinations; the part in Figure 11 is the one that Chris said fit the best. While this description was close, Chris was not fully satisfied by our account, but no more effective description could be obtained. Given my traditional theory

Figure 11. Approximation of the harmonic implications of the second fill in "Turn"

background, I had supposed that this series of chords was in some way leading to either the A or the D, but Chris stamped out this reading. He explained that the 2-bar melodic fill had no tonal implications and pointed to nothing outside bar 19.

Because, in Chris's experience, the melody notes are all heard against or imply the E power chord, we are safe to infer that E is the root of the chord, the B is a chord tone, the A is a scalar tone and the G is either a blues alteration against an implied E major or a free third against an ambiguous E power chord. What we are unable to do is determine if the E chord implied in this bar is a I chord, IV chord, V chord, or serves any other function in any other broader key area. Further unclear is what tonal quality and implication the implicit C, G/B, A, and G might have. If I sing the melody slowly to myself, I can hear the C and the G both as I chords when they appear, but my experiences are only relevant to the discussion inasmuch as I am able to share Chris's experience. As James observed (1974, 48), all research is guided by the researcher's allegiance to one of two distinct and competing ends: garnering truth or avoiding falsehood. Given the practical limits placed on the research by the participant's patience and schedule, and having no pressing need to draw hasty conclusions, I shall leave the point unresolved. We can note, however, that Chris was always concerned with avoiding tedious repetition in his songs; distinct from but harmonically related to the first fill, these bars fit in with Chris's goal.

More than any other part of the song, the third and fourth sections of the verse are tied to the vocals and the meaning of the lyrics. In bars 20 and 21, the D power chord returns; an area unto itself, it is neither implied by the previous, difficult-to-interpret fill nor leads into the A area fill in bars 22 and 23. The vocal part descends chromatically from D to B-natural; the D chord is clearly a I, either power or major, and the melodic line also centers on D. Chris observed that the descending line's contour mirrors the lyrics: "Slipping slowly." The return to the melodic fill in bars 22 and 23 again places us in the new key area of A. The final section of the verse again involves a melody centering around D. The guitar descends in power chords from D to C, B, and B-flat. Here Chris intended for the music to sound as if it were "falling apart;" Ken, he said, played some "sick" sounding chords, and Steve played out-of-time fills to give a more disturbing effect. The

March 12, 1993, performance didn't employ these "sicker chords," and because the analysis of the changes that KB played is similar to that of the changes in the chorus, I shall move on to that analysis directly.

Up to this point, there are few tonal relationships between the chords. The A and D both form discrete areas, and the reader may be inclined to believe that Chris either did not understand what I meant by "tonal center," or the very concept of tonality itself was irrelevant to his experience. The chorus contradicts those assertions. The changes to bars 28 through 30 (the first three bars of the chorus) are some of the most familiar in contemporary rock, D5/ B-flat5/ C5, while the melody circles around the pitches E, F, and D. At first no surprises are present. In bar 28, Chris agreed that the D note is a center for the melody, and as above, the quality implied by the power chord is either D major or the power chord itself. As such we are forced to describe the F note in the melody as a blues alteration against the implicit major third or a minor third against the neutral power chord. In the chords, Chris agreed that the D is a I; revealing his ability to hear tonal relationships across chords, Chris clearly indicated that the B-flat and C chords both were also part of the D area. As such, Chris hears the B-flat and C chords as flat VI and flat VII chords respectively, tension chords that imply and forcefully push us back to the D as I.

But the part is significantly more complex than it appears at first. Recall from the above that during bar 28, Chris heard the D chord as a major or power I; as a result, the scalar quality present in the experience of the chords is of D major. At bar 29, the B-flat implies the D. But what kind? The i, flat VI, flat VII (that is, the turn around to the natural minor one) is one of the most common in rock.[6] But this is not a sufficient description of the experience, because Chris strongly maintained that the D is not minor. I, flat VI, flat VII is another common chord change in Western music; here, the area is D major throughout, but the flat VI and flat VII are substituted from the minor to give the composer greater melodic latitude. Since we know that the D chord is a power chord or a major, we would seem to have our answer. We do not. Listening and attending to our experience, Chris and I felt that the B-flat was indeed a flat VI pushing us to the D, but the D it implied was a D minor and not a D major. In Chris's experience, the tonal implication of the piece changes from D major to D minor as we move to bar 29; the C chord is a flat VII of a minor D, not a major D. Given this, the F note in the melody at bar 28—which had been a blue note against the implicit F-sharp of the unstated D major—becomes in bar 29 the scalar (minor) third of the implicit D minor, and it retains that scalar quality in bar 30 against the C.

Before going on, we must note that the I/ flat VI/ flat VII/ could be misunderstood as a deceptive cadence, that is, a series of chords implying a minor i and surprisingly resolving to a major I. This description is inapplicable for two reasons. First, the B-flat and C do not end up leading to a D, but a G. The D major *precedes* the B-flat, and, as such, if any deceptive reinterpretation is present, it is that of the B-flat and not the C. More important, however, the term *deceptive cadence* implies a great surprise when the deceptive chord emerges; here the B-flat is no great surprise. Chris explained that one of the aims of this song was to get an aggressive, minor feel without blasting the listener with minor progressions. Though the F melody note against D power chord is a blues alteration and not a minor third proper, it paves the way for the B-flat chord and the minor tonality. This passage in no way represents a deceptive cadence because no surprise shift to major, or minor, is present.

By bar 31, the B-flat and the C do not lead us to the D, as I or i, but to the G; simultaneously, the melody resolves to the G's fifth, a D note. Chris and I quickly concluded that the G is not minor, but how does the G relate to the other chords? When writing the tune, Chris had no reflective plans on how the tonality should operate, but he was adamantly opposed to the tedious repetition of D, B-flat, C, D that dominates so many rock songs. To avoid that repetition, Chris moved to the G, and listening, he explained that the G is less a IV of any D, and more "by itself." In traditional music scholarship, the IV is seen to be the second most stable of all the chords derived from the major scale, and I was concerned that Chris might mistake the relative stability of the IV for the autonomy of a brief change in key area. This fear was quickly dispelled, however, when we examined the return to the D; that change, Chris said, is felt as a bit of a surprise, which supports the description of the G as a brief, independent area.

Moving through bars 32, 33, and 34, we see the earlier functions repeated: the D is a I with blues alterations tensing against it, and when the B-flat emerges it is grasped as a flat VI chord of D minor. The move to F, the relative major of D minor, is a standard one in rock; such shifts between relative major and minor are usually used to mark off different sections of a song, and the move is slightly more unusual in the middle of a chorus. Little listening was required to achieve the description that the F is indeed heard as a I, and as a result, the B-flat's implications of D minor is "surprisingly" resolved to the relative major. Interestingly, the melody descends diatonically from a G to end on the D pitch, and Chris asserts that the E and F are definitely heading toward the D. This "heading toward" gives the D a tonic stability that is in direct contradiction to the tonicity of the F as major I; I asked Chris about the D over the F chord, and he said that all that matters is that the parts do not clash. A harmony vocal part added to the line involves a unison E over Chris's E and a F over the D, giving more weight to the F as tonic. Interpreting this section, I asked Chris if there can be relative independence of the tonal implications of the vocal line and the chords as long as there is no strong dissonance; Chris saw no reason to oppose this view, but he was also was quick to assure me that none of this was planned.

Concluding the first chorus, the vocal melody is sung staccato so as to represent a clear break between the end of the chorus and the bass fill that leads the song into the second verse. In the second chorus and out-choruses, the bass fill is replaced with a G chord, which Chris says operates in the same way as the G in bar 31, that is, as a brief key area. Interestingly, the melody of the backup vocals descends from F to D. I did not explore the point with Chris at the time, but it is no wild hypothesis to guess that E and F lead us to a D as center, and that again we have a disjunction in the tonality of the vocal line and chords.

Implications of the ethnographic description for tonality, temporality, and the subject

The foregoing description is the ground-level data of a phenomenological ethnography of musical sound; more than mere description of experience, however, the data can be used to explore the notion of tonality.

As music theory is commonly taught, consonance and dissonance are inherent aspects of musical sound, and the tonal relationships in a piece somehow emerge from the inherent structure of the composition. Assuming the existence of such relationships rather than interrogating experience, such an orientation is antiempirical and problematic. Husserl's first discovery in establishing a radically empirical philosophy was that all experience involves subjective and objective poles; ignoring either one severely compromises the integrity of the research. Applying this to the present inquiry, we discover that tonality—the centrality of a pitch in a melody or chord progression, the scalar implications inherent in the experience of a part—is an extant phenomenon; however, tonality is a property of the subject's experience as a whole and not merely its objective pole. The objective aspect of experience here refers to "the notes themselves." As always, the objective is best understood as just exactly those aspects of the world that are there for any capable subject engaged with, or "grasping," the world. Tonality is not a property of the objective notes themselves, but of the subject's engagement with those notes. In the Ozimek data, we see that the D chord in the first bars of the verse (bars 12 and 13) could have been a IV of A, that the notes in the first fills (bars 14 and 15) could have implied an A major or A minor, that A could have been a V chord or a I chord, and so on. In other words, what we see is that the notes never fully specify, never fully determine the experience. What determines the experience is the subject's grasping of those notes.

But "the subject's engagement" or the "subject's grasp" is a broad metaphor. Can we be more specific about what this means? When Chris hears the B-flat chord in the second bar of the chorus (bar 29) as a flat seven, what we really mean to say is that he hears it as a tension that *implies* a resolution to the D major. Speaking in phenomenological and concrete terms, we see that to *imply a resolution of the D chord means to hear the absence of the D,* that is, *to protend the D chord while the B-flat is sounded.* Chris's experience of tonality is thus his experience of a chord in the moving now-point colored by the chords held in protention and retention, and his perceptual engagement is in fact the conjunction and disjunction of immediate, retained, and protended experiences. Phenomenologists refer to the dynamic gestalt of experiences protended, experiences held in the now-point, and experiences retained as "the living present"; all the experiences we have are situated within this temporal "thickness." What I suggest here is that *tonality and harmonic function are an effect of the organization of phenomena in the living present.*

The D and A chords in the verse illustrate these ideas with greater nuance. What is meant by hearing the D as IV and the A as I, the D as I and the A as V or, as in Chris's actual experience, hearing both A and D as I chords as long as each lasts? Hearing the D as IV in bar 12 would mean to be holding the A tightly in protention and retention, waiting for the return of the A with tense expectancy. Hearing the D as I in bar 12 would also mean holding the A in retention, but in a very different way; hearing the D as I versus hearing it as IV differ in the way that the A is held in retention and protention. When the D is held as IV, the A is more intensely present in retention and protention, pushing for its return to the now-point. When the D is held as I, the A is still held in protention and retention but less intensely; it is held as mere possibility, as an occurrence that would not surprise if it arose but is not so urgent a potential occurrence that it may come about at any moment.

An example modified from Ihde (1976) will make the point. I am sweeping the floor while waiting for an important phone call; as I sweep, the patch of floor just out of sight and the sound of the bell are present to protention and retention in very different ways. The sound of the ringing bell is present in protention alone and quite intensely; its intense presence in protention as a possibility and its absence in the now-point and retention makes the overall experience of the living present quite anxious. Alternatively, as I look about my feet and sweep, I of course protend and retain the patches of linoleum that I cannot see. These, however, I protend and retain differently from the protention and retention of the bell; I protend them as mere possibility. They lurk with no special intensity and may emerge into temporal centrality at any moment. Applying this example to "Turn," the tension and intensity of the V chord in protention parallels that of the bell. Both color the phenomena in the now-point with anticipation; the light intensity and mere possibility of the IV chord in protention parallels that of the floor just out of my view.

But what are we to make of the situation in which both A *and* D are I chords? Here James's (1967) ideas of conjunction and disjunction are critical. If we hear the A as V and the D as I, the various moments of the living present are tightly bound to one another. When the D arrives as I, the recent A is retained as a resolved past, and that retention strongly colors the A in the now-point; this tight figure/ground of now-point and retention conjoins the elements of the living present. In the case where the A and D are both held as I, there is a greater disjunction in the living present. When the D is first grasped as I here, the A lurks dimly as a possibility in protention and retention. When the A as I emerges, however, the just past D is disjoined— separated and held away—from the now-point. When the D reemerges, the just past A is similarly disjoined. Separated from one another, the past chords do not color the present chord with their typical tonal implications.

In sum, our experience of tonality is an effect of our organization of the living present, our engagement with the world in its processuality. Some readers may accuse me of straying into metaphysics with this idea; the charge might read that tonality is experienced as a quality, and my application of Bergson and Husserl treats these experiences as an epiphenomenon of some extra-experiential reality called the "organization of the living present." The charge is false, I believe, but it illustrates an important point. There is no doubt that tonality, tension, and release are lived experiences; however, careful phenomenological description also reveals that musical experience is composed of protended sound, sound in the now-point, and retained sound. It is only when we focus intently on the objective pole of experience, rather than the experience as a whole, that the full breadth of the living present is obscured. Saying that experiences of tonality are an effect of the organization of the living present is not metaphysical, because "the organization of the living present" is simply the experienced arrangement of temporal phenomena. Just as one's experience of the plus sign (+) is an effect of the experienced arrangement of horizontal and vertical lines in lived space, one's experience of tonality is an effect of one's experienced arrangement of sound in lived time. Both the phenomena and their arrangement are present in experience, and the experienced quality of tonality is an effect of that arrangement.

A more important point must be clarified, however. All music scholars know that tonally ambiguous musics exist, and it could be argued that the reality of ambiguous tonality does not preclude the possibility that there are musical "texts" that do fully define harmony. As a result, this view suggests, tonality is not merely an aspect of the subject's perceptual practices, but is actually inherent in the sound itself. This critique is mired in objectivist views that do not appreciate the complex dialectic between the subject and the world referred to by the passage from Merleau-Ponty quoted in Chapter 1. As Ihde shows in *Experimental Phenomenology*, to say that experience depends on the subject's grasping of the world is not to confuse perception and imagination. Ihde explores multistable figure/ground drawings, such as the Rubin's Goblet diagram. Using what Husserl called "variational method," Ihde guides the reader through different ways of grasping the image and shows that the experience is not fully determined by the "objective drawing." At *the same time*, however, he shows that neither is the experience a mere imaginative caprice; it is hard to see a map of Connecticut in Rubin's Goblet and still claim to be engaged with an other or constituting a perception.[7]

Returning to this potential critique of my phenomenology, I observe, as Ihde does, that, of course, the thing which is there for everyone, "the objective musical sound," limits the kinds of experience one may make of them. Hammering away on the D note on the melody at bar 12 leads the listener to hear the D as I, while Chris's jumping away from the microphone cues the audience to hear the different parts of the verse as different areas. The point is *not* just that others use our actions, as mediated in sound and gesture, to partially share experience; the point is that the tonality and musical sense is inherent in the *subject's lived experience* and not some putative metaphysical realm of the objective text. To posit tonality is to posit a subject grasping musical sound and hearing tensions and releases. To say the tonality is objectively in "the music" is really only to say that any subject listening to the music will always experience the tonality one way, that the tonal cues of rhythm, accent, gesture, and so on allow no multistability. However, such monostable cases, be they many or few, always rely on a musical tradition of norms and commonplaces of tonality, and musical tradition itself implies the existence of a perceptual subject thus acculturated.

Even setting aside this defense, however, we can ground the dialectical impulse of phenomenology and the critique of the objective text in philosophy rather than ethnography. The existence of cues and strictures in musical sound, even if they could be inherent in the sound and independent from a musical history and musical culture, still requires the existence of a subject to grasp them, to animate them in the flux of the living present. It is the living present itself that ultimately necessitates that our study object be the full experience of the subject; it is the living present itself that ultimately nullifies the idea of "text" or "musical sound itself" as anything but the objective pole of experience. Tonality only exists in a living processual present, in a now melting into a recent past and accepting a near future. Without a subject there is no now; no present, past, or future; no here nor there. Text, musical sound, and, most broadly, objective reality, no matter how limiting to experience, all require a subject for their constitution. Tonality implies a temporal subject.

By the same token, we must not misread phenomenology's emphasis on the subject and fall into a subjectivist metaphysics. The subject is no underlying principle or subconscious, generative system; the subject is present in experience as the ordering of the phenomena. This is true of all experiences, although in daily life we usually background the subjective pole of any phenomena. Here, we must not confuse two different senses of the word "subject." At any given moment I may experience my body or my thoughts as "self"; a moment later, I may distance myself from my body or thoughts and experience them as merely "mine." As James observed in *The Principles of Psychology* (1983), this marking of individual phenomena as "me" or "mine" is highly contingent. But there is another sense of the word "subject" that is not contingent. All experience comes about as an interaction of a subject with an object; as a result, the subject is present in experience as the arrangement of phenomena. In visual perception, for example, the subject is embedded in the experience as the perspectival arrangement of the visual objects, as the organization of the visual field into objects near and objects far away. Understood in this way, the emphasis on the subject is not metaphysical but fully experiential.

Shifting back from philosophy to ethnography, we can of course recognize that all such musical cues to tonality are specific to particular musical traditions at particular moments. With the ethnographic goal of partially sharing experience in mind, we must not merely focus on the presence of culturally specific cues; we instead must focus on the subject's employment and interpretation of those cues. Perhaps more important, we must look at how implicature and imaginative phenomena are mixed into perceptual experience and influence the meanings produced. In the Chris Ozimek example, the major sound of the third-free power chords (even in the presence of minor thirds in the melody!) shows how important such implicatures and imaginative phenomena are.

Setting aside the broader implications of these data, a world of more specific concerns about the processual dimension of experience opens itself up to us. For example, the analysis given above explores the living present on the short temporal span of two or three bars, but the span of the living present is clearly much wider. As we listen to the chord changes in a composition from a familiar genre, we are also aware of our location in the section and the location of the current section in the overall form. These levels in turn are related to our experience of previous performances of the song. For example, the reader will surely have observed that repeated listenings to a song may make surprising chord changes less shocking; alternatively, our ability to frame experience tightly enables us to be surprised by an unexpected chord, even after repeated listening. These points place limits on the accuracy of descriptions that do not explicitly account for the changes that occur in the research participant's engagement with the song from one event to the next. Some aspects of the song, however, are more stable than others; thus, while no two of Chris's experiences of "Turn" are identical, he does not seem to grasp the tonality of the piece in substantially different ways across the series of experiences (although that may have been changed by the fieldwork process itself). Chapter 8, focusing on death metal guitarist Dann Saladin, will explore both the organization of the living present on larger temporal scales and the impact of the personal and historical past on situated musical experiences. Comparing Dann's and Chris's experiences across musical cultures will reveal the social base of temporal engagement and hint at the limitless possibilities of temporal form. With history and society always come issues of affect and purpose, and, toward the end of Chapter 8, I shall begin to draw all of these issues together.

Some additional ethnographic notes

The description thus far covers the tonality of the main sections of the song and provides enough raw material to help us ground the idea of tonality in the actions of the engaged temporal subject. What it leaves out, however, is a detailed discussion of Chris's broader goals in music making and his surrounding social context. In an upcoming work, I shall explore these points by looking at the links between perceptual practices, musical purposes, and ideas about gender and masculinity in American commercial hard rock. Also excluded in this chapter are a host of other aspects of the musical sound of the tune. An exploration of these would have provided the reader with a fuller sharing of Chris's musical experiences, but the endemic problem of richness (that is, that experience always exceeds its descriptions) prevent us from exploring these points in detail. A brief discussion, however, will give the reader some glimpse of the richness of this music.

Largely similar across performances are the instruments' timbres. Playing and hearing "Turn" on March 12, 1993, at Flash's, Chris didn't merely hear power chords, but the carefully groomed distortion of Al's Jackson guitar playing full blast through his Marshall stack. The distorted sound fleshes out and energizes the three-note power chords and unison lines, and the meaning of these guitar timbres—heavy, sustaining, and powerful—is an important area for exploration (see Walser 1991). The drum groove also is essential for providing texture and rhythmic impetus in the song. Steve's unusually powerful rhythmic feel and use of extra large bass drums gave Dia Pason a heaviness that contrasted sharply with both Chris's sweet, melodic vocals and the other bands of this style. The guitar timbres, vocal timbres, and rhythmic feels represent a vast area for ethnographic inquiry.

I explored above the note choice and phrasing of Chris's vocal melody, but I set aside the interplay among the lyrics, embellishments, and vocal timbres; among these features, "form-function relationships" abound. For example, the first line of the song "Sidewalk walking, round the blocking" refers to Ken's leaving Dia Pason and taking a step backward in his career; Chris explained that to support that meaning he adds a taunting, bratty nasality to his voice at the beginning of the phrase and a falloff at the end of the line. Line 2 accuses Ken of insulting Chris behind his back—"Turn your back and look who's talking." Chris stated that he spits out the first six words on the downbeats, as if underlying the accusation with an index finger thumped against Ken's chest; to invoke the greater aggressiveness of this line, Chris explained that he shifts his vocal quality to a rougher, harder-edged tone. Chris's expert manipulations of timbre and embellishment are critical to his experience and help to give the song its affective power.

Other compositional devices are key to Chris's musical experience. For example, the repetitive, undulating contour of the chorus melody, originally sung by Chris alone, was intended to give a "roller coaster-y" or "drunken" effect, a sonic form mirroring Ken's circuitous movements from band to band. Employing devices like call and response and layering (bars 28 through 31), or multipart expansion (bars 33 and 34),[8] Chris uses a wide palette of arrangement techniques to keep the song fresh and interesting. Such arrangements are the parts of the song that Chris most fervently hopes the audience will notice and the parts he monitors most closely in the other players' performances. Each of these devices—as well as their complex dynamics of progressive and situational change across performance events—could act as the object of a phenomenological ethnography.

Tonality, Temporality, and the Perceptual Subject (2)

Dann Saladin and "The Final Silencing"

The discussion of Chris Ozimek's "Turn for the Worse" illustrated how tonality, seemingly an inherent aspect of the musical sound, is actually an effect of the subject's practices of perceptual engagement. But the complex dynamics of tonality and the endless variety of temporal forms in experience can be better appreciated if we explore some musical experiences from a different scene. To that end, I now turn to a music that is as far away as possible from Chris's and yet still falls under the general rubric of "rock"— death metal.

Some background to "The Final Silencing"

By the time I began interviewing Dann, Sin-Eater, the band with which he originally wrote and performed "The Final Silencing," had been broken up for six months. Though Sin-Eater was in the process of writing other songs when the musicians went their separate ways, "The Final Silencing" (henceforth FS) was the last song they composed and performed and by all accounts was their finest piece. Again, to orient the reader, I have provided a transcription (see Figure 12).[1] Dann's initial impulse was to write a song featuring the keyboards he had recently bought. He composed most of the sections of the song on his own, and during the first rehearsal of FS he got only as far as teaching the other players the parts. Dann missed the second rehearsal; in his absence the other players did the bulk of the arranging work. Later they showed Dann the order and bridging materials they composed, and during the next few rehearsals the song's form was finalized.

The Final Silencing

Figure 12. "The Final Silencing"

201

Figure 12. "The Final Silencing" (*continued*)

Figure 12. "The Final Silencing" (*continued*)

Figure 12. "The Final Silencing" (*continued*)

Figure 12. "The Final Silencing" (*continued*)

Figure 12. "The Final Silencing" (*continued*)

Figure 12. "The Final Silencing" (*continued*)

Figure 12. "The Final Silencing" (*continued*)

Figure 12. "The Final Silencing" (*continued*)

Figure 12. "The Final Silencing" (*continued*)

Figure 12. "The Final Silencing" (*continued*)

Figure 12. "The Final Silencing" (*continued*)

Figure 12. "The Final Silencing" (*continued*)

213

Figure 12. "The Final Silencing" (*continued*)

Dann wrote the lyrics as well. Dann's grandfather died in the mid-1980s, but it was not until 1991 that he really began to explore his grief. Surprised to find a well of untapped emotions, he resolved to write a song about the loss; Dann composed the lyrics to FS and fit them to the music during the final stages of arrangement with the band. FS was performed several times, and recorded in the studio twice—once for a poor-quality demo and once for a seven-inch record made under much improved conditions at Terry Salem's basement studio. At the time of this writing, Dann was recording a rather different version of the song with his current band, Blood Coven.

During the four interviews in which we discussed the song, Dann and I played guitars and used a tape of the seven-inch to facilitate the conversation; a video of the June 20, 1992, performance of FS at Flash's also exists. Again, in this discussion I shall focus on the rhythm guitar parts and their tonality. These guitar parts involved no improvisation, and Dann grasps them in perception in a fairly similar manner across the event. With both the *noema* and *noesis* of the experience relatively stable, I shall speak below of "Dann's experience of FS"; such statements are to be understood as limited generalizations about the similarities of experiences across the series and are in no way meant to imply an ahistorical musical structure.

Introductory sections to FS

The seed idea for the intro (bars 1 through 4) is the keyboard part at bar 1.[2] The part is played four times, and is then repeated four more times with the guitars harmonized above in parallel minor thirds. As always, the notes as objective pitches are only a starting point for ethnographic and phenomenological description. To go further, we must ask, Is there a tonal center to the part? If so, where is it? What are the scalar or tonal qualities of the part? Is there a pulse behind the part? Are the pulses grouped, and if so, how? Is the part heard as a melody, as an outlining of chords, as pure texture, or some other form? What is the affective quality of this part and how is it constituted? How does this part connect to others in the section and to the next section? In short: How is the part heard?

We began our exploration with the tonality. Dann was very familiar with the idea of tonic and had no trouble asserting that the E was the tonal center; however, the scalar quality of the line required more exploration. Playing the part at home before the interview, several possibilities presented themselves. I observed that all the notes but the B-flat fall into E minor. Thus, the B-flat could be read as a mere chromatic passing tone, a tension releasing to the B-natural. Alternatively, the passage could be in the fourth mode of B harmonic minor, with several notes missing; in this case, the B-flat would be a raised fourth and a scalar tension to the natural fifth. As always, the pitches never fully determine one's grasping of them, and in this case, neither of these standard options described Dann's experience.

Assured that I was only interested in a description of his experience of the line, Dann explained that he does not hear the B-flat as a tension to the scalar B. As a result, the B-flat is neither a chromatic neighbor tone nor a weak scalar tone, but a structural tone in its own right. As a note choice that "strengthens the feel of the riff," Dann said that the B-flat sounded "drastic" and "lends itself to being a little more eerie sounding, a little more . . .

moody," than if he had used the A-natural or the B-natural in its place. As such, the B-flat, a tritone from the tonic E, is crucial to the part's sound. Melodic tritones are central to death metal. Dann recalled that one of his many guitar teachers described the tritone by comparing intervals to the steps in a stairway; unlike the other intervals, the melodic tritone gave the listener the unsettling impression of going down the stairs and skipping a step. After this discussion, it was not difficult to establish that the G was a strong scalar tone and the F-sharp a weak scalar tone that heightened the E's centrality. As a description of the harmonic functions of the pitches, Dann and I agreed that the piece implied E aeolian, but with a structural B-flat added.

Viewing the part more fully, we agreed that the line was a melody, with the B-flat as a structural point in the melody's contour and the B-natural an embellishment to that shape. When I asked Dann about the time of the part, he said he never thought in terms of time signatures and didn't know what the time of the part was. I asked him, however, if tapping a pulse behind the part would have been natural when he wrote it; he assured me it was, proceeded to tap out the ten pulses for the phrase, and agreed to my assertion that those pulses were implicit in the part. He further agreed that the part formed a unit and that the E fell on a downbeat. Given all this, Dann agreed that the designation of 10/8 was a valid description of the rhythmic implications inherent in his experience of the part.[3]

The importance of the melodic contour was highlighted as we turned to the harmony guitar lines that emerge in bar 5. Trained in a music theory where diatonic harmonies are the default case, my concern was discovering if the parallel minor thirds change the part's tonal implications. Parallel harmonies are common in both death metal in general and Dann's music in particular, and he said that with keyboards, guitar, and two basses playing the original melody in unison, the harmony part on a single guitar fails to change the original tonality. Dann explained that because the part was dynamically faint, it acts almost "subconsciously" and gives the section an "eerie" feel; further, Dann explained, a diatonic (nonparallel) harmony would draw too much attention to the part and diminish the overall effect. I suggested that parallel harmony may emphasize the most important aspect of the part, its melodic contour, and Dann agreed. In retrospect we can see that the parallel harmony also adds a further layer of harmonic richness to the section and is characteristic of Dann's music in general.

To Dann's mind, the first section of the tune is more than eerie; it also leaves the listener a bit uncertain as to what will come next. After a brief bridging fill that allows the musical ideas to flow smoothly together, the next section (bars 11 through 24) gives the listener the impression that the band is settling into a predictable pattern. Initially, Dann intended that the section would consist of the guitars and basses playing the chord progression at bar 11: /F E/. Not surprisingly, Dann explained that the progression powerfully reasserts the E as the tonal center. On top of the chords, the lyrics lay out the main theme of the song—the inevitability of death—and act as a prologue to the ensuing narrative of Dann's grandfather's funeral.[4] Establishing the tonality and presenting little melodic or harmonic material, the chords parallel the lyrics by serving as a prologue; the minimal melodic movement also serves to highlight the vocals.

Early on the bass players found these ringing chords too simplistic; as a result, Chuck composed the bass part (bars 25 through 28); this was later harmonized up an octave by the second guitarist, Erik.[5] With the chords clearly announcing E as the tonal center, I was not surprised when Dann explained that E was also the center of the bass part; however, the scalar quality of this passage was much less clearly defined. When Dann said that the section has no key, I responded by suggesting that the part might be a pitch axis.

A device not found in Chris Ozimek's pop metal, pitch axes occur when one pitch is clearly felt as the tonal center, but all eleven other pitches are equally structural and likely to occur. If a diatonic scale is a seven-note pitch collection with one note as a tonic and the fifth, third, sixth, second, fourth, and seventh present in a descending order of stability, then a pitch axis is a twelve-note pitch collection with a tonal center and equal weight given to all eleven other pitches. Though only nine pitches are actually present in the line, Dann said that the part gave the impression that the full chromatic spectrum could be evoked at any moment. Looking at the song in retrospect, I suggest that the presence of both the flat second and natural second, as well as the flat second and natural seventh, give the listener the sense of chromatism that is central to the concept of pitch axis. Further exploration would be necessary to discover if all the pitches in the part were experienced as having equal tonal stability, but because Dann did not write this part and it was less important than others in the tune, I did not explore these questions.

This part serves other functions as well. Primarily, it provides a shift of tempo, groove, and density; such shifts are crucial to Dann's song writing. Throughout our interviews Dann represented his songs as intellectually demanding and opposed them to the perceived musical banality of pop and rock. But the complexity of the overall form and individual parts does more than serve purely intellectual functions. The shifts in tempo and groove keep the music from getting boring, and the affective contrasts between the parts make the entire song more emotionally powerful. Before FS, Sin-Eater had specialized in slow, "doomy" songs. While the band was adept at this style and all the other members were devoted to it, Dann observed that audiences were tiring of programs composed solely of dreary, slow-tempo tunes. This section was meant to address these concerns. Where the first parts of the song (bars 1 through 10) evoke uncertain and eerie moods and the section at bars 11 through 24 acts as a prologue to later themes in the music and lyrics, the part at bar 25 breaks the song out of the doomy mode. Dann explained that this part, less emotional but more energetic, keeps the song formally interesting and provides affective contrast as well.

After nine repetitions of this part, the tempo shifts abruptly and the two basses play a slower version of the main verse part; almost inaudible on the seven-inch record, the two bassists play in call and response, with each musician trading off two notes of the line. Again, the quick shift in tempo provides affective contrast and keeps the music interesting. The formal foreshadowing of the upcoming section and the abrupt shift in tempo perfectly illustrate the dialectic of smooth and sharp section transitions. Bar 46 marks the end of the introduction.

The verse and tonality

The verse part[6] (bars 47 through 56) is the beating heart of the tune. Displaying neither the pure energy of a grind section nor the depressing emotionality of a doomy section, the verse's medium tempo and heavy groove provide just the right feel for moshing, while its chords invoke an irresistible anger and aggression. Central to the tune, Dann and I explored this part in great detail.

Establishing the meter posed no great problem. Dann frequently taps his foot while composing, and those taps coincide with the rhythms at which he head-bangs on stage. Playing and tapping, Dann gave a pulse for every two chords. When asked about the logical grouping of the part into units, he explained that one repetition of the part (F♯ G C B G G♯ D C♯)[7] formed a unit, with heavy accents on the first and third pulses. Given all this, we had little difficulty in concluding that the part is in 4/4 time, with each chord lasting an eighth note. Dann added that the simple rhythm and heavy accents make it especially good for moshing. When I observed that John's drum part accented the off-beats, Dann responded that the simple rhythms of the guitar part prevented John's dense drumming from confusing the audience.

While the discovery that the part is in 4/4 time is straightforward, the status of the claim and the method used to achieve it are not. Dann explained that he never reflectively plans to write a part in a time signature. Instead, he hears a part in imagination or experiments on his instrument until he discovers an idea that appeals; inherent in the experience of the part thus composed are grouped pulses. As a result, time signature can be understood as a description of rhythmic experience and not as either a transcriptional device or an aspect of objective musical sound.

It is worth digressing to note that this compositional sequence—imaginative or bodily experimentation, followed by aesthetic judgment[8] (and later phenomenological description)—is equally important for the harmonic aspects of the music as well. On most occasions, Dann does not plan to use a certain scale or device. On the contrary, he experiments with a part, makes an aesthetic judgment, and modifies the part to improve weak points. Harmonic designations of the kind constructed in our fieldwork process are largely after-the-fact descriptions of the structures inherent in the prereflective process of perception. As such, scale must be viewed as a partial description of musical experience rather than an underlying system that generates composition and perception. I shall return to this point in greater detail below.[9]

Turning to the tonality of the verse, we established that the section was less a series of chords that established an underlying harmonic rhythm, and more a melody harmonized in power chords (fifths and octaves). It was also clear that the roots of the chords were the center of the part; like the parallel minor thirds in the intro, the fifths of the chords simply acted as a harmonic embellishment that thickened the sound but in no way disturbed the primacy of the roots. As a result, we may look at the melody "/F♯ G C B G G♯ D C♯/" and set aside the fifths. Dann's first move was to say that the piece was broadly in F-sharp locrian; indeed, all the pitches except G-sharp and C-sharp fit in that mode. Recognizing the subtle distinctions possible in the music, I asked Dann if he heard the part in F-sharp locrian (that is, with the G and C possessing the stability of weak scalar pitches) or merely F-sharp minor with two alterations (that is, with G and C appearing as variations of the implied scalar G-sharp and C-sharp). Dann stuck firm with locrian, and an analogy—mine—will clarify the distinction.

The natural minor provides the ear with a unique scalar sound. Natural minor can be described formally as a scale with a root, major second, minor third, natural fourth, natural fifth, flatted sixth, and flatted seventh. Transposing a familiar melody, such as "The Star Spangled Banner," into the parallel minor would, for most listeners, invoke a sound in which the minor third, sixth, and seventh were heard as alterations of the major sound, in which each occurrence of an alteration would invoke the note from the major scale by its very absence. When we hear most songs in minor keys, however, the minor third, sixth, and seventh do not invoke the major ones by their absence; on the contrary, we hear the minor third as stable and structural. The locrian is much less familiar in Western popular music, and as such it is easy to conflate locrian with altered minor. But Dann and other death metal composers use locrian all the time. In fact, Dann has an oft-told narrative about how he argued with a music teacher who held that the locrian is not musically useful. This should clarify the important difference between experiencing the flat nine and flat five as an alteration of the minor and experiencing those pitches as locrian per se. With the F-sharp falling on a heavily accented first beat, F-sharp is clearly the tonal center, and the next three chords in the part are all heard as locrian scale tones.

The entire part, however, is not in locrian, and from here interesting complexity arises. Dann explained that he could have written the entire part in locrian (resulting in /F♯ G C B G A D C/), but the G to A move and the D to C move would take away some of the part's spice and interest. As a guitar player, I learn parts by visualizing patterns on the fretboard, so I asked Dann if the part emerged from the geometry of the neck; Dann said it did. The pattern the part makes on the fretboard emphasizes the predominance of half-step moves: F♯ G, C B, G G♯, D C♯. As such, Dann agreed that the second half of the part (G, G♯, D, C♯) is more a half-step transposition of the first part of the lick than it is an alteration of the locrian scale. But exact transposition of motifs is common and predictable in death metal, and Dann explained that his constant goal was to avoid predictable parts. Hence, the part ends with D and C-sharp, not C-sharp and C.

Dann and I established that he hears the G and G-sharp as part of a G locrian area and as a parallel to the F-sharp locrian motif. Knowing that the D and C-sharp are heard as a variation of the first motif, we still have not established how they are grasped in their tonal aspect, and several possibilities presented themselves. First, the D could be an alteration of the flatted sixth degree of the G locrian scale (and, as a result, would be "better" spelled E-double-flat), and the C-sharp ("better" spelled D-flat) could be the locrian's (scalar) flatted fifth. As half-steps and fifths are the intervals commonly employed in Western music for leading a bass line back to the tonic in a cadence, another possibility could be that the D was merely a chromatic passing chord to the C-sharp, and the C-sharp the fifth of the F-sharp. Further, we could be in a G pitch axis, some other harmonic implications could be present, or we could even have a brief period of atonality.

After assuring me that the questions were valid, Dann played the part again and listened. Playing the part slowly, as the basses do at bars 43 and 44, the tonal relationships are more clearly presented to the ear, Dann said; here, the D seems to lead us to the C-sharp and the C-sharp back around to the F-sharp. Playing the part quickly, as is done in the verses proper, the tonal relationships are more difficult to hear, and the D and C-sharp imply the F-sharp much more weakly. When played quickly, Dann said, the tonality is much less important than the moshy rhythm and drive of the part. Pursuing the point, I offered that when the part is played faster, it appears less as a melody with tonal implications, even less as a contour, and more as a pattern of intervals or play of half steps. Dann agreed entirely with this interpretation.

The description thus far well serves the ethnographic aim of sharing Dann's experience. We can pause at this point to explore the broader implications of these complex data. The idea of the foregrounding and backgrounding of different aspects of phenomena was introduced in Chapter 5. Extending my analysis of the organization of the living present begun in Chapter 7, I hope to gain additional insights into the dimensions of temporality in musical experience. What is meant when I say that Dann foregrounds the tonality when he listens to the slow version of the verse part? What would be meant if he foregrounded the contour (something he doesn't do) or if he foregrounded the play of intervals? When Dann plays the chords slowly, he is more aware of their tonal relationships, of their active leading into one another; when played quickly, the intervals stand out more, or are more clearly present in experience. Such an analysis is fine as a first step, but the "aspects" of tonality, contour, and interval are aspects of the part as a whole, not the individual note phenomena; these emerge when the subject engages with a series of moments in the flux of the living present. As different organizations of the *noema* in the living present, we can observe the following: as pure quality, to foreground the tonality means, in the second half of the bar, to hear the D leading to the C-sharp and the C-sharp leading to the F-sharp. In terms of the subject's organization of the living present, "foregrounding the tonality" means protending the C-sharp and the F-sharp while the D is sounded and protending the F-sharp while the C-sharp is sounded; more than merely protended, the C-sharp and F-sharp must be present intensely and as absences waiting to be fulfilled, like the sound of the ringing telephone in the example in Chapter 7.

As pure quality, foregrounding the contour, which Dann does not do, would mean being aware of the overall melodic arc of the part. In terms of the subject's organization of the living present, "foregrounding the contour" means intensely holding on to the first chord, the last chord, and all the chords that reflect important changes in pitch direction. In the first two beats, the F-sharp is critical as a starting place for the contour and the C is critical as a place where the direction changes; the B is important inasmuch as it is a downward turn from the C, but the G only functions to flesh out the general upward contour with a slightly smaller leap. Similarly, the G starts off the second arc of the contour, while the G-sharp, D, and C-sharp play analogous roles to G, C, and B, respectively. "Foregrounding the contour" means to hold those chords important to directional changes in the greatest intensity, be they in protention or retention. While the chord at the now-point is never fully backgrounded, protentions and retentions across the living present are more tightly held than usual, because the *overall* contour only emerges when the subject grasps the part as a whole.

As pure quality, hearing the part more as a pattern of intervals or a play of half steps means being less aware of contour and tonal relationships and being more aware of the intervals of the successive chords. In terms of the subject's organization of the living present, "foregrounding the play of intervals" means focusing on the minor seconds as the polar opposite of focusing on the contour. Here the subject must intensely grasp together certain pairs of chords, one held in the now-point, one held in protention or retention (F-sharp and G, C and B, G and G-sharp, D and C); there is less conjunction between all the chords in the living present as a whole, but there is greater conjunction between the adjacent chords. Further, the subject may grasp the relationships between the pairs, together in retention or protention, and conjoin those pairs with other intensely grasped pairs.

Given all this, we easily see it is no accident that Dann hears the part one way when it is played slowly and another when it is played quickly. When the part is played slowly, the chords ring longer; the passive synthesis that holds the *noema* of the sustained bass notes together requires no effort on the part of the subject; as a result, it is easy for the future protention necessary for tonal implications to emerge in the subject's living present. When the part is played fast, however, each chord rests in the focal center of the now-point for a shorter period of time, so it is harder to generate and maintain tonal expectations. The shift between adjacent chords is hard to miss when they are played fast; as such, the half-step intervals stand out more and the tonal richness is more backgrounded. These conclusions about the relationship of tonality to the organization of the living present bear upon a variety of issues, including the relationship between affect and experience. That discussion, however, can be held off to the end of the chapter.

Introductory sections through the verse:
A first look at lyrics, form, and affect

Returning to the ethnographic data, we can expand our understanding of Dann's experience by looking at the affective component of the part as well as its relationships to the lyrics and the form. Having moved through several levels of prologues, the verse emerges as the first substantial section of the tune, in both music and lyrics. The words here depict the thoughts and feelings of a mourner at a funeral, which Dann based on his experiences at the passing of his grandfather. Beginning with the basses, the part is slow and doomy; when the band enters and the piece moves into double time, Dann said, the part takes on a more "aggressive," "angry," and "upbeat" feel.

Dann reiterated that his decisions about the types of parts to use in a song are influenced by concerns about the band's success. Many metal players, Dann among them, explained to me that in the extremely up-tempo genres of metal, the emphasis on speed and energy often detracted from the music's expressiveness and affective power; similarly, the use of too many slow parts tended to alienate contemporary audiences. As a result, Dann was constantly concerned with balancing doomy parts, low-emotion speed parts, and medium-tempo expressive parts. The arrangement of the sections into an overall form brings other interests into play: the desire to present a piece of music with powerful emotional impact and the need to harmonize the meanings of the music and the lyrics. In terms of audience building, the tune starts out slow, a device that may attract fans of doom metal but repel other fans; the section from bars 11 through 24, Dann explained, functions like movie music by setting a mood and implying that further action is soon to come. The action builds with the fast section at bar 25 but is unpredictably broken by an abrupt switch to the slow tempo at bar 43—another attention-grabbing move. When the moshy (and, for metal, hooky) verse emerges, we are finally in the body of the tune.

The same affective contour of the overall song form, however, can be read in terms of its relationship to the lyrics and the emotions surrounding the loss of a loved one. Dann explained that the numerous changes between the sections give the listener a sense of confusion about the direction of the song. This sense of confusion, Dann explained, ties in with a major theme of both the song and Dann's overall beliefs—the uncertainty of the afterlife. In the course of our interviews, Dann repeatedly told me that he dislikes the undue concern with the afterlife that he saw in traditional Christianity and American culture. Unconvinced by accounts of the nature of death, again and again Dann proclaimed that people should focus on the present and not be concerned with heaven, hell, nonbeing, or any other putative afterlife experience. Dann explained that his desire to depict the afterlife as the ultimate uncertainty is supported by these constant, unpredictable section changes.

More than unpredictable, the shifts in affective tenor also correspond to the complex feelings that come with mortal loss. Moving into the body of the song at bar 43 the part is slow and morbid-sounding. It is more than just depressing; the slow tempo reflects a level of confusion, explained Dann, evoking the ambivalent tug between anger and depression that mourners feel. When the up-tempo verse proper starts (bar 47), the anger reasserts itself—anger directed at both the situation and the confusion that death presents to us. Dann and I agreed that the song evokes a wide range of feelings associated with death: anger, grief, helplessness, sadness, and depression. The fact that listeners experience the overall form of a piece of music, I believe, requires us to expand our idea of the living present to include larger time scales. Further the presence of form-function relationships holds pregnant implications for a phenomenology of affect in music. Data from the next section of the song can help us to shed light on these topics.

The bridge and tonality

With the intellectual tools developed in the previous sections, we shall be able to examine the bridge more quickly. The bridge section (bars 58 through 105), was originally composed as the series of power chords that are played in bars 58 through 67. At practice, Erik wrote the part later played by the guitar on the left side of the stereo field on the seven-inch record (bars 78 through 84).[10] Listening to the two parts, Dann felt that there was still something missing. Experimenting with different parallel harmonies, he settled on parallel perfect fifths (center-right guitar, bars 78 through 84); still feeling that the parts didn't fulfill his affective and formal intentions, he finally composed the other melodic part (center-right guitar, bars 68 through 74). Because they were composed first, the chord changes are the best place to begin an examination of this section.

Dann explained that when he composed the piece, and when the part initially appears to the listener, the A sounds like a tonic; as a power chord, the harmony is not explicitly laid out at this point and could imply major, minor, or neutral tonality. Dann explained that to his ear, the part is ambiguous, but is closer to a major than any other sound. The C-sharp and G-sharp of the C-sharp power chord all fit within A major, and given introductory music theory it would seem likely that the C-sharp would be heard as the iii chord. Accustomed by now to the contrary nature of Dann's tonal imagination, the reader will not be surprised that Dann hears the C-sharp as a distinct break with the previous part and therefore a key change to some form of C-sharp. Dann is not just being willfully perverse, here; having some familiarity with death metal at this point, I also heard the C-sharp as a new I or i—even before Dann and I discussed the piece.

This method of constituting the part is not capricious. First of all, the chord appears heavily accented on a strong beat after the A chord had died away. Turning from *noema* to *noesis*, we can observe that one of the overriding interests of death metal players in general and Dann in particular is to create abrupt and tonally challenging music; it is no surprise that to those weaned on pitch axis, chromatism, and occasional lapses into atonalism, a leap up a major third, heavily accented on a downbeat, would be grasped as a new key area. More surprising is Dann's ensuing narrative about the affective quality of intervals. Dann explained that major has a grand sound to him, but the melodic leap of an ascending major third sounds "gloomy." It is not merely Dann's perception that contradicts the simplistic associations "major = happy, minor = sad"; illustrating the point in his room one night, Dann played the interval from A 220 to the C-sharp a third above; to my great shock, I heard the ascending major third as "gloomy."[11]

Having moved from an A as a tonic with an ambiguous scalar quality to C-sharp as a tonic with an ambiguous scalar quality, the guitars descend a half step to C. Dann explains that when the first C appears in the song, he hears the move as abrupt and discontinuous; the C sounds as if it is neither part of the previous chords, nor leading toward any chords, nor a center itself. When the G appears, however, the descent of a perfect fourth helps Dann grasp the G as a I, and the C is reinterpreted in retention as a IV. Dann describes the trill between B and C as an embellishment of the G chord, leading us by a perfect fifth to the E, heard as vi.

Moving from qualitative description to an examination of the structuring of the living present, we can say that as the A is sounded, many tonal configurations emerge as possibilities in protention; of these, the major configuration is most strongly evoked. When the C-sharp emerges, the A is retained and a distinct contrast appears between the unfulfilled protentions of the A major and the protended possibilities implied by the C-sharp in the now-point. The situation here is the opposite of that in the verse of "Turn for the Worse." There, when the D emerged, the A chord was present as part of the halo of possibilities that lurked in protention and made the D appear as a tonic. When the A emerged, however, the just-past D (and the fulfilled protention of the A as V) were *disjoined* from the A in the now-point; as a result of this highly disjoined organization of the living present, the A in the now-point was grasped as a I chord. An analogous disjunction was made when the D reemerged.

"Turn" and FS are similar in that both present us with a series of chords that fit within the halo of protended possibilities, and yet neither establishes a sense of coherent tonality across chords. There is, however, an important difference between the cases. In "Turn," the protended chord is heard as a new I because the now-past possibilities and the newly emerging present chord are so disjoined that the new chord appears as a I. In FS, both Dann and I were so accustomed to hearing abrupt changes (and so resistant to hearing straight major sounds) that we refused to hear the new chord as a fulfillment of the A major possibilities—even though the pitches do not preclude it. As a result, we protended a new set of possibilities (with C-sharp as I). Unlike "Turn," the moments of the living present are tightly conjoined; it is precisely the *experienced contrast* between the protentions implied by the A as I and the protentions implied by the C-sharp as I that is the grounds of the qualitative experience of key change.

As I suggested in Chapter 7, it is important to keep in mind that I am not suggesting that the qualitative experience of tension and release, of harmonic implication and tonality, is an illusion. As experience, the quality of tonality is concretely lived and certain. Nor am I saying that the organization of the living present is some subconscious process. Though rarely thematized, the organization of the living present—the constantly changing intensities and relationships of phenomena in protention, now-point, and retention—is concretely lived and actively achieved (Ihde 1976). My point is that that quality of the tension or release is a result of the organization of the living present; not an effect of the phenomena by themselves but an effect of the relationships between phenomena, the sense of tension or release is no less concretely experienced.

The subsequent moves in this progression can also be understood in terms of the organization of the living present. Dann explained that at its first emergence, the C is a distinct break from the C-sharp; here, the conjunction and ensuing contrast of the C in the now-point with the C-sharp in retention is the ground of the experience. When the G emerges, it is grasped as a I with its characteristic halo of tonal possibilities; such possibilities not only lurk in protention, they are conjoined with the retained C. Thus, the C changes quality and becomes a IV after it has passed into retention.

Dann observed that on the first repetition of the part, the C is a distinct break; interestingly, this first emergence can either refer to Dann's first interaction with the song or the first repetition of the part in a performance. Given this, however, we must immediately ask if the second repetition of the part in the song, subsequent repetitions, or subsequent listenings impinge upon the experience, causing Dann to protend the G and hear the C as a IV when the C first emerges. This point, raised briefly at the end of Chapter 7, is crucial for a variety of reasons. Primarily, it forces us to make our description of Dann's experience much more concrete, speaking, not of "Dann's grasping the part in general," but of Dann's grasping of the part at this or that moment in his history of experiences with the tune.

Perhaps more important, however, is that this section brings up a broader issue: how Dann may be surprised by his composition at all. Dann has played FS hundreds of times; he composed the parts, varied them, and taught them to others. How could Dann ever not protend exactly the next chord he is going to play?

The solution to this puzzle rests in the process of framing and the difference between reflection and perception. It would seem at first glance that Dann would know that the G chord is to follow the C, and therefore, that there would be no way that the C could not be heard as a IV of G. The word "know," however, is extremely vague in this instance. To hear the C as a IV chord means to hold the G chord in protention as a I and conjoin that present C and the protended G. No other experiences are relevant to hearing the C as IV. Dann may actively think "I am going to go to the G chord"; he may prepare his hand to grasp the G, or may even protend the G chord but insulate the C chord from it—none of these will make the C a IV. Only if he protends the G and conjoins the C to it will the C be a IV chord, because to hear the C as a IV means to perform that organization of the living present.

With this in mind we can see the data in a much clearer light. There is no question that prior experiences with the song could influence a listener to protend the G and conjoin it with the C; by the same token, a listener may forget where the song is going or engage so intently with the current performance that past experiences do not impinge on present graspings. With training, the listener may even freely manipulate that organization for its own sake. In the interview, in fact, Dann left room open in his description of the C chord. On the first repetition of the part in a performance, Dann said he usually heard the part as a distinct break; as the section wore on, however, he would be more likely to protend the G. The broad point here is not that performance events transcend history, but that the active achievement of perception is never fully determined by past events. I wasn't able to penetrate the data deeply enough to differentiate Dann's first and most recent experiences of FS; however, I have pushed the analysis one step closer to concrete description. In fact, this point leads the way to a level of the living present *in between* the intrasectional level and the interperformance level: the protention and retention of sections in the living present.

But first let us finally finish up the analysis of the bridge. Given the G as a I, the trill between the B and C were all within G major; they lead the part forward to the E, which Dann strongly heard as a vi of G. Translating these terms into the language of protention and retention is at this point a simple task: the notes of G major are all protended throughout this section; the G is protended most strongly, the other chords and notes are protended more weakly, and all are conjoined together to give the characteristic tensions and releases of the major chord series. What is interesting here, is that the move of the C to the G, and the use of the E as a pivot chord (that is, both vi of G and v of A) are traditional harmonic moves found throughout Western music. This constant switching between varieties of tonal organization is critical to Dann's music, and to the sense of "chaos" and "abruptness" that he values in death metal.[12]

After the first repetition of the chords, several tracks of guitars emerge. The part Erik composed in rehearsal starts with a melodic fragment using the fourth, major third, and root of the A chord, and is then transposed in parallel to fit the C-sharp, C, and G chords (left guitar, bars 78 through 84); Dann's harmonizes this line in parallel perfect fifths (center-right guitar). Dann plays a single note line—composed later but appearing first in the song—at the center-right portion of the stereo field (bars 68 through 74). Over the A chord he plays C-sharp, the major third, and over the C-sharp chord he plays the F and E, both the major and minor thirds. Against this, Erik plays the part at the left side of the stereo field, which arpeggiates the power chords and foreshadows the line composed of scalar degrees 4, 3, and 1 that he wrote. After additional repetitions, Dann plays a slight variation of his last part up an octave.

The tonal organization of these parts is not surprising. First, Dann explained that the major thirds here solidify the interpretation of the A and C-sharp as major, although Dann wasn't clear about whether they retroactively make the earlier iterations of the chords major. As before, the parallel perfect fifths thicken the timbre and texture but in no way imply a change in harmonic orientation. As we saw before, Dann felt that these parts alone did not achieve the sound he desired. Though Dann's part emerged from aural experimentation and not musicological reflection, he agreed in our interview that Erik's part laid out the tonal relationships too clearly. Employing both thirds on the C-sharp and the perfect fifth over the G, his part returned some of the ambiguity to the tonality and gave the section an overall sense of "chaos"; the introduction of rhythmically independent guitar melodies, somewhat unusual in death metal, furthers the sense of chaos and imparts what Dann called a sense of "openness" and "spontaneity." This combination of the grand sound of the major chords with the gloom of the minor third and the chaos of the progressively changing tonality precisely defines Dann's affective goals for this section. Such chaos, gloom, and grandeur also fit the lyrics of the section. In a rich and impossibly deep voice, Dann expresses his complex feelings of loss: "I was strong. For the rest. I still cared. You. Now you're gone. But you live. In my mind."

The chorus: Tonality and affect

Two theoretical issues remain to be examined in this chapter: the organization of the living present on the level of the section and the so-called form-function relationships that link grasped musical structure to lived and felt affective content. The data in this section are particularly relevant to the issue of affect.

The bridge proceeds through almost five repetitions of the chord cycle before the chorus (bars 106 through 116) emerges. Again, the series of power chords that forms the part is best understood as a melody, not a chord progression laying out harmonic rhythm; again, the power chords thicken the texture, but the fifth of the power chord doesn't influence the tonality. Given our earlier analysis, Dann and I were able to come to a description of this section quickly. Dann had no doubt that E was the tonal center here, and as usual, the pitches of the roots—E and F for the first phrase, E, B-flat and C for the second—opened up a range of possibilities. Dann rejected my suggestion that the part could be an E pitch axis or a E locrian, and held fast that the part was phrygian with a flatted fifth.[13]

In purely formal terms there is, of course, no difference between locrian and phrygian with a flatted fifth; however, as we have observed, purely formal interpretations are limited abstractions from the full lived experience. As a result, we are in a precisely reversed situation to that of the first half of the verse: there, Dann heard the passage as F-sharp locrian and not merely as F-sharp minor with two altered notes; here the passage is heard as E phrygian with an alteration and not E locrian. In both sections the experience is more articulated and detailed than either pitch *noema* or the formal analyses would allow.

As before, Dann's particular perceptual grasp of the part is not capricious. Dann hears the part as clearly divided into two 2-bar phrases with a triplet feel breaking up the pulses. The first phrase employs only the tonic and the flat second, which is the trademark sound of the phrygian. While locrian also has a flat second, it is only fully defined by the pitches when a flat five is present; taken by itself as a phrase, the move from one to flat second so highlights the flat second as to place us in phrygian. With the phrygian so strongly established, the second half retains the phrygian feel—even to the extent that the B-flat is heard as an alteration of the locrian flat five. Described in terms of Dann's organization of the living present, the E is a tonal center; all the pitches of the phrygian scale with an altered fifth are held as possibility throughout the entire passage. The tonic is held most intensely, giving a sense of resolution when it arises and a sense of tension when nontonic pitches are present. As in all tonal passages, there is tight conjunction across the entire phrase, enabling the tensions and releases described above.

Turning to the affective dimension, Dann and I observed that the part's slow triplet time produces an extremely heavy effect. To get a more visceral description, I suggested that the part evoked the same sense of heaviness as do the "walkers" from the film *Star Wars: The Empire Strikes Back*; the walkers, giant tanks supported by mechanical legs, were the main ground forces of an invading army and moved in titanic, lumbering steps. Dann agreed that the weight and menace of the walkers is in line with the feel of the first phrase of this part. The second half of the phrase, however, with its large leap and altered tonality give the section a floating and ethereal quality. The part's affective power is magnified by the contrast between the heavy first phrase and the lighter, floating quality of the second. As I have observed before, experienced contrasts must be understood as the conjunction of opposites across the living present; here, that means the tight conjunction of the retained heaviness of the first part is conjoined with the floating quality of the second, increasing the power of both. Here, affective organization parallels the overall organization of the living present.

This parallel is particularly important when we recall that the division of musical phenomena into affective and perceptual aspects is, for most experiences, an after-the-fact operation. Returning to experience, as Husserl urges us to do, we discover that the sound itself is a gestalt of affective and sensual qualities;[14] only in reflection do we separate the subjective/affective component from the objective/sensory parts. This division is not an error, because we know that others may grasp the sound in different ways and hear different affects. This division is not a full truth either, because it leads us to the false conclusion that the sensory aspects of the experience are there for themselves and the affective components are merely subjective additions. To the contrary, the sensory aspects are there for experience and exist as experiences before they are subjective or objective. Integral to the experience, the affective components are *not* the product of individual whim; they are the result of the subject's grasping of the world in perception and are deeply influenced by the subject's social history. As a result, they offer us a partial but direct connection with the experiences of others.

This last point is crucial. If we think of experience as individual islands of appearance floating inside an objective reality, then sharing experience is at best problematic and at worst fictional. But when we treat experience as objective reality grasped—when we treat perception as practice—then *the sharing of experience between individuals means engaging with the world in a manner similar to the other*. While two can never grasp the world in identical ways (and while one person can never grasp the world exactly the same way twice), insight and a directness of sharing can occur when I and the other engage with the world in similar ways. Returning to the case of music, no one doubts that simple association between musical form and affective content accounts for much of the affect in musical experience. But there is also no question that some affective content emerges from the subject's engagement with musical sound.

Further, composers and performers exploit this situation to achieve their effects. Much of music's affective power comes when a composer creates musical forms that lend themselves to be grasped in a particular way by those with similar social-musical histories. These observations must be tempered by Alan Merriam's great caveats about musical uses, laid out in his *Anthropology of Music* (1964): not all music is played with the intent of sharing or eliciting affect; some composers or musicians may intend to elicit affect that they in fact do not feel, and others may intend to elicit affect only in themselves. Further, we must observe that sharing is always partial, and this is so for a wide variety of reasons: The musical *noema* never fully determine the manner in which they are grasped; no two listeners have the same social-musical history; even if they did, two different listeners would always be free to grasp the music in different ways. Nevertheless, we can still agree that similar modes of engagement, mediated by similar musical forms, can have similar affective consequences. In semiotics, a related set of linkages is referred to as form-function-meaning relationships; to emphasize the subject's role in constituting meaning, I shall refer to the situation as form-engagement-affect relationships.

Before returning the idea of form-engagement-affect relationships to death metal, I must first establish the Merriamesque uses of this music. Sharing structures of lived experience with Dann, I repeatedly stopped the interview process to ask Dann if he wanted listeners to hear the parts as he did. Often, he responded that he would never tell anyone how to listen to his music; instead, he wanted to know what others heard. This would seem to run counter to the idea that Dann was trying to set up musical *noema* that would lend themselves to being grasped by others with the intended affects. In phenomenological terms, Dann's performance would thus be the conjuring of a rich field of *noema*, a vast sonic playground with which listeners may engage as they like. I have no doubt that there is some truth in this view. At the same time, however, much of the material in our interviews suggested that Dann *is* concerned with more direct sharing of both *noesis* and affective *noema*. Dann was very clear about the intended affective content of the music; moreover, he was able to specify the kinds of crowd responses he expected and desired in certain sections. Thus, while Dann has no explicit phenomenological ideology of partial sharing, he does have a desire to share affect through his music, and there is no question that some of this sharing is achieved through form-engagement-affect relationships.

For example, in the bridge Dann created a series of chords that, for a listener with a social-musical history similar to his, would be difficult to grasp with clear tonal implications; he and Erik further muddy the waters by writing a large number of independent, tonally ambiguous, and tonally contradictory parts. It takes no great leap of imagination to understand that grasping chords that are tonally ambiguous or contradictory may lead to a sense of confusion, that grasping numerous independent parts in a music that is filled with homophony would give a sense of openness and spontaneity. In the verse, the crescendo across the span of the riff and its ascending contour both lend themselves to greater intensity and presence in the listener's experience; such high intensity easily connects with the "uptempo" and "aggressive" emotional content of the part. The clear and insistent rhythm of the riff—an unbroken series of eighth notes—is perfect for coordinating aggressive moshing, a form-engagement-affect relationship that entails other aspects of the performance.

Of course the *noema* never fully determine the phenomena; a person's organization of perception and his or her lived social history always has an impact on how the affects emerge in the full experience. A listener familiar with the atonalism in twentieth-century Western classical composition may grasp the verse part as traditional and orderly. A lover of big band jazz who values music for its uplifting lilt may grasp the verse part's tonality as ambiguous and chaotic but feel that those affective aspects are distasteful and annoying, rather than artful and empowering. After several years of additional experience with composition, Dann may be so familiar with these musical devices that the chaotic power of ambiguous chords may be grasped more as a dated symbol and less as an effective device.

Most important, in any given context, Dann has the ability to control how the music is grasped; all listeners have this ability, and the amount of control they possess depends on both their training and contingent, situational factors. *This ability to hear music in different ways, this perceptual ability to do otherwise, constitutes a level of agency that is crucial to musical experience.* As a result, the organization of the living present is a kind of practice and connects with the larger themes we have examined. Purely textual, nonexperiential readings of artifacts (as well as all schemes of analysis that describe fixed, unconscious systems of competence) are ultimately problematic, because they represent the practices of meaning establishment as mechanical processes rather than as social achievements.

At this point, we see the first links among the momentary, situated practices of perception and musical goals, broader projects, social context, and agency. Such links are of the first importance; before examining them, however, we must recognize that in most cases it is a complex interplay of form-engagement-affect relationships and cultural association that influence a part's affective content. The verse will illustrate the point. Dann repeatedly asserted that simple tonal chord progressions were to be associated with emotionally banal commercial music. In Dann's experience, and presumably in the experience of other death metal fans, the verse part cannot be grasped in terms of any one scale. Instead, their socially trained ears are led to grasp the part either as an almost atonal pattern of minor seconds or as a contour that sets up and then deforms the locrian sound.

Given the cultural association between the locrian sound and grim emotions, is it hard to imagine that an energetic passage that is grasped as locrian and locrian-deformed would be grasped as angry? If the minor second is seen in this culture as an extremely tense interval, is it hard to imagine that a passage grasped as a complex pattern of minor seconds would have a tortured, angry sound? Might we even say that, just as the organization of the living present constitutes and is coterminous with the tonal quality of the individual chord *noema*, the grasping of the chord *noema* as an atonal minor second pattern itself constitutes and is coterminous with its rageful affective component? And have we finally reached a place in our discussion where we can say that the subject simply is the grasping of the *noema*? That we are present to ourselves as subjects not as the bodies we see before us or in mirrors, nor in the self-presence of thoughts, but in the organization of experiences that we constitute for ourselves and understand only through careful observation? That the subject—the self or the other—is found only as the organized aspect of the world in experience? These questions obviously cannot be answered here. The description and analysis presented above, however, do allow us to conclude that form-engagement-affect relationships are a reality in musical experience.

The transition from the chorus into the second verse

The main riff in the chorus repeats three times, the first with guitars, basses, and synthesizer, the second and third without the synthesizer but with vocals. After the third repetition, the band plays a series of held chords that are then repeated on the basses alone. This progression, /D G♯/ G B/, leads us back into the verse.

In many forms of American popular music, the term *turnaround* refers to a brief series of chord changes that occurs at the end of a section and returns the ear back to a tonal center. Turnarounds often employ chromatic substitutions and extensions and surprise the ear with unusual note choices, but in a traditional turnaround there is no question that all the chords are pointing the listener back to a tonic chord. I heard this brief bridge—a 2-bar passage at the end of a section—as a turnaround and, after explaining the concept to Dann, I asked him if he heard it that way. After some reflection, Dann explained that, given my definition, the part was not a turnaround because its ambiguous tonality could lead to any number of new keys. Knowing Dann's love for tonal ambiguity, I suggested that the part was death metal's version of a turnaround—a turnaround that confused, rather than led, the listener. Dann felt comfortable with this reading.

This moment in the fieldwork process was also interesting because, to my listening, the part clearly leads to an E or F-sharp. As a result, it required effort to fail to protend the F-sharp to which the section leads. Given my jazz training, my practice of engagement is not capricious in that the progression /D G♯/ G B/ could easily be given extended harmonies (D 9, G♯ flat-9 sharp-5, G 13, B 7 suspended 4) and used as a jazz turnaround. Dann's (to me, novel) grasping of the part was an object lesson in the organization of experience.

The second verse, the solo, and tonality

The bridge at the end of the chorus leads into a second verse. Because Erik is the only singer in this section, Dann was free to run around the stage here and always took advantage of that opportunity. For this reason, Dann always felt the second verse was the most intense section in the song.

The solo follows the second verse (bars 129 through 148). Dann composed the basic part (bar 129) at home and intended it to be played fast. Erik and Chuck, however, were committed to the doomier style of metal and wanted to play it slowly, and so a compromise was eventually reached. Dann plays one up-tempo cycle of the part by himself, and then the entire band joins in for four more cycles at a slow tempo. To Dann's surprise, Erik wanted to use the part as a background to a guitar solo, and in the recorded version of the song, he solos over the first three slow cycles. The entire band plays the part together on the fourth cycle, and then the chorus returns.

During our interviews, Dann explained that the part's chromatic and unpredictable nature made it unsuitable for soloing; in my interviews with John and Rob, they said that they felt the same way. At the time, I found this difficult to understand. Even if we adopt the style of perception typical of death metal musicians, the part seemed to be in some kind of E. Dann explained that the part has two tonal centers. The first three beats of the bar (E G F♯ E C and B) all fall neatly within E minor, with the F-sharp as a scalar passing tone leading to the E and the entire part leading to E's fifth scale degree, B. The second part, lasting just one beat, is a D/D-sharp trill, which Dann hears as a embellishment of the D. Dann was eager to disabuse me of the notion that the D and the D-sharp lead up to the E. For him, they are there by themselves. After three repetitions of this bar, the D/D-sharp trill is replaced by an F5 chord, which marks the form and helps to keep the band together; Dann referred to this F5 as a "clincher chord."

Our previous readings can shed light on this section. Once again, given the pitch collection and standard conceptual tools, there would seem to be little doubt that we are in E throughout the section and that the extraneous pitches can be easily explained: the F chord could be seen as flat second chord, or, more likely, a flat five substitution for the B five; E minor can accommodate both the D and D-sharp in either the natural or harmonic modes, and both pitches can be seen as leading toward the E. As I have observed above, such a reading is in no way an objective description of the music, but itself is contingent upon a very specific kind of organization of the living present—one in which E is retained and protended throughout the entire part, and the other scalar pitches are retained or protended with greater or lesser intensity relative to their position in the traditional scalar hierarchy of strong and weak tones.

Given the importance of the minor second in Dann's music, however, we should not be surprised that Dann hears the D as tonally independent. Of course, that independence is heightened because it falls on a downbeat, because it lasts longer than any of the notes, because it is the only embellished note, and because its embellishment increases its dynamic and sustain, effectively producing an accent. Perhaps more important, however, is the fact that the trill builds a minor second into the pitch itself. As we saw in the discussion of the verse part, Dann tends to focus on the intervalic relationships of melodically adjacent pitches, rather than subsuming many pitches within an area. As such, it is no surprise that the D would be disjoined from the other notes in the part (Berger, in press).

But there is more here. Even though he initially said that E is the center for the first three beats and D for the last beat, in further conversation he continued to emphasize the extreme chromatism of the part. This initially struck me as very odd. Given E and D as centers, it is not clear that any notes are outside the scale because Dann didn't specify what kind of D key area we are in. Even given E-natural minor as the center for the part, a very narrow reading, only the D-sharp is outside the scale. The part in experience, however, is chromatic if we attend, not to the scalar structures as a whole, but to the play of half steps. The experienced "chromatism," and the attendant implications of a weak tonality, are increased if we conjoin all the pairs of adjacent minor seconds (G and F-sharp, B and C, D and D-sharp, later E and F) to one another more tightly than we conjoin the broader part in its two scalar sections (E, G, F-sharp, E, C and B as a unit; D and D-sharp as a unit). Further, if we make a noncontinuous conjunction of the *pairs* of half steps (G and F-sharp conjoined to B and C, and D and D-sharp), an entirely different sound emerges—one that by definition emphasizes the half steps and, in an unexpected way, is "more chromatic."

In terms of broader conclusions, we can see that even a selection from a traditional pitch collection can be experienced as "chromatic" if the half-step intervals are highlighted in perception. Further, it does not matter that the intervalic relationships formally imply the self-identical pitches and the scale, because, as William James observed, the conjunctions and disjunctions within experience are as real and important as the phenomena thus conjoined (James 1967, 42). In terms of form-engagement-affect relationships, the notes chosen in the composition set up the listener for a certain kind of perceptual engagement that, in turn, has affective significance; there is no guarantee, however, that the listener will achieve the intended experience. In the solo, we can easily see how the selection of minor second intervals in the composition—and the performance of the D and D-sharp trill—could lead the listener to Dann's experience of the part as chromatic and thus chaotic and aggressive. It is also clear that an exoteric listener like myself could grasp the part as a straightforward example of E minor. Understanding how Dann heard the part as chromatic, we can comprehend his incredulity at Erik's choice of the section for his solo.

The closing sections and form

With the solo in place we have seen all the main parts of the song. After the solo, the band moves directly into a repetition of the chorus. The death metal turnaround from the chorus ends the section and leads us back to the sustained /F E/ progression. Over these chords Dann sings:

So the story must end. As I greet the hand of death, I just sit back and laugh, for now I'm free from pain.

After woodchucking on the E, the basses repeat a fragment of their melody from the second part of the introduction (bar 167), and the guitars harmonize in parallel. A nearly retrograde variation of the first part of the introduction is then played by all the string players. One bass continues that line, the other plays a separate part, and the two guitars play an arpeggiated E-minor figure. The song ends with the entire ensemble playing a series of unmetered hits on an E power chord.

In terms of formal and affective considerations, Dann explained that the ending proper begins with the /F E/ part. For Dann, the mere return of that prologue signals that we are in the final parts of the song. In the introduction, the /F E/ part served as a prologue because its lower density, here grasped as lower energy, sets a tone for later musical and affective developments. In the ending, that energy drop "winds down" the listeners from the frenetic energy of the body of the tune, preparing them for the final sections and the end of the song itself. Dann agreed that his repetition of the other parts serve similar functions—marking the ending by recapping the major themes and winding the song down.

More detail and nuance can be found in the affective and formal aspects of the near retrograde variation of the 10/8 section. Where the original part was merely eerie, Dann explained, the retrograde inversion evoked a clear sense of uncertainty. Holding forth in tones reminiscent of Vincent Price, Dann explained, "You don't really know where it [the final 10/8 section] is going. Sounds real mysterious I think. Wondering where you are going. [*Pause.*] Maybe to heaven. [*Pause.*] Maybe to hell." In retrospect, it seems to me that this elusive quality emerges from the variation of the melody. The first melody articulated the root, octave, and flatted fifth on successive strong beats, effectively declaring that E was the tonal center; in contrast, the concluding variation ascends slowly and provides the structural E and B-flat later in the line. The elusive quality of the retrograde section is further heightened by its abrupt replacement with the arpeggiated E-minor chord. Pursuing his aesthetic of unpredictability, Dann explained that the complex pattern of final hits was meant to leave the listener uncertain about where the song would end.

With the major parts of the song recapped, we are now in a position to knit together some of the various allusions made to the broader organization of experience. The discussion of tonality has focused almost exclusively on the organization of the living present on the level of the phrase. But if we are committed to a return to experience, we must recognize that the living present has much greater temporal span.[15] The initial illustration of the idea of protention and retention came from language; there, the goal was to show that we must retain our awareness of the early part of a sentence to make sense of each incoming word. To continue the parallel, we must realize that to make sense of the sentence, we must retain the preceding parts of the paragraph, and perhaps the chapter and the book, as well.

It is critical to recall here that retention and memory are two very different things. To remember an earlier part of the paragraph or book means to make a phenomenon that was once present but is now absent part of the living present once again; retention means to hold phenomena in the living present continuously. Thus, to make sense of this sentence, the reader does not merely glance back, with eye or memory, at the topic sentence of the paragraph; on broader levels, neither does he or she stop to recall or reread the FS data or even the introduction of the chapter. To follow the thread of the argument means to retain past ideas (to let the meaning of the topic sentence lurk in retention) and allow their conjunction with the newer phenomena to give added sense and meaning. Understood in this way, the word in the now-point is given only limited sense by its conjunction with retained words in the sentence; the meanings of entire passages or whole arguments are only achieved when present sentences are related to the living retention of past sentences and paragraphs. The failure of retention on the broader levels illustrates the point equally well: when we are forced to remember actively or glance visually at a topic sentence or introduction, it is not memory we are really after but retention. In those situations, we reread the phrase or replay it in memory to reconstitute the retention and achieve the sense that was lost when retention failed.

The point here is that phenomena of short duration are nested within larger retentions and protentions. We have already seen this point in two places. The affective impact of the chorus was achieved by retaining the entire first phrase (bars 106 through 107, the aggressive E and F), while the entire second phrase (bars 108 through 109, the light and floating E, B-flat, and C) emerged. It was the lived contrast, the retention of the entire first phrase during the emergence of the entire second phrase, that really entailed the full experience of the part.

Staying on the intrasectional level, we can see that all of the sections involving repetition have a similar form. Setting aside the special picking effects of the guitar, the *noema* of the verse part repeats over and over; however, the full experience is anything but static. The first repetition of the entire part sets up protentions of exact repetition; given rock music's typical forms, most listeners protend a cycle of four repetitions. Listening through the verse, however, the full experience of the second, third, and fourth repetitions are different from each other, because each new iteration is differently situated in the living present on the scale of the section as a whole. The first iteration emerges with a corona of protention and no other sectional retentions; the last emerges with three full cycles in retention and a protention of some kind of sectional change. I discussed this general point with Dann and a wide variety of musicians, and the agreement was universal: even the exact repetitions of a phrase sound different because they are differently colored by retentions and protentions.

Throughout the chapter I have alluded, in casual language, to intersectional protention and retention. I observed that some of the affective power in FS depends upon tempo and groove changes across sections (bars

46 and 47, bars 105 and 106, bars 120 and 121). But it is not merely because the groove and tempo, for example, of the bridge are temporally adjacent to the groove and tempo of the chorus that the transition has impact. The impact does first require the establishment of tempo and groove as a set of relatively stable rhythmic protentions and retentions within the framed level of the bridge section, but that alone is not enough. It is the failure of the new groove to fulfill the old groove's protentions, conjoined with a section's worth of those fulfillments lurking in retention, that achieves that impact.

We may bring our discussion of the intersectional level to completion by exploring the grouping of sections together and the form of the song as a whole. In Dann's experience, the first several sections of the song (the 10/8 section, the long lick, the /F E/ section) go together; they are experienced as a unit with tight conjunction across the sections and a looser relationship to the rest of the song. Before the verse proper emerges, there is a broad protention that a large quantity of musical material is coming up.

When the verse itself emerges, this new section is not tightly conjoined with the past sections, but is set off—disjoined—and experienced as the start of a new group of sections. As the following body sections emerge (the bridge, chorus, second verse, solo, and second chorus), they too are conjoined together and form a unit. More than just a group of parts, the sections are retained together and provide an overall affective contour. Thus, the song shifts from the moshy and aggressive feel of the verse, to the more open and chaotic feel of the bridge, to the strange mix of heaviness and ethereal confusion of the chorus, and so on; this lived contour of changing affects gives the song as a whole its complexity and power. Not only is the affective contour grasped as it emerges, but each new unit is colored by the past as well. For example, when the second chorus emerges, most of the body of the song has passed. The retained first chorus makes the second chorus familiar, preventing the song from seeming like an amorphous mass of material. Further, the bulk of the song lurking in retention colors the second chorus with the sense that the music is progressing through a form, thus adding a level of energy and power. After the last chorus, a new group of sections is begun; conjoined, and opposed to the introduction and the body, this new group offers a sense of winding down and completion.

Many phrases or techniques in FS could be understood as framing devices—markers that indicate location in the musical form. Such devices are important, but their significance and operation can easily be misunderstood. Used by the players to keep track of their location in the form, the "clincher" F chord in the solo section is such a framing device. When the players hear it, they know that they have just completed four cycles of the solo section's chord progression. The various bridging fills (bars 9 and 10, bar 57) and the death metal turnaround not only mark the end of the section unit but lead the listener's ear into the sections that follow. The low density of the first /F E/ section signals the listener that we are in a prologue, and the restatement of the earlier themes renders the various parts of the closing sections as markers of ending. The thunderstorm sound effects at the beginning and end of the tune frame the song as a whole.

Framing devices are not just features of the score; they are used by listeners to help guide their organization of protentions and retentions on large time scales. This organization may operate in several, slightly different ways. Some framing devices are customary in a musical tradition. For example, every blues fan knows that certain turnarounds, when played with a diminuendo, indicate the end of a song. When blues fans hear the first few chords of the turnaround, they protend the rest of the turnaround (followed, perhaps, by a silence), and these protentions color the present chords with a sense of near completion. Similarly, any striking feature of a musical work may become a marker for listeners who have become familiar with the piece. Fast-forwarding a tape of FS to the middle and hearing "All must shake the hand of fate" (bar 132), Dann may strongly protend the opening chords of the solo section and more weakly protend the rest of the body and the closing sections. Finally, some elements of an individual musical work may become framing devices in the context of a listener's abstract knowledge about the genre. For example, death metal fans know that few metal tunes are made up of nothing but sustained chords; because of this, the /F E/ section at the beginning of FS serves as a cue that more and denser material will soon be forthcoming. On their first listening to the tune, metalheads conjoin the /F E/ section with "open" protentions on a large temporal scale—protentions of substantial but unknown musical material. On later listenings, these open protentions are filled in with an abstract, large-scale protention of the body and the closing sections. It should be noted here that construction of phenomena on large temporal scales requires a high amount of engagement with the music; as a result, this last level of description only speaks to Dann's most intense experiences of FS.

Conclusions

With this level of musical experience addressed, I have come to the end of my ethnographic description of "The Final Silencing." As in the discussion of "A Turn for the Worse," my narrow focus has passed over many features of the music. In terms of *noema*, the vocals and their timbre, the lyrics, the drum parts, and the relationships across instruments could all be examined in greater detail. In terms of *noesis*, a much greater range of material remains to be explored. Further work could inquire into the different ways in which Dann grasped FS depending on the situated context — rehearsal, performance, composition, or ethnographic interview. Examining the historical series of Dann's experiences with FS, one could compare two or more specific events in which Dann grasped the song. Of course, comparisons of the FS experiences of bass players and drummers, musicians and audience members, and listeners from different musical scenes could all provide fascinating topics of study. My approach to Dann's experience in this chapter was to examine his most intense experience of FS; a different view would explore Dann's lightly engaged experiences of the song. By the same token, this particular interpretation focused on the coherence of Dann's experiences within and across events; a different approach would be to explore and highlight the fragmentation and change in Dann's various experiences of the song.

With a detailed description of the tonality and a lighter discussion of the affective and overall sectional structure laid out, I have made steps toward the ethnographic goal of the study: the partial sharing of experience among Dann, myself, and the reader. Two tasks lie ahead. In the next chapter, I shall draw together some broad theoretical generalizations about musical experience and the practice of perception. In Part III, I shall use the ethnographic data I have presented so far to help explore the relationship between Dann Saladin's musical life and larger social and historical contexts.

NINE

Conclusions
Perceptual Practice and Social Context

The previous chapter explored the perceptual practices by which the retentions and protentions of notes and chords in the living present are constituted to form meaningful tonal phrases. This inquiry serves as a case
study of a more general question: How are the various facets of individual
musical experiences organized, and what is the relationship between particular facets of an experience and the experience as a whole? Each type of musical phenomenon is defined by such a set of relationships, and Husserl's
notion of the synthesis of identification can help us to understand this
point.[1]

I see a guitar across the room. In my experience, the guitar always
presents one of its faces to me: now the front, now the back, now a side. As
mere momentary "appearances," the surfaces of the guitar are different
each time I view them. Our full experience of the guitar, however, is not of
a cubist fragmentation of "appearances"; on the contrary, when we truly
return to experience, we realize that we apprehend those surfaces as different surfaces *of* the same guitar. To reduce experience to a mere series of appearances is, in James's terminology, to privilege the disjunctions of experience over its conjunctions (1967, 42–43). Husserl coined the term *synthesis
of identification* to refer to the constitution of unified phenomena from
their various perspectives, facets, or aspects (1960, 41–43). Such a conjunction synthesizes the various momentary views into a unit, which we then
experience as autonomous from us and other. All unitary and repeatable
phenomena are constituted through a synthesis of identification.[2]

These ideas extend the lines of argument presented in Chapter 8. When
I established that a series of notes were taken together to form a phrase, I
was exploring how the phrase was constituted as a unified phenomenon

through a synthesis of identification. When I examined the protention and retention of notes within the phrase, I was exploring the temporal relationships among the various facets of the phenomenon. Every category of musical phenomena is constituted through a characteristic synthesis of identification; two examples will suggest the possible application of these ideas.

First, take the notion of a "drum groove." To hear the part in Figure 13 as a "drum groove" means to grasp the *noema* in a very specific way. There is no question, of course, that each particular *noema* of bar 1 is a unique spatiotemporal event, but when we hear the part as a groove, we do not hear the various drum beats and cymbal hits as radically discrete. Instead, we grasp them as part of a unit, and each successive bar is heard as an iteration of that unit. Further, any fills (Figures 14 and 15) or participatory discrepancies are informed by our protentions and retentions of past groove units. In phenomenological terms, we can say that the various *noema* of bar 1 are grasped in the synthesis of identification and are experienced as a unit that repeats.

A chord progression, experienced as a statement of harmonic rhythm, is constituted through a very different synthesis of identification. To hear the part in Figure 16 as the progression /A-7/ D7/ Gmaj 7/ (/ii7/ V7/ I7/) means to grasp the *noema* in a very specific way. All of the notes in the first bar, for example, must be synthesized together and taken as a unit here. As a

snare
bass drum
high hat

Figure 13. An example of a rock groove

Figure 14. A fill played against the implied groove

Figure 15. A second fill played against the implied groove

Conclusions / 243

Figure 16. Synthesis of identification in harmonic rhythm

statement of the harmonic rhythm, that unit must be conjoined to protentions of the upcoming D7 and the tonic G-major 7 chord. The differences between the drum groove as a type of phenomenon and the chord progression as a type of phenomenon could not be more stark. The elements of a drum groove are synthesized into temporal units on the level of one or two bars; the elements of a chord progression can be synthesized to form much longer phenomena. The drum groove sets up rhythmic and timbral protentions, while the chord progression sets up harmonic and melodic protentions as well. The various elements of the groove (drum beats, cymbal hits) are synthesized together even if they are slightly non-metronomic; in fact, according to participatory discrepancy theory, drum grooves are improved if their elements are varied in time. The elements of a chord progression (pitched notes) may be detuned and still synthesized into a unit, but few would suggest that the chord progression is neccesarily improved by such detuning.

Even this brief comparison of the synthesis of identification in the drum groove and the chord progression suggests questions for future study and huge areas of research. First of all, it should be clear that phenomena are synthesized at various levels. Individual notes and chords constitute chord progressions as unified phenomena; notes and chords, however, are not monads but multifaceted phenomena, and the problem of the relationship of a phenomenon to its facets is a rich one. As the discussion of the relationships among the sections of a song showed, phenomena are taken together to make up larger-scale entities in experience; this is also an important vein for future research. Further, not all types of phenomena have clearly demarcated boundaries. The reverb-soaked "washes" and soundscapes of various kinds of electronic music are such an example, and exploring the concept of discrete phenomena could prove instructive. Future research should examine how the participants from various musical cultures constitute the facets, phenomena, and larger-scale entities of their musical experience.

But even before such research has been performed, the examples we have explored point the way toward new perspectives. Comparing the synthesis of identification in the drum groove and the chord progression suggests how dissimilar and unique are the various phenomena that emerge in musical experiences. When we reflect on the diversity of musical phenomena that populate experiences cross-culturally—drum groove, harmonic rhythm, *pathet*, *raga*, timeline—we begin to glimpse the endless ways in which experience can be constituted. To appreciate the complexity of this issue, however, we must further recall that many different kinds of musical phenomena are constituted *at the same time* in any given musical experience. In "Turn for the Worse," for example, a drum groove, a chord progression, and an undulating melody are all simultaneously constituted by the listeners and related to one another in complex ways. When we recall that each of these seemingly natural phenomena is culturally specific, and that their juxtaposition is the product of a highly contingent musical and social history, we begin to appreciate the sociality of musical experience.[3]

Returning the discussion to the larger themes of the section, it is clear that the synthesis of identification is a kind of perceptual practice. Thus, temporal phenomena such as drum groove and harmonic rhythm are neither inherent in the musical sound nor universally obvious; they are actively constituted by the subject—a subject whose every action is influenced by and oriented toward situated and broader social contexts. We often think of musical cultures as differentiated by the artifacts produced under their aegis. One of the main purposes of Part II has been to show that the subject's perceptual engagement with the world—the *noesis* as well as the *noema*—is culturally specific as well. Deeply informed by my music school training, for example, I initially grasped the power chords of the solo section as all within the E-minor key area. Dann, immersed in the sonic universe of death metal and valuing chaotic sounds, heard the part as chromatic and ambiguous. Analogous differences in perception occurred in our discussion of the bridge and the chorus. Phenomenological ethnography—the never-completed attempt to constitute the world as the other does—attempts both to bridge and to highlight the social basis of our perceptual practices.

We are now at a point where we may synthesize the three major themes of Part II: the practice of perception, the organization of the living present on broad time scales, and the critical role of affect in musical experience. Chapter 8 showed that the organization of the living present does not occur only at the level of individual phrases; our experiences of particular phrases are themselves nested within protentions and retentions of other sections and the form of the song as a whole. By extension, it is not hard to see that our experiences of entire songs may be nested within protentions and retentions of the entire event, and the event in turn is experienced within the context of the subject's past. This is not to say that every event in the subject's life is retained at every moment in the living present; the retentions of lived events cannot be infinitely piled up. But as the existential phenomenologists have shown, the living present is experienced as nested within a horizon of history and society (Ihde 1976). Just as we experience the surfaces of the guitar as facets of a real other that always hides some dimensions from us, we experience all situated practice as nested within the temporal context of our past lives and the spatial context of the world outside the event—a world of other places outside of our view and a world of other people we do not know individually, but whom we know exist "out there."

My past experiences are connected to events in the present situated context in a wide variety of ways. Past experiences may directly influence situated practice, with or without our reflective awareness. Constraining and enabling, past experience impinges on present practice by providing unreflected-upon assumptions and socially based intuitions. This universe of meanings is what allows all subjects to answer the question, What's going on here? when they enter one of the routine situations of their society. It is exactly this domain that ethnography has traditionally tried to illuminate—the domain of culture. By the same token, subjects may reflectively draw upon past experience, interacting with stocks of cultural knowledge and responding creatively in the event. It is this active manipulation of culture that has so interested scholars in the last twenty years, from Del Hymes's "Folklore's Nature and the Sun's Myth" (1975) and Barbara Kirshenblatt-Gimblett's "A Parable in Context" (1975) to any number of contemporary studies.

The central point is that if we wish to get a richer understanding of a subject's perceptual practices, we must examine the past experiences that inform them. David Sudnow's brilliant body-phenomenology of jazz piano, *Ways of the Hands* (1978), shows both the power and the limitation of a "microlevel" focus. In that work, Sudnow shows how he, as a jazz musician, actively engages with the piano, constituting physical space and musical time in culturally specific ways. Sudnow's discussion of situated practice is both unique and profound; however, phenomenology need not stop at the so-called microlevel. *Ways of the Hands* doesn't tell us *why* the pianist wants to make music that sounds like jazz, what emotions are evoked in his playing, and how he is located in a social history that enabled that playing. The discussion of the relationship of the organization of attention to larger social and political ideologies in Chapters 5 and 6, and the discussion of Dann's perception of the solo section in Chapter 8 have been attempts to answer these kinds of questions.

If our goal is to achieve partial sharing and to understand the subject's experience, to stop at the situated constitution of perception would leave us with only part of the story. We must go further and ask, for example, What past social experiences have led Dann to use music in the ways that he does? What are his goals in music making and what are the concrete consequences of that action? Knowing that Dann wants to make intellectually and affectively powerful music, we may ask specifically, What kinds of emotions does the music stir and why does he want to evoke those emotions? Most important, we must ask what kinds of everyday experiences impinge upon his music making. These questions focus on practice at the medial level and have been partially explored in Part I. My larger point is that music's affective content and meaning are the link between musical structure and the broader aspects of the participant's social life.

Even this level of discussion, however, leaves us with only part of the story and, in effect, a partial distortion. We are all aware that our own situated experiences are nested within the context of our own past lives and a contemporary world that is there for us to explore. Further, it is directly given in experience that the world existed before the horizon of our past experiences, what Alfred Schutz calls the world of our predecessors (1967, 207–14). This is the social history into which we are thrust and which is not of our own choosing. Dann's social experiences, his musical uses, and his aesthetic projects did not arise by themselves; they came into being and were informed by the past acts of others. Rich musical ethnography must take this context into account.

It may seem that such a history cannot be understood phenomenologically, that history is outside of experience and independent of individual subjects. As I have suggested in Chapter 1, however, nothing could be further from the case. The historical past is a history *for* experience and a history in experience: history is there for experience inasmuch as past events, no matter their span, can potentially be grasped by a historically reflecting subject. Taken in this way, the currents of history can be understood as cross-situational phenomena; such phenomena are grasped in reflection as chains of contexts, actions, and consequences across large spans of space and time. Further, history is there as experience inasmuch as the experiences of our predecessors can be partially shared with anyone reflecting historically. Understood in this way, the study of history is the ethnography of the past, and partial sharing is enabled through the office of durable mediators: artifacts, remains, historical documents, and memories. In understanding history in this way, the researcher follows the basic phenomenological method. The work emerges from the certainty of the subject's concrete experience, moves outward to understand the world as experience, and achieves a partial understanding of others as particular subjects.

Conceptualized in this way, it is clear that Dann's music, Chris's music, Larry's music, and Jerome's music cannot be richly understood without situating their constitution of perception within broader social and historical contexts. Determining which parts of that immense domain were consequential for their musical practices is, of course, complex. As a case study in cross-situational phenomenology, Part III will refocus the inquiry once again to exclude everything but Dann Saladin, death metal, and the social and historical context of deindustrialized Akron, Ohio.

Just as we experience situations as nested within our own personal history and the history of our predecessors, we are also aware that the present has consequences for our descendants. This future orientation evokes James's famous reflex arc—the complex connections among perception, reflection, and action—and reminds us that we as scholars are actors in the world of our research participants. As a result, Part III will focus on the tensions and reciprocities between the most proactive aspect of social inquiry—critical scholarship—and the ethnographic project of partially sharing the experiences of research participants.

PART THREE

MUSIC, EXPERIENCE, AND SOCIETY: DEATH METAL AND DEINDUSTRIALIZATION IN AN AMERICAN CITY

TEN

Death Metal Perspectives
Affect, Purpose, and the Social Life of Music

*Subjects at Work: A Phenomenological Approach to the
Dialectic of Garnering Participant Perspective and Doing
Critical Scholarship*

Descriptive ethnography: Garnering participant perspective

Taken in conjunction with the data on the metal performance event in Chapter 3, the foregoing discussion of affect and musical structure has moved our ethnography of death metal to the edge of the situated context itself. If we are to share, in part, the participants' experiences, however, we must do more than describe their situated contexts, perceptual practices, and experiences of musical affect. As the link between musical structure and broad social and historical context, emotion is more than a beating heart and churning stomach; likewise, musical activity is more than playing guitar or organizing perception in the performance event. Any momentary affective quality is informed by a complex relationship with the subject's goals in the situation, and all exercises of agency exist in relationship, however complex and contradictory, with the subject's broader values and plans. This is not to say that all people have coherent, reflectively formed projects that direct their conduct. It is to say, however, that each momentary experience of affect and situated action exist in a relationship with, and are informed by, a meaningful social past and a set of expectations of the future, however fragmentary or contradictory that context may be. If we seek to understand the perspectives of our research participants, we must explore these projects, expectations, and contexts.

Observing that a piece of music is infused with a quality of aggressiveness, for example, is only the starting point of our description of the participant's experience; merely adding contextual and bodily dimensions to the account does not suffice for a thorough description. The righteous rage of an American Christian metal band and the disgusted rage of an English hardcore outfit are not the same; neither is it the case that the affect in each band's music is the same, but the ideologies associated with them are different. The quality and texture of affect is inextricably entwined with the values, projects, meanings, and ideologies for which they are enacted. Not only is the rage to wipe away sin qualitatively distinct from a titanic disgust with English society, but the quality and texture of the rage itself is not fully separable from the desire to wipe sin away or the cleansing act itself. To begin to appreciate musical experience, we must not understand only the narrow musical goals of the situated actor; we must also understand the broader purposes within which those goals are nested and the social and historical context that informs them. Thus, we must not just ask, What is the structure of the tonality here, or What does this guitar part *feel* like? Though those are necessary for thorough research, we must go further to ask, Why do the participants want to create these aggressive sounds? How do their musical goals and larger projects connect with other aspects of their social experience?

Our lives are composed of experience. Doing humanistic ethnography means partially sharing those experiences, engaging with the world as the other does, and understanding the other's life on his or her own terms. In this enriched sense, understanding the other's experiences does not merely mean reading an abstract description of his or her position in the social structure, but grasping the meanings of his or her actions and projects in the broader context of his or her social life. When the experiences of the other—framed as representations and tumbling through the reader's mind—are taken on their own terms, taken with a high degree of sharing, felt with great affective, power and (within that literary frame) marked as self, then a level of sharing has occurred and a kind of intimacy has been established. The self in all its political and historical concreteness is partially transcended. And while descriptions of broad-scale patterns of practice and trains of context and consequence may teach us about the nature of larger social forces, humanistic phenomenology can help us to transcend our individual boundaries, if only partially.

The problem of contemporary ethnography
and the idea of critical phenomenology

Along with the goal of sharing experiences comes the goal of abstracting generalizations about experience from the data at hand. The larger theoretical project of this section is to explore the possibilities of doing critical scholarship under the aegis of phenomenology.

At first glance, the idea seems absurd. How can a scholarship grounded in the subject's experience ever be critical of that subject's experience? What, in fact, can the ethnographer say that the subject cannot already say better from direct experience? The question is not a parochial concern of phenomenology or social theory; on the contrary, it goes to the heart of contemporary folklore, anthropology, sociology, and cultural studies. From at least the time of Boas, one of the ethnographer's main tasks has been the garnering of "native perspective." With the complex situations of the postcolonial and postmodern world, that ethnographic project has run into seemingly intractable problems. Rightly shamed by anthropology's colonial past and rightly fearful of participating in the injustices of contemporary globalization, some postmodern ethnographers have turned to collaborative work and experimental writing to embrace the perspective of the other more fully (see Marcus and Fischer 1986; Clifford and Marcus 1986). Other postmodern ethnographers have followed the antihumanistic strands of their tradition and given up the notion of the subject. Throwing aside the quest for the other's perspective, these scholars seek to critique power relations by exploring superorganic entities such as the Site or Discourse (for example, Dorst 1989).

The problem of the subject is paralleled by the tension between garnering participant perspective and doing critical scholarship. When ethnographers claim social utility for their work, they usually do so by referring to one of two noble ends. On the one hand, pursuing the deep insight that experience is culturally constructed, some scholars seek to show how perception depends on social context and how facts and values are relative to those who perceive them. On the other hand, led by a praiseworthy commitment to social justice, other work seeks to criticize inequitable social relations and expose ideas that cause dominated groups to participate in their own undoing. There has always been a tension between these ends, and, in the present intellectual context, that tension can no longer be denied. Here I shall show that an existential and phenomenological response to the problem can provide a way out. I shall start by showing that, from the perspective of existential phenomenology, critical scholarship is tenable, useful, and, in some cases, morally unavoidable. I shall then suggest that tensions between the perspective of the research participant and ethnographer can be resolved by understanding and accepting the subjectivity of both parties; dialectic interaction between the two, I argue, is the best method for dealing with this tension. Finally, I explore the politics of death metal as a case study in critical phenomenology.

Doing critical phenomenology:
The dialectic of partial sharing and social critique

The idea that critical scholarship conflicts with phenomenology is a fallacy that comes from confusing phenomenology with a facile subjectivism. Husserl held that experience is the apodictic (unquestionably certain) ground of all knowledge. Applying this notion to the study of specific cultures (the "*hylētic*" particulars of social research) we can say that partial sharing and social interaction must be taken as the apodictic ground of ethnography. Such a position places the subject in the center of all inquiry and makes phenomenology a kind of humanism. But Husserl did not have an unquestioning allegiance to the immediate, given experience. In *Cartesian Meditations* (1960), he claimed that no single, momentary phenomenon exhausts all the possible ways that an object can emerge in experience; for him, doing phenomenology meant rigorously exploring the various ways the object can be grasped in perception and fantasy variation to reveal its possibilities and boundaries.

Returning once again to *Experimental Phenomenology*, Ihde effectively illustrates these ideas through the use of multistable drawings (1977, 92), the most helpful for the issue at hand being the famous Necker cube. Ihde's text and accompanying diagrams teach the reader how to view this simple line drawing as either a box viewed from above or a box viewed from below; Ihde shows how these two distinct visual experiences are given as the certain ground for the discussion and cannot be erased. He cautions us, however, that the exploration of these figures cannot stop at this initial stage, and he carefully reveals a wide variety of other ways of grasping the drawings (94–96). Ihde's discussion emerged from his introductory class on phenomenology, and the research proceeded in a somewhat ethnographic fashion. Concerned with partially sharing his students' perspectives on the drawings, he treated every given experience as the certain ground of the research. He did not, however, simply accept his students' initial experiences of the object as complete; he and the students explored the drawings together to reveal the full range of their possibilities. Further, Ihde did not naively accept any report of his students' experiences. For example, Ihde recognized that there is a limit to what any one drawing will yield; one cannot grasp the Necker cube and yield the same experience as that of the divided hexagon (102) without adding several lines and moving from perception to visual imagination. Because the world exists first in and for perceptual experience before it is reflected upon, and because the world is there to be shared, Ihde had grounds for being critical of his students' descriptions of their experiences.

Using an introductory class in phenomenology as a metaphor for ethnographic research is instructive but problematic. As I have suggested throughout, our reflective descriptions of experience are distinct from and never fully account for the experiences they attempt to describe. Just as students may think that there are only one or two ways to grasp the Necker cube, the professor's broader experience may allow him or her to see further possibilities. This is not to say that ethnographers are teachers and ethnographic subjects are their students (even less do I wish to carry the teacher-student power relation into the ethnographic process). I do suggest, however, that subjects can misunderstand their experiences; as a result, critical research is phenomenologically tenable.

I wish, however, to make a much stronger claim. In an oblique reference to Freud, Husserl recognized that certain "psychological resistances" (1931, 180) may cause us to misunderstand and misdescribe our experiences. Likewise, we can recognize that multistable Necker cubes are one thing, but experiences like anger, work, and power are quite another. Such phenomena are not merely more complex than the Necker cube; vast political interests come into play in their interpretation. Advertisers, public relations workers, politicians, clergy, educators, and legions of other ideologists strive daily to influence our interpretations of society and history, of action and its consequences. The politics of representation, not to mention the hide-and-go-seek of depth psychology, enter in here, and I need only reference these massive areas of study to suggest the utility of critical work in a social world of power relations. But my claim is not merely that critical scholarship is tenable or useful; in many spheres of social life, the ethical dimensions are *unavoidable* and critical scholarship is the only defensible alternative.

As we have observed, phenomenological ethnography proceeds by partial sharing. This approach presupposes that the ethnographer is a subject, a contingent and responsible moral agent sharing not only the experiences but the very world of the ethnographic subjects. The point is well articulated by Robert Georges and Michael Owen Jones's conception of the "results" of social scientific and humanistic research. In *People Studying People*, their classic book on field methods (1980), they urge researchers to view the results of their work, not merely as the deductions drawn from the data or even the production of the ethnography itself, but as the full range of consequences that emerge from the fieldwork.[1] These consequences include the writing of the book, the relationships between the research participant and the fieldworker, the changes that result in their lives, and the social consequences that emerge from the book's publication. Such a broad vision of results has implications for the ethics of fieldwork. More important, however, it reveals the ethnographer for what he or she is—a subject among subjects, emerging from a social history that he or she cannot control, and responsible for the consequences of his or her activities, scholarly and otherwise, that he or she can never fully predict.

The scholarly actions significant to the present discussion are the representation of the subject's experiences and the act of criticism. For tightly focused research into some spheres of practice, the ethnographic project can often proceed solely in the descriptive mode. For example, a sharply bounded study of techniques in some genre of expressive culture may merely depict the research participant's views of the experience and proceed with little fear of ethical dilemmas. Some limited form of criticism may ensue if the ethnographer discovers some contradiction or incoherence in the participant's account; in many narrowly framed research problems, however, these may be resolved with cooperative exploration and dialogue. Here, the scholar's tight focus and choice of research problem place political issues outside the bounds of the study. However, when we begin to take an even slightly wider view, or if we choose to directly examine power relations, then the tension between garnering participant perspective and doing critical scholarship may become unavoidable.

The dilemma is sharp and painful. On the one hand, we have the important goal of understanding another's experiences; on the other, we cannot deny that one can be misled in understanding one's own experience. In some situations, the research participants will have a rich understanding of their social situation, and there will be no tension between ethnographer and participant perspectives. But what does the fieldworker do if the participant actively denies that he or she is the victim of an injustice that the fieldworker sees as clear and manifest? What does the fieldworker do if the participant spews out hatred and lies? Extreme cases will illustrate the point. How does the fieldworker react to the abused child that denies the beatings? The alcoholic who denies he or she has a problem? The brainwashed cult member? How does the fieldworker react to the participant who stoutly holds that anyone who can't find work deserves to starve? That African-Americans are inherently inferior to European Americans? That a wife should be controlled and dominated by a husband? That Jews command the world economy and should all be fed into the gas chambers? Ideologies that deny the victim's own oppression are wrong on phenomenological grounds because they conflate the participant's reflective descriptions with the fullness of their experience. Ideologies of hatred are wrong on phenomenological grounds because they deny the experiences and legitimate the suffering of the murdered, the raped, and the subjugated. To blandly represent such positions crowns them with the aura of scholarly authority; to hold a facile subjectivist relativism, to accept all views as merely one version of the truth, is to be guilty of complicity; simply to avoid the issue distorts the participant's experience and whitewashes the situation.

When we recognize that the ethnographer is always a responsible subject among responsible subjects, then ethical issues are unavoidable—all the more so when that ethnographer explicitly focuses on power relations or broadens a narrow technical inquiry to embrace the fullness of a participant's life. Because, as William James observed (1962), failing to act is a kind of action, critical phenomenology is not merely tenable or useful. Here the ethical dimension of the research is unavoidable and critical work is the only responsible option.[2]

But even the painful confrontations given above do not capture the full situation. While ethnographers of the Ku Klux Klan or the American Nazi Party may feel no moral difficulty in critiquing the blatantly hateful positions of their research participants, most ethnographers work with far more difficult and subtle situations. For example, all of Western Marxism turns on the question of how capitalism has survived in a world of increasing injustice and suffering, how monied interests are able to dominate great masses of people with relatively little physical coercion. As I have suggested throughout, theoretical orientations that posit reified "structures" or "discourses" are false on phenomenological grounds. Any easy reliance on the notion of false consciousness that is not based in careful ethnography runs the risk of doing violence to the subjectivity that it claims to respect. As a general statement of method, the subject position of both the ethnographer and the research participant necessitates that we take a dialectical approach to garnering participant perspectives and doing critical scholarship. Cutting off either side of the dialectic endangers either project.

Both sides of the equation require careful attention. On the one side, to do critical work that fails to explore the research participant's experience dehumanizes that participant and sets up the kind of power relation that the critical scholarships of Marxism or feminism seek to avoid. Perhaps more important, the failure to achieve the partial sharing of ethnography in critical scholarship also distorts the phenomena and endangers the critical project. No account of objective social conditions (even understood as the context formed by the intentional and unintentional consequences of intentional action) can effectively explain social reality. Because ethnographic subjects make history with their agency, we must understand their lived experiences and interpretations, no matter how hateful or misled. To conflate the scholar's interpretation with the objective and the participant's perspective with the merely subjective is the first step toward setting the scholar outside of the world, the first move in denying the scholar's subjectivity, the first phase in the occlusions of scientism.

As both phenomenologists and logical positivists have suggested, truth is inherently subjective; this does not mean that anything goes, but that truth is always the truth for a subject. Any denial of this fact in human research does an injustice to both the research participant and the ethnographer. As a result, ethnographic data collection must be understood as partial sharing and the ethnographer must be understood as a subject among subjects. Ideally, this is achieved through the intimacy of face-to-face ethnography, but it can also be achieved through the mediations of historical documents or archeological evidence. And while there are clear-cut cases of hatred or self-deception that must be condemned out of hand, the social situations of most historical subjects call for careful and nuanced analyses; here, the subject's own perspectives are often as valuable as that of any "outside" observer. To ignore the subject's experiences and their social context is to threaten the entire critical project. When the fieldworker first begins to feel that the participants are engaged in some hateful beliefs or practices or that some self-deception obscures the participants' understanding of their experiences, the fieldworker must make a strenuous attempt to achieve partial sharing. The great ethnographies of the past have shown that garnering the participants' perspectives can yield powerful new ethical insights; as a result, all value judgment must be temporarily suspended to overcome in part the ethnographer's presuppositions.

The process of partial sharing is potentially limitless, however, and when the ethnographer is convinced that hatreds or self-deceptions are present, he or she must engage in critical work. To take what research participants say at face value, to assume that those participants can have a complete understanding of their experiences, is to deny the very subjectivity of those participants, deify them, and place them outside the world. To avoid critical work when hatred or self-deception are clearly present, to lapse into a spineless relativism, is to run the risk of complicity. Such a fate defeats the very humanism that the relativism is meant to defend.[3]

Of course the more relativistic reader at this moment will ask on what grounds the ethnographer can place himself or herself (let us say herself) into a community and appoint herself as a judge of hatred and self-deception. The relativistic reader may claim that by appointing herself as judge and jury of the participant's misconceptions, the ethnographer is in fact giving herself a higher authority and again placing herself outside the world. Such an argument is largely grounded in the fact that anthropology and folklore have generally focused on disempowered and marginalized groups. Burdened by a shameful legacy of complicity in colonization, for example, a European or urban ethnographer would seemingly have little right to criticize Third World or rural others. But when we see that the ethnographic subject may be a sweatshop owner, a child abuser, or Klansman, then the need for critical work begins to emerge. When we admit that the disenfranchised do not always have the fullest understanding of their social circumstance, the problem begins to stand out. When we understand that *all* research participants are engaged in complex webs of power relations, that *all* subjects (ethnographers and research participants) have dirty hands, then the tension between garnering participant perspective and doing critical scholarship appears in sharp relief.

The relativistic reader may, however, push these concerns aside and hold fast to her first claim. If, the relativist argues, the ethnographer is phenomenologically bound to admit her own position as a limited subject, on what grounds can she claim a higher moral authority and a less clouded vision than the research participant? The question brings our entire debate to a head and would seem to have no answer. But as Alan Watts (1958, 28–29) observed, the solution to any truly vexing paradox is found by moving through the difficulty, not away from it.

The relativist is correct: the ethnographer may have a broader knowledge than the research participant and a clearer view. Or she simply may not. The participant may have a vested interest in a power relation or may be too occluded by false consciousness to understand her own subjugation. Or the ethnographer may indeed be wrong. But the ethnographer's fallibility, the very emblem of the partiality and contingency of the subject, does not absolve her from action, critical work, and responsibility; in the language of Jean-Paul Sartre, it condemns her to it. Again we return to James: being limited subjects in a world of contingencies, we cannot avoid acting. Failing to engage in critical work has its consequences just as critical ethnography does. As a result, both relativistic abstention from critique and vigorous critical scholarship are kinds of actions. Truly radical relativism, the lack of academic authority, and the ethnographer's inevitable subjectivity thrust the ethnographer into the world. Whether the ethnographer chooses to abstain from comment or write a polemic, she is taking an action for which she is responsible.[4] Action and nonaction form a moral continuum in history.

This train of argument would seem again to thrust us into radical relativism with any move allowable and nothing resolved; on the contrary, we have finally reached our conclusion. In fact, the ethnographer can do anything she wants to. She is free to act as she chooses, to critique or abstain from critique. The most strident Frankfurt School critic and most radical postmodern relativist can agree that ethnographers have taken both paths and will continue to do so in the future. What this line of argument shows, however, is that in either case the ethnographer must accept responsibility for her actions in research, critical, "objective," or abstaining. The moral dimension of fieldwork is in many settings unavoidable, and abstaining from critical work is merely one move among many in the moral continuum of history. Above, I have suggested that serious dangers may be associated with abstaining. In some situations, however, it may in fact be the best route—though abstention is not an escape from the continuum but merely one move within it. How the consequences play themselves out depends, of course, on the exigencies of each ethnographic situation.

In any situation, however, the ethnographer must constantly affirm her subjectivity and responsibility; to avoid this is to be guilty of Sartre's bad faith. In critical work, the ethnographer must admit that her critiques are a subject's critiques and not some absolute critique, that the values they promulgate are her own values and not some paradoxical "objective" values. Again, the extremes illustrate the point. Working with a Nazi research participant (and I must make it clear that none of my research participants are fascists and I in no way intend to imply any critique of them here), the fieldworker must make every attempt to understand the experiences and perspectives of the anti-Semite. This in no way prevents the ethnographer from criticizing the Nazi. Further, the fieldworker must acknowledge that her critique—Jews do not run the world economy, it is wrong to commit genocide—is hers. It does not exist by itself, but for the subject (and, I would argue, for any subject). As such, the ethnographer takes responsibility, and may receive credit, for holding the position. She may argue tenaciously, and even fight, to prove its truth. But to avoid bad faith she must hold that that truth is a truth, not for itself, but for the ethnographer as subject—and, in the Nazi example, for any subject.

The main methodological consequence of the subjectivity of the ethnographer and the research participant is that ethnographic work is a dialectic between two subjects. Given the face-to-face intimacy of the fieldwork setting, this dialectic should ideally take the form of the primordial dialectic—the dialogue—but of course there are situations where this is impossible. Having established the subjectivity, fallibility, and situatedness of both the research participant and the ethnographer, described the partiality and the possibility of sharing, and suggested the necessity of dialogue, it is time to recall that theoretical work is always best achieved when yoked with data. The remainder of this section takes the politics of the death metal underground as a case study in critical phenomenology and focuses on the experiences of Dann Saladin. Following the scheme elaborated above, the balance of this chapter presents a descriptive ethnography and seeks to share in part Dann's situated musical goals, larger aesthetic projects, and encompassing social beliefs. The following chapter provides a critical dialogue between Dann and myself on issues of race and class in the death metal scene and American society. While the details of his biography, his perspectives on the scene, and his broader views are all specifically Dann's, many of the themes in this section echo those found in Chapter 3. Dann's self-conscious opposition to the perceived banalities of rock and the perceived political dogmatism of hardcore, his use of music to explore emotions and overcome obstacles, and his commitment to the ideals of critical thinking, personal motivation, and personal responsibility are not idiosyncratic to Dann, but are found broadly throughout the death metal underground. While it is always difficult to generalize from depth ethnography to larger patterns, the description and dialogue given in this section can point the way to larger insights and perspectives.

Purposes in History and Society: An Ethnography of the Politics of Death Metal

Background

To understand Dann's broader goals and aims, we would do well to know the man a bit better. Dann Saladin was born in 1971 in Summit County. As a child Dann loved cartoons, soldier toys, and all forms of martial play. The youngest of three children, his father worked as a manager in plastics factories and his mother kept house. Throughout the 1970s and 1980s the Saladin family moved constantly as different jobs beckoned his father, and the moving was not always easy. Although Dann bears no wounded inner child crying to be healed and voices only the highest praise for his parents' childrearing, throughout our interviews Dann alluded to the problems typical of a child from a peripatetic family. Dann would just start to make friends and the family would move. With Dann and his brother separated by only a year and a half, sibling quarrels occurred all the time, the worst happening during a transitional period in which the family was living in a cramped motel. In his early high school years, Dann's family moved to Richmond, Indiana, a small town on the Ohio border. He made friends but the sleepy pace of the town drove Dann to distraction, and he was thrilled when the family moved back to Kent, Ohio (just outside of Akron) while he was still in high school. Today, Dann credits the frequent moves with giving him a strong sense of independence.

Dann's life story is similar to that of other metalheads outlined above (see Chapter 3). In his early teens, he developed his first real interest in music. While he recalls his first Kiss album and the commercial hard rock of the late 1970s with a distant affection, his real passion for music exploded during his first year back in Ohio when an acquaintance lent him a Metallica tape. Leaving for the weekend to visit friends in Richmond, Dann listened to the tape on his Walkman incessantly; he had never heard anything that powerful, musically intricate, or intense; by the end of the weekend, Dann was hooked. He soon became interested in both hardcore and metal, and what followed was a series of musical involvements that virtually all of my heavy metal research participants reported: hunting down new metal recordings, learning an instrument, joining bands, going to shows, and constantly searching for heavier music.

An outsider in high school, Dann dressed in jeans and metal T-shirts but spent his time with the punk crowd. When he graduated from high school, his parents offered to pay for some higher education, and Dann spent one semester at a local college. Never fond of school, Dann was wrapped up in his bands and the music scene and made poor grades. His parents said they would not pay for him to get Ds, and constant fights between him and his brother over the car they shared spurred him to quit school and get a job in a plastics factory. After college Dann held a variety of blue-collar jobs. At the time of our interviews he was working more than fifty hours a week in a nonunion factory job polishing metal molds for a few dollars per hour over minimum wage. Sharing the basement of his parents' house with his brother and eating frequent meals upstairs, he is able to afford payments on a pickup truck and own some musical equipment, a stereo, a television set, and a VCR. Dann's father works for himself as a consultant to the plastics industry. His sister, a polyglot, attended Earlham College and ever since has been in the Air Force translating Russian. Dann's brother didn't attend college and works in construction in the Akron area.

After being in a series of punk and metal bands in high school, Dann eventually formed Sin-Eater. The band's intense practice schedule and unusually large instrumentation (two basses, two guitars, two vocalists, and a drummer) gave Dann a serious musical outlet. He worked hard on the band, composing much of the music, setting up the shows and rehearsals, and doing endless promotional work through mail, zines, and flyers. Tensions between the musicians tore the band apart in September 1992, and Dann continued writing songs, doing mail, and keeping in contact with the scene while he searched for new musicians to play with. In the summer of 1993, Dann formed a joke band named Scumlord that played contemporary hardcore and kept him occupied until more serious opportunities arose. Filled with short parody songs, the band made two cheap demos and played a handful of shows. Since I left Ohio, Dann has formed a new

Dann Saladin at home.

group, Blood Coven, that briefly involved some of the old members of Sin-Eater and plays some of their songs.

All told, Dann and I had twelve interviews together. Lasting between two and five hours, most took place in his basement bedroom. The walls were covered with a bricolage of band posters, the tables and shelves with countless fanzines, tapes, CDs, boxes of old correspondence, records, notes for new songs, fantasy statuary, books, and musical equipment. As a basement, the room is dark by nature and made darker by soft lighting and Dann's gothic decors. In each interview Dann would wear jeans or shorts and a T-shirt from an underground band. Early on in the interview process I made a personal game out of trying to decipher the band names encrypted in intricate, gothic lettering on his shirts; eventually giving up, Dann helped me decipher the shirts at the beginning of each interview. A listener of broad tastes, Dann has a record collection including music from the entire span of underground punk and metal, as well as some mainstream rock, sound tracks, and experimental music. One evening I found Dann sitting in the darkened room, apparently doing nothing. After a short while I noticed a very quiet sound, and Dann explained to me that we were listening to the soundtrack from Francis Ford Coppola's *Dracula*. On another occasion, a few days before Halloween, I remarked that the room was all decked out for the holiday; we both smiled at the naïveté of the comment, and Dann said, "Everyday is Halloween to me." Beyond our interviews, I saw several of Dann's performances, and we attended a variety of shows and social functions together.

Proactive, motivated, and critical:
Representations of Dann's identity

The elements of Dann's life story connect smoothly with his self-representations and larger musical and social beliefs. Over and over again, Dann represented himself as a critical thinker, robust individualist, and ardent self-motivator—a man actively engaged with making something of himself. Hardy individuality is not merely represented as some inherent aspect of his character; Dann values critical thought and self-motivation in others, propounds them in his music, and holds them up as the hallmark of the death metal underground. These characteristics were illustrated in our discussions of religion, everyday life, the meanings of the underground music scenes, and politics.

In our second interview, for example, Dann explained that he had recently shifted from a strident atheism to a more tolerant agnosticism. Although admitting that there may be a life after death and a superhuman will, and while voicing a tolerance for others' private religious lives, Dann held that in most cases religion is nothing more than an attempt by clergy to wield power and control the minds of their flock. Again and again in our interviews, Dann explained that religion's obsession with life after death distracts people from their lives in the present, and that he, Dann, is concerned with enjoying his life and achieving his goals in *this* world. And though Dann is tired of the endless hardcore songs that deride televangelists, he is quick to agree with their sentiments.

Dann's strong sense of self can also be found in his dealings with the Satanic elements of the death metal underground. Dann, and most metalheads, emphasized that Satanism is actually a very small part of the American metal scene, and Dann's relationship with that part of the scene is particularly revealing. Many people avoid metal because they fear its Satanic elements, but Dann's confidence in his ability to handle himself never allowed such fears to stand in his way of exploring the black metal sector of the scene. Further, Dann has always listened to Satanist bands and been willing to weigh the opinions and ideas expressed by them without fear of being overwhelmed by demonic influence. Though not a Satanist himself, he is sympathetic to one of their main tenets: Aleister Crowley's dictum "Do what thou wilt shall be the whole of the law." While Dann feels that this position must be moderated with a sensitivity to others, he explained that this emphasis on personal action and personal motivation is consistent with his own beliefs and the death metal underground as a whole. Dann is also sympathetic to the Satanist critique of Christianity, although he in no way advocates burning down churches or any other blasphemous activities.

Dann's depiction of himself as critical and proactive extended beyond religious issues to include his musical life. Most frequently, in our interviews, he accomplished these representations by juxtaposing his own beliefs and actions with the ill-considered dogma and apathetic involvements of those around him. Discussing his bands, for example, Dann explained that he and a few others were always the ones to write and arrange the songs, do the mail, and post flyers. Lazy, or merely uninspired, most of the other players made only the smallest contributions to songwriting and promotion, and Dann said that no amount of encouragement on his part would get them to be more active. On one occasion I observed to Dann that people at metal shows all tended to dress alike—black concert T-shirts and worn but not ripped jeans. Dann explained that people dress that way because they feel that they have to; he, on the other hand, has dressed this way for years and wears whatever he wishes at shows. Over and again, the differences between underground metal and commercial hard rock came up in our talks. Dann explained that he and other death metal fans engage intently with concerts or recordings. Careful to admit that there are good rock bands and interested rock listeners, Dann went on to explain that most radio music is banal background noise and most rock listeners have little aesthetic sensitivity. Further, Dann had numerous narratives of discovering musical gems in genres that most people simply ignore: Japanese noise bands, gothic punk, experimental guitar music, movie soundtracks, television commercials, and cartoon music.

This identity via opposition extends beyond Dann's musical life. Dann is often frustrated by the ease with which his friends acquire the beliefs of those around them or slip into apathetic routines. In one interview, Dann held up Karl (not his real name) as an example of the follower mentality. In high school, Dann relates, Karl was a punk's punk: he wore the standard punk garb, listened to the right punk music, displayed the classic punk attitude, and toed the party line of local punk beliefs. While the two were good friends, Dann always felt that Karl's punk persona was forced. Karl later joined a vegetarian reggae band, and Dann feels that Karl's subsequent vegetarianism was a direct result of the other band members' constant teasing. Discussing the issues of animal rights, Dann felt that Karl's vegetarianism was poorly thought through and forced.

If Karl was easily led, Dann admitted that he could at least find and hold down a job. Dann illustrated his proactive approach to life by explaining a typical day and opposing himself to his "apathetic" friends. Up at 5:30 A.M.,

Dann punches in at his job by six-thirty. He takes half an hour for lunch, keeps himself going with caffeinated sodas, and clocks out at five. When he gets home, he showers, grabs a quick dinner, and is off to practice; afterward, he relaxes with his girl friend and by 11:00 or 12:00 he is asleep again. His six-day workweek must also accommodate composition, mail, posting flyers, shows, household chores, and social events. All this is made easier by his recent job change. Before polishing molds, Dann was an assistant foreman at a plastics factory. Though the work was far from stimulating, his supervision of several people and machines gave the work a frenetic pace; eagerly sought by his employers for his industriousness, he worked six 10-hour days a week plus two weekends a month. The ten-and-a-half-hour day polishing molds is long, but requires so little attention that he once discovered that he had fallen asleep at work and kept on polishing. The youngest worker in a group of forty- and fifty-year-olds, Dann is horrified at the idea of sitting on a bench, tediously polishing molds for the rest of his life.

In juxtaposition to all this activity, Dann repeatedly derided Frank (not his real name) as the consummate slug, in and out of dead-end jobs since high school. Dann was amazed when, in one winter in the early 1990s, Frank took a seasonal job to end his latest spell of unemployment. Why work a job you know will end in six weeks, Dann asked, when you can get something permanent and stick with it? But Dann's proactivity is not a simple Protestant work ethic; Dann was much more fed up with Frank's iffy commitment to the underground. Dann said that members of Frank's band say he is notoriously unreliable in returning phone calls, showing up for practice, and doing band promotion. Even in recreation, Dann juxtaposed his own interest and vitality with others' apathy. Dann described his own frequent outings to shows, visits to friends in other cities, and adventuresome road trips; in sharp contrast, Dann said, all Frank did was smoke marijuana and hang out with his girlfriend.

And Dann's representation of Frank was not an isolated case. Again and again, Dann represented specific people around him or generalized others as apathetic and incurious. Early on, Dann explained to me that he didn't want the standard-issue life that so many Americans live: go to school, get married, have 2.3 children; work at a pointless job, come home, eat dinner, go to bed, get up, and do it again. In our interviews, Dann's careful listening, constant national and international correspondence, clubbing, and diverse social engagements were served up as testaments to his curiosity and involvement with life. Beyond his musical involvements, Dann spoke of his interest in popular science literature and spontaneous road trips with friends to serve as evidence for a proactive and energetic style. And most frequently, his active involvement in the scene and general curiosity was set up as a broad critique of the stultifications of contemporary American society and the apathy of those around him.

With all of these descriptions of Dann's critical views, the reader may draw the false impression that Dann is judgmental and doctrinaire in his individuality. While he is critical of the (perceived) banality of American popular culture and the sin of sloth, he is always careful to temper his critiques by stressing the value of tolerance. When lobbing his broadside attacks at religion, Dann was careful to stress that people should be free to believe anything they want to believe, and it is the soapbox proselytism, not the views themselves, that Dann finds most offensive. An omnivore, Dann has nothing against Karl's vegetarianism per se. Myself a vegetarian on ethical grounds, I discussed the topic with Dann at length and found him open to and tolerant of my views. Throughout our conversations, Dann was quick to express tolerance for difference and often referred to the problems of racism and hatred in America; at the same time, Dann offered that the tolerant individual must understand why the racist is a racist. Tolerance is a central theme throughout the death metal underground.

Aspects of the death metal scene (1):
The values of personal choice and tolerance

My discovery that Dann describes himself as a proponent of critical thought, curiosity, and robust individuality was no *tour de force* of ethnographic inquiry. The point simply could not be missed, and on the repeated occasions when I fed these perceptions back to Dann, he confirmed them wholeheartedly. And while I did no statistical study of the scene, all of my other death metal research participants spoke of the importance of critical thinking, individualism, and self-motivation. As abstract statements of values, those ideas would be present in any ethnography of death metal. But the issues become more nuanced and complex as we move from Dann's broad representation of himself to his view of the death metal scene and the values he claims are propounded there. While similar themes are brought out here, nuances emerge precisely in the space between values and their enactment in social life, between ideologies[5] and action. Significantly, Dann's vision of the death metal underground is largely formed in opposition to the hardcore underground.

Early on in the interviews, Dann began setting up the opposition between (what he saw as) hardcore punk's preachy and tedious politics and death metal's emphasis on critical thinking and individual action. In the second interview Dann voiced his dislike of gore metal—a narrow, underground metal subgenre whose lyrics solely depict images of graphic violence. Purely for shock, the gory imagery entails no creativity and leaves the listener bored. But to Dann, this music is nowhere near so tedious as the hardcore and thrash with which he used to involve himself. Dann explained that the underground is largely divided between the punk and metal scenes. As we saw in Chapter 3, the relationship between the two is complex; the scenes are fairly distinct, but many listeners are familiar with both musics and occasionally attend both kinds of shows. Further, punk has always been more explicitly political than metal. After many years of involvement with the hardcore scene, Dann became bored by what he saw as the monotonous politics of punk lyrics. Hardcore bands, Dann said, would hunt in the newspaper for topics and themes for songs; after hearing hundreds of tunes condemning televangelists, deforestation, and the killing of whales, Dann had had enough. He began to distance himself from the punk scene in the late 1980s. In 1993 Dann made a partial return to this scene with Scumlord, a group intended as a parody of punk's dogmatic and preachy style.

More than merely uncreative, the punk scene bothered Dann because of its divisiveness, authoritarianism, and hypocrisy. While some bands just employ the yelled vocal style and simple musical structures of punk to create the underground equivalent of good-time party music, most punk bands have a political thrust. Such bands, Dann explained, are not content merely to state a position; they have to win converts and won't listen to anyone who disagrees with them. Hardcore itself is divided between right- and left-wing bands, but Dann saw the two as more similar than different. As extremes of the spectrum tend to become indistinguishable, Dann explained, the constant preaching on both sides made that scene nearly unendurable. And with their inflated rhetoric, the bands' intolerance led to fights, name-calling, and a politics of division that threatened to destroy any unity the underground as a whole might have. Dann reserved his greatest wrath for straight edge, a hardcore genre formed around the opposition to drug and alcohol use. Dann claims that Cleveland's straight edge bands are not just preachy and boring; they're the worst substance abusers and greatest hypocrites in the underground. Karl's unthinking acceptance of vegetarianism can stand as an emblem of all that Dann found distasteful about the dogmatism of the Ohio punk scene in the late 1980s and early 1990s.

Musical reasons also contributed to Dann's disenchantment with the hardcore side of the underground: one variety of thrash evolved into speed metal—a genre defined largely by extremely fast tempi and an accelerated polka beat referred to as grind drumming. This obsession with tempo sacrificed emotion for pure energy, said Dann, and produced the flat, boring music that Sin-Eater sought to avoid. Also at this time, several noted thrash bands, including Metallica, gained more mainstream attention; in so doing, Dann said, they acquired just the out-of-touch rock star image that underground participants despise, and their music lost its cutting edge. While Dann never completely left the punk scene, he began to focus his energies on death metal.

Dann explained that, in opposition to the self-conscious rhetoric of hardcore, the metal side of the underground is oriented toward "freedom" and "personal choice." Politically, death metal is dead center, said Dann; metal bands want you to "feel your way" through each issue, make judgment calls, and question received wisdom. Confronted with a new issue, Dann said, a left-wing or right-wing punk would thoughtlessly toe the party line; metalheads, on the other hand, would be more careful to consider each issue on its own merits. "It's live for yourself," Dann explained, "live for freedom from anything that would be trying to force you to submit." Crowley's "Do what thou wilt" philosophy was a perfect statement of this perspective. When I asked if this emphasis on the individual was a reaction against the hardcore scene, Dann was quick to answer yes. Further, he allowed that the stultifying authoritarianism of the American high school and dead-end factory jobs contributed to death metal's emphasis on critical thought and individual choice. While there is explicitly political death metal, the lyrics of most bands focus on occult themes, grim nihilistic musings, and stories of personal tragedy.

Part and parcel of the death metal emphasis on individuality and critical thinking is the notion of tolerance. Skinheads and hardcore punks, Dann claimed, not only preach and proselytize; their interactions frequently threatened to explode into violence. In sharp contrast, Dann said, anyone is welcome at a death metal show—skinheads, straight edge punks, commercial hard rockers, and so on. How a punk treats a person depends on what that person believes or which group they belong to, Dann said; how a metalhead treats a person depends on how they behave. Dann is adamant about tolerance and unity in death metal in particular and in the underground as a whole, and he bemoaned the endless fights that broke out in the underground of the early 1980s.

Aspects of the death metal scene (2):
The practices of music making and the uses of rage

We now shift our focus from abstract values to the social practices and projects of the death metal underground; in so doing, we can begin to ground the sweeping generalities of self-representation in the concrete particularities of daily life. Indeed, when we speak on the abstract level of value and belief we almost *necessarily* speak in truisms and platitudes because such talk posits a deep layer of meaning that is somehow divorced from and later applied to action. Values and beliefs, however, are not deep guiding structures or consistent existential projects; like flows of reflections in situated practice, the beliefs and values that accompany our day-to-day lives are just as much an effect as a cause of action.[6] This is not to say that long-range plans or abiding values do not exist, but that all such plans and values are informed by our social history, geared toward the perceived possibilities of our life, and constantly reconsidered and negotiated in and by our daily practice. Here, our focus is on situated practice (understood at the level of "the kinds of things we tend to do these days") and the projects and values that are enmeshed with them—specifically, music making, music listening, and the uses to which those practices are put.

Why do people make and listen to death metal? Listening to underground musics, I could not help noticing the relentless aggression in both the hardcore and metal, and midway through the research process Dann and I discussed the topic in detail. I asked Dann if metalheads listen to death metal to experience anger and power; his first response was to avoid the idea that underground fans use music to bring about a rage solely for the pleasure of releasing it at the event. He explained that metal's anger is "a vent for life anger" and the frustrations that accrue in the workaday world. While most metalheads know the songs' lyrics from reading the inserts in the recordings, the shows themselves are primarily a place for a cathartic release of the rage that accrues in daily life. All of the underground musicians with whom I spoke voiced a clear and familiar litany of fears and complaints. Environmental destruction, civil unrest, the declining economic fortunes of working-class Ohio, and the daily frustrations of dead-end jobs were cited as pieces in the larger puzzle of pessimism and rage. Dann and other metalheads complained that the Parents' Music Resource Center has tried to depict metal as the cause of teenage disobedience, drug use, and suicide; the PMRC is wrong, the metalheads claim. Metal is used as a release from anger; it is not its source.

But Dann held that anger, or its turned-in corollary, depression, is at the base of most of the world's music, and he cited country music as an example. What made underground hardcore and metal fans stand out was their treatment of these emotions. Where the depression invoked by country musicians and listeners is a kind of crying-in-your-beer sadness, said Dann, people involve themselves with underground music to experience an "anti-procrastination and proactive" rage. Repressed anger and the hopelessness that emerges from it are exactly what limit people and sap them of their motivation and energy, Dann said; people play and listen to death metal to draw that anger out, jump-start individual action, and acquire the energy to overcome impediments and restraints.

It is exactly at this point that all of the detailed work on the constitution of musical experience pays off. It would be far too easy to caricature death metal as merely aggressive music. While anger and aggression are clearly present in death metal, the ethnography of musical sound has shown that musicians, moshing crowds, and listeners come together at events to evoke, explore, and utilize a wide range of related emotions and qualities: anger, rage, aggression, pure and explosive energy, grandeur, depression, lumbering heaviness, confusion, and countless others. People do go to the mosh pits to blast out their rage in cathartic release, but the pit is just one place in the show and the moshy parts are just one moment in the songs. Dann emphasized that grindcore or speed metal may focus on pure energy or rage, that some hardcore musics are nothing more than an underground version of good-time music, and that the worst and most divisive and sermonizing punk may promote rather than explore anger or aggression. However, the rage of the underground as a whole is largely a response to, not a generator of, anger and aggression. While agreeing that some people may go to a metal show just to mosh and have a good time, Dann believes that people use death metal to explore the grimmer sides of their experiences, to ignite their frustrations like a bomb, and to overcome the obstacles in their lives.

Dann's observations lead me to broader thoughts about the history of metal. Throughout my interviews I tried to master the complex sets of generic classifications of the participants in the underground. As Dann played each example and I learned to distinguish industrial from thrash and grindcore from doom metal, I realized that the music's affective content and sonic structures are ultimately inextricable in experience. The clicky snare drum sound of 1970s progressive metal is irreconcilably different from the gated reverbs and huge snare sounds of 1990s industrial, and each bears a unique aggression. Almost all of my metal research participants have observed that each successive genre in the history of metal has developed unique musical structures. These new structures are not pursued merely as an end in themselves; on the contrary, with each new style the musicians and listeners have experienced new dimensions of heaviness, doom, sadness, or aggression. Because affective qualities and musical structures cannot be separated in living experience, the history of metal must be understood as the story of the creation of new emotions.

Further lured by academic abstraction, I move from speculations about metal history to thoughts about general aesthetics. Most people do not enjoy being angered, frightened, or saddened. Why then do we listen to heavy metal, watch horror movies, or read tragedies? In daily life, rage, fear, or sadness erupt because of negative events, real or imagined. In the framed sphere of music or literature, however, we are able to experience these emotions without having to suffer the consequences. Experiencing rage without actually having to suffer humiliation or violence, experiencing fear without actually being threatened, experiencing sadness without actually undergoing a loss, we are freed up to attend to the affect itself and treat the affect as an aesthetic object on its own terms. One may further inquire, What is interesting about these emotions? These questions contain the seeds of their own answers because emotions and affects are *by definition* interesting. To account for our interest in particular things, we append an affective, aesthetic, or valual adjective to the factual noun—an angry cut, a beautiful painting, a glorious sunrise. But anger, beauty, or glory themselves require no affective or emotional justification because affects and values are the *grounds* of interest. Inside the performative frame, we are free to experience and appreciate rage or depression, because we need not worry about the consequences.

Nevertheless, such broad generalizations can blind us to the complex reality of practice. Musical uses (such as the exploration of emotions) and aesthetic projects (such as the creation of new musical forms and affects) are always tied to broader contexts. Even music intended as purely autonomous sonic structure is tied to social and historical context by its creator's ideology of formal experimentation and the material conditions through which the music is made. "The subject" is always a specific person in a concrete historical situation engaged with particular goals for particular reasons. The metalheads' music making practices are more than examples of an aesthetic exercise, more than moments in a project of creating new emotions. Death metal's heaviness and affects have not sprung from the pristine individuality of the composer's soul; they have been constituted by the practices of social actors operating within numerous contexts, including the development of pop metal and the deindustrialization of Britain and the United States. The participants' exploration of grim emotions has not occurred as some autonomous aesthetic project but is used to serve the broader purposes of casting away obstacles, motivating the self, and clearing a path for action.

Tying together the threads of the discussion, we can see how the metalheads' musical uses mesh with their larger values and beliefs. It is just the uncritical and apathetic lifestyle Dann so derided in Frank and the general population that death metal performance is intended to overcome; a good death metal show blasts away the apathy that metalheads find everywhere around them. The rhetorical strategy of stating positions rather than preaching them and the lyrical themes of personal choice and occult power connect with the broad values of individualism, critical thinking, and personal motivation. Illustrating his ideology of tolerance and openness, Dann explained that death metal rage could be applied to any kind of stumbling block people have in their lives.

Aspects of the death metal scene (3):
Building communities of sound and affect

Again and again, Dann and others referred to the practices of community building in the underground in terms reminiscent of the most romantic folklore scholarship. For example, Dann fondly recalls his first club show: the then underground band Anthrax at Cleveland's Fantasy nightclub. Still short at sixteen or seventeen, Dann recalls how he and his friend Erik were dropped off by Dann's wary parents; the huge line and mixed crowd of punks and metalheads was more than a bit intimidating. Once inside, those feelings evaporated. It was "intense being around that many people that were all there for one thing," Dann recalls. "They wanted to hear good heavy music . . . there were even a couple of kind of jocky guys sitting for a while, they had short hair, muscle shirts." But even the jocks were amiable and enjoyed the music.

More than the subject of a quaint anecdote, the idea of community building is both in the forefront of Dann's mind and central to his underground practice. When Dann isn't writing music or rehearsing, he works on correspondence. "Doing mail" entails writing to musicians and fans around the country and the world, ordering and reading fanzines, and promoting his music through flyers and demos. The massive boxes of letters, shelves full of fanzines, stacks of demos, and two huge card files of addresses attest to the effort Dann puts into doing mail. Dann's sense of scene boosterism extends far beyond mail. He supports local bands by attending the bulk of the metal shows in the Cleveland and Akron areas. Weekend trips to metal shows and fests in Milwaukee, Pittsburgh, Erie, and Cincinnati are common, and Dann's friends know that he can always be called upon to come to their out-of-town shows. A careful follower of the scene, Dann was my constant source of information about national and local acts, shows, zines, new genres of underground music, local bands forming, local bands breaking up, demos, parties, picnics, road trips, and all forms of gossip.

And where commercial hard rockers may know their scene or do promotion, the self-conscious attempt at community building is much stronger in the underground. Dann does not do mail, attend shows, and keep up contacts in the scene solely to promote his music. While his desire for a successful career plays a part in these actions, reciprocity, not selfishness, is a more accurate depiction of his motivations. Dann explained that to make a living in the scene, there has to be a scene there to support you in the first place. If you want zines to promote your demo, Dann explained, you have to promote the zines by buying them and passing them around to friends. If you want crowds to attend your shows, you have to support area bands and get out to their shows. Other bands are partners, not competitors, because only a thriving and diverse lineup of bands will help bring about an active and supportive underground. In short, Dann's interests and the scene's interest run together; working for himself and working for the community go hand in hand.

Dann is motivated by more than a simple sense of reciprocity; he revels in the convivial spirit and international scope of the death metal community. While some mainstream rock stars or sports figures may be known worldwide, Dann explained, their star status insulates them from the fans; metal's small size and emphasis on community enables an "intimacy" between musicians and fans that is absent in sports or mainstream rock. Dann has numerous stories of "hanging out" with famous underground musicians at shows; while some are arrogant, many are friendly, accessible, and well informed about the local scenes. Dann explained that walking down the street, a guy with a Cleveland Browns T-shirt and a guy with an Oakland Raiders T-shirt would have no connection with each other; at worst, they might start a fight. But a guy with a Napalm Death T-shirt and a guy with a Sepultura T-shirt would have something in common, an instant connection. Some of Dann's favorite metal narratives come from the Milwaukee Metal Fest, a yearly event that attracts metalheads from all over the country. At the fest, he said, he would frequently start up a conversation with a complete stranger only to discover that he and his interlocutor were longtime corespondents. Dann enthusiastically points to these interactions as symbols of metal's solidarity.

The idea of the scene as an international community brings out Dann's most expansive pronouncements. Discussing the Brazilian band Dorsal Atlanticus in connection with international scene unity, Dann explained, "That's the future, it's an international language, it's a bond between me and five guys in fucking Brazil that I've never met before. . . . And I can't speak their language and they probably can't speak mine but there's a bond there. Fifty years ago, there was nothing like this. You look at the world today, and you say well no wonder, there was no unity at all. . . . Metal may be small, but it's so involved. And it's growing. Locally it seems that it may be shrinking, though. People aren't getting out, and nobody has money. It's my only hope for the future."

At this point, I could not help observing to Dann the irony of a romantic community built around images of aggression, violence, and death. At first Dann agreed that there was a paradox. In his reading of metal history, however, heavy music emerged from the creativity of Black Sabbath and the bands that followed them, and the metal community formed around the participants' common interest in the music. Whether the scene or the music came first was irrelevant, Dann said; what was important was the idea of people coming together to listen to heavy music and using it to face the difficulties in their lives.

Discussing Dann's pessimistic view of modernity and his celebration of small-scale communities, I could not help recalling the romantic tradition in folklore scholarship and Henry Glassie's existentialist communitarianism in particular. As I began to lay out Glassie's vision of the folk community as a way of overcoming the void, Dann interrupted me and eagerly explained that the death metal scene is just such a folk group. When I pointed out the irony of overcoming the void through images of the void,[7] Dann was quick to correct my misreading. He agreed that the images of aggression and destruction may be in opposition to the idea of a tightly knit community; however, the purposes to which those images are put—the exploration and overcoming of grim affect and apathy, the group support of the pursuit of personal goals—affirms the building of community. Later on in the interview, I conjured the image of Irish village storytelling and Serbo-Croatian epic singing, and he immediately identified. For Dann, death metal is the same thing.

ELEVEN

A Critical Dialogue on the Politics of the Metal Underground
Race, Class, and Consequence

With this celebration of the death metal scene in place, we have the main outlines of Dann's vision of the underground. Discussing death metal with historian Stuart Svonkin, I was reminded that community is an essentially neutral term. Small-scale communities may be convivial and supportive, but they may also be mean-spirited and provincial. Massive bureaucracies will not be found in a society of two hundred, and neither can face-to-face social interaction occur among everyone in a society of two hundred thousand; however, nothing decrees that either will, *on balance,* be better or worse than the other. While I have only the greatest respect for Dann Saladin as a musician and social observer, I could not help questioning some of his interpretations of the death metal scene. As I suggested in the previous chapter, all scholarship exists in a moral continuum of history. In this continuum the most objective ethnography, the most partisan polemic, and even the failure to publish must all be understood as political acts with moral consequences. Aware of this Sartrean dilemma, in August 1993 I wrote several entries in my field notes responding to Dann's interpretations, and, a few weeks later, discussed them with Dann in our tenth interview.

This conversation took the project from descriptive ethnography to critical scholarship. Critical evaluation is, of course, very different from ethnographic description, but they have one thing in common: in both, the object of concern is practices and their social consequences. As a result, the discussion in the previous chapters can help us make sense of the vexed relationship between music and politics.

As we have observed throughout, music does not exist by itself; it is constituted in social practice and is thus bound to society through social contexts and social consequences. As I have suggested in Chapters 9 and 10, larger social contexts, such as those of race and class, deeply inform the musician's goals in music making; as chapters 6 through 10 have shown, these goals, in turn, influence the musician's practices of composition, performance, and perception. But just as music is influenced by context, it may have broad social consequences as well. Listeners constitute meaningful experiences of music; these meanings may play a substantial role in the participants' lives, which in turn may affect their actions and, through them, larger and larger social contexts. Music and its related practices are political, therefore, not because they may discuss hot-button issues or involve large sums of money, but because they can be consequential for the rest of the listener's experiences and, through those experiences, may be consequential for the larger society. Understood in this way, the participant's experiences of musical meanings are the mediator between musical sound and larger political significances.

None of this is to say that we must naively accept the research participant as the sole arbiter of the political significance of music or its related practices. Meanings arise in experience as a complex gestalt of sound, lyrics, other expressive forms in the performance event, audience-performer interaction, and contextualizing cultural practices; neither the participants nor the scholar can fully capture the richness of those meanings in words. For example, while few of the commercial hard rock musicians I spoke with stated that men are always the protagonists in their music, the image of men as active and women as passive is a background meaning in the musical experiences of local rock fans. Further, the social consequences of those musical meanings may ripple outward in byzantine and complex ways that the musicians and the listeners may have neither thematized nor intended. For example, while most commercial hard rock fans do not go to shows actively seeking to contribute to patriarchy, their experiences of sexist imagery may make it easier for them in other contexts to accept men as actors and women as passive observers. Though this example is not particularly challenging, the larger point is to criticize any form of political interpretation that seeks only the scholar's reading of the text. While the scholar may have unique insights into the participants' musical experiences, the politics of music is grounded in the consequentiality of the music for the lives of the participants and other members of their society, and that consequentiality is always mediated through the participants' experiences, however well or poorly they describe them. If a meaning is not present in the participants' experiences, how can it be consequential for their lives or the broader society?

The emphasis on consequences is meant to illustrate the continuity of the so-called microsocial and macrosocial and is not meant to replace rich interpretation with simplistic pragmatism. Interpretations—and in particular, nuanced interpretations of sonic experiences—are essential because rich lived meanings are what are consequential for the participants' lives and the larger society. Further, the possible consequences of those meanings may be blindingly complex: like mathematical curves in a two-dimensional graph, the consequences of musical practices may end abruptly in finite inconsequentiality or stretch out with endless repercussions. For example, transmitted through a variety of media, musical action may reach unintended audiences and yield unexpected meanings; mediated through a score, a computer, or a CD, today's obscure music may have untold consequences at some later date, while the current craze may disappear without a trace. The very absence of musical action itself may be highly consequential, and a music's main effect may be to prevent action—which is, of course, a kind of action in the flow of history. A music's most important effects may terminate in the lives of a few individuals or boil out into the widest contexts and any domain of social life.[1] While consequences may be difficult to predict, this should not lead us into despair and back toward a priori interpretative schemes; it is just the world of experiences, practices, and consequences that those schemes are meant to explain. It is precisely because different elements of our lives may affect one another and because others' lives can be consequential for our own that the study of expressive culture is more than vocational education for artists or tedious formalism for the idle.

This structure of consequentiality means that critical, progressive scholarship involves two phases. The first phase is descriptive and seeks to understand the full range of contexts and consequences that bind sound phenomena to the rest of social life; the previous chapters have pursued such a descriptive program. Next is the critical phase. Here the scholar explores the full range of the music's consequences and tries to determine whether or not they serve the ends of social justice, diminish inequitable power relations, or help to give subjects more choice. The term *consequences* here must be understood broadly and include personal, local, regional, national, and global consequences, as well as consequences in race, class, gender, or any other area that impinges on power relations, social justice, and human experience. As I have suggested in Chapter 10, there are good reasons that, wherever possible, the progressive scholar should pursue this last key phase in critical dialogue with the participants. While the participants may misinterpret their own experiences or misjudge the larger social consequences of their acts, they may also have insight that the progressive scholar misses.

To make critical assessments without engaging in critical dialogue is to assume that the scholar's position is not merely correct—which, of course, it may be—but that it is of a different order from the opinions of the research participants. To exclude them is to preach to the converted or assume that the participants have nothing to contribute to the dialogue and have no capacity for change. The last two positions are particularly problematic: if we feel that regressive positions—ours or others'—cannot be redeemed through inquiry, then I am not sure what the point of our critical work might be.

With all this in mind, I engaged Dann in dialogue, and our conversation revolved around the issues of race and class. I shall begin this chapter with a report on our dialogue and end by examining the complex range of death metal meanings and consequences that this conversation unearthed. While the Althusserian Marxist may have little use for Dann's perspective and the postmodern relativist little use for mine, I felt that both Dann and I came away from the conversation with a richer understanding of the scene. At the very least, I hope that by presenting this dialogue I shall help to return progressive politics to the basement bedroom, the living room, and the club. Any value in the dialogue should be credited to Dann and myself; any flaws in the presentation are, of course, mine alone.

Critical Dialogue

After discussing one of Dann's songs for about two hours, I suggested that we turn to some political issues. I pulled out some notes I had taken on the politics of the scene and fed back to Dann my understanding of his views of the underground. Dann confirmed my readings: that the underground is divided between hardcore and metal; that hardcore is explicitly political; that many metalheads view hardcore as dogmatic and preachy; that metal focuses on themes of individual action, tolerance, and fantasy; that metal's themes are a reaction against the perceived dogmatism of hardcore and the stultifications of bad schools and dead-end jobs; that most in the underground are familiar with both scenes but are more interested in one side than the other.

The first topic we talked about was the notion of radical toleration, and two previous interviews contextualized our discussion. In our second interview, I noticed a small swastika among the many stickers plastered across Dann's guitar. At first, the sight of the swastika surprised me; I didn't know Dann very well at this point and wasn't sure what the symbol meant to him. After ten or fifteen minutes I asked him about it. He said he was neither a Nazi nor an anti-Semite but "a pro-person person." Quick to condemn the evils of the Holocaust, Dann explained that genocide "was one of the biggest things that led to Hitler's downfall. Why he [Hitler] felt that the Jews were horrible is beyond understanding." This said, Dann explained that you had to respect Hitler's ability to accumulate power; sporting the swastika was meant as a sign of respect for that power, not a show of hatred. While I am aware that some readers will find this to be incredible, I was, and am, completely convinced of Dann's sincerity. I responded by saying that I understood that Dann wasn't a neo-Nazi; however, the swastika is a very powerful symbol, I said, and as a Jew, I knew that some Jews would be unable to see someone using that symbol as anything but an enemy. Dann became thoughtful at this point, and after several moments explained that he never considered the symbol that way. Several weeks later, the swastika was removed from his guitar.

The issue of toleration came up again with respect to Steve, a local figure who created a series of demos known as the "Nut Screamer" tapes. Steve would go to amusement parks, underground shows, and other public places and explode in an uninterrupted stream of virulent, almost nonsensical racist and sexist invective; his demos alternated recordings of these rants with short noise band pieces. Well known in the area, these demos were treated as an amusing curiosity by some in the scene. When we happened upon the topic of the Nut Screamer tapes in our fifth interview, Dann began by condemning the racist views; as we discussed the tapes, Dann asked me why the word "nigger"—used so frequently in Steve's tirade—was so powerful and inflammatory. Why would an African American be offended by the word "nigger" or why would a woman be bothered by being called a whore? If you know you aren't a whore, Dann asked, why does the term bother you so? I responded by saying that there are crushing power relations between whites and blacks—with which Dann agreed completely—and that such language is offensive because it celebrates the broader hate in the society, twists the knife that is already deep in the flesh. Dann again considered the idea thoughtfully, explained he had never thought of it that way, and agreed that my interpretation may be correct. We discussed race for a little while longer before continuing on with the interview.

In neither of these situations did I have any simple options. If I said nothing about the swastika or the racist tirades we stumbled upon, Dann would have realized I was censoring my thoughts, and I would have felt duplicitous and complicit. But reading the preceding paragraphs, I can't help feeling that the reader will find my comments patronizing—Alan Alda among the metalheads come to show them the way to tolerance and decency. A reader from the Anti-Defamation League will find my remarks too weak; the postmodernist will find them too strong. While there are many field situations in which "no comment" is the best solution, Dann was eager to discuss weighty issues, and I felt that the best I could do was to state my opinion honestly and discuss my responses with him as an intelligent other. In any event, the larger point is that racist rhetoric is present in the scene and protected by an atmosphere of radical "tolerance."

Both of these events were in my mind when we began our discussion of the politics of the underground in interview 10. I started by asking Dann if death metal's radical toleration may have the negative consequences of making racism and sexism seem normal and acceptable. After a long pause, Dann said "Yeah, maybe, I would almost say so." He added that it takes a strong mind and a good education to understand a person from a different background, and that those qualities are also necessary for understanding another's prejudices. Not being African American, female, or gay, Dann explained, he had a hard time understanding what it is like to experience prejudice. Dann offered that he is marginal only inasmuch as he is a longhair and that he could go to a barber to change that; besides, he said, a certain romance and power came from sporting the metal look. Dann explained that he could imagine how African Americans would be fed up with stereotypes. He added, however, that some black youths do get involved with the stereotypical drugs and crime, largely because they feel that they will be penalized no matter what they do. Drawing us back to the topic, I gave Steve the Nut Screamer as an example of the negative side of toleration. Dann agreed that Steve was difficult to take and explained that some of Steve's views were rooted in a highly troubled home life. Addressing the broader issue, Dann said "There is so much tolerance [in the scene], things that ordinarily would be not tolerated become tolerated."

When I suggested that the issue might not always be handled well in death metal, Dann said that metal's broad toleration was not a negative thing. "I think it's a vast array of acceptance," he said. That acceptance does not involve *supporting* offensive views like racial hatred, Dann suggested, it just means "accepting the fact that it [racism] is there, it's going to happen, so I just have to learn to deal with it." Dann illustrated by contrasting the different segments of the underground. Within punk, Dann explained, the tensions between the strident antiracist hardcore bands and racist skinhead groups have led to intolerance and even violent confrontations. At one show, he said, his band shared the bill with death metal, skinhead, hardcore, straight edge, and noise bands. All evening long, the straight edge punks were very clear about their dislike for skinheads, and during one performance, a straight edge musician pulled out a baseball bat and menaced some of the skins. When Ronny, the show's organizer, saw this, he immediately shut down the band and threw them off the stage. Neither good nor bad, toleration simply works, Dann said, and it does so by making the scene a place where everyone is included. Pretend I am a militant antidrinker, he suggested. At a show I would tolerate drinking and drinkers, but in any other arena I would speak my mind and oppose alcohol. As such, this extreme tolerance is really only operative at the shows proper, and "doesn't become inbred in what a person is thinking." The scene forms a common bond, which obliges people to tolerate things they may not like. As such, a racist at a show has to tolerate black people, and the blacks must temporarily tolerate racism. I don't support hate, Dann said, but a certain amount of this broad-based tolerance "has to work."

It is moments such as these that make critical dialogue such a valuable tool. While it would be easy to condemn death metal's radical tolerance, Dann's explanation of the exigencies of the scene helps us to see the situation in a different light. In the context of wildly diverging politics and preachy dogmatism, the ideology of all-embracing tolerance has a very legitimate appeal; in the context of occasionally violent divisiveness, radically tolerant practices prevent broken bones and canceled shows. But if radical toleration has positive consequences, it does seems to encourage just the regressive normalization of racism that Dann and I were concerned about earlier. For example, in another interview, a local musician I shall call Dave told me that while skinheads, not metalheads, sang about racial hatred, metal's toleration did very much include a tolerance for racism; a Klansman would be perfectly welcome at any of his performances, he said. Dave owned some of the Nut Screamer tapes, and when I asked him about them, he explained that while he himself was no longer a racist, Steve's tirades were merely "his opinion," something to which everyone is entitled. Responding to Dave's hypothetical Klansman at a metal show, Dann said that if black people found out later that they had attended a show with a Klansman, "they might think, 'well, then, that's their deal, they're not bothering me at this particular time. And outside of this show I'll probably never see them anywhere, so let them do what they want on their weekends.'" While this position is absurd to me and the problems of tolerance are all too real, the social conditions of the underground offer metalheads few obvious alternatives to radical toleration—exclusion and violence or radical toleration and the normalization of hate. Metal's ideology of tolerance has both progressive and regressive consequences, and both celebration and condemnation are simplistic responses.

I wanted to explore these ideas further with Dann, but dialogue is essentially an open-ended activity, and at this point the discussion changed course. As I began to respond to this last idea, Dann brought up the well-publicized case of Jan Demjanjuk, a Ukrainian American from the Cleveland area accused of having been an SS guard in World War II. As in other discussions, Dann prefaced his remarks about Demjanjuk by saying that, because he was not black, gay, or female, he, Dann, was part of no disadvantaged group. To me, this comment reflected the widespread American denial of class, and I responded by saying that while Dann was not a woman or a minority, he was a nonunion factory worker earning six and a half dollars an hour with few benefits. Dann denied that blue-collar workers were in any way disadvantaged, and the conversation that ensued slowly moved back and forth between the topics of class in general and class in the underground.

We can make the discussion more meaningful if we pause to explore the larger historical contexts of heavy metal and the cultural criticism that has sprung up around it. As many writers have suggested (Weinstein 1991, Walser 1993, Gaines 1990) deindustrialization is a key context for heavy metal. Deindustrialization is a process in which a region's economy loses its industrial base; the main mechanism of the current American deindustrialization is disinvestment, the failure to fund new factories and maintain old ones. Milking factories for their profits, allowing equipment to become obsolete, and closing shops, American business has, since the 1970s, consistently disinvested in the country's main industrialized regions; attracted to nonunionized workers, low taxes, and lax environmental and safety regulations, investments have been redirected into other regions in the United States and overseas economies (Bluestone and Harrison 1982, Rodwin 1989). According to Markusen and Carlson (1989), the Midwest is one of the regions hit hardest by the phenomenon, and they explain that the region's job loss and economic devastation is the result of structural, not cyclic, changes in the region's economy. The result of these processes is a "postindustrial" economy in which blue-collar wages have remained stagnant for almost thirty years, the union movement is substantially weakened, and disparities between rich and poor constantly increase. Once America's tire capital, Akron is a case study in deindustrialization: as mentioned in Chapter 2, the Akron Development Office reports that the only tires currently made in Summit County come from a few specialty shops for race cars. Young men and women whose parents held union jobs in the tire factories now work dead-end service-sector jobs, hold poorly paid nonunion factory jobs in other industries, or are unemployed.

The frustrations of blue-collar life in a declining economy are a crucial context for heavy metal, and the most substantial critiques of the genre have centered on this issue. Originating in the deindustrialized English

Midlands of the 1970s, metal has found its most loyal American audiences in the devastated Midwest and Northeast, and both qualitative and quantitative scholarship shows that the music's audience has largely come from working-class youth (Walser 1993; Weinstein 1991; Hakanen and Wells 1990, 62–63; 1993, 60, 66). While conservative critiques of metal have been based on interpretations of the lyrics and music (and have largely been debunked, see Walser 1993, 141–44, 151–52; Weinstein 1991, 258–63; Epstein, Pratto, and Skipper 1990; Verden, Dunleavy, and Powers 1989), the attacks from left-wing music critics and social commentators have focused on the class dynamics of metal. With the important exception of Robert Walser and Donna Gaines, left critics have assailed metal's themes of fantasy and aggression as an unproductive, adolescent ventilation of working-class tensions. For example, E. Ellis Cashmore condemned metal as one of the "great force[s] of political indifference of the time" (1987, 263). Comparing metal unfavorably with the more politically involved subcultures like reggae, punk, and two-tone, Cashmore's conclusion was that metalheads "sensed the intensifying futility of trying to improve their material lives and so convinced themselves that what really mattered was that portion of their lives over which they could at least exert some control" (264).

Across the political spectrum, all of the critics use the methods of social commentary; the intended audience for their writing is other critics or the general population, and dialogue with the metalheads themselves is never considered. One of my main goals in fieldwork was to give the metalheads a forum for responding to these attacks, and as the conversation turned to class issues, I was eager to get Dann's opinion of these criticisms.

Back in the interview, we began by exploring the notion of class in general. Dann started our discussion by arguing that if you build a business empire, you deserve the fortune that you earn. I responded by saying that many people that are wealthy have inherited, rather than earned, their fortune; more important, for every person that moves from poverty to wealth, there are thousands of others upon whose work that fortune is built. Dann acknowledged that there is unfairness in the system, but said that capitalism generally rewarded knowledge and hard work. I couldn't agree with this position, but Dann persisted. His job in the plastics factory was completely mindless, he said; realistically, would you pay more than minimum wage to have someone flip burgers at McDonald's? While I admitted that many blue-collar jobs require few skills, I said that many executive positions were equally mindless, and that many people did no work at all and inherited fortunes. But this is all beside the point, I said, and briefly recounted Marx's critique of profit: in industrial capitalism, one person owns a factory; other people work there, turning raw materials into products. The owner sells the products at a price determined by adding together the cost of the raw materials, the wages, the depreciation of the equipment, and an extra sum—the profit—that the owner keeps. In this view, the capitalist's contribution to the process has only been the ownership of the equipment; the worker's labor transformed the raw materials into products, and therefore profit is really unpaid labor.

Dann paused and reflected on this. Acknowledging that the situation was unfair, he said, "There's a lot of really, lot of really sick things going on like that. In a way it is sick, and I have to say I respect you for looking at things like that, because it's a very humanistic way of looking at things. But on the same token it's kind of a every-man-for-himself world." Dann admitted that this was a harsh view, but he said it's a "sink-or-swim world and you got to do what you can to swim. And somehow some of these guys are building boats." Besides, most of these people working the low-skill jobs are "too dumb or maybe just too uneducated to realize they're being exploited." The owner of his company, Dann explained, owns a house on Lake Erie, a nice boat, another factory in Akron, and rental property. "I know that he's making money on the money he's not paying me, but then again by the same token . . . I could not see paying somebody a vast amount of money for doing my job because my job is nothing." I asked if Dann could see paying someone a vast amount of money for this guy to sit on his boat. No, Dann said, but who knows what he did to start this company; maybe he did something great and deserves to kick back. Dann said that he himself has worked since high school to earn his musical equipment, stereo, TV, VCR, and truck; the factory owner's possessions are earned personal property in the same way that Dann's truck and guitars are, he said, "just on a much larger scale." Responding to Dann's idea that the average worker was lazy and ignorant, I said that, yes, there do exist apathetic, directionless people in the world. "My friends!" interrupted Dann, laughing. But apathy and lack of direction, I said, arise from a lack of opportunities, from looking at the world and seeing nothing but dead-end jobs. Dann agreed, but, he said, it is each individual's responsibility to overcome his or her apathy, to find and make his or her own opportunities in the world.

At this point, the abstract conversation began its return to the topic of class in the underground. Earlier, discussing Jan Demjanjuk's alleged atrocities, Dann had said that most of the Nazi guards couldn't be held responsible for their actions, because they were in a situation where they could either collaborate or be killed themselves. At this point, I asked how Dann could forgive Demjanjuk's alleged capitulation to larger social forces and be so hard on people he knew that were mired by apathy. Dann's response was both thoughtful and pointed:

It's true, society sucks. It does. [*Pause.*] And it's very hard to overcome what's happening in society. I mean, I look at the future, and I'm scared as hell. [*Pause.*] I really am. But also, to me, it's my responsibility to do my best to overcome that [the difficulties of blue-collar life], just as it would be his [Demjanjuk's] responsibility to, you know, risk his life and not do that [not collaborate]. But everyday there's millions of people making the wrong decisions. . . . I can see myself being scared and saying, "Either I have to kill these people, or I'm going to be killed. Then I'm going to kill these people." I can see myself in that situation; I can see myself being scared, and I can see myself making that decision [to collaborate with the Nazis. But] I cannot see myself saying, "OK, I can either work like I am now, and support myself, and try to do my best as I can with this band and get something out of it; or, I can not work and half-ass the band and let the future take hold of my fate." [*Pause.*] No. I cannot see myself letting go to that decision, to the second. No. No way. To me it is my responsibility to do the best that I can with my life.

Once again, critical dialogue provides new insights. The value of personal motivation that Dann argues for here is of a piece with death metal's emphasis on personal responsibility and the individualistic ideologies found throughout American culture; it is just this radically individualistic perspective for which progressive critics attack metal. While it is easy to talk about the false consciousness of working-class individualism, Dann's comments show how ideologies of motivation serve genuine needs. This is not to deny that capitalism has structural inequities or that an emphasis on the individual at the expense of the social may help maintain power relations. It is, however, to observe that people require both short- and long-term solutions, and that any time people are frustrated and blocked, ideas of motivation will play a crucial part in their lives. Dann's comments reminded me of events in my own experience, and I related to Dann the story of Ella (not her real name), my close friend's sister. A child of divorced, working-class parents, Ella graduated from high school with poor marks and missed the deadlines for applying to community college. Unfazed, Ella answered phones at an office complex for six months; when the next term arrived, she informed her family that though she had no long-range plans, she wasn't going to enroll in school, and that the phone job was good enough. My friend's family went wild trying to get her out of that dead-end job and into school, and they used just the kinds of ideas that Dann championed here. The story of Ella illustrates how, when faced with real-world situations, the ideology of personal motivation is hard to dismiss. Dann took the story as a case in point.

Dialogue provides no simple answers, however, and I could not agree with Dann that capitalist labor relations are somehow fair because we live in a dog-eat-dog world, nor could I agree that the social inequities we are born with are mitigated by the negligible meritocractic impulses of capitalism. But just as the examination of values in Chapter 10 became more concrete by exploring death metal practices, our dialogue provided new perspectives when the topic moved to the politics of the underground.

I began by feeding back my understanding of Dann's interpretation of the musical uses of metal: metalheads use the energy of the music to overcome apathy and spark personal motivation. Dann replied that my reading was close, but not exactly right, "Even more so than that, it's [metal is] a way of discarding anything that would oppress you . . . not necessarily jump-starting, but just breaking away from the things that would oppress you from doing what you consider your life to be." Someone might look down on me, Dann said, because I work a "lame job" and live in my parent's basement; but my life, to me, is music. The energy in metal, he said, is a way of tearing down the obstacles that limit you—people telling you to give up your music, cut your hair, or get a real job. Metal could motivate a person to be a dentist, explained Dann, if he felt that to be his calling.

At this point, I explained to Dann the progressive critique of metal: while metal may ventilate working-class frustrations, its emphasis on fantasy and personal responsibility draws attention away from the social and economic causes of those frustrations—deindustrialization and the inequities of capitalism—and only makes the situation worse. Considering, Dann replied that he could understand this view and why a liberal or Marxist writer would condemn metal. However, Dann continued, metal's anger is focused on personal change, not political or "structural" (Dann's term) change. Given the political climate of contemporary America, said Dann, large-scale social change is "far-fetched"; metal is a tiny subculture and any "rebellion" would instantly be crushed. As such, "the metal scene kind of dwells on changing yourself; that makes more sense to me." I responded that there were many gradations of political involvement between the depoliticized focus on one's own life and full-scale rebellion. Dann responded that that in fact may be what is happening. If you try to make too drastic a change too quickly, Dann explained, "it flops"; any change must begin with the building of community, and this is already going on in death metal. And while metal fans aren't "bent on creating this huge amount of change," that change may be beginning almost unconsciously. In any case, if it is going to happen, it must arise naturally from within and cannot be forced. "If you get these political people saying, 'Look, start directing this anger at something,' people are going to be, like, 'Fuck you. This isn't about that. This is about being, doing what we want to do, not about doing what you're telling us to do.'"

Seeking to reconnect some of the various ideas in the conversation, I asked Dann to respond to a passage in my field notes: "It seems to me at this point that there is a double-edged sword to the politics of anger in the metal underground. In reaction to sermonizing and repressive control in both music (hardcore) and social life (the school, the factory, religion) a kind of individualism has arisen. The positive sides of this are well elaborated by Dann. There is a reaction against passive consumption and the banality of popular culture, an emphasis on free thought, the building of an underground community against the mainstream, and a toleration for and sensitivity to others. Additionally there are the positive uses of anger: catharsis; the building of a community that supports anger; the aesthetic exploration of anger, and the use of anger as a personal motivator." Dann agreed that this was a fair representation of his views. Continuing with the field notes, I said, "But there seems to be a negative side to this anger, a radical individualism within the communalism. As such: does the complete disaffection with politics and the free-floating anger disengage emotions from their social causes? Is the anger channeled into personal ends and diverted from changing repressive social situations?"

These comments served to open up the conversation onto broader topics. Dann's first response was that while there was some political metal, he and most metalheads used music as entertainment and as an outlet for creativity, not as a soapbox for social change. Further, Dann argued, there have been more than enough underground songs about politics; the thrash bands of the 1980s like Metallica and Megadeath beat these themes into the ground. "If I hear one more song about televangelists," he said, "I think I am going to die." While I agreed that these themes were overplayed, I observed that these comments made Dann seem unconcerned about larger political conditions. Dann said that in any political conditions you can still take responsibility for your own actions and make something of yourself; I responded that such personal action is always informed by social contexts. Dann asked, "What 'social context' would really affect me? . . . There aren't a lot of laws that really strongly affect me." Although he wouldn't break the law just for the sake of disobedience and although most laws simply reflect common sense, he said, his actions are guided by his own moral principles and desires and not the dictates of the government. I responded by suggesting that political conditions do impact our lives. How do you feel, I responded, about the opportunities for employment that surround you? What would you do if birth control were outlawed? How would you feel if the minimum wage were sharply reduced? Dann responded that such drastic change is unlikely to happen in this country. A ban on birth control would fail, Dann said, just as Prohibition did; birth control would go underground, and he would still get condoms. I agreed that an underground economy would develop, but suggested that the condoms would be less reliable and more expensive. Context matters, I said, because context and individual agency together determine the consequences of our actions—not agency alone. Dann agreed.

As the evening wore on, the conversation began to open up onto wider topics. We discussed the problems of welfare and the disparities between wealth and poverty in America. Dann said that we won't solve the world's problems in one evening, and that he does the best he can to be responsible for himself and help others. Tired, we ended the interview there.

Conclusions

With these ideas in place, we can begin to tie together some of the diverse threads of this conversation. If, as I have suggested above, music's political significance is grounded in the lived meanings of the music and their various social consequences, then our first methodological principle must be a sensitivity to the complex and open-ended range of meanings and consequences that music may entail. The discussion of race in the underground is a case study. Death metal tolerance has contradictory consequences in the underground. On the one hand it is a genuinely progressive ideology that stands in resistance to any kind of prejudice; at the same time, however, it has the unintended consequence of giving space to racist imagery and larger racist perspectives. From this research, it would be difficult to judge the social consequences of any death metal practices for the larger society, but it seems likely to me that both currents would exert their influences on the metalheads' actions outside the scene. Embracing an attitude of radical toleration and chastened by their own feelings of marginalization, I suspect that metalheads would be more accepting of ethnic, racial, or religious minorities than the population in general; at the same time, I think the metalheads would also be more tolerant of racism or homophobia in the public arena.

The question of class in the underground offers a different set of issues and no simple assessments. On the one hand, there is truth to the claim that metal distracts blue-collar youth from the social roots of their predicament. Both the metalheads and the progressive critics are in agreement that metal emphasizes the individual over larger political contexts. Dann's strident arguments at the end of the interview all stress individual action and personal motivation and downplay the significance of social context in general and class in particular; my fieldwork suggests that these attitudes are common in death metal and integral to its ideology of personal motivation and personal action. In the English-speaking world,[2] metal is primarily a working-class phenomenon of the deindustrialized period, and there is little doubt that much of the rage in metal has its roots in class frustrations. Inasmuch as death metal may attract the most frustrated blue-collar youth and dissipate their potentially progressive energies in politically disengaged activity, there is validity in the progressive criticism.

Accepting that there is some truth in this perspective, dialogue is still useful, however, because it helps us to make sense of this expressive culture from the perspectives of the participants. Much of the emphasis on personal motivation and personal responsibility in the underground is a reaction against the preachy sermonizing of hardcore. The music of the best known "left-wing" bands criticizes environmental destruction, televangelism, political corruption, and racial hatred. While there are some songs about wealth and poverty and some class-conscious bands, little contemporary American hardcore speaks to the experiences of blue-collar youth, articulates the concept of class, or avoids strident rhetoric. As a result, it is easy to understand why hardcore is so frequently the object of the metalheads' wrath; the appeal of metal is equally obvious, validating as it does the individual's capacity for action and critical thought. Of course, this issue is not the provincial concern of a small youth subculture. The rhetoric of "personal choice and personal responsibility" and its attendant disengagement of the individual from his or her social context are crucial themes in American politics. My conversation with Dann took place just thirteen months before the 1994 Republican sweep of Congress—a victory largely credited to the so-called angry white male. As American liberalism abandoned any pretense of concern for the working class and revealed itself incapable of dealing with the problems of deindustrialization, it is no surprise that blue-collar voters abandoned it in droves. When the "left" of mainstream politics—really, liberal centrists—stands for women's rights, minority rights, environmental protection, and the social safety net but cannot even articulate the notion of class, blue-collar men will certainly find little attraction there. This is not to suggest that class is more important than race or gender, but to observe that all progressive politics in America will be hobbled if mainstream politics cannot even admit the existence of class in anything but the most veiled terms.

The examination of larger issues, however, takes us away from a fuller examination of the politics of death metal. While there is truth that death metal does ventilate class tensions, it would be degrading to metalheads to argue that metal is nothing more than a safety valve. When I first began to work on metal, I thought the music was about anger; after reading an earlier draft of this work, Deena Weinstein suggested I reconsider this position and offered the notion that metal was about power and aggression, not anger. Later, carefully thinking about Dann's comments, I realized that all of these emotions are secondary. When metal is viewed from the outside, the observer first sees its titanic rage. The music is so powerful that it is difficult to get past this quick interpretation, and it is here that analysis of musical sound and ethnographic dialogue is so important to understanding the political significance of the music. The ethnography of musical sound in metal shows that the songs involve constant shifts among anger, aggression, sadness, depression, grandeur, surprise, and explosive energy; the critical dialogue on metal's beliefs and practices shows that the music is used to explore emotions and overcome their stultifying effects. Metal is about action and action denied; it is about frustration and about exploring and responding to the whole emotional complex that emerges from that frustration. Metal is not a mechanical venting of psychosocial steam, although steam is vented in the mosh pit; metal is an arena in which the participants engage with emotions denied in daily life. As Viktor Frankl observed (1963, 157–58), to say that people are driven by their emotion is to say that they are determined by them; metalheads use the music precisely so they *won't* be driven by their emotions, precisely so they *won't* be driven by rage or held back by depression.

At this point it is important to recognize that metal's audience is not uniformly blue-collar, nor are all frustrated working-class youth metalheads. Any persons whose musical past can help them to constitute metal in a meaningful way can use the mosh pit to explore their emotional lives. This is not to deny that most metalheads come from working-class backgrounds or to downplay the social causes of those listeners' frustrations; it is to say that death metal is a creative response to difficult conditions with real benefits for the participants' lives. In a world with little hope for social change, in a world where class is (to use the terminology of phenomenological Marxism) occluded, the liberating emotional exploration of death metal performances serves genuine needs. And it is not merely the case that metal offers short-term emotional utility at the expense of a long-term obfuscation of class consciousness; anything that helps to liberate the individual might turn out to have progressive consequences. While the ideologies of death metal do emphasize the "individual" and construct him or her as distinct from the "social," there is no explicit rejection of political action. If, as Dann has said, death metal could free a person from his or her stumbling blocks to realize his or her potential as a dentist, then there is no reason that metalheads may not realize themselves as activists as well. "Feeling his way" through the progressive critique I described, Dann said that, in fact, this may be what is happening.

But we cannot end the discussion with a simple celebration of metal. While death metal performances at their best consecrate the humanity of their participants, and while the music may some day open into larger political engagements, none of this contradicts the idea that death metal's radical individualism obscures the social causes of social inequity. An objection might be raised here: "Metal helps metalheads get through their lives. Other kinds of music are not judged by their ability to bring about social justice, so why should metal be judged in this way?" The problem with this response is that it confuses progressive scholarship with a simplistic advocacy. If we only celebrate our research participants, if we only present their position as true and don't criticize their contradictions, then we are dehumanizing them by deifying them. All music need not bring about social justice, but to be unwilling to criticize elements of a musical culture that contribute to the participants' own undoing is to be complicit in that undoing. To be willing to criticize the metalheads for the unintended racism of their radical tolerance and unwilling to criticize them for the unintended classism of their radical individualism is to say that race matters but class doesn't. Criticism is not personal attack. Progressive scholarship should neither engage in a dialectical dithering nor a simplistic either/or celebration or critique; the best method is a both/and approach that both celebrates the progressive and criticizes the regressive, while engaging the participants in dialogue. Death metal is at once a fragile and embattled subculture and a warm and convivial community; an oasis of open-mindedness and a safe harbor for hatred; a barrier to seeing the social roots of the life of limited options and a life-affirming and potentially transformative examination of that life. None of this is to suggest that if metal were more politically engaged that some liberatory Marxist revolution would spontaneously come about. But society is both produced and reproduced by the practices of its agents, and it would be equally wrong to assume that the existence of a vibrant minority of politically engaged blue-collar youth would be inconsequential in American society. Moshing in the pit, talking politics in a basement bedroom, or watching in the practice room as bands remold rock clichés into heavy metal thunder, anyone involved in metal can see that the possibilities are endless.

In late October 1993 a friend of mine visited me in Cleveland. Knowing she was eager to get out and see live music, I asked Dann about upcoming metal shows in the area. He told me that every year on Halloween a bunch of his friends rent a hall in Akron, throw a party, and play for it. He gave me sketchy directions, and two weeks later my friend Rebecca and I drove around an industrial area of Akron in a cold sleet trying to locate the party. The sign on the front of the building was unlit, and we drove by the place several times before we found it.

Stepping inside, Rebecca and I arrived just in time to hear Scumlord do their set. The band sounded good. Chatting with Dann afterward I began to take in my environment. Paper streamers, skeletons, and witches had been hung on the walls, and folding tables and chairs took up about half the space in the dingy room. Huge metal buckets sat in inopportune places all over the place, catching the drops of water that poured in through the torn acoustical ceiling tiles. I had been wondering what kind of place this was from the moment Dann first mentioned the party, and once there I asked several people what the room was used for. No one knew. A small kitchen just off the area where the instruments were set up held a keg and had the neglected look that all public kitchens do. There was no doubt that this place was in bad shape, and when I went to the basement to find the men's room, the paneling was ripped in several places and one of the cement walls was literally crumbling.

Nevertheless, it wasn't a bad party. About half the people were in costume, including one man with an elaborate getup reminiscent of Pinhead from the Hellraiser movies. In this roomful of metalheads, most of the people not wearing costumes wore jeans and black T-shirts with imagery that was perfectly appropriate for the occasion. Observing this, I couldn't help thinking back to Dann's comment in our last interview: "Everyday is Halloween to me." Finally the band that sponsored the event, Catastrophic, started playing. They were phenomenal, and both Rebecca and I

OUAM Hall

were entranced; the whole room was totally caught up in the grinding, revelatory power of the music. Unable to turn off my ethnographer's curiosity, I was still wondering what kind of a hall could attract customers and still be so dingy and decrepit when I stepped outside between songs to get some air. Looking carefully at the sign on the front of the building, I read, "JR O.U.A.M., Goodyear Heights Council 369." The place was an old union hall.

Picture the scene. Akron, Ohio, was once the tire capital of the world. Hobbled after years of deindustrialization, the children of tire workers stood that night bathed in the sounds and images of a glorious rage. The room itself, once home to a force for labor equality, is not merely crumbling, but completely unrecognized by the participants. All of the elements of social change are present—rage, community, skills, and talent—yet things remain the same. Death metal is neither an example of false consciousness nor a coping mechanism for the stresses of an unequal world. It is a promise unfulfilled.

TWELVE

Conclusion
The Scope of Ethnomusicology

In the final days of my stay in Cleveland, I began to think about how I would conclude this ethnography. While driving to a final interview or doing some other repetitive task, I kept thinking in terms of dramaturgical or cinematic tableau. In a dramaturgical tableau Chris Ozimek and Al Ricci would be set in a standard scene performing some characteristic activity like writing a song in the practice room or posting flyers at a club. Posed and blocked, they freeze at some critical moment that is both typical and revealing. At other times, I thought that cinematic tableau would be more effective. Here, for example, Dann Saladin and John Ziats would be filmed at a bar chatting. Dann has just finished setting up his amp, John has just placed the last flash pot on the side of the stage. We cannot hear their words—a metal soundtrack obscures them—but we see their lips move, and their silent gestures in some way capture the feeling of the scene more effectively. Thick fog from the last band's set blurs our vision as the camera pans across the bar, revealing Rob Toothman drinking a beer with some friends. The camera pulls back but the action continues, diminishing in size and enveloped by the smoke.

In both of these tableaus the effect of the trope is to give the impression that the actions and experiences described earlier will continue indefinitely. Tableau is reassuring if the images it captures in amber are positive ones, chilling if the images are negative. In either case, tableau is the trope of the synchronic. Synchronic time, the only time comprehensible by structuralism, is the time in which small activities and changes are captured within the rubric of larger, changeless systems. Thus, in the synchronic time of the Dann Saladin tableau, we imagine Dann going through all of the activities depicted in the ethnography. Nevertheless, the series of shows does not add up to a career; the songs written do not add up to an ever-growing corpus; the moment-to-moment changes are not part of the never–self-identical flow that is history. We think in synchronic terms whenever we conceptualize "a period" of our lives. Casting my mind back to my sophomore year of college, I recall scenes in tableau: going to class, playing music with friends, working, making lunch. I don't think of a particular lunch as the thirtieth of the semester, incrementally closer to the end, incrementally further from the beginning, and fully unique in the flow of the semester. I think, and thought, of each lunch as an example of a type, a set of acts caught in a larger, changeless period. The trope of the synchronic is a common one because it is almost impossible to think of each and every event as located uniquely in history, impelling us through history, and in fact constituting that history.

The trope is common—common, but misleading. While our reflective descriptions may obscure the differences between particular events, in immediate experience the events themselves are unique and colored by their ever-expanding past. The thirtieth lunch I ate that sophomore semester, however identical it might have been to all those that preceded it, is unique in experience precisely because it is colored by those past lunches. And as attractive as a romantic tableau might be, it does great violence to the fullness of the experiences. During the writing of this work, Winter's Bane, Max Panic, and Dia Pason all broke up, the Whisler Quartet disbanded, and Leonard Burris and Jerome Saunders left Cleveland to further their music careers. Though Rizzi's scaled back its live music offerings, Dick Schermesser still plays there, and Bill Roth, Jack Hanan, Eric Gould, and Alvin Edwards are all actively performing. The late 1980s style of commercial hard rock was routed from the scene by a variety of alternative musics, and both Flashes and the Akron Agora closed. Blood Coven, Dann Saladin's group, is currently recording a new version of "The Final Silencing," while Erik Rueschman performs in area clubs with Somnus. Timmy Owens went on to sing with Judas Priest. More recently, Winter's Bane reformed with a slightly different lineup, and the Akron Agora reopened as a country bar. As necessary as it is to our sense of things to capture the seeming permanence inherent in the fact of expectation, it is also necessary to see each new event—no matter how similar to the past—as part of the flux of history. As a result, I leave Dann working on an unfinished piece of music, each new band a unique one, each new gig a change in his musical career leading on a trajectory of unknown destination. Entrenchment, incremental growth, development, stagnation, discontinuous shock—the arc of that trajectory is left to agency, society, and contingency.

With the ethnography and theoretical work in place, we are finally in a position to view as a whole the scope of ethnomusicology. Ethnomusicology extends across the entire reach of experience, from the minutest micro-constitution of the temporality of sound phenomena to the broadest historical (geological or even cosmic) cross-situational trains of events, grasped in reflection and consequential for practice. Ethnomusicology covers this vast area because that entire range is there for the subject as experience and may be consequential for that subject. In this way, ethnomusicology is merely a fragment of the living human sciences, selecting from the expanding world of experiences all those that connect to music. In this sense, the best model for the scope of ethnomusicology is David Buchan's monumental *The Ballad and The Folk* (1972). In that great work, Buchan extends his view from the smallest details of balladry, to the situated practices of ballad performance, to the broadest economic and geographical trains of events that impinge upon and are affected by the ballad practices. The ground of this unimaginable scope is the scope of experience, which is to say, the scope of the subject and the scope of the World:

The unfinished nature of phenomenology and the inchoative atmosphere which has surrounded it are not to be taken as a sign of failure, they were inevitable because phenomenology's task was to reveal the mystery of the world and of reason. If phenomenology was a movement before becoming a doctrine or philosophical system, this was attributable neither to accident nor to fraudulent intent. It is as painstaking as the works of Balzac, Proust, Valery, or Cézanne—by reason of the same kind of attentiveness and wonder, the same demand for awareness, the same will to seize the meaning of the world or of history as that meaning comes into being. In this way, it merges into the general effort of modern thought.
— Maurice Merleau-Ponty, *Phenomenology of Perception*

Notes

✧

1. An Introduction to Central Issues in Ethnomusicology and Folklore (pp. 1–28)

1. Finding a word to describe the people with whom one does fieldwork is a difficult and unsatisfying experience. The traditional "informant" sounds too much like informer, "collaborator" evokes images of the Vichy government, and "respondent" suggests passivity. Given this problematic situation, I have chosen "participant" to indicate someone that becomes involved in an academic research project. I also use "participant" to refer to anyone who partakes in a musical event. Where the two senses of the word might be confused, I use the term "research participant" to refer to someone who specifically takes part in an academic project and "musical participant" to refer to a person attending a musical event or engaging in musical activity.

2. See Berger (1991, 20–21) for a discussion of the trope of the text-context sandwich.

3. Though primarily grounded in performance theory, Briggs suggests that phenomenology is useful in determining which levels of context are relevant to a particular performance event (1988).

4. Many of the issues of this period were prefigured in the Fillmore-Gilman debate of the end of the nineteenth century (Fillmore 1888, 1895, 1899; Gilman 1891, [1908] 1977). There, Fillmore held that Native Americans intended to sing tempered European intervals but failed, while Gilman held that their performance of these non-European intervals reflected an entire, culturally unique musical system. For a discussion of this debate, see Berger (1991).

5. Though in no way representative of the breadth and subtlety of Nettl's work, the chapter on function in his *Study of Ethnomusicology* (1983, 147–61) represents this kind of perspective.

6. For a related analysis of the contemporary musicology of rock, see my discussion of Stan Hawkins's work on Annie Lennox's "Money Can't Buy It" (Berger, in press).

7. For a more complete introduction to phenomenology, the reader should consult Kohák (1978), Ihde (1977), or Hammond, Howarth, and Keat (1991).

8. For a fuller discussion of the problem of the other in phenomenology, see Berger and Del Negro (in preparation).

9. On the dialectics of theory and data in folklore research, see Berger (forthcoming).

2. Commercial Hard Rock in Cleveland, Ohio (pp. 31–55)

1. The term "bodily stylistics" comes from folklorist Giovanna Del Negro (1997, 1999). I am indebted to her for making me aware of the importance of bodily stylistics and the practices of seeing and being seen in display events.

2. In recent years a number of popular music scholars have taken everyday musical activity as their focus (for example, Finnegan 1989; Straw 1991; Cohen 1993; Guilbault 1993, 1997; Shank 1994; Erlmann 1996). Most relevant to the present study is the work of Ruth Finnegan. Throughout her excellent study, *The Hidden Musicians*, Finnegan strongly emphasizes the fact that all musical "worlds" are brought into being by the actions of their members. Further, she points out that such actions may form scenes (or, in her terminology, "pathways") with varying amounts of social cohesion and that scenes may interpenetrate one another and the surrounding society in complex ways (188–90, 323–25; also see my discussion of Finnegan in Chapter 1). Focusing on the role of musical ideologies in the establishment of music scenes, Straw (1991) uses rather different theoretical apparatus to explore related issues of fragmentation and cohesion in the social base of music. Combining the methods of social history and ethnography, Jocelyne Guilbault (1993) and Barry Shank (1994) explore how musical coalitions emerge and change over time. In this chapter and the next two, I hope to develop this general concern with music making activity by employing insights from Anthony Giddens. Giddens's work helps us to reconcile situated conduct and larger social forces and understand the different ways that social formations may be organized. Attending equally to structure and agency, I will explore the different ways in which concrete musical practices, the social and musical ideologies of the participants, structural features of the regional society, and the "macro-level" contexts of race and class interact to constitute musical scenes of varying levels of stability. For other discussions of Giddens's practice theory and music making conduct see Monson (1996, 13–14) and Erlmann (1996, 18, 242).

3. Throughout this book, I have used the real names of the research participants with whom I have worked. In the few instances where a participant requested anonymity, I have created a pseudonym and altered minor details of his or her life story. When an identity has been obscured, I have indicated it in the text.

4. The Fender Stratocaster, or strat, is one of the most common guitars in all of popular music. Thin, with two sharply angled cutaways near the neck, it has been imitated by countless companies and is common in commercial hard rock.

5. In her valuable discussion of the dynamics of music composition in rock, Weinstein (1993, 217) distinguishes three kinds of compositional processes: "proprietorship" (leader composition), "duopoly" (two main composers), and "the cooperative" (group composition). For another perspective on the process of group composition in rock, see Shank (1994, 141–45) and Finnegan (1989, 167–69); also interesting is Keil, Keil, and Blau's discussion of group composition in American polka music (1992, 176–80).

6. Here, I am using the word "groove," to mean "repeating drum pattern." Rock musicians and ethnomusicologists also use the word "groove" to refer to the sense of rhythmic vitality and energy found in a successful musical performance. For a more detailed discussion of the former sense of the word groove, see Chapter 4.

7. The Roman numerals here are a standard nomenclature for representing chords. Lower-case Roman numerals represent minor chords, upper-case represent major chords. The numbers themselves refer to the scale degree on which the chord is based. Often, Arabic numbers follow the Roman ones to indicate the diatonic extensions of the chords; thus a V9 chord is a major chord built on the fifth scale degree with the flatted seventh and major ninth extension added.

8. A number of theoretical works explore the dialectics of contextualized creativity and stocks of cultural knowledge. From a Marxist approach, for example, V. N. Vološinov's *Marxism and the Philosophy of Language* (1973, 99–106) explores how past knowledge of semantics interacts with situated context to produce unique

utterances; from an ethnography of speaking perspective, Dell Hymes's "Folklore's Nature and the Sun's Myth" explores how stocks of knowledge interact with emergent innovations in folklore performance (1975).

9. Though some of my commercial hard rock and metal research participants could read traditional Western music notation, none wrote down their parts. Most singers, however, did write out their lyrics at some stage of the composition process.

10. In a polemical piece in *Popular Music*, Philip Tagg (1994) argues for a homology between musical sound and social organization in the rave subculture. Dave Hesmondhalgh's critique of Tagg's homology argument (1995) is in line with a number of elements of this discussion: specifically, the problem of interpreting both music and society and the difficulties of reconciling internal differences within a culture with a unified interpretation of its music. For related ideas, see Erlmann (1996, 14–17, 82), Guilbault (1997, 36–37), and my discussion of Feld (1982) in Chapter 1.

11. As I shall suggest in Chapter 11, a music cannot be deemed progressive or regressive based on the scholar's interpretation of its style of interaction or ideological content; a music's political content is based on the meaning of that music in the participants' experiences and the consequences of those meanings for the participants and the society as a whole. This is not to say that the participant is the only judge of a music's meaning, or that musical participants always describe the meanings they experience accurately. This is to acknowledge, however, that the politics of music is grounded in the consequentiality of that music for the lives of the participants and other members of their society, and that that consequentiality is always mediated through the participants' experiences, however well or poorly they describe them.

12. For one of the finest explorations of the relationships among expressive practices in a situated context, see Barre Toelken's exploration of folklore in Navajo family life (1979, 93–103).

3. Heavy Metal in Akron, Ohio (pp. 56–75)

1. For an excellent debunking of the connection between Satanism and metal, see Walser (1993, 141–44, 151–52) and Weinstein (1991, 258–63).

2. The progressive history that my research participants described is in some ways at odds with the academic histories told by Deena Weinstein and Robert Walser. In the 1970s and early 1980s, the boundary between commercial hard rock and metal was somewhat blurry. Deena Weinstein includes 1970s hard rock bands like Led Zeppelin, Rush, and Van Halen in metal's roots and posits a schism within metal that produced two distinct lineages within the subculture: the overall thrash/speed/death lineage that my research participants accept and the "lite metal" tradition of bands like Poison and Winger that are the immediate precursors of the commercial hard rock scene described in Chapter 2. My metal research participants excluded the 1970s and 1980s hard rock bands from their history and defined themselves in opposition to the contemporary commercial hard rock scene. On the development of heavy metal from a musical style into a robustly stable subculture in the early 1980s, see Straw (1984, 119).

3. It is important to note that while the term "heavy" is rich and polyvocal, no one in rock or metal uses it in the sense of the 1960s counterculture: in rock and metal, "heavy" never means deep or profound, as in "heavy, man."

4. For an excellent discussion of the range of distorted timbres in popular music, see Art Thompson's valuable articles in *Guitar Player* (1992, 1997).

5. For a discussion of the tensions among different subgenres within metal, as well as a brief review of the musical and aesthetic features of the genre as a whole, see Friesen and Epstein (1994).

6. The notion that identity in expressive behavior is constructed across or between group boundaries has a long history in folklore scholarship. For classic statements of these concepts, see Bauman (1972) or Abrahams (1981). For an examination of the ways in which oppositional identity plays itself out in musical rhetoric, see Ingrid Monson's discussion of John Coltrane's version of the Broadway standard "My Favorite Things" (1996, 106–20). Guilbault (1997) develops related ideas in connection with post-colonial theory.

4. Two Jazz Scenes in Northeast Ohio (pp. 76–116)

1. For an excellent discussion of the dynamics of leaders and side players in a different region and style, see MacLeod (1993).

2. My approach here has affinities with the social history sections of the recent popular music studies of Barry Shank (1994, esp. 16 and 30–90) and Jocelyne Guilbault (1993). In these works, the emergence of music scenes is conceptualized as similar to the formation of political coalitions. Here, I do not seek to trace out a social history, but to illustrate how diverse, historically informed actors interact in the present to constitute a loosely knit scene. In a related connection, also see Finnegan's discussion of the shared skills and knowledge possessed by musicians in the fragmented jazz scene of Milton Keynes, England (1989, 88).

3. Many of the musical practices I discuss in the rest of this chapter and the next one are also documented in the important jazz ethnographies of Paul Berliner (1994) and Ingrid Monson (1996). Both Berliner and Monson examine the musicians' achievement of groove, the negotiations between the soloist and the rhythm section, and the distinction between mastering the defining features of the song and creatively applying techniques of improvisation. Berliner's study situates these practices within the context of the musician's ongoing acquisition of improvisatory skills, while Monson focuses on the issues of indexicality and interaction. Here, I hope to provide insights that complement these studies by showing how these jazz musical practices emerge within the larger framework of the player's organization of attention, and how that organization of attention is tied to the player's broad aesthetic and social projects.

4. The use of these terms is not fully standardized in educational discourse. Some teachers refer to beats 1 and 3 of a 4/4 bar as "on-beats" and beats 2 and 4 as "off-beats." Independent of the terminology, however, the concept is the same. In basic Western music theory, the various moments of the bar fall in a hierarchy from strong to weak. The first beat is the strongest. The third beat is weaker, beats 2 and 4 are weaker still, and the subdivisions of the beat (the eighth notes, sixteenth notes, thirty-second notes, and so on) are even weaker.

5. Melodic patterns are often represented with a nomenclature of numbers, caret symbols, and underscores. Given a scale of any tonality whose degrees are represented by numbers (1, 2, 3, 4, 5, 6, 7), this nomenclature represents the notes of the first upper octaves by preceding the number with a caret symbol (thus, $^\wedge 1$, $^\wedge 2$, $^\wedge 3$, $^\wedge 4$, $^\wedge 5$, $^\wedge 6$, $^\wedge 7$). Similarly, the first lower octave is represented by adding an underscore (_) to the number ($\underline{1}, \underline{2}, \underline{3}, \underline{4}, \underline{5}, \underline{6}, \underline{7}$).

6. In jazz theory, "key area" refers to a group of bars within a song that are all in the same key; a key area is distinct from the key of the song as a whole.

7. Monson cites her research participant Michael Carvin as the source of the terms *solid* and *fluid* (1996, 51). In her interpretation, the interplay between solid

and fluid parts is crucial for both jazz drumming (51–69) and the overall operation of the jazz ensemble (66–72).

8. In a related connection, see Finnegan (1989, 174–75).

5. The Organization of Attention in Two Jazz Scenes
(pp. 119–148)

1. For a more detailed discussion of the dialectics of theory and data in folklore research, see Berger (forthcoming).

2. The one difficulty of this metaphor is that it may lead the reader to equate the full phenomena with our narrow, momentary experience of it. Husserl has rightly pointed out that the experience of an object entails an awareness of both the immediately visible faces and a horizon of faces invisible but potentially available upon future inquiry. His notion of objective reality existing "in" experience is at least partially rooted in a phenomenology of space in which "objectivity" is understood as a spatial multifacetedness that transcends momentary presentations (1931, 89–90; 1960, 39–41). While in some ways misleading, the Rubin's Goblet drawing helps us gain a clear entrance into the ideas of foreground, background, and gestalt. For a phenomenological discussion of the concepts of foreground and background that is illustrated by reference to multistable figures, see Don Ihde's *Experimental Phenomenology* (1977).

3. Throughout the discussion, I have used the expression "the focusing of attention" to describe our organization of experience. Such an expression—and its parallel, "the structuring of consciousness"—may seem an innocuous way of referring to the processes I am interested in exploring; the usage certainly fits in with the commonsense understanding of "attention" or "consciousness" as some metaphysical substance that must be poured onto an object for it to enter into experience. As a mere turn of phrase the expression poses no harm, but the concepts it suggests are seriously problematic and need to be addressed. The project of William James's *Essays in Radical Empiricism* ([1912] 1962) is a critique of the notion of consciousness. Writing within the tradition of empiricism James sought to ground knowledge in experience, and a rigorous examination of experience revealed that no such substance called "consciousness" (or "attention") could be found. James concluded that consciousness was not a thing in itself; on the contrary, the term is used to explain the fact that we do not merely experience the world but are able to construct knowledge about it. James suggested that there is one "substance" in the universe— namely, experience—and that our living reality is assembled by the conjunction, or gluing together, of pieces of experience. The details of his argument are not important here, but the central point is both clear and essential: it is a mistake to think of the organization of experience as the dispensing of consciousness and the constitution of perception as the animation of physical or ideal objects with the living breadth of attention. Understood in this way, the "organization of attention" must be seen as "the arrangement of experiences relative to one another."

Such a position may seem to be at odds with a phenomenological orientation that requires experience to be conceptualized as a duality of subject and object. Discussing the neo-Kantians, James himself explicitly rejects such a duality (James 1967, 4–5). But Husserl, in trying to remove the problematic implications of the notion of the stream of consciousness, expressed a similar view (1931), and in fact, James's radical empiricism and phenomenology are not incompatible. The resolution of this seeming contradiction lies in the insight that the subject is not some fictitious entity called consciousness and the object is not some other entity that is thus animated by the subject; on the contrary, subject and object are both part of experience. The subject is there in experience as the ordering of phenomena, and the world is there in experience as that which is constituted and ordered; both the ordering and the ordered are aspects of experience as a whole. The topic of this chapter, therefore, is *not* the animation of objects by consciousness but rather the active organization of experience.

4. Here and throughout this chapter, "groove" is mainly used to refer to the energetic and flowing rhythmic feel of a successful jazz performance. As I have suggested in Chapter 4, the word can also be used to refer to a repeated pattern of drum beats (i.e., the standard rock "groove" or the standard bossa nova "groove"). For a theoretical discussion of the various senses of the word groove, see Monson (66–69).

Grounded in the ideas of Charles Keil, a body of work has emerged connecting "participatory discrepancies" (nonmetronomic ensemble coordinations) to the experience of groove (in the former sense of the word); for a review of this literature, see Keil (1995). My fieldwork confirms the importance of groove and seeks a different perspective on the topic by looking at the connections among groove, perception, and the organization of attention. See Berliner (1994) and Monson (1996) for their discussion of the role of groove in jazz.

5. On the importance of the relationship between the bass line and the drums for groove in jazz, see Monson (1996) and Berliner (1994).

6. See Caton (1993, 320–22). Also, see Caton's discussion of the dynamic ways in which the reflexive subject shifts between foreground and background in experience (323). Also see Ihde (1976, 143–46).

7. Monson explores a parallel issue when she examines how jazz musicians negotiate and reestablish ensemble coordination after one of the musicians has lost his or her place in the form (1996, 156–70).

8. While I differ from Schutz on many points in the analysis of the organization of the living present, his discussion of the relationship of musical experience to time consciousness (1976, esp. 37–42, 46–48) is basic to any phenomenology of music. In a similar connection, also see Ingarden (1989, 49–52 and 97–99).

9. The following discussion of Bill's playing focuses on his experience while comping. Bill takes a few solos (not enough for his taste) and trades fours with the other players. Unfortunately, space does not permit a thorough discussion of his organization of attention in that phase of the event.

10. There are some important differences between the way Eric and I use the term *background* with respect to the changes. To Eric, backgrounding the changes does not mean placing the sound of chords at the edge of experience; on the contrary, to him the term meant placing the mental computations necessary for note choice and voicing into the subconscious and outside of experience. The differences here are important. In my usage, I refer to the backgrounding of the *sound* of the chord; in Eric's usage, he refers to the backgrounding of the underlying musical calculations that enable voicing. In Eric's usage, backgrounding places a backgrounded entity outside of experience; in mine, backgrounding places an entity at the background or edge of experience. While these are substantial differences, Eric's use of the term background to refer to *nonchordal* elements of the musical experience was quite similar to my usage.

11. Larry Glover is slightly older than Alvin, Leonard, Eric, and Jerome. Though he tends to move in somewhat different circles from the four Cleveland musicians on whom I have focused, Larry is familiar with their east side jazz scene, and his perspectives are relevant to the topic at hand.

12. The social basis of the organization of experience has complex dynamics. One typical dynamic is for a broad musical goal to effect a particular, situational aim, and for that particular aim to require a certain technique of attention. For example, the jazz players all aim to have a tight band. This goal itself is culturally specific (for example, some punk musics have no such value), and one instance of this

goal specific to jazz is tight bass and drum coordination. To serve this goal, the technique of attention called "locking in" emerged. But the social basis of the organization of attention need not be mediated in such a complex manner. The jazz player's invitation of the audience's attention is a case in which the value and the technique of attention are coterminous.

13. For a more detailed discussion of the dialectics of theory and data, see Berger (forthcoming).

6. The Organization of Attention in the Rock and Metal Scenes (pp. 149–173)

1. See Bennett's discussion of the role of the PA and stage monitor system in rock performance (1980, 159–68). It is interesting to note that while Bennett was generally enthusiastic about the ability of monitor speakers to deliver the band's sound to the musicians, the players I spoke with were rarely satisfied with the stage sound they experienced at clubs.

2. Other similarities with jazz can be found as well. For example, the rocker's organization of experience during group composition at rehearsals is similar to the jazzer's organization of experience in performance. In both settings, mutual attention to the other players is crucial.

3. For a discussion of audience-performer interaction in rock from a Lacanian perspective, see Shank (1994, 118–61).

4. In a related connection, see Bennett's discussion of the sound check in rock music (1980, 161–65). Here, Bennett suggests that when testing out the sound system before the audience has arrived at the club, the rock musician attempts to hear the music, not as it sounds on the stage, but as it will sound to a listener on the floor.

5. As I suggested earlier (Chapter 5, note 3), it is important to keep in mind that "attention" is a shorthand way of referring to the organization of experience. As a result, the sentence "the players are aware of the listeners' attention to them and the affective tenor of their attention" can be rephrased in this way: a crucial part of the player's experience is the lived realization that the audience members are orienting themselves toward the band so that the band can emerge more fully in their (the audience's) experience; further, the affective tenor with which the band is constituted in the audience's experience is also present in the *band's* experience.

6. For a more detailed discussion of rhythmic protention, see Berger (1997).

7. For some early discussions of the idea of melody as temporal gestalt, see Schutz (1976, 37–42, 46–48) and Ingarden (1989, 49–52 and 97–99). In the work of both authors, the musical composition is represented as unambiguously determining how the melody will be parsed in experience. The goal of Chapters 7 and 8 is to shed light on the listener's role in the constitution of these gestalts and show how that constitution is influenced by the listener's social and cultural context.

7. Tonality, Temporality, and the Intending Subject (1) (pp. 174–199)

1. For an excellent discussion of the advantages and disadvantages of the audio feedback interview technique in ethnomusicology, see Stone and Stone (1981).

2. See Berger (1997) for a discussion of the perception of rhythm in heavy metal.

3. The transcription is based on Dia Pason's March 12, 1993, performance. Because of Chris's interests and my own focus of analysis, I have given a schematic rendering of the drum part and have omitted the guitar solo altogether.

The reader should also note the conventions used in this transcription. The guitar is traditionally tuned to a concert E, and guitar music is written an octave higher than it is sounded. The guitarists and bassists in Dia Pason tuned their instruments a major second below the traditional tuning, a practice common in commercial hard rock; further, they refer to the lowest note of the instrument as an E, regardless of its concert pitch. Combining both sets of conventions, the transcription is an octave and a second higher than it is sounded. Unless otherwise noted, the basses are an octave below the guitars.

4. For an excellent discussion of power chords in rock and metal, see Walser (1993).

5. On Schutz's and Ingarden's treatment of melody as a temporal gestalt, see Chapter 6, note 7.

6. In some forms of music theory, this i chord could not be seen to be a true one because there is no V7 chord or leading tone to support it. Instead, the i would actually be a vi, tending to a I a minor third above. However, this reading is so dogmatic and distanced from the experiences of my participants that we need not concern ourselves with it.

7. Steven M. Friedson's discussion of Don Ihde's work (Friedson 1996, 128–62) has important connections with my own research. Both Friedson and I seek to show how an individual musical form can be experienced in more than one way and to illustrate how the subject is involved in the act of perception. Friedson applies these ideas to the "mottos" (basic drumming patterns) of the healing ceremonies of the Tumbuka of northern Malawi and suggests that the mottos possess a kind of rhythmic multistability. In a rich analysis, Friedson shows that Tumbuka listeners generate different perceptual experiences of the same pattern by variously grouping the drum strokes into units of two or three. Showing the different perceptual experiences that can be constituted from a given guitar part, my discussion of tonality in rock and metal parallels Friedson's analysis.

From here, however, he and I take these ideas in different directions. Friedson's discussion applies variational method to the composition and performance of new sonic forms as well as to the perception of existing rhythms and shows how the numerous drum patterns of a given rhythmic mode can be derived as variations of the mode's main motto. Further, Friedson examines the relationship between different sense modalities in the act of music making. Where Friedson develops the variational method by tacking between perception and performance, I focus specifically on perception and explore the subject's organization of the living present. Using Husserl's *Phenomenology of Internal Time Consciousness*, I reveal how the constitution of different sonic experiences from a single musical form comes about through the listener's differing arrangements of protentions and retentions. Further, I examine the interplay between culture and agency in those perceptual acts and interpret auditory perception as a kind of social practice.

8. In other performances, a third backing vocal part was added on the words "give it up" in bars 33 and 34.

8. Tonality, Temporality, and the Perceptual Subject (2)
(pp. 200–241)

1. The lowest string of the guitar is traditionally tuned to a concert E. In metal, however, bands tune lower, often as much as a perfect fourth. On the recording of FS discussed here, Sin-Eater tuned down to B. Independent of the concert pitch, most metal musicians refer to the lowest note on the instrument as an E. Dann and I followed this practice in our conversation, and I have kept with this usage in this

chapter and transcription. Further, the guitar is traditionally transcribed an octave higher than it is sounded; combining these conventions, the transcription of FS is written an octave and a fourth higher than it is sounded. Unless otherwise noted, the basses play an octave below the guitars.

2. Also see Berger (In press).

3. The social interactions by which the song is produced add a great deal of complexity to Dann's experience of the rhythmic aspect of the part. While Dann composes the guitar parts, John is free to write any drum part behind Dann's guitar that he desires; it is very common for John to write parts that go counter to the more obvious rhythmic implications of Dann's composition. For example, in my interviews with John, we explored the drum part for bars 1 through 8 of the intro, and found that by changing the bass and snare parts (bars 5 through 8) he is able to shift the feel of the entire band from 10/8 to 5/4. The exploration and description, however, take us too far afield from the present discussion. For a detailed discussion of John's drum parts, see Berger (1997).

4. When he initially composed the tune, Dann knew that lyrics must go on top of these mood-setting chords. One of Dann's main concerns in songwriting is avoiding the pat and predictable. As such, he usually holds off writing the lyrics until after the rest of the song is composed, and then writes lines whose scansion is unrelated to the rhythms of the chords. In this instance, Dann knew that he wanted the section to last for four or eight bars, but allowed the exact length to be flexible enough to accommodate the lyrics he would later compose.

5. Because of problems in the mix-down, this part is almost inaudible on the demo recording.

6. As I suggested in Chapter 3, the terms *verse, bridge,* and *chorus* are used in a much vaguer way in death metal than they are in commercial hard rock. In this chapter, I follow Dann's usage.

7. Just as metal musicians commonly refer to the lowest note on the instrument as E regardless of the concert pitch to which they tune (see note 1), they also use enharmonic spellings of note names that contradict the practices taught in introductory theory courses. Metal musicians generally prefer spelling notes as sharp rather than as flat (G-sharp, rather than A-flat), and these spellings hold none of the theoretical implication that they would in academic discourse. For example, the second note of G phrygian is commonly spelled as G-sharp. Throughout, I have followed Dann's spelling of the notes.

8. This process can be described as follows. (1) The construction of a new phenomenon in imagination or with body and instrument. (2) Simultaneous with step 1, the careful attendance to that phenomenon that highlights its affective or aesthetic dimensions. (3.1) If the phenomenon is worthy, memorization or transcription, followed by a return to step 1 to construct or constitute a new phenomenon. (3.2a) If there is a problem, reflective judgment about the positive and negative aspects of the phenomenon created. (3.2b) Alternatively if there is a problem, a new and intense attendance to the phenomenon that highlights the phenomenon's positive and negative aspects. (4) (optional) Reflective plan about how to correct the offending aspects of the phenomenon. (5) Construction or constitution of a variant of the first phenomenon guided explicitly or implicitly by step 3.2a or 3.2b. (6) Simultaneous with step 5, careful attendance to the new phenomenon. Because each part exists as a gestalt of its aspects, the change of any one aspect will color all the other aspects of the phenomenon, thus changing the phenomenon as a whole in ways not fully predictable and necessitating steps 5 and 6. This process continues with creating phenomena, judging/attending, (reflecting), creating variant and so on until the individual is satisfied, he or she moves on to create a new phenomenon, or quits out of frustration. Optionally, flows of reflection may accompany and guide every step as well.

The process is as true of cooking, drawing, dancing, or writing as it is of composing music, and the differences lie in the rate of change of the media and its mutability/erasability. Live sound, recorded sound, transcribed sound, live sound improvisation, food (each kind of dish with its own dynamics of change and mutability/erasability), sketches on computer screen or Etch-a-Sketch, sketches with unerasable material that can be layered over, sketches with unerasable material that can't be layered over, bodily movements, bodily movements as recorded on camera, verbal art, writing with pencil, writing with pen, writing with word processor—the unique rates of change and mutability/erasability of each of these media affect the dynamics of the processes outlined above in distinct ways. (For related ideas, see Sawyer 1995.)

Two points here are significant. (1) On this level of abstraction, the process may be universal for all human aesthetic activity. (2) The dynamics of that activity depend upon the fact that phenomena are holistic. In other words, phenomena are a gestalt of their various aspects; while their aspects are partially separable in reflection or focused perception, they interact in complex ways to form whole phenomena. Thus, the correction of a flaw of any one aspect may result in unpredictable interactions between old and new aspects and may result in unpredictable aesthetic effects; the holistic nature of phenomena necessitates the reperformance, and, in fact, the whole process. This concept could be useful for scholarship in a variety of areas, but the implications of these ideas must be explored in other contexts.

9. There are cases in which Dann does start the compositional process with a reflective plan to employ harmonic materials or devices. Such cases reinforce the conclusion given above. Reflectively employed here, scale is no subconscious structure but an intellectual tool used to influence the imaginative or bodily construction of musical ideas.

10. There are three tracks of guitars on the seven-inch record; they are panned left, center right, and right in the stereo field and are labeled in this way in the transcription.

11. Listening and reflecting at a later date, folklorist Giovanna Del Negro suggested to me that the interval sounds "happier" when the notes have short time values, but gloomier when the pitches are allowed to ring. While the point may be explored in more detail, it should be clear that there is no way to experience the interval by itself, and that aspects of musical sound are never fully separable from performance events or social contexts.

12. Also interesting is the unusual 10-bar phrasing of the part, and the harmonic consequences of that phrasing for the E and the A. In my listening, the E feels more like a i than a vi, and the 10-bar phrasing weakens the A's centrality.

13. In one version of the song, Erik adds a part to the second half of the riff. Not surprisingly, Dann hears Erik's part as a harmony to his own focal melody line. The part adds only one new pitch, G-sharp, which, again, can easily be understood as an alteration of the phrygian.

14. For a detailed discussion of the relationship between the affective and the valual dimensions of perception, see Berger (1991).

15. On the experience of the unity of a musical composition on large temporal scales, see Ingarden (1989, 99–103). Also, see Bennett's brief discussion of the rock "set" as a large-scale temporal whole (1980, 151).

9. Conclusions (pp. 242–248)

1. For a rather different approach to these issues, see Schutz (1976, 50–57).

2. As we have seen throughout, the emphasis on the fact that perception is constituted should not lead the reader to confuse perception and imagination.

While there may be many ways to constitute sound in experience, perception means engagement with the world, and the synthesis of identification is not infinitely malleable.

3. Ingarden suggests related ideas when he argues that small-scale gestalts like chords or individual melodies are synthesized into higher-order experiences like ensemble texture and orchestral arrangement and that such large-scale gestalts can have unique "qualities" (1989, 53–56). Unfortunately, Ingarden's interpretation of these qualities is rather narrow. Such qualities, he argues, may be melodic, harmonic, or rhythmic but never "dynamic, agogic, or timbric" (56). Further, in Ingarden's thought, these qualities are always located in the quasi-ideal space of the musical work rather than in the listener's culturally specific encounter with that work. Also see Ingarden's useful discussion of the relationship between individual notes and phenomena of brief duration such as individual melodic phrases and chords (49–52).

10. Death Metal Perspectives (pp. 251–275)

1. For a related discussion of the social consequences of fieldwork, see Cohen (1993, 134).

2. Though Sartre does not deal explicitly with fieldwork issues, many ideas in this argument are inspired by his approach to the ethics of the existential subject (1955, 1956).

3. For related ideas, see Lawless (1992).

4. Weinstein's *Heavy Metal: A Cultural Sociology* (1991) is an excellent example of abstention. Weinstein explicitly attacks both left and right critics of heavy metal for failing to relate to metal on its own terms. The goal of her work is to present an "objective" description of heavy metal upon which others may ground policy decisions. The critical point here is that even if Weinstein is able to present an "objective" description (understood as I have explained above, see my discussion of objectivity in Chapter 1), failing to engage in critique or celebration has social consequences; as a result, abstaining from action and "objective" description are just as political and ideological as the more explicit left and right critiques. None of this is to attack Weinstein; acts of abstaining or "objective" description may in fact be the most progressive option in some situations. On the contrary, my goal is to suggest that abstention, objective description, critique, polemic, celebration, and critical dialogic ethnography are *all* actions in the moral continuum of history.

5. In the contemporary academic environment, "ideology" is used in two very different ways. In the neutral sense, ideology is simply taken to mean a coherent set of ideas. In the critical sense, the term is used to indicate a set of ideas that cause dominated groups to participate in their own undoing. Throughout this discussion, I shall use the term in the neutral sense.

6. For an abstract discussion of the relationship between reflection and action, see Giddens (1979, 56–57); for a discussion of these issues in the context of a music scene, see MacLeod (1993, 181–82).

7. For a different perspective on the contradictory themes within metal, see Harrell (1994, 99–102).

11. A Critical Dialogue on the Politics of the Metal Underground (pp. 276–294)

1. For a rich interpretation of music's unintended political consequences, see Jeff Goldthorpe's (1992) excellent discussion of the impact of early 1980s hardcore on the rhetoric of various late 1980s progressive movements in San Francisco. Also

see Guilbault's comprehensive discussion of the concrete influence of Zouk music on the economic and social life of the French Antilles (1993, 30, 204–8) and Lipsitz's discussion of the political consequences of various popular musics throughout the world (1994a, esp. 135–56).

2. Metal is also popular in Latin America, Scandinavia, and East Asia; the remarks in this chapter do not necessarily address the scenes in those countries.

Glossary

✧

NOTE: The explanations of musical terms in this glossary are meant to describe how these words were used by the musicians and listeners of the metal, rock, and jazz scenes of northeast Ohio in the early 1990s; they are not intended as prescriptive or authoritative definitions.

Alternative: A loose collection of rock music genres and scenes emerging in the early 1980s and gaining wide acceptance in the 1990s. Most alternative scenes are in some way opposed to commercial hard rock and pop. Alternative includes such subgenres as grunge and college rock. *See* **college rock, commercial hard rock,** and **grunge.**

Bebop: A genre of jazz developed during the 1940s and early 1950s emphasizing small ensembles, virtuosic improvisation, an elaborated harmonic palette, and melodic lines of flowing, swung eighth notes.

Bridge: A section in the form of rock songs. The bridge usually serves to connect two other sections of the song, such as the verse and the chorus. *See* **chorus, intro, outro,** and **verse.**

Chorus: A section in the form of rock songs. The chorus usually contains a memorable repeated fragment of melody and lyrics called a hook. *See* **bridge, intro, hook, outro,** and **verse.**

College rock: A loosely defined subgenre of alternative rock. Characteristic features may include chimey guitar timbres, complex vocal harmonies, or obscure lyrics.

Commercial hard rock: A genre of rock music featuring distorted guitar timbres and traditional rock song forms. Commercial hard rock was the dominant form of rock music throughout the late 1980s.

Comp: Abbreviated form of "accompany." This term is most frequently used by jazz musicians.

Cover: To perform a song composed and performed by another band or musician. This term is most frequently used by rock musicians.

Death metal: A genre of underground heavy metal characterized by growly, unpitched vocals. *See* **heavy metal** and **underground.**

Demo: Abbreviated form of "demonstration recording." A recording produced by a band for sale on the local level or for promotion.

Drum riser: The stand upon which a drum kit rests.

Epochē: Literally, "bracket," the term is used in phenomenology to refer to the process by which claims about the subjective or objective status of an experience are set aside so that the phenomenon may be viewed on its own.

Fusion: A loosely defined genre of music that emerged in the late 1960s and early 1970s and combined elements of jazz, rock, and funk. Also referred to as jazz/rock fusion.

Fuzak: A portmanteau word combining the terms *fusion* and *Muzak,* fuzak is a derogatory term used by some jazz musicians to refer to fusion.

Glam: An abbreviated form of "glamour metal," not to be confused with 1970s "glam rock." *See* **glam metal.**

Glam metal: A genre of 1980s commercial hard rock that combines elements of heavy metal and pop and whose performers employ elaborate makeup, costumes, and stage antics. For some, the term is almost synonymous with "pop metal." In differing contexts the term may have derogatory or neutral connotations. While sometimes abbreviated to "glam," it is not to be confused with 1970s "glam rock." *See* **pop metal.**

Grunge: A genre of alternative rock music combining heavy guitar timbres and rough, melodic vocals. A response to L.A. pop metal, many grunge bands came from Seattle and passed from relative obscurity to mainstream success in the early 1990s. The term can also refer to the characteristic guitar timbres of the genre and its associated fashions. *See* **heavy, Seattle sound,** and **pop metal.**

Hardcore: An abbreviated form of "hardcore punk." *See* **hardcore punk.**

Hardcore punk: A genre of music and set of subcultures emerging from punk in the early 1980s, often abbreviated to "hardcore." Hardcore is characterized by brief songs, a sharp dislike of individual displays of virtuosity, and politicized ideologies.

Headbang: To bow one's head and rock it up and down in time with music. This activity is usually performed while listening to heavy metal.

Headbanger: Members of the heavy metal subcultures.

Headliner: The featured band in a program of rock or metal music. The headliners are usually the last to perform in an evening.

Heavy: A term used by rock or metal musicians to refer to distorted guitar timbres, stiff and aggressive drum grooves, rough nonpitched vocals, or the overall ensemble texture of a piece of music.

Heavy metal: A group of musical genres. Heavy metal often employs distorted guitar timbres, individual displays of virtuosity, and complex song forms. Underground metal includes death metal, thrash, speedcore, grindcore, and other genres. *See* **underground.**

Hook: A repeated fragment of melody or chords, usually occurring in the chorus of a rock song. The hook is intended to attract the listener's attention and help him or her remember the song.

Intro: An abbreviated form of "introduction." A section in the form of rock songs, the intro is the opening section in the form. *See* **bridge, chorus, outro,** and **verse.**

Jazz/rock fusion: *See* **fusion.**

Living present: The experienced moment. This concept from phenomenology is intended to draw attention to the fact that the present is not experienced as an infinitely thin "now," but as a temporal thickness that includes anticipations of the near future and retentions of events just passed. *See* **protention** and **retention.**

Melograph: A device for mechanically transcribing music.

Metal: An abbreviated form of "heavy metal." *See* **heavy metal.**

Mosh: A variety of audience behavior in heavy metal and punk involving body checking and other forms of rough physical contact.

Noema: The object of an experience. A *noema* never exists by itself and always requires a subject to constitute it. *See* **noesis.**

Noesis: A mode in which a subject engages with an object (*noema*) to constitute an experience. Perception, imagination, and memory are examples of *noetic* modes. *See* **noema.**

Noise band: A band performing music intended as chaotic and random. Noise bands may employ standard rock instruments, electronic equipment, and everyday, "nonmusical" sounds. Their pieces generally do not use meter, scale, pitch, or other traditional structures.

Outro: A section in the form of rock songs. The opposite of an intro, the outro is the closing section of the song. *See* **bridge, chorus, intro,** and **verse.**

PA: Abbreviated form of "public address system."

Phenomenon: An entity in experience. All phenomena are composed of *noema* and *noesis*. *See* *noema* and *noesis*.

Pop metal: A genre of commercial hard rock popular in the 1980s that combines elements of heavy metal and pop. *See* **glam metal**.

Post-bop: A broadly defined group of jazz genres emerging after bebop that further extended bebop's harmonic palette and deemphasized the use of vertical improvisation. *See* **bebop**.

Power chord: A term used by rock musicians to refer to chords composed of a root, a perfect fifth, and an octave. Occasionally, the term is used to refer to chords composed of a root, a perfect fourth, and an octave or a root, a tritone, and an octave. Power chords never contain a third. Designated by the chord symbol 5 (for example, E5), power chords are essential to most forms of rock music.

Protention: A phenomenon that has emerged (as potential) into the near future of the experienced moment. *See* **living present** and **retention**.

Retention: A phenomenon that has moved into the recent past of the experienced moment. *See* **living present** and **protention**.

Seattle sound: An ensemble texture popularized by alternative rock bands from Seattle. The texture is characterized by highly distorted guitar sounds and low-pitched, melodic vocals with rough vocal timbres. *See* **grunge**.

Stratocaster: A model of electric guitar made by the Fender Corporation and widely used in rock music. Many guitar manufacturers have copied the characteristic Stratocaster double cut-away body shape, and any guitar using that shape is loosely referred to as a "strat."

Strat: An abbreviated form of "Stratocaster." *See* **Stratocaster**.

Textual empiricism: Any variety of academic research that treats texts as autonomous objects of study rather than as the end product of social action.

Underground: Usually an abbreviated form of "heavy metal underground" or "hardcore punk underground," although the term can be used to refer to both. The underground is a network of subcultures and supporting music businesses often thought of by its members as existing in opposition to the mainstream music industry.

Verse: A section in the form of rock songs. The verse is typically repeated three times in a song, with each repetition employing the same melody and a different set of lyrics. The verse usually precedes the chorus. *See* **bridge, chorus, intro**, and **outro**.

Woodchucking: A technique of electric guitar performance in which the musician plays a series of muted single notes or power chords on the low E or A strings. Woodchucking is central to most forms of heavy metal and commercial hard rock music. *See* **power chord, heavy metal**, and **commercial hard rock**.

Zine: An abbreviated form of "fan magazine" or "magazine." In underground hardcore punk and heavy metal, a zine is an amateur or small-scale magazine used to promote bands and discuss the subculture. *See* **hardcore punk, heavy metal**, and **underground**.

Selected Bibliography

Abrahams, Roger D. 1968. Introductory remarks to a rhetorical theory of folklore. *Journal of American Folklore* 81:143–57.

———. 1981. Shouting match at the border: The folklore of display events. In *"And other neighborly names": Social process and cultural image in Texas folklore*, edited by Richard Bauman and Roger D. Abrahams. Austin: University of Texas Press.

Ames, David W. 1973. Igbo and Hausa musicians: A comparative examination. *Ethnomusicology* 17:250–78.

Bartók, Béla. [1924] 1981. *The Hungarian folk song*. Edited by Benjamin Suchoff and translated by M. D. Calvocoressi. Albany: State University of New York Press.

Bauman, Richard. 1972. Differential identity and the social base of folklore. In *Towards new perspectives in folklore*, edited by Richard Bauman and Roger D. Abrahams. Austin: University of Texas Press.

———. 1977. *Verbal art as performance*. Rowley, Mass.: Newbury House Publishers.

———. 1986. Performance and honor in 13th-century Iceland. *Journal of American Folklore* 99:131–50.

———. 1989. Performance. In *The international encyclopedia of communications*, edited by Erik Barnouw. Oxford: Oxford University Press.

Benedict, Ruth. 1969. *Zuni mythology*. New York: AMS Press.

Bennett, H. Stith. 1980. *On becoming a rock musician*. Amherst: University of Massachusetts Press.

Berger, Harris M. 1991. Armloads of crystals: A general theory of music and emotion. Master's thesis, Indiana University.

———. 1997. The practice of perception: Multi-functionality and time in the musical experiences of a heavy metal drummer. *Ethnomusicology* 41 (3):464–88.

———. Forthcoming. Theory as practice: Some dialectics of generality and specificity in folklore scholarship. *Journal of Folklore Research*.

———. In press. Death metal tonality and the act of listening. *Popular Music*.

Berger, Harris M., and Giovanna Del Negro. In preparation. Bauman's *Verbal art* and the social organization of attention: The role of reflexivity in the aesthetics in performance.

Berger, Harris M., and Cornelia Fales. 1997. An historico-cognitive approach to the study of timbre perception: "Heaviness" in the perception of heavy metal guitar textures. In *Working Papers of the Sound and Video Analysis and Instruction Lab*, vol. 1, edited by Cornelia Fales. Indiana: Indiana University Folklore Institute.

Bergson, Henri. 1913. *Time and free will*. Translated by R. L. Pogson. New York: Macmillan.

Berliner, Paul F. 1994. *Thinking in jazz: The infinite art of improvisation*. Chicago: University of Chicago Press.

Blacking, John. 1970. Tonal organization in the music of two Venda initiation schools. *Ethnomusicology* 14:1–57.

———. 1972. Deep and surface structures in Venda music. *Yearbook of the International Folk Music Council* 3:91–108.

———. 1973. *How musical is man?* Seattle: University of Washington Press.

———. 1979. The study of man as music maker. In *The performing arts: Music and dance*, edited by John Blacking and Joann W. Kealiinohomoku. New York: Mouton.

Bluestone, Barry, and Bennett Harrison. 1982. *The deindustrialization of America: Plant closings, community abandonment, and dismantling of basic industry.* New York: Basic Books.

Boas, Franz. 1955. *Primitive art.* New York: Dover.

———. 1966. *Race, language, and culture.* New York: Free Press.

———. 1970. *Tsimshian mythology.* Reprint, New York: Johnson Reprint.

Botkin, Benjamin. 1944. *A treasury of American folklore: Stories, ballads, and traditions of the people.* New York: Crown.

Bowman, Rob. 1995. The Stax sound: A musicological analysis. *Popular Music* 14: 285–320.

Bradby, Barbara, and Brian Torode. 1984. Pity Peggy Sue. *Popular Music* 4:183–207.

Briggs, Charles L. 1988. *Competence in performance: The creativity of tradition in Mexicano verbal art.* Philadelphia: University of Pennsylvania Press.

———. 1993. Genre versus metapragmatic dimensions of Warao narratives: Who regiments the performance? In *Reflexive language*, edited by John A. Lucy. Cambridge: Cambridge University Press.

Bright, William. 1979. A Karok myth in "measured verse": The translation of a performance. *Journal of California and Great Basin Anthropology* 1:117–23.

Buchan, David. 1972. *The ballad and the folk.* London: Routledge and Kegan Paul.

Bunzel, Ruth Leah. 1929. *The Pueblo potter: A study of creative imagination in primitive art.* New York: Columbia University Press.

Burrows, Edwin. 1936a. *Ethnology of Futuna.* Bernice P. Bishop Museum Bulletin, no. 138. Honolulu: Bernice P. Bishop Museum.

———. 1936b. *Music of the Tuamotus.* Bernice P. Bishop Museum Bulletin, no. 109. Honolulu: Bernice P. Bishop Museum.

———. 1945. *Songs of Uvea and Futuna.* Bernice P. Bishop Museum Bulletin, no. 185. Honolulu: Bernice P. Bishop Museum.

Butler, Gary. 1992. Indexicality, authority, and communication in traditional narrative discourse. *Journal of American Folklore* 105:34–56.

Caton, Steve C. 1993. The importance of reflexive language in George Herbert Mead's theory of self and communication. In *Reflexive language*, edited by John A. Lucy. Cambridge: Cambridge University Press.

Cashmore, E. Ellis. 1987. Shades of black, shades of white. In *Popular Music and Communication*, edited by James Lull. Newbury Park, Calif.: Sage.

Clifford, James, and George E. Marcus, eds. 1986. *Writing culture: The poetics and politics of ethnography.* Berkeley and Los Angeles: University of California Press.

Clifton, Thomas. 1976. Music as constituted object. *Music and Man* 2:73–98.

Cohen, Sara. 1993. Ethnography and popular music studies. *Popular Music* 12 (2):123–38.

Cooper, Robin. 1977. Abstract structure and the Indian raga system. *Ethnomusicology* 21:1–31.

Cubbit, Sean. 1984. "Maybellene": Meaning and the listening subject. *Popular Music* 4: 207–24.

Dégh, Linda. 1969. *Folktales and society: Story-telling in a Hungarian peasant community.* Translated by Emily M. Schossberger. Bloomington: Indiana University Press.

Del Negro, Giovanna P. 1997. "Our little Paris": An ethnography of the *passeggiata* in central Italy. In *Industry, technology, labor, and the Italian American commu-*

nities: Selected essays from the 28th annual conference of the American Italian Historical Association. Staten Island, N.Y.: American Italian Historical Association.

——. 1999. "Our little Paris": Gender, popular culture, and the *passeggiata* in central Italy. Ph.D. diss., Indiana University.

Densmore, Frances. 1939. *Nootka and Quileute music.* Bureau of American Ethnology Bulletin, no. 124. Washington, D.C.: GPO.

——. 1972. Northern Ute music. Reprint, New York: Da Capo.

Derrida, Jacques. 1973. *Speech and phenomena and other essays on Husserl's theory of signs.* Translated by David B. Allison. Evanston: Northwestern University Press.

Dorst, John D. 1989. *The written suburb: An American site, an ethnographic dilemma.* Philadelphia: University of Pennsylvania Press.

Dundes, Alan. 1980. Textured text in context. In *Interpreting folklore.* Bloomington: Indiana University Press.

Epstein, Jonathon S., David J. Pratto, and James K. Skipper, Jr. 1990. Teenagers, behavioral problems, and preferences for heavy metal and rap music: A case study of a southern middle school. *Deviant Behavior* 11:381–94.

Erlmann, Veit. 1996. *Nightsong: Performance, power, and practice in South Africa.* Chicago: University of Chicago Press.

Feld, Steven. 1982. *Sound and sentiment: Birds, weeping, poetics, and song in Kaluli expression.* Philadelphia: University of Pennsylvania Press.

Fillmore, John Comfort. 1888. *Lessons in musical history.* Philadelphia: Theodore Presser.

——. 1895. What do the Indians mean when they sing and how far do they succeed? *Journal of American Folklore* 9:138–42.

——. 1899. The harmonic structure of Indian music. *American Anthropologist* 1:297–319.

Fine, Elizabeth C. 1984. *The folklore text: From performance to print.* Bloomington: Indiana University Press.

Finnegan, Ruth. 1989. *The hidden musicians: Music-making in an English town.* Cambridge: Cambridge University Press.

Fletcher, Alice Cunningham. 1893. *A study of Omaha Indian music.* Archeological and Ethnological Papers of the Peabody Museum, vol. 1, no. 1. Cambridge, Mass.: Peabody Museum of Archeology and Ethnology.

Fletcher, Alice Cunningham, and Francis La Flesche. [1911] 1972. *The Omaha tribe.* Reprint, Lincoln: University of Nebraska Press.

Foley, John Miles. 1992. Word-power, performance, and tradition. *Journal of American Folklore* 105:275–301.

Ford, Charles. 1995. "Gently Tender": The Incredible String Band's early albums. *Popular Music* 14:175–83.

Frankl, Viktor E. 1963. *Man's search for meaning: An introduction to logotherapy.* New York: Washington Square.

Frazer, Sir James George. 1911. *The golden bough: A study in magic and religion.* London: Macmillan.

Friedson, Steven M. 1996. *Dancing prophets: Musical experience in Tumbuka healing.* Chicago: University of Chicago Press.

Friesen, Bruce K., and Jonathon S. Epstein. 1994. Rock 'n' roll ain't noise pollution: Artistic conventions and tensions in the major subgenres of heavy metal music. *Popular Music and Society* 18:1–18.

Frith, Simon. 1981. *Sound effects: Youth, leisure, and the politics of rock and roll.* New York: Pantheon Books.

——. 1988. *Music for pleasure: Essays in the sociology of pop.* New York: Routledge.

Gaines, Donna. 1990. *Teenage wasteland: Suburbia's dead end kids.* New York: Pantheon Books.

Garofalo, Reebee. 1987. How autonomous is relative: Popular music, the social formation, and cultural struggle. *Popular Music* 6 (1):77–92.

———. 1992. *Rockin' the boat: Mass music and mass movements*. Boston: South End.

———. 1997. *Rockin' out: Popular music in the USA*. Needham Heights, Mass.: Allyn and Bacon.

Georges, Robert A., and Michael Owen Jones. 1980. *People studying people: The human element in fieldwork*. Berkeley and Los Angeles: University of California Press.

Giddens, Anthony. 1979. *Central problems in social theory: Action, structure and contradiction in social analysis*. Berkeley and Los Angeles: University of California Press.

———. 1984. *The constitution of society: Outline of a theory of structuration*. Berkeley and Los Angeles: University of California Press.

———. 1993. *New rules of sociological method: A positive critique of interpretive sociologies*. 2nd ed. Stanford: Stanford University Press.

Gilman, Benjamin Ives. 1891. Zuni melodies. *Journal of American Ethnology and Archeology* 1:66–91.

———. [1908] 1977. *Journal of American Ethnology and Archeology, volume 5: Hopi songs*. Reprint, New York: AMS Press.

Glassie, Henry H. 1982. *Passing the time in Ballymenone: Culture and history of an Ulster community*. Philadelphia: University of Pennsylvania Press.

Goldthorpe, Jeff. 1992. Intoxicated culture: Punk symbolism and punk protest. *Socialist Review* 22 (2):35–64.

Guilbault, Jocelyne. 1993. *Zouk: World music in the West Indies*. Chicago: University of Chicago Press.

———. 1997. Interpreting world music: A challenge in theory and practice. *Popular Music* 16 (1):31–44.

Hakanen, Ernest A., and Alan Wells. 1990. Adolescent music marginals: Who likes metal, jazz, country, and classical? *Popular Music and Society* 14:57–66.

———. 1993. Music preference and taste cultures among adolescents. *Popular Music and Society* 17:55–70.

Hammond, Michael, Jane Howarth, and Russell Keat. 1991. *Understanding phenomenology*. Oxford: Basil Blackwell.

Harrell, Jack. 1994. The poetics of destruction: Death metal rock. *Popular Music and Society* 18:91–104.

Hawkins, Stan. 1996. Perspectives in popular musicology: Lennox and meaning in 1990s pop. *Popular Music* 15:17–36.

Hebdige, Dick. 1979. *Subculture: The meaning of style*. London: Methuen.

Herndon, Marcia, and Norma McLeod. 1979. *Music as culture*. Norwood, Pa.: Norwood Editions.

Hesmondhalgh, Dave. 1995. Technoprophecy: A response to Tagg. *Popular Music* 14:261–63.

Hood, Mantle. 1963. Musical significance. *Ethnomusicology* 7:187–93.

———. 1971. *The ethnomusicologist*. New York: McGraw-Hill.

Husserl, Edmund. [1913] 1931. *Ideas: A general introduction to pure phenomenology*. Translated by W. R. Boyce Gibson. London: Allen and Unwin.

———. [1931] 1960. *Cartesian meditations: An introduction to phenomenology*. Translated by Dorion Cairns. The Hague: Martinus Nijhoff.

———. [1929] 1964. *The phenomenology of internal time-consciousness*. Translated by James S. Churchill and edited by Martin Heidegger. Bloomington: Indiana University Press.

Hymes, Dell. 1962. The ethnography of speaking. In *Anthropology and human behavior*, edited by T. Gladwin and W. C. Sturtevant. Washington, D.C.: Anthropological Society of Washington.

———. 1975. Folklore's nature and the sun's myth. *Journal of American Folklore* 88:345–69.

Ihde, Don. 1976. *Listening and voice*. Athens: Ohio University Press.

———. 1977. *Experimental phenomenology: An introduction*. New York: Putnam.

Ingarden, Roman. [1957] 1989. The musical work. In *Ontology of the work of art*, translated by Raymond Meyer and John T. Goldthwait. Athens: University of Ohio Press.

Irvine, Judith T., and J. David Sapir. 1976. Musical styles and social change among the Kujamaat Diola. *Ethnomusicology* 20:67–86.

Jackson, Michael. 1989. *Paths toward a clearing: Radical empiricism and ethnographic inquiry*. Bloomington: Indiana University Press.

Jairazbhoy, Nazir. 1977. The "objective" and the subjective view of music transcription. *Ethnomusicology* 21:263–74.

James, William. [1912] 1962. The will to believe. In *Essays on faith and morals*, selected by Ralph Barton Perry. Cleveland, Ohio: World.

———. 1967. *Essays in radical empiricism*. Gloucester, Mass.: Peter Smith.

———. 1983. *The principles of psychology*. Cambridge, Mass.: Harvard University Press.

Josephson, Nors S. 1992. Bach meets Liszt: Traditional formal structures and performance practices in progressive rock. *Musical Quarterly* 76:67–92.

Johnston, Thomas F. 1973. The cultural role of Tsonga beer-drink music. *Yearbook of the International Folk Music Council* 5:132–55.

Jolles, Andre. 1965. *Einfache Formen*. Halle: Max Niemeyer.

Kauffman, Robert. 1980. African rhythm: A reassessment. *Ethnomusicology* 24:393–415.

Keil, Charles. 1995. The theory of participatory discrepancies: A progress report. *Ethnomusicology* 39:1–20.

Keil, Charles, Angeliki V. Keil, and Dick Blau. 1992. *Polka happiness*. Philadelphia: Temple University Press.

Kirshenblatt-Gimblett, Barbara. 1975. A parable in context. In *Folklore: Performance and communication*, edited by Dan Ben-Amos and Kenneth S. Goldstein. The Hague: Mouton.

Kittredge, George Lyman. 1905. Disenchantment and decapitation. *Journal of American Folklore* 18:1–14.

———. 1907. Ballads and rhymes from Kentucky. *Journal of American Folklore* 20:251–77.

———. 1908. Two popular ballads. *Journal of American Folklore* 21:54–56.

———. 1909. Ballad singing in Nova Scotia. *Journal of American Folklore* 22:327–31.

———. 1929. *Witchcraft in old and New England*. Cambridge, Mass.: Harvard University Press.

Koetting, James. 1970. Analysis of notation of West African drum ensemble music. In *Selected Papers*, vol. 1. Los Angeles: University of California at Los Angeles Institute of Ethnomusicology.

Kohák, Erazim V. 1978. *Idea and experience: Edmund Husserl's project of phenomenology in "Ideas I."* Chicago: University of Chicago Press.

Kolinski, Miczyslaw. 1961. *Studies in ethnomusicology*. Vol. 1. New York: Folkways Records and Oak Publications.

———. 1965. *Studies in ethnomusicology*. Vol. 2. New York: Folkways Records and Oak Publications.

Korson, George Gershon. 1938. *Minstrels of the mine patch: Songs and stories of the anthracite industry*. Philadelphia: University of Pennsylvania Press.

————. 1943. *Coal dust on the fiddle: Songs and stories of the bituminous industry.* Philadelphia: University of Pennsylvania Press.

Krohn, Kaarle. [1926] 1971. *Folklore methodology.* Translated by Roger L. Welsch. Austin: University of Texas Press.

Kunst, Jaap. [1950] 1974. *Ethnomusicology.* 3rd ed. Reprint, The Hague: Martinus Nijhoff.

Lawless, Elaine J. 1992. "I was afraid someone like you . . . an outsider . . . would misunderstand": Negotiating interpretive differences between ethnographers and subjects. *Journal of American Folklore* 105:302–14.

La Flesche, Francis D. [1914] 1970. *The Osage tribe: Rite of the chiefs, sayings of the ancient men.* Reprint, New York: Johnson Reprint.

————. 1928. *The Osage tribe: Two versions of the child naming rite.* Annual Report of the Bureau of American Ethnology, no. 43. Washington, D.C.: GPO.

————. 1930. *The Osage tribe: Rite of the Wa-xo-be.* Annual Report of the Bureau of American Ethnology, no. 45. Washington, D.C.: GPO.

————. 1939. *War ceremony and peace ceremony of the Osage Indians.* Annual Report of the Bureau of American Ethnology, no. 101. Washington, D.C.: GPO.

Leder, Drew. 1990. *The absent body.* Chicago: University of Chicago Press.

Lipsitz, George. 1990. *Time passages: Collective memory and American popular culture.* Minneapolis: University of Minnesota Press.

————. 1994a. *Dangerous crossroads: Popular music, postmodernism, and the poetics of place.* London: Verso.

————. 1994b. *Rainbow at midnight: Labor and culture in the 1940s.* Chicago: University of Illinois Press.

List, George. 1974. The reliability of transcription. *Ethnomusicology* 18:353–77.

Lomax, John Avery, and Alan Lomax. 1938. *Cowboy songs and other frontier ballads.* 2nd ed. New York: Macmillan.

Lord, Albert Bates. 1960. *The singer of tales.* Cambridge, Mass.: Harvard University Press.

Lüthi, Max. 1948. *The European folktale: Form and nature.* Translated by John D. Niles. Bloomington: Indiana University Press.

MacLeod, Bruce. 1993. *Club date musicians: Playing the New York party circuit.* Urbana: University of Illinois Press.

Manuel, Peter. 1993. *Cassette culture: Popular music and technology in North India.* Chicago: University of Chicago Press.

Marcus, George E., and Michael M. J. Fischer. 1986. *Anthropology as cultural critique: An experimental moment in the human sciences.* Chicago: University of Chicago Press.

Markusen, Ann R., and Virginia Carlson. 1989. Deindustrialization in the American Midwest: Causes and responses. In *Deindustrialization and regional economic transformation: The experience of the United States,* edited by Lloyd Rodwin and Hidehiko Sazanami. Boston: Unwin Hyman.

McAllester, David P. 1954. *Enemy way music.* Papers of the Peabody Museum of American Archeology and Ethnography, vol. 41, no. 3. Cambridge, Mass.: Peabody Museum of Archeology and Ethnology.

Merleau-Ponty, Maurice. [1945] 1989. *Phenomenology of perception.* Translated by Colin Smith. London: Routledge.

Merriam, Alan P. 1964. *The anthropology of music.* Evanston: Northwestern University Press.

Middleton, Richard. 1985. Articulating musical meaning, reconstructing musical history, and locating the popular. *Popular Music* 5:5–44.

Monson, Ingrid. 1996. *Saying something: Jazz improvisation and interaction.* Chicago: University of Chicago Press.

Moore, Allan F. 1993. *Rock: The primary text.* Buckingham, Eng.: Open University Press.

Nketia, J. H. Kwabena. 1988. The intensity factor in African music. *Journal of Folklore Research* 25:53–86.

Nettl, Bruno. 1954. *North American Indian musical styles.* Memoirs of the American Folklore Society, vol. 45. Washington, D.C.: American Folklore Society.

———. 1964. *Theory and method in ethnomusicology.* [New York]: Free Press of Glencoe.

———. 1974. Thoughts on improvisation: A comparative approach. *Musical Quarterly* 60:1–19.

———. 1983. *The study of ethnomusicology: Twenty-nine issues and concepts.* Urbana: University of Illinois Press.

Paredes, Americo, and Richard Bauman, eds. 1972. *Toward new perspectives in folklore.* Austin: University of Texas Press.

Parmentier, Richard J. 1993. The political function of reported speech: A Belauan example. In *Reflexive Language,* edited by John A. Lucy. Cambridge: Cambridge University Press.

Polhemus, Ted. 1994. *Streetstyle: From sidewalk to catwalk.* New York: Thames and Hudson.

Pred, Allan Richard. 1990. *Making histories and constructing human geographies: The local transformation of practice, power relations, and consciousness.* Boulder, Colo.: Westview.

Pred, Allan Richard, and Michael John Watts. 1992. *Reworking modernity: Capitalism and symbolic discontent.* New Brunswick: Rutgers University Press.

Radway, Janice A. 1984. *Reading the romance: Women, patriarchy, and popular culture.* Chapel Hill: University of North Carolina Press.

Reichard, Gladys A. 1928. *Social life of the Navajo Indians with some attention to the minor ceremonies.* New York: Columbia University Press.

Reid, James. 1977. Transcription in a new mode. *Ethnomusicology* 21:415–33.

Roberts, Helen H. [1926] 1967. *Ancient Hawaiian music.* Reprint, New York: Dover Publications.

———. [1936] 1970. *Musical areas in North America.* Reprint, New Haven, Conn.: Human Relations Area Files Press.

Rodwin, Lloyd. 1989. Deindustrialization and regional economic transformation. In *Deindustrialization and regional economic transformation: The experience of the United States,* edited by Lloyd Rodwin and Hidehiko Sazanami. Boston: Unwin Hyman.

Rodwin, Lloyd, and Hidehiko Sazanami, eds. 1989. *Deindustrialization and regional economic transformation: The experience of the United States.* Boston: Unwin Hyman.

Sartre, Jean-Paul. 1955. *No exit and three other plays.* Translated by Stuart Gilbert and Lionel Abel. New York: Vintage Books.

———. 1956. Being and nothingness: An essay on phenomenological ontology. Translated by Hazel E. Barnes. New York: Philosophical Library.

Sawyer, R. Keith. 1995. Creativity as mediated action: A comparison of improvisational and product creativity. *Mind, Culture, and Activity* 2:172–91.

———. 1996. The semiotics of improvisation: The pragmatics of musical and verbal performance. *Semiotica* 108: 269–306.

Schutz, Alfred. [1932] 1967. *The phenomenology of the social world.* Translated by George Walsh and Frederick Lehnert. Evanston: Northwestern University Press.

———. [1944] 1976. Fragments on the phenomenology of music. Edited by Fred Kersten. *Music and Man* 2:5–72.

Seeger, Charles. 1957. Towards a universal music sound-writing for musicology. *Journal of the International Folk Music Council* 9:63–66.
———. 1958. Prescriptive and descriptive music writing. *Musical Quarterly* 44: 184–95.
Seitel, Peter. 1972. "Proverbs: A social use of metaphor." In *Toward new perspectives in folklore*, edited by Americo Paredes and Richard Bauman. Austin: University of Texas Press.
Shank, Barry. 1994. *Dissonant identities: The rock 'n' roll scene in Austin, Texas.* Hanover: University Press of New England.
Sherzer, Joel. 1987. Poetic structuring of Kuna discourse: The line. In *Native American discourse: Poetics and rhetoric*, edited by Joel Sherzer and Anthony C. Woodbury. Cambridge: Cambridge University Press.
Smith, F. Joseph. 1979. *The experiencing of musical sound: Prelude to a phenomenology of music.* New York: Gordon and Breach.
Stone, Ruth M. 1982. *Let the inside be sweet: The interpretation of music event among the Kpelle of Liberia.* Bloomington: Indiana University Press.
———. 1988. *Dried millet breaking: Time, words, and song in the Woi epic of the Kpelle.* Bloomington: Indiana University Press.
Stone, Ruth M., and Verlon L. Stone. 1981. Feedback, event and analysis: Research media in the study of music events. *Ethnomusicology* 25:215–26.
Straw, Will. 1984. Characterizing rock music cultures: The case of heavy metal. *Canadian University Music Review* 5:104–20.
———. 1991. Systems of articulation, logics of change: Communities and scenes in popular music. *Cultural Studies* 5 (3):368–88.
Sudnow, David. 1978. *Ways of the hand: The organization of improvised conduct.* Cambridge, Mass.: Harvard University Press.
Sydow, Carl Wilhelm von. 1948. *Selected papers on folklore.* Copenhagen: Rosenkilde and Bagger.
Tagg, Philip. 1994. From refrain to rave: The decline of figure and the rise of ground. *Popular Music* 13:209–22.
Taylor, Archer. [1962] 1985. *The proverb and index to "The Proverb,"* edited by Wolfgang Meider. Bern: Peter Long.
Tedlock, Dennis. 1972. *Finding the center: Narrative poetry of the Zuni.* New York: Dial.
Thompson, Art. 1992. Fuzz tone user's guide. *Guitar Player* 26 (10):68–79.
———. 1997. Fuzzbox shootout. *Guitar Player* 31 (6):74–86.
Thompson, Stith. 1955. *Motif index of folk literature.* Revised ed. Bloomington: Indiana University Press.
Toelken, Barre. 1979. *The Dynamics of folklore.* Boston: Houghton Mifflin.
Vander, Judith. 1988. *Songprints: The musical experience of five Shoshone women.* Urbana: University of Illinois Press.
Verden, Paul, Kathleen Dunleavy, and Charles H. Powers. 1989. Heavy metal mania and adolescent delinquency. *Popular Music and Society* 13:73–82.
Vološinov, V. N. 1973. *Marxism and the philosophy of language.* Translated by Ladislav Matejka and I. R. Titunik. New York: Seminar.
Walser, Robert. 1991. The body in the music: Epistemology and musical semiotics. *College Music Symposium* 31:117–24.
———. 1993. *Running with the Devil: Power, gender and madness in heavy metal music.* Hanover: University Press of New England.
Waterman, Christopher. 1990. *Jùjú: A social history and ethnography of an African popular music.* Chicago: University of Chicago Press.
Watts, Alan. 1958. This is IT. In *This is IT and other essays on Zen and spiritual experience.* New York: Random House.

Weinstein, Deena. 1991. *Heavy metal: A cultural sociology*. New York: Lexington Books.

———. 1993. Rock bands: Collective creativity. *Current Research on Occupations and Professions* 8:205–22.

Whiteley, Sheila. 1990. Progressive rock and psychedelic coding in the work of Jimi Hendrix. *Popular Music* 9:37–60.

———. 1992. *The space between the notes: Rock and the counter-culture*. London: Routledge.

Woodbury, Anthony C. 1987. Rhetorical structure in Central Alaskan Yupik traditional narrative. In *Native American discourse: Poetics and rhetoric*, edited by Joel Sherzer and Anthony C. Woodbury. Cambridge: Cambridge University Press.

Index

Illustrations and glossary definitions are in **bold** typeface.

Abrahams, Roger, 7
Accompaniment patterns, jazz, 96–97, 105–9, 125–29, **311**. *See* Chords
Action and nonaction, moral implications, 259, 267, 278
Aesthetics, 126, 128–29, 130–31, 143, 272
Affect: and attention dynamic in commercial hard rock, 153–54, 156; and feedback loop in music, 159–60; in "The Final Silencing," 222–25, 229–33, 237; in jazz performance, 130; lyrics and, 214; in metal scene, 165–68, 269–75, 271, 290–91; role in musical experience, 10–11, 247; social context for, 12–14, 251–52
African American jazz scene: biographical sketches, 86–91; compared with European American jazz scene, 78, 92–94, 99–109, 112, 139–40, 146; musicians' experience in, 138–45
Agency: and change, 6; and ethics of fieldwork, 257–58; in musical experience, 7, 12–13, 14, 116, 170–72, 232. *See also* Subject of experience
Age of participants, 39, 78, 85, 92, 96
Aggression: and audience behavior in metal scene, 71–73; and metal's musical development, 57; and metal sound qualities, 58–59; politics of metal underground, 269–73, 288, 290–91; variations in affect in metal scene, 252
Akron, Ohio: commercial hard rock scene in, 33, 35–37, 296; and deindustrialization, 283; jazz scene in, 76–78, 84, 85
Akron Agora night club, 35–37, **36**, 296
Alternative rock, 34, 35, 38–39, **311**
Anthropology of Music (Merriam), 10, 11, 231
Apathy, metal musicians' view of, 265–67, 272–73, 285–86
Arrowsmith (band), 51
The Atomic Punks (band), 42, 49, 184
Attention, organization of: commercial hard rock, 73, 150–58, 169, 170; jazz, 112, 145–48, 152–53, 165, 169, 304n10; jazz scene,

African American, 138–45, 146; jazz scene, Whisler Quartet, 125–38, 145–46; metal scene, 73, 158–68, 221–22, 225–28, 238–40; social context for, 122–25, 169–73; sociology of, 43–44, 132–33, 154–58; theoretical issues, 303–4n3, 305n5
Audiences: African American musicians' attention to, 138, 140–41, 142–43, 144–45; behavior of, 31; commercial hard rock, 37–41, 43–44, 154–58; jazz, 102, 111–12; metal, 34, 64, 68–69, 70–72, 165–66, 168; sound experience for, 115–16, 223; Whisler Quartet's attention to, 132–33, 135, 136–37
Avant-garde jazz, 87, 88, 92

Background/foreground elements of experience. *See* Foreground/background elements of experience
Background vocals, and rock music composition, 47
The Ballad and the Folk (Buchan), 297
Barber, Ken, **41**, 153, 184, 199
Barlow, Jon, 115
Bartók, Béla, 8
Bass guitar: commercial hard rock, 47, 150–51; metal, 58, 159, 161, 217. *See also* Double bass
Bauman, Richard, 5, 7, 38
Beat. *See* Groove
Bebop, **311**. *See also* Post-bop
Bennett, H. Stith, 18, 116
Bergson, Henri, 132, 195
Berliner, Paul F., 14, 302n3, 304nn4, 5
Big band, 78, 107, 135
Blacking, John, 9, 49
Black metal, 57
Black Sabbath (band), 57
Blood Coven (band), 214, 263, 296
Blue-collar workers, and metal scene, 61, 283–84, 290, 291
Blues music, 46, 78, 188
Boas, Franz, 4

Bodily stylistics, 32, 37–41, 42–43, 68–69, 299n1
Body awareness: commercial hard rock, 153; jazz, 130, 136, 140, 145; metal, 164
Bop Stop, 102
Bowman, Rob, 17
Bradby, Barbara, 16
Brass instruments, jazz, 89–91, 107, 143–45
Bridge section of compositions, 46, 224–28, 311
Briggs, Charles, 6
Buchan, David, 297
Burris, Leonard (pseudonym), 90–91, 112, 296
Burrows, Edwin, 10

Capitalism and class inequity, 284–85
Carlson, Virginia, 283
Carr, John, 41, 218
Carter, Ace, 83
Cartesian Meditations (Husserl), 254
Cashmore, E. Ellis, 284
Cassette Culture (Manuel), 17
Catastrophic (band), 293
Change and agency, 6
Chapman, George, 41
Cheap Trick (band), 54
Chomsky, Noam, 6
Chords: in metal, 219–20, 233, 235–36; in jazz, 95–96, 104, 126–27, 134; notations for, 300n7; pivot, 228; power, 184–85, 313; progression of, 243–44
Chorus section of compositions, 46, 94, 229–33, 311
Christen, Steve, 40, 42, 43, 54, 183, 199
Chromatism, 235–36
Cinematic music, power metal as, 67
Class, socioeconomic, 14–15, 17, 61, 66–67, 283–91
Cleveland, Ohio, music scene in, 33, 34–35, 76–78, 85, 87–88
Clifton, Thomas, 23
Club settings for music performance: commercial hard rock, 35–37, 296; jazz, 100–2, 130, 140–41; metal, 67–68
Cohen, Sara, 15–16
College rock, 34–35, 38–39, 311
Commercial hard rock: attention organization in, 73, 150–58, 169, 170; audiences for, 37–41, 43–44, 154–58; composition practices, 44–50, 114–15, 153, 183–84, 186–89, 190; defined, 311; developments in study of, 16–17; geographical setting,

33; group identity in, 77; influence on death metal, 301n2; vs. jazz, 80, 82–83, 92; vs. metal culture, 31, 59–62, 69, 265; musicians' style, 42–43; performance elements in, 31, 53–56; physical space, 35–37; purpose and meaning in, 50–53, 74–75. See also "Turn for the Worse" (song)
Community, sense of, in underground metal, 273–75, 276. See also Social context
Competence in Performance (Briggs), 6
Competence vs. performance, 6
Comping patterns, 96–97, 105–9, 125–29, 311
Complementarity and reciprocity in experience, 145–46
Composition: commercial hard rock, 44–50, 114–15, 153, 183–84, 186–99; jazz, 94–99, 102–6, 108–10, 114, 134; metal, 62–65, 114–15, 167; process of, 307–8n8. See also "The Final Silencing"; Form, musical; "Turn for the Worse"
Concert vs. club setting for jazz, 140–41
Conjunction and disjunction in musical experience, 195, 236, 242
Consciousness, structuring of, 303–4n3. See also Attention, organization of
Consequentiality, and politics of metal underground, 276–79, 287–89
Constitution of perception, 1, 13, 14, 21–22, 119–20, 124. See also Perception; Practice
Context and meaning, 7. See also Social context
Contour, awareness of melodic, 221–22
Cooper, Robin, 9
Cosmopolitanism, 25
Cover bands, 60, 311
Critical phenomenology, 24–25, 254–61, 279–94
Critical thinking, metal's championing of, 66, 264–66, 267, 269
Cross-cultural communication, 120–21, 147, 245
Cross-situational reality, 25–28
Crowley, Aleister, 264
Cubbit, Sean, 16
Cuing, 161–62, 164
Cultural studies, and interpretive ethnography, 32
Culture: and agency, 12–13, 14, 116, 170–72; expressive, 7, 31–33; systematicity of, 85–86. See also Social context
Cuyahoga County, Ohio, 33

Dance floors, 36

Davis, Miles, 88, 89
Death metal: characterizated as proactive, 264–67; composition style, 64, 252; eclecticism of, 60–61, 66; origins of, 57–58, 261–62, 301n2; performance event analysis, 67–73; politics of, 17, 61, 261–64, 279–94; vs. power metal, 60–61, 64–65, 67; social practices, 252, 269–75; values of, 66–67, 113, 265–69, 276–79, 279–82. *See also* "The Final Silencing"
Deceptive cadence, 192
Defining background, 124
Def Leppard (band), 51
Dégh, Linda, 7
Deindustrialization, 17, 283–84
Demjanjuk, Jan, 283, 285
Densmore, Francis, 8
Depression, and death metal themes, 270–72
Descriptive vs. critical ethnography, 278–79
Dia Pason (band): at Akron Agora, 40–43; attention dynamic among, 150–53; audience interaction, 154–56, 158; break-up of, 296; composition and rehearsal, 44–48; performance style of, 53–55; photo, 40; on purpose of music, 50–51. *See also* "Turn for the Worse" (song)
Diffusionist anthropology, 3
Disjunction and conjunction in temporality of musical experience, 195, 236, 242
Doom metal, 57–58, 61
Dorsal Atlanticus (band), 274
Double bass, in jazz, 83, 96, 106–8, 125–33, 139, 141. *See also* Bass guitar
Double constitution. *See* Practice
Dried Millet Breaking (Stone), 13
Drummer: commercial hard rock, 45, 47, 150–51, 170; jazz, 82–83, 97–99, 108, 125, 134–35, 139; metal, 58, 158–62, 164–67, 170, 218
Du Bois, W. E. B., 14
Dundes, Alan, 7

Eclecticism: jazz, 84–89, 91, 112, 141–42, 143; metal, 60–61, 66
Economic context: class dynamics of metal scene, 17, 61, 66–67, 283–91; and Ohio music scene, 33; and popular music studies, 14–15
Edwards, Alvin (pseudonym), 89–90, 112
Einfache Formen (Jolles), 4
Electric guitar. *See* Guitar
Emotional intensity, and heavy metal, 57. *See also* Affect

Entering into the music, 141, 142, 153–54
Epochē, 19–20, 26–27
Equipment, band: and attention, 150, 152, 153; and composition style, 46; expense of, 36; importance of drum monitors, 159; in Whisler Quartet, 102
Erlmann, Veit, 13
Escapism, rock music as, 50–51
Ethics of fieldwork, 255–61, 276. *See also* Value judgments; Values
Ethnography: descriptive vs. critical role of, 278–79; and expressive culture, 7, 31–33; fieldworker's role in, 147–48, 175–76, 187–99, 255–61, 276; humanistic, 4–5, 12, 32; methodological issues, 2–3, 24, 76–77, 251–61, 299n3; purpose of, 246
"Ethnography of Speaking" (Hymes), 6
Ethnomusicology: and cross-situational reality, 25–28; and song analysis, 187–99, 240–41; medial vs. micro levels of analysis, 32, 119–20; and participants defined, 299n1; phenomenological basis for, 22–25, 120–21; scope of, 295–97; theoretical development, 10–19; transcription issues, 8–10
Ethnopoetics, 5
European American jazz scene: compared with African American jazz scene, 78, 92–94, 99–109, 112, 139–40, 146; biographical sketches, 79–84. *See also* Whisler Quartet
European Folktale (Lüthi), 22
Evolutionism in ethnomusicology, 8, 10
Experience: and ethnographic methodology, 2–3, 251–61; as flow of perception, 110, 126, 133, 145–48; folklore as, 7–8; listener's role, 115–16; phenomenological approach, 19–23, 120–21; and study of immediately lived meaning, 31. *See also* Attention, organization of; Living present, experience of; Phenomenology; Subjective nature of experience
Experimental Phenomenology (Ihde), 196, 254
Exton, Brian, 40, 183–84

Fanzines, 62
Fashion, 32, 37–40, 42, 68–69, 265
Feedback interviews, value of, 33
Feedback loop, and affect, 159–60
Feeling the form. *See* Protention
Feld, Steven, 12
Fieldworker's role in ethnography, 147–48, 175–76, 187–99, 255–61, 276

Fillmore, John Comfort, 10
Fills, 47, 108
"The Final Silencing" (song): affective component, 222–25, 229–33, 237; bridge section, 224–28; chorus sections, 229–33; closing sections, 236–40; composition of, 200–15; ethnographic depth of, 240–41; introductory section, 215–18; solo section, 234–36; transcription, 201; transitions, 233–34
Fine, Elizabeth C., 5
Finnegan, Ruth, 18, 34, 75, 114
Flash's night club, 215
Fletcher, Alice C., 8
Flow of experience, 110, 126, 133, 145–48
Folklore, study of, 3–8. *See also* Ethnography; Ethnomusicology
Folklore Methodology (Krohn), 3
The Folklore Text (Fine), 5
Foreground/background elements of experience: commercial hard rock, 152, 155–56; jazz, 123–25, 128, 135, 143, 304n10; metal, 163–64, 167, 221–22; philosophical basis for, 303n2. *See also* Attention, organization of
Form, musical: commercial hard rock, 31, 46–48, 63–64; and ethnomusicology, 10–19; form-function relationships, 199, 231–33; jazz, 94–95; metal, 63–64, 161–62, 164; and transcription issues, 8–10. *See also* Composition; Protention; Sound, musical
Formal phenomenology, and cross-cultural communication, 120–21
Form-engagement-affect relationships, 231–33
Form-function relationships, 199, 231–33
"Fragments on the Phenomenology of Music" (Schutz), 132
Framing devices, 240
Frankl, Viktor, 291
Frazer, Sir James, 4
Freelancing, and jazz band organization, 77–78
Friedson, Stephen M., 14
Frith, Simon, 14–15
Functionalism in ethnomusicology, 10–12
Fusion, 78, 83, 90, 92, 311
Fuzak, 311

Gaines, Donna, 57, 284
Gender issues in metal music, 61, 72
Generational issues, 39, 78, 85, 92, 96

Genre problem, 4, 13–14
Georges, Robert, 255
Gestalt, in musical experience, 123, 125–26, 132, 150–51, 152
Giddens, Anthony, 11, 26, 74, 170, 300n2. *See also* Practice
Glam metal, 34, 38, 39, 52–53, 311–12
Glassie, Henry, 7, 275
Glover, Larry, 143, 144
Gore metal, 57, 61, 267–68
Gothic (band), 40
Gould, Eric, 88, 88–89, 91, 107, 112
Grateful Dead subculture, 38, 39
Grindcore, 57
Groove: in commercial hard rock, 45; defined, 300n6, 304n4; and drummer's role, 243–44; jazz, 95, 98–99, 107, 110, 125–26, 134, 135–36; metal, 59, 307n3; and pianist's role, 135–36; variations in, 217–18
Group-oriented composition style, 44–48, 49, 62
Grunge music, 34, 39, 312
Guilbault, Jocelyne, 13
Guitar, 45–46, 47, 58, 150–51, 158–59. *See also* Bass guitar; Double bass
Gutted (band), 69

Halford, Rob, 57, 165
Hanan, Jack: biographical sketch, 83; eclecticism of, 84, 85; experience of music, 125–32; performance style of, 108; photo, 84, 100; purpose in playing, 110
Hardcore. *See* Punk rock
Hard rock. *See* Commercial hard rock
Harmonic analysis, 45–46, 64, 103, 105–6. *See also* Tonality
Harmonic rhythm, 95, 126–27
Hayes, Dennis, 65, 158
Head, Count, 82
Head-banging, 70
Head section of jazz composition, 94, 95–97, 99, 103, 134
Heavy Metal: A Cultural Sociology (Weinstein), 17
Heavy metal music: attention dynamic in, 73, 158–68; vs. commercial hard rock, 31, 59–62, 69, 265; composition style, 62–65, 114–15; and ethnomusicology, 16–19; glam, 34, 38, 39, 52–53, 311; groove for, 59, 307n3; history and social organization, 31, 56–62, 301n2; perceptual subject in, 219–22, 224–36; performance event,

67–73; social context, 66–67, 73–75, 113–14. *See also* Death metal

Hebdige, Dick, 14

Heterosexuality, and audience for commercial hard rock, 39

The Hidden Musicians (Finnegan), 18

Hip-hop style, 35

History, 247

Hits, and rock music composition, 47

Hood, Mantle, 8

Hook, **312**

Horns, jazz, 89–91, 107, 143–45

Humanistic ethnography, 4–5, 12, 32

Humanistic phenomenology, and cross-cultural communication, 120–21

Husserl, Edmund: and *epochē* concept, 19–20; on experience and knowledge, 254; protention, 126, 132; and subjectivity of experience, 22; synthesis of identification, 242; variational method, 196

Hymes, Dell, 4, 6

Identity issues, 24, 62–63, 77, 78, 264–69

Ideology and action, 267, 309n5

Ihde, Don, 122, 132, 143, 163, 194, 196, 226, 246, 254

Imagination vs. perception, 196

Improvisation, jazz: in composition, 94; control over, 143–44; learning process, 79; and musical freedom, 107; parameters of, 138–39, 141, 143, 145; and reflection, 130, 135, 137, 139, 142–43, 146; sound experience of, 104

Individualism: and jazz scene, 77–78, 84–86; and metal scene, 264–69, 286–88, 289–90, 292

Ingarden, Roman, 22

Intending subject, 12, 186–99. *See also* Agency

Interpretive ethnography and cultural studies, 32

Intervals, affective quality of, 225

Intro section of composition, 46, 64

Iron Maiden (band), 57

Jairazbhoy, Nazir, 9

James, William: on action vs. nonaction, 257; conjunction and disjunction in experience, 195, 236, 242; on consciousness, 303–4n3; on nature of subject, 197; on purposes of research, 190; subjectivism of experience, 259

Jazz fake book, 102

Jazz/funk, 89

Jazz music: African American attention dynamic in, 138–45, 146; attention of organization in, 43–44, 112, 145–48, 152–53, 165, 169, 304n10; composition/knowledge, 94–99, 102–3, 105, 108, 114, 134; environment for in Ohio, 76–78; patterns of practice, 79–94; performance and purpose, 99–113; research basis, 76–77; social context for, 74–75, 113, 129, 304–5n12; theoretical perspective, 14; Whisler Quartet attention dynamic in, 125–38, 145–46

Jazz-rock fusion, 78, 83

Johnston, Jeff: attention dynamic in Max Panic, 151–52, 153–54, 157; on purposes of band, 55; on composition style, 45; photo, **41**; on purpose of participation, 52–53

Johnston, Thomas, 11

Jolles, Andre, 4

Jones, Michael Owen, 255

Judas Priest (band), 57, 166

Keil, Charles, 300n5, 394n4

Kid Wicked (band), 41

Kinetic sculpture, representation of experience as, 121

Kiss (band), 261–62

Kittredge, George Lyman, 3, 4

Knowledge, musical. *See* Composition; Form, musical; Sound, musical

Koetting, James, 8

Kolinski, Miczyslaw, 10

Krohn, Kaarle, 3

Kunst, Jaap, 10

La Flesche, Francis, 8

Launching, 72

Leader-composer style of composition, 48–49, 62

Leder, Drew, 153

Let the Inside Be Sweet (Stone), 13

Listening, 17, 133. *See also* Songs, musicians' experience of; Sound, musical

Listening and Voice (Ihde), 122, 132, 143, 163, 194, 226, 246

Living present, experience of: defined, **312**; in "The Final Silencing," 221–22, 225–26, 229–33; and practice of perception, 245–46; and tonality, 195–98

Locrian mode, 219–20, 229, 233

Lord, Albert, 4

Lüthi, Max, 4, 22

Lyrics, 130, 190–91, 199, 214, 307n4

Macrosocial/microsocial aspects of study, 27, 49–50
Manuel, Peter, 13, 17
Marimba, 79
Markuson, Ann R., 283
Max Panic (band): attention dynamic in, 151–52, 153–54, 157; composition style, 45, 49; disbanding of, 296; performance style, 54, 157; photo, **41**; and purposes of music participation, 52–53
Mead, George Herbert, 125
Meaning in musical experience: commercial hard rock, 50–53, 74–75; as constituted in practice, 2, 13, 119–20; and context, 7; and ethnomusicology, 10–19; immediately lived, 31; importance to participants, 15; and shared experience in death metal, 113; and sociology of attention, 24, 43–44. *See also* Living present, experience of; Purposes for music participation
Medial level of practice, 32, 119–20
Melody composition: commercial hard rock, 45–46, 190; jazz, 103, 105, 108–9; metal, 219–20
Merleau-Ponty, Maurice, 20, 297
Merriam, Alan, 10, 11, 231
Metallica (band), 262, 269
Metal music. *See* Death metal; Heavy metal
Metaphysics, 6–7, 11
Methodology. *See* Ethnography; Ethnomusicology
Middleton, Richard, 16
Midwest region of U.S., and deindustrialization, 283
Milwaukee Metal Fest, 274
Monitor mix, adjustments to distortions of, 159–61
Monson, Ingrid, 14, 107, 130
Moore, Allan F., 16–17
Moral issues. *See* Ethics of fieldwork; Values
Moshing, 64, 70–73, 166, 218
Mr. E's Tavern, 67–73, **68**
Multistable drawings, 254
Musical scenes, as in opposition to other scenes, 34
Musicians: commercial hard rock, 150–53; jazz attention dynamic among, 125–32, 134–36, 137, 138–40, 141–42, 143–44; metal attention dynamic, 158–62; narratives of metal, 59; purposes for participation, 50–53. *See also* Performance; *specific musical groups*

Native perspective, 12–13, 15–16, 253
Necker cube, 254–55
Neil Zsa Zsa, 51
Nettl, Bruno, 8, 114
Networks, fan, 61–62
New Orleans–style jazz, 78
New York jazz scene, 79–80
Nirvana (band), 34
Noema: defined, **312**; and protention, 238; role in perceptual experience, 21; and synthesis of identification, 243; and tonality experience of music, 221–22, 225, 231–32
Noesis, 225, 245, **312**
Noise band, **312**
"Notch in the Bedpost" (song), 176
"Nut Screamer" tapes, 280, 282

Objective vs. subjective aspects of experience: and attention organization, 303–4n3; dialectic of, 21–22, 182–83, 193, 196–97; and *epoché*, 19–20; folklore studies' focus, 5; musical transcription, 9–10; partial sharing, 230–31
Object of experience, role in perception, 124. *See also Noema*
Object of study, 4–7, 9–10, 22, 23, 27
Omega Institute, 83
The Ontology of the Work of Art (Ingarden), 22
Oppositional identity, 62–63, 78, 265–66, 267–69
Oral poetry, 5
OUAM Hall, **293**
Outro section of compositions, 46, 64
Owens, Timmy, 57, 65, **65**, 67, 158, 166–68
Ozimek, Chris: attention dynamic in Dia Pason, 150–51, 153; audience interaction, 154–56; composition style, 48; performance style, 42–43, 54; photo, **40**; on purpose of music, 50–51. *See also* "Turn for the Worse" (song)

Parameters of improvisation, 138–39, 141, 143, 145
Pareimiology, 7
Parents' Music Resource Center (PMRC), 270
Partial sharing: and ethnographic research, 24, 254–61; in musical experience, 21–22, 156, 175, 230–32, 247–48
Participants: defined, 299n1; importance of meaning to, 15; perspectives of, 12–13, 15–

16, 123, 253; social context of meaning for, 24. *See also* Audiences; Musicians
Participatory discrepancy theory, 244
Pathway concept, 18
People Studying People (Georges and Jones), 255
Perception: analysis of musical, 242–48; feedback loops in, 159; vs. imagination, 196; musical experience as flow of, 110, 126, 133, 145–48; as practice, 2, 13, 14, 21–22, 119–20, 230–31, 243, 245–46; vs. reflection, 227; social context as basis for, 11–12, 25, 245, 246–48; subject's role in, 7, 9–10, 20–21, 124, 219–22, 224–36, 238–40
Perceptual subject, 219–22, 224–36, 238–40
Percussion: commercial hard rock, 45; jazz, 79, 81, 86–89, 105–9, 135–37, 138–43. *See also* Drummer; Groove
Performance: bodily stylistics in, 32, 37–41, 42–43, 68–69, 299n1; commercial hard rock, 31, 53–56, 157; jazz, 99–113, 130, 138–39; metal, 61, 67–73, 158–59; physical settings for, 35–37, 67–68, 100–2, 130, 140–41, 296; study of, 4–7. *See also* Attention, organization of; Protention
Personal action and motivation, 66–67, 264–65, 286–87, 290
Personal narrative, and heavy metal's development, 59–60
Personal responsibility, as death metal theme, 66–67
Perspective, participant, 12–13, 15–16, 123, 253. *See also* Subjective nature of experience
Phenomenological sociology, 6
Phenomenology: and cross-cultural communication, 120–21, 147, 245; and ethnographic method, 22–25, 120–21, 252–61, 279–94, 299n3; and experience of song, 187–99; importance of, 297; and metaphysics, 6–7; and nature of experience, 7–8, 19–23, 182–83; and practice theory, 19–28
Phenomenology of Internal Time-Consciousness (Husserl), 132
Phenomenology of Perception (Merleau-Ponty), 297
The Phenomenology of the Social World (Schutz), 26
Physical spaces for musical event, 31, 35–37, 67–68, 100–2, 130
Piano, jazz, 81, 86–89, 105–9, 135–37, 138–43

Pitch axis, in metal composition, 63, 217
Playing behind/ahead of the beat, 108
PMRC (Parents' Music Resource Center), 270
Poison (band), 51
Polhemus, Ted, 38
Politics: of band composition techniques, 49; and consequentiality, 276–79; and metal underground, 17, 61, 66–67, 261–75, 279–94; and musical content, 301n11
Popular music, influence on jazz musicians, 90
Popular music studies, 14–19. *See also* Ethnomusicology
Pop vs. underground metal, 34
Porter, Keith, 159, 160, 161, 164–65
Post-bop jazz style, 76, 78, 89, 92, 113
Postindustrial economy, 283
Power and aggression, as metal themes. *See* Aggression
Power chord, 184–85, **313**
Power metal, 57, 60–61, 64–65, 67
Power relations, 24, 93, 111–12, 143–44. *See also* Class, socioeconomic
Practice: and attention organization, 170–71; complexity of, 59–60; and death metal scene, 270–73; as doubly constitutive, 1, 13, 14, 21–22, 119–20, 124; perception as, 2, 13, 14, 21–22, 119–20, 230–31, 243, 245–46; and phenomenology, 19–28; themes among genres, 113–16; theoretical issues, 26; as unifying force for jazz musicians, 86. *See also* Giddens, Anthony; Social context
Practice Theory. *See* Giddens, Anthony; Practice
Press roll, 97
The Principles of Psychology (James), 197
Proactive stance of death metal, 265–67
Progressive metal, 57
Protention: commercial hard rock song analysis, 193–95; defined, **313**; jazz performance, 126–27, 131–32, 137, 138–39, 141; metal performance, 162–64, 221–22, 225–26, 227–28, 238–40
Pulse, 98
Punk rock: compared with commercial hard rock, 34; and death metal, 57, 60, 267–68, 290; defined, **312**
Purposes for music participation: commercial hard rock, 50–53, 74–75; jazz, 109–13; metal, 66–67, 73–75, 113–14. *See also* Meaning in musical experience

Index / 331

Racial issues: in jazz scene, 76–77, 78, 92–94; and metal underground, 61, 66–67, 279–81, 280–82, 283, 285; popular music studies, 14–15; tensions in Ohio, 33
Radical tolerance, 279–82, 289. *See also* Racial issues
Rage, and death metal affect, 252, 269–73
Ratt (band), 51
Receding background, 124
Reciprocity of experience, 145–46
Reflexivity in experience: in commercial hard rock, 153–54, 186; in jazz, 130, 135, 137, 139, 142–43, 146; in metal, 165, 168, 219; vs. perception, 227; problem orientation of, 125–26; vs. protention, 132; and social context, 49
Regional considerations, in jazz scene, 92
Rehearsal styles, 45, 47–48, 100
Reid, James, 8
Relativism and ethnographic research, 258–60
Religious issues, 57, 61, 83, 264–65
REM (band), 34–35
Retention, 193–95, 227–28, 237–38, 239–40, **313**
"Rhetorical Theory" (Abrahams), 7
Rhythm. *See* Groove
Ricci, Alfredo: attention dynamic in Dia Pason, 150–51, 153; audience interaction, 154, 155–56, 158; and experience of song, 199; on performance style, 54; photo, 40; on purpose of music, 50–51; role in band, 42, 43
Rizzi, Joe, 80, 81, 111
Rizzi's Jazz Lounge, 76, 100–5, **101**, 296
Rizzo, Phil, 81
Roadies, 39, 40
Roberts, Helen, 8, 10
Rock: The Primary Text (Moore), 16–17
Rock music. *See* Commercial hard rock; Heavy metal
Roth, Bill: and audience interaction, 165; biographical sketch, 82–83; on drummer's musical knowledge, 97–98; eclecticism of, 84–85; experience of music for, 131, 134–35; and Hanan's musical role, 125–26; on musical knowledge, 96–97; performance style of, 107–8; photo, **82**, **100**; purposes in playing, 110
Rubin's Goblet, 123, 196
Rueschman, Erik, 64, 217, 228, 234, 296
Running with the Devil (Walser), 17

Saladin, Dann: on affect of metal music,

269–73; attention dynamic for, 158–59, 165; biographical sketch, 261–63; breadth of musical practice, 66; on community building in metal scene, 273–75; compositional style, 63–64; and fan correspondence, 62; identity representations, 264–67; on performance style in metal, 70, 71; personal style of, 263–64; photo, **63**, **263**; politics of metal underground, 279–83, 284–94; values of, 267–69. *See also* "The Final Silencing"
Salem, Terry: attention issues, 158, 159, 160, 161, 164–65; photo, **65**; purpose for music participation, 65, 67
Satanism, 57, 61, 264–65
Saunders, Jerome: biographical sketch, 86–88, 296; eclecticism theme of, 91, 112; performance style, 105–6, 107; photo, **87**
Sawyer, R. Keith, 114, 115
Saying Something (Monson), 14
Schermesser, Dick: biographical sketch, 80–82, 296; experience of music for, 127, 128, 134–37, 139–40; and jazz fake book, 102; performance style, 105–6, 107; photo, **81**, **100**; purposes in playing, 110–11
Schutz, Alfred, 6, 22, 26, 132, 145, 247
Scooped-mids death tone, 58
Scumlord (band), 262, 268, 293
Seattle sound, 34, 39, **313**
Sections, musical composition. *See* Composition
Seed ideas for songs, 45–46, 63, 64
Seeger, Charles, 8
Seitel, Peter, 7
Self, experience of: commercial hard rock, 153–54; jazz, 130, 136, 140, 145; metal, 162–65
Sensorium. *See* Perception
Sexism, and metal underground, 280
Shadow Play (band), 159
Shank, Barry, 13
Silent Men, 37–38, 39, 43
Sin-Eater (band), 64, 158–59, 262–63. *See also* "The Final Silencing"; Saladin, Dann
Situational phenomenology, 22–25
Skanking, 72
Skinheads, 281
Slam dancing, 64
Small ensemble jazz, 78
Smith, Brandy "Chuck," 64, 217
Smith, Joseph, 23
Smoking, as common to club ambience, 36
Social context: for affect, 12–14, 251–52; and

agency, 12–13, 14, 116, 170–72; attention organization, 122–25, 169–73; as basis for ethnography, 254–61; in commercial rock, 48–50, 113–14; and cross-situational reality, 25–28; in ethnomusicology, 10–19; and folklore analysis, 4, 7; in jazz scene, 74–75, 84–86, 113–14, 129, 132–33, 304–5n12; in metal scene, 39, 59–60, 62, 66–67, 73–75, 113–14, 269–75; musical practice elements, 2, 32–33, 73–75, 147; music as shared experience, 231–32; nature of experience, 21–22; perceptual practice, 11–12, 25, 245, 246–48; situational phenomenology, 22–25; transcription issues, 8–10. *See also* Politics

Society gigs, 80, 82

Socioeconomic class. *See* Class, socioeconomic

Sociology of attention, 24, 43–44, 132–33, 154–58

Solo section of compositions: commercial hard rock, 46, 153; jazz, 94, 103–5, 106, 109–10, 131–32, 136, 143–44; metal, 64, 234–36

Songprints: The Musical Experiences of Five Shoshone Women (Vander), 13

Songs, musicians' experience of: composition history, 183–84, 200–15; ethnographic analysis of, 193–99, 240–41; introduction, 174–76; phenomenological description, 187–99; tonality and method, 184–87; transcription issues, 176–83. *See also* "The Final Silencing"; "Turn for the Worse"

Sound, musical: and affective experience, 230; audience experience of, 115–16, 223; and ethnomusicology, 16–17; jazz, 94–99, 129; metal, 52–53, 58–59, 62–65, 217–18, 223–24; and participants' purposes, 51–52. *See also* Form, musical; Songs, musicians' experience of

Sound and Sentiment (Feld), 12

Sound Effects (Frith), 14–15

Speed metal, 57, 268–69

Spirituality, 57, 61, 83, 264–65

Spork, Kirk (KB), 42, 43, 49, 54, 184

St. Paul, Lou, 65, **65**, 67, 158, 165

Stage antics, 154–55

Stage diving, 72

Stone, Ruth, 13

Structuralism, 9, 11, 12

Structuration, 26

Structures, musical. *See* Composition; Form, musical

Study object, problem of, 4–7, 9–10, 22, 23, 27

Subculture (Hebdige), 14

Subjective nature of experience, 22–25, 123, 259–61. *See also* Objective vs. subjective aspects of experience

Subjectivism vs. phenomenology, 254, 258

Subject of experience: as central focus of study, 120, 253; dialectic with objective world, 21–22, 182–83, 193, 196–97; fieldworker as, 255–58; intending, 12, 186–99; perceiver's role as, 7, 9–10, 20–21, 124, 219–22, 224–36, 238–40; social origin of, 21. *See also* Agency

Sudnow, David, 246

Summit County, Ohio, 33

Svonkin, Stuart, 276

Synchronic time, 295–96

Synthesis of identification, 242–45

"Take the 'A' Train" (Ellington), 95–96, **96**, **97**

Tale migration, 3

Taylor, Archer, 3–4

Taylor, Cecil, 87

Technology, and music experience, 17

Teenage Wasteland (Gaines), 57

Tempo: commercial hard rock, 151–52; jazz, 98, 134; metal, 59, 161, 217–18, 223–24. *See also* Groove

Temporality, 193–98, 236, 238–40, 242, 243, 245–46

Textual empiricism, 3–4, 8, 22, **313**

Texture, musical, 7, 142

Thinking in Jazz: The Infinite Art of Improvisation (Berliner), 14

Thompson, Stith, 4

Thrash metal, 57, 60–61, 268–69, 288

Timbre, 46, 58

Time and Free Will (Bergson), 132

Time signature, 98

Tolerance, as metal theme, 66, 267, 269, 273, 279–82, 289

Tonality, experience of, 62–63, 95, 184–99. *See also* "The Final Silencing"; "Turn for the Worse"

Toothman, Rob, 64, 159

Torode, Brian, 16

Transcription: folklore, 5, 8–10, 13; song, 176–83, 201–14, 306–7n1, 306n3

Transitions, and tonality experience, 233–34

Tribute bands, 60

Trombone, jazz, 90–91

Trumpet, jazz, 89–90
Turnaround, 233–34
"Turn for the Worse" (song): composition background, 183–84; phenomenology of, 187–99; vs. "The Final Silencing," 225–26; tonality in, 184–87; transcription, 176–83, **177**, **190**

Underground metal. *See* Death metal

Value judgments in ethnography, 24–25, 147–48, 258–59, 278–94
Values, death metal, 66–67, 113, 265–69, 276–79, 279–82
Vander, Judith, 13
Verbal Art as Performance (Bauman), 7
Verse section of compositions, 46, 222–24, 234–36
Vibraphone, 79, 137–38. *See also* Whisler, Larry
Violence theme, and moshing, 71–73. *See also* Aggression
Vocabulary, jazz, 104
Vocals: commercial hard rock, 47, 190–91, 193, 199; metal, 57, 58, 166–68
Voice leading, 106–7
Von Sydow, Carl Wilhelm, 3

Walking bass line in jazz, 96, 108, 127–28
Walser, Robert, 17, 46, 58, 284
Waterman, Christopher, 13
Watts, Alan, 259
Ways of the Hand (Sudnow), 246
Weinstein, Deena, 17–18, 301n2, 309n4
Western art music tradition, 8–10, 81, 86, 114
Whirlwinds, 70
Whisler, Larry: biographical sketch, 79–80; experience of music for, 128, 134–35, 136, 137–38; performance style, 103–5; photo, **79**, **100**; purpose in playing, 109
Whisler Quartet: audience's attention experience, 132–33; disbanding of, 296; musicians' experiences with, 125–32, 134–38; performance experience, 99–105; photo, **100**; routine of, 80; as study object, 76
Winter's Bane, 64–65, **65**, 67, 158–59, 166–68, 296
Woodchucking, 63, **313**
Working class and metal scene, 61, 283–84, 290, 291

Ziats, John: attention dynamic in metal, 158, 159, 160, 161, 164, 165; as composer, 64
Zouk (Guilbault), 13–14